ON THE HILL

ON THE HILL

The Story of Shorter College

ROBERT G. GARDNER

SHORTER COLLEGE
Rome, Georgia
1972

© 1972, Shorter College
Library of Congress Catalogue Card number 72–78515

Printed in the United States of America
by Kingsport Press, Inc., Kingsport, Tenn.

Preface

This is not the first time that the story of Shorter College has been told. Luther Rice Gwaltney wrote an eyewitness article for the 1898 *Iris*. A. W. Van Hoose prepared splendid essays in 1910 and 1915. A fiftieth anniversary history was published in a 1923 *Chimes* by Paul M. Cousins. B. D. Ragsdale in 1933 and 1938 and Mrs. Lydia Dixon Sheppard in 1940 brought the story up to their own day. The college catalogues have always contained historical sketches.

Despite its bulk, the present volume omits much that might be considered important. First, items will appear, throwing light on certain sections and rendering them inaccurate or partial. Second, many members of the faculty and staff have not been included because of a general rule that has been employed. Those serving at least five years and almost all those returning to serve their alma mater have been discussed. Virtually no others are to be found in these pages. Third, another, and even larger, book could be written about the accomplishments of students and members of the faculty and staff before coming to and after leaving Shorter College. Unless these accomplishments have been related directly to the college, they too have been omitted.

No doubt to the surprise of one or two of the thousand upperclassmen who have heard me extol the virtues of consistent footnotes and a complete bibliography, I have thought it unnecessary to include either. However, this information is available if the interested reader wishes to see it. I have attempted to examine, scan, or read everything in the Shorter College Memorabilia Room: catalogues, annuals, bulletins, magazines, newspapers, record books, scrapbooks, publicity releases, handbooks, photographs, and other artifacts. Trustee minutes and college audits have received careful scrutiny. The extant Rome newspapers and the *Christian Index* from 1873 to 1911 have been consulted column by column and since 1911, with greater selectivity. Annual minutes of the Southern Baptist Convention, Georgia Baptist Convention, Cave Spring Baptist Association, and Floyd County Baptist Association have provided much of value. Finally, by mail, telephone, and personal conversation, I have received a multitude of facts and impressions from literally hundreds of persons. If I were to list the names of all who have helped me, I would have little space left for the chapters!

I do think it necessary—and pleasant—to record my words of appreciation to an indispensable few. While carrying a full teaching load in 1968–1969, I initiated a study of Shorter's early years with no thought of a consequence such as this book. President Randall H. Minor heard of my work and requested me to complete it. He has reduced my classroom responsibilities, has read each chapter, and has supervised the entire project with a businessman's eye. My thanks go to him for interest and support that have not lapsed into editorial restraint.

Each chapter has been examined by Mrs. Robert Powell, who has also given countless hours in making the Memorabilia Room usable, and by Miss Mabel Thompson. For the assistance of these two I am grateful.

Representing Kingsport Press, Inc., Mrs. Wilma Kilgore, Craig Pippin, and Kenneth Gilley have furnished technical counsel reflecting a professional competency that has been of value to me.

Miss Susan Gardner, my efficient secretary, my daughter, and a Shorter senior, has compiled a multitude of names and figures so necessary for this kind of study. David Gardner, my adviser on design, my son, and a sophomore at the Georgia Institute of Technology, has helped to make the volume much more attractive than otherwise it would have been.

One other person would prefer not to be mentioned, I know without asking, but she must be included. In four years this lovely lady has shared this book for exactly 1,461 days—and some have been twenty-five hours long. Her work in the Memorabilia Room was pleasant for her and important for me. She has rejoiced with me on the good days when creativity was at its peak, and has remained optimistic on all the others. She has heard about the book as it was being researched and written, read it with a critical eye several times, offered suggestions that I have usually accepted, proofread every galley that came along, and prepared the index. To my wife I owe more than I can accurately express.

August 1, 1972   Robert G. Gardner

Contents

PART ONE: ON COLLEGE HILL

PART TWO: ON SHORTER HILL

Note: A detailed table of contents is located at the beginning of each chapter.

Old Shorter

PART ONE

ON COLLEGE HILL

1873-1910

1
"A Gift to our Daughters"

Mrs. Martha Harper Baldwin sat in her home at Monticello, Georgia, enjoying the hours that she spent sewing for the poor. Almost three years earlier she had been widowed by the death of her husband, John Baldwin. Alfred Shorter had been his partner in business and, more recently, her financial adviser. A warm friendship had grown up between Mrs. Baldwin and Shorter, and he had become impressed with her gentle, womanly character. Into the room where she worked came her very purposive adviser, accompanied by the Reverend James McDonald. "Why should we wait any longer?" asked Shorter. "Let us be married at once." In response, Mrs. Baldwin stood, shook the threads from her dress, and with the scissors still hanging from her waist repeated the vows that made her Mrs. Alfred Shorter.

Meantime, four hundred miles away in southern Virginia, that wedding went unnoticed. Instead, a three-year-old boy, Luther Rice Gwaltney, whiled away the hours in a most unspectacular way, playing around the house and yard.

Unknown at the time to any of them, these three persons were to combine their insights and abilities thirty-nine years later to found a college "on the hill."

Who were these persons?

An educator and clergyman, Luther Rice Gwaltney was the son, grandson, and great-grandson of Baptist preachers. Born in Isle of Wight County, Virginia, in 1830 and named for his father's most famous friend, he was educated at home, at a nearby academy, and at Columbian College, Washington, D. C., receiving the Bachelor of Arts degree in 1853, the Master of Arts degree in 1857, and the Doctor of Divinity degree in 1876. After teaching five years in Virginia and two years at Columbian College, he was ordained in 1855. Subsequently he led Baptist churches in Greenville, North Carolina, and Edgefield, South Carolina, for thirteen years. For one year he was professor of Latin and mathematics at Chowan Female Collegiate Institute, Murfreesboro, North Carolina, and for several years in Edgefield he combined teaching with his pastorate. Gwaltney was married twice—to Miss Louisa Davidson of Virginia, who died in Edgefield leaving two children, and to Miss Sophia B. Lipscomb of South Carolina, who bore him seven children. "No home is complete without a little baby," he asserted. His reputation grew as an eloquent preacher, an experienced and successful teacher, and a gentleman of deep piety and broad culture. Of average size and wearing a long beard, he became pastor of the Rome Baptist Church, which then had about 250 members, in

11

1869 at the age of thirty-eight. During the next four years the presidency of three female colleges was tendered to him, but he remained in Rome. Always interested in temperance, he helped for a time to edit a newspaper and took a leading part in a lodge devoted to that cause. The townspeople found him to be patient, gentle, courageous, and friendly, and this "laborious and gifted pastor" grew in their affections.

The other founder of the college, Alfred Shorter was born in Wilkes County, Georgia, in 1803. While yet a child he was made an orphan by the death of his parents and was subsequently reared by relatives near Eufaula, Alabama. It is said that he eventually left them with his total possessions in a hand satchel and a pet rooster under his arm. At the age of sixteen he found employment as a clerk in the store of John Baldwin of Monticello, eventually becoming a partner in it. In 1834 he married Baldwin's widow, Mrs. Martha Harper Baldwin, who was four years his senior. She had been left $40,000 by her late husband and encouraged Shorter to invest it in real estate in Georgia, Alabama, and Mississippi. Although the Shorters had no children, they reared her niece and nephew, Martha and Charles M. Harper. In 1837 they moved to Floyd County, and in 1847 Shorter built a handsome white mansion, Thornwood, located one mile out of town on the road to Alabama. Possessing acute business judgment, he traded in cotton, merchandise, and real estate. His farming interests were extensive and his slaves numerous. He was part-owner of a local steamboat line, banks, and an insurance company. At one time he saw the Rome Railroad Company, of which he was a principal investor, operate an engine named *The Alfred Shorter* between Rome and Kingston. For almost twenty-five years he owned two bridges crossing the Etowah and Oostanaula rivers in Rome, charging toll for their use. Having almost no formal education, he nevertheless read rather widely, especially enjoying Charles Dickens. A man of clear and powerful mind, modesty, and integrity, his calm and placid manner led many to feel that he was stern and difficult to approach. His intimates, however, found him to be kindly, gentle, wise, and deeply pious. Quietly active in church affairs, he and Mrs. Shorter regularly occupied their pew on the extreme right hand side of the Rome Baptist Church. At various times he was a trustee, treasurer, and member of several committees of the church. His financial contributions to it were extensive. Centering her life in her church and home, Mrs. Shorter was described as hospitable, generous, humble, and unostentatious. "She was the mother to the orphan, and a friend to the friendless, a benefactor to the poor and a reliable support in every noble undertaking." As a younger lady she had formed and taught children's Sunday school classes and had initiated a matrons' prayer meeting in her home. Though her strength gradually failed, she nevertheless maintained a keen interest in her church, supporting it with her attendance and money. In 1873 the Shorters—both in their seventies—were serenely cheerful and moderately vigorous, surrounded by relatives who loved them and friends who esteemed them, comfortably situated in their unobtrusively elegant country home.

Colonel and Mrs. Alfred Shorter

Rome in the 1870s

The Rome that Gwaltney and Shorter knew in the early 1870s was a growing city of about three thousand, slowly recovering from the disastrous effects of the recent war. Surrounded by the suburbs of Forrestville, East Rome, Hillsborough, Dahomeny, and DeSoto—which were eventually taken into the city—it was located in Floyd County, which had a population of about eighteen thousand. Looking up Broad Street from the new depot serving the Rome Railroad Company and the Selma, Rome and Dalton Railroad, one could see stretching for several blocks fine brick business establishments: the Rome and the Choice hotels; Ayer and McDonald, hardware; J. G. Daily, undertaker; Woodruff and Morgan, cotton buyers; Whiteley's livery stable; S. Carnochan and Sons, saddlers; Allgood and Hargrove, bankers; Billy the Barber; Patrick and Omberg's department store; Veal and Company, jewelers; DeJournette and Son, grocers; Coleman and

13

Sargeant's restaurant and bar; Mesdames Attaway and Wilkinson, milliners; Warner's Photographic Gallery; and M. N. Cutter's tailor shop. A. Shorter Caldwell sold musical instruments; Thomas Fahy, dry goods; Seay and Walker, stoves; and A. S. Patrick, books and stationery. Also in the downtown area were the courthouse and city hall, the offices of several lawyers and physicians, the presses of the *Courier* and the *Commercial*, and the four churches, Baptist, Episcopal, Methodist, and Presbyterian. Elsewhere in and near town were the J. J. Vandiver lumber and coal yard, J. N. Wimpee's carriage shop, the J. M. Wardlaw boarding house, the Rome Hollowware and Stove Manufacturing Company, Noble Brothers Foundry, an axe and hoe handle plant, cotton gins, and warehouses. Recreation of various sorts was furnished by billiard parlors, a dancing academy, meetings of lodges, the Grange, the Memorial Association, and the Young Men's Literary and Social Club, programs held at the city hall by local entertainers and visiting troupes, drills of discharged Confederate military units, traveling menageries and circuses, riverboat excursions on the Coosa, and the local fair in the fall.

Romans had favored the Baptist-sponsored Hearn Academy operating successfully in nearby Cave Spring since 1839 and had doubtless wished for a similar school of their own. Briefly in 1857 they had probably supported a female school apparently operated at the Rome Baptist Church by the pastor, Shaler G. Hillyer. They had also given assistance to the two short-lived Baptist schools in nearby Cedartown and Cassville—Woodland Female College and Cherokee Baptist College for young men—just prior to the war and had doubtless been sobered by their failures.

In 1873, of course, Rome was not without her own educational institutions. Thomas M. Holleyman operated a preparatory school for young ladies and girls. Professor Proctor's Select Male High School accommodated many of the young men and boys. Other smaller secondary schools also existed. Under Presbyterian auspices, the Rome Female College had been in operation intermittently since 1853, enrolling 164 pupils and graduating 10 in the current year.

In this city, Gwaltney and Shorter established a college.

Founding the College

In 1872 Luther Rice Gwaltney, pastor of the local Baptist Church, conceived the idea of "a college for the daughters of Cherokee, Georgia," to be located in Rome. During that year, preliminary dis-

14

cussions were carried on with many civic leaders, but no definite conclusions were immediately reached. Conversations were continued into the summer of 1873, when it was finally decided that the Cherokee Baptist Female College should be organized. At a general meeting of persons interested in the venture, held on Saturday, August 2, 1873, probably in the basement of the Rome Baptist Church, a board of trustees was elected and financial pledges were made. Alfred Shorter became president of the board, with John W. Janes serving as secretary. Three others were then named: Major J. C. McDonald, D. B. Hamilton, and Gwaltney. On August 12, application for a charter was

President Luther R. Gwaltney

made to the Superior Court of Floyd County by thirty-two men listed as stockholders. The charter was duly granted on September 20 and confirmed on November 12, providing for the appointment of "a board of eleven Trustees, who shall be members of some Baptist Church in good standing and who shall hold their offices for the term of five years and until their successors are selected and qualified." Only ten of the first trustees are known—the five already named, plus Captain A. M. Jackson, Colonel Charles G. Samuel, Thomas J. Perry, Abner Echols, and Henry W. Dean. Alfred Shorter remained as president of the board and John W. Janes as secretary.

The site selected by the trustees was then known as Shelton Hill, located on Maiden Lane (an exceedingly appropriate name that was soon changed to Elm Street) between Alpine and Cherokee streets (now East Third Avenue between East Third and East Fourth streets) and described as "far enough to escape the bustle of active business

15

life, yet near enough to be convenient to all sections of the town."
An eight-room brick residence with outbuildings was situated just off
the crest of the hill, which was then much higher than the present
summit. The buildings stood in a splendid grove of oaks on a plot
covering three acres. On the southern brow were earthen fortifications
with embrasures for cannon, probably used by Union forces in 1864.
Negotiations for this purchase were made on August 4, and agreement
was reached for the sum of $7,500—with one-third to be paid in cash
and the remainder to be covered by notes.

The structures were soon made suitable for accommodating the day
students. The main building was repaired, while the outbuildings
were converted into one long, narrow school hall. An assembly room
was provided and then enlarged before the completion of the first
academic year. Indicative of an early interest in music, initial purchases included "two magnificent pianos and a large Estey organ."
Subsequently the grounds were described as "well kept and orna-
mented with beautiful shrubbery and choice flowers."

The first known advertisement for the new school appeared in the
Rome *Tri-Weekly Courier* for August 19, 1873. A descriptive circular
was said to be available, but no copy of it is known to have survived.

The faculty was initially headed by Gwaltney. At a called conference held on Sunday, August 10, 1873, the Rome Baptist Church
responded to a request from the college trustees by permitting him to
become temporary president for one year *"without any compensation*
(except that his daughters shall be taught without charge), he to
devote not more than 3 hours time each day to the duties, and the
position not to interfere in any respect with his pastoral duties." In
addition, he was also professor of moral and mental philosophy until
his first departure from Rome in 1876. For the first few months, he
was apparently assisted in administrative details by David Blount
Hamilton, a Rome lawyer and preacher who was married to Mrs.
Shorter's niece.

Four or five others were on the faculty when the school opened on
Monday, October 6, 1873. Mrs. H. C. Cooper, mother of J. P. Cooper,
a later benefactor of the institution, left her own successful school to
become principal of the preparatory department and professor of
English and history in the collegiate department. For fourteen years
she was to be associated with the college—longer than anyone else on
the downtown campus except for Gwaltney. Mrs. S. E. Harper was
principal of the primary department for four or five years. Two sisters,
Misses Sallie and Kate C. Hillyer, instructed in vocal and instrumental

16

music and in art for five years each. Perhaps Miss Ione Newman taught calisthenics, as she is known to have done for eight to ten years in this early period. In the first advertisement, Miss Rosa Cooper was also listed on the faculty, but evidently she did not teach. The editor of a Rome newspaper commented: "The faculty is an excellent one, both as to scholarship and high moral worth . . . . Altogether, the college will open under the happiest auspices."

Attendance during the first year reached a total of 124 students. About 80 were present at the opening of school. By the following January, the number had jumped to 110. The cumulative figure in-

President Alexander S. Townes

cluded 46 in the primary department, 43 in the preparatory department, and 35 in the collegiate department. About 10 students in the first two departments were boys. Approximately 6 boarding students were kept in the home of the president or in other nearby homes; all others were day students from Rome and its environs.

Throughout the fall of 1873 a full-time president was sought, and in November one was elected. On January 5, 1874, Alexander Sloan Townes assumed that office, becoming also professor of English and ancient and modern languages. Born in 1842 at Greenville, South Carolina, he was a graduate of Furman University. After serving four years in the Confederate army and later teaching in his native state, he studied a variety of ancient languages for two years in Germany. He then married a widow, Mrs. Lavinia Brooks White of South Carolina, and they had one son. Thereafter he was the successful president of the Georgia Female College, Madison, and principal of

17

the Greensboro (Georgia) Female High School, before coming to Rome with his wife and family. Characterized as "a very quiet and amiable gentleman, with none of the blow and bluster of many with far less merit as educators," he led the college during three semesters of slow growth.

The curriculum was described in the first college catalogue issued in August of 1874. The course of study for the primary and preparatory departments included spelling, reading, writing, arithmetic, and geography. The former added lessons in vocal music, while the latter added English grammar, history, and composition. The collegiate department was divided into seven schools—English, ancient languages, modern languages, mathematics, natural science, mental and moral science, and history. Each offered courses extending two to four years, and it was recommended, in the interests of preserving health and doing "full justice to the studies pursued," that no pupil enroll for more than four schools at the same time. Apparently this was not strictly followed, for one would thereby have consumed six academic years in securing a full diploma. Serving pupils in each of the departments were the instructors in music and art. Lessons in piano (no organ was mentioned), with facilities for practice, were provided. Drawing in pencil and crayon and painting in oil were also taught. Reports were made to parents every five weeks regarding attendance, deportment, and scholarship.

Expenses for two terms extending over forty weeks were nominal. Day students in the primary department were charged $25 for tuition; in the preparatory department, $40; and in the collegiate department, $60. Board and room, at the home of the president or one of several nearby "excellent private families," was $150. "Washing" and "Incidental Expenses" were $22. If desired, piano lessons added $70, while art lessons added $20 to $40. For a minimum of $232, then, a young lady could be maintained at the college for a full academic year, and the total cost would seldom exceed $342. Scholarships covering the full cost of tuition were given to daughters of clergymen and to no more than two orphan children sponsored by each Masonic and Odd Fellows' Lodge.

Three types of academic awards were made. At the conclusion of any year a "Certificate of Distinction" could be conferred for the work done during that year. After passing a comprehensive examination by any one school, a student could receive a "Diploma" with the title of "Graduate" in that one school. A "Diploma" with the title of "Full Graduate of Cherokee Baptist Female College" was available for any graduate of all seven schools who prepared an essay of approved merit.

Since the normal age at graduation was about eighteen, it would appear that the young ladies actually received an education comparable to that offered by a modern secondary school.

Rules were made to secure "politeness and courtesy" and "lady-like deportment." Regular and punctual attendance at classes was required. Communication between pupils during recitation and study hours was forbidden. Boarders were not allowed to visit or to receive visitors except on Saturday, and never were they to patronize the stores in town unless accompanied by one of the teachers. "In no case will the young ladies be permitted to receive attentions from gentlemen." "While no denominational views will be taught," efforts were made "to inculcate regard for personal religion and reverence for the Word of God." It was therefore stated: "Boarders are expected, if not Providentially hindered, to attend Church and Sabbath School on the Sabbath regularly. Each one will attend the church desired by her parents."

The first academic year concluded with public examinations on July 6 to 8 and a concluding ceremony and concert on July 9. For three days the students from all departments were subjected to written and oral tests in the college chapel and assembly room, attended by their families and friends, trustees of the college, and a board of visitors appointed for the occasion from the professional, business, and educational leaders of the community. Archibald J. Battle, who was then president of Mercer University, gave the annual address at the Baptist Church on Thursday morning, speaking for fifty-three minutes on the theme, "The education of woman sanctified by pious devotions to God." While there were no graduates at this time, the ceremony was notable in that three of the first four presidents of the college were present: Gwaltney, Townes, and Battle. That evening in the city hall, "crowded almost to suffocation," the music students of Miss Sallie Hillyer were presented in the first Grand Concert, while many paintings were exhibited by the students of Miss Kate Hillyer.

The Second Year

Classes convened on August 31, 1874, with about 80 students present by the end of the first week. The number slowly grew to almost 100 in December. Bad weather immediately after the Christmas holiday reduced the number to 60, but once again it slowly regained its former level. The cumulative figure for the entire year was reported as 134, and the average number for the first two years as 100.

The school occasionally received visitors who described activities

19

therein. David Butler, editor of the *Christian Index*, heard a number of students read compositions previously assigned to them. Commenting on their abilities, he observed: "If they had help at home, the hand of the helper was not so easily seen as the one that wrote the doom of Belshazzar on the wall of Babylon." While in the primary department, he continued: "We heard a little class sing a part of the multiplication table to the tune of 'Yankee Doodle'—to us a new way of learning music and mathematics." This was apparently a favorite form of instruction with Mrs. Harper; other visitors later observed the same exercise.

Although they could not vote, the young ladies of the collegiate department displayed an interest in local politics. W. H. Felton and William H. Dabney were opposed for a seat in Congress. The pro-Dabney newspaper in Rome noted with satisfaction: "The Cherokee Baptist College girls are being trained up in the way they should go—for Dabney, so when they are older they will not depart from the Dabney men. For yesterday some of these girls . . . announced the 'official vote' of a meeting of the College girls, which summed up 93 for Dabney and 4 for Felton." The editor concluded: "Every unmarried man on the *Commercial* is now energetically setting his cap for one of these same little Dabney girls." They obviously exerted no political influence beyond the walls of the college, however, and their candidate lost.

The earliest known extracurricular organization at the new college was the R.O.K. Society, founded by Gwaltney probably in 1874. Supposedly only the members knew that the letters stood for "Reapers of Knowledge." Initially its membership was comprised of the young ladies in the collegiate department, but soon they invited various adults to become honorary members. The club had an official monogram, the design of which has since disappeared. Its motto came from Virgil, *Haec olim meminisse juvabit* ("it will be pleasant to remember these things hereafter"). Although the group apparently met regularly for literary discussions, its other functions were recreational and financial, and it sponsored receptions for the graduating classes and presented public programs of entertainment in order to make money for its projects. In February of 1875, which is the first record of the society that remains, it utilized the city hall for a program of music, tableaux, pantomimes, and farce, "funds to be applied in purchasing Library and other needed appliances of the Society." Adults were charged 50¢ and children, 25¢; over $100 was realized by the group. It should be observed that this is the first known reference to a library at the college. Four months later, in connection with the commencement season, the society held a reception from 8:00 to 12:00 P.M. at the W. I. Brooks home, honoring its own honorary members and the graduate of the college, Miss Mary Darlington. A visitor described the event, adding: "These lovely resorts were well patronized during the evening, and we are willing to wager that Cupid had not a single dart left in his quiver." For the next three years, similar entertainments and receptions were sponsored by the group—as well as one woman's suffrage meeting at the city hall.

Sadness came to the little college early in 1875, contributing to the premature resignation of the president. Mrs. Townes had been an

Miss Mary Darlington

invalid for a long time because of "consumption," but her condition became increasingly grave and she died. For the remainder of the term a sister of President Townes was placed in charge of the boarding department. Not long before graduation, it was reported in a local newspaper: "Mr. Townes felt that, in the death of his wife, it was not expedient for him to remain as the President . . . longer, and therefore tendered his resignation in consequence . . . ." This was "reluctantly accepted" at a meeting of the trustees on June 8, 1875, to become effective after the graduation service on June 23. With the expressed consent of the Rome Baptist Church, Gwaltney was again elected temporary president. Obviously Townes and the trustees parted in goodwill, for two of his stepdaughters later graduated from the college.

The closing exercises grew even more complex in 1875 when the college had its first full graduate. For a week the students were tested, both publicly and privately, in written and oral form. The baccalaureate sermon was delivered in the Rome Baptist Church at the Sunday

21

morning service on June 20 by the Reverend J. J. F. Renfroe, associate editor of the *Alabama Baptist*. The entertainment by the freshman and sophomore classes and the Grand Concert were held in the city hall on Monday and Tuesday evenings. At the former, President Townes distributed certificates of distinction to those who had passed their courses during the year. At the conclusion of the concert, he was presented "a neat gold-headed cane" by the junior and senior classes. The graduation exercises were in the Baptist Church Wednesday morning, June 23, with one full and four partial graduates. Miss Mary Darlington, the first full graduate of the college, was a sister of the lawyer and educator for whom Darlington School in Rome is named. Each of the graduates delivered her composition, and President Townes awarded the diplomas in "a brief but touching address."

After leaving Rome, Townes spent the remainder of his life in South Carolina. He married Miss Elvira Sayle McKellar of that state in 1879, and five children were born to their union. President of the Greenville Female College for sixteen years and of the Greenville College for Women for fourteen, he took an active layman's interest in Baptist denominational affairs. He died in 1909.

Shorter's First Gift

Attendance decreased alarmingly from an encouraging total of 134 during the second year to a depressing total of 108 during the third. Undoubtedly the loss of a full-time president contributed significantly to this decline.

Nevertheless, Gwaltney remained popular with his associates. He received special attention on his forty-fifth birthday, November 10, 1875, due to the secret preparations of teachers and pupils. A newspaper article vividly recounted the event: "They decorated his chair and desk with evergreens and flowers, and his table with appropriate presents. The Reverend gentleman was totally surprised, but, as usual, was master of the occasion. He acknowledged the compliment in well chosen terms—feelingly alluded to the warm attachment growing up between them—cheerfully gave his testimony as to their good behavior and fidelity to their duties—and, finally, to cap the climax, decreed a holiday for the day." The almost inevitable cheer was not recorded.

Six months later another holiday was given. On May 10, 1876, the citizens of Rome observed Memorial Day by marching to Myrtle Hill Cemetery where the soldiers' graves were decorated and a patriotic speech was made. The teachers and pupils of the college marched in the parade and attended the graveside ceremonies—a practice which was to continue for many years, finally being halted during the Simmons era.

Throughout these first three years the trustees were constantly considering an expansion of the physical plant. Plans were announced to raise $20,000 "to perfect our buildings and get all necessary apparatus." It was anticipated that much of this sum would be used in the erection of a chapel building. Later they passed a resolution calling for the construction of a music building. While envisioning a glowing future, they nevertheless faced a present, stern reality, making only minor additions to the existing structures.

It became increasingly obvious to Gwaltney that the school needed additional financial assistance. The national panic of 1873 had not stayed the opening of the college, but by 1875 monetary conditions in Rome were stringent. He later recalled: "Its buildings were insufficient; its accommodations were poor; its equipment very meager, and I realized that the demands which Georgia and the South would make on an institution for women, could in no sense be met by the advantages afforded by the Cherokee Baptist Institute." If an increase in student enrollment were to be achieved, larger facilities would be necessary, and efforts had been made to raise funds for this purpose. Instead of success in this regard, however, the stockholders were unable even to meet current payments due on the purchase of the building. Accordingly, Gwaltney continued: "I knew that the people as a whole were not able to build a college, and I looked around me for some man whom God had blessed with wealth; some man who loved God; some man whose breadth of intellect, whose love for his fellow man and whose willingness to consecrate a part of his wealth to posterity, would enable him to see the vision that I had seen, and catch the spirit which Almighty God had given to me." One man quickly came to mind, a member of the Rome Baptist Church and president of the Cherokee College trustees, Alfred Shorter. Gwaltney addressed a letter to him in the early part of 1876, urging him to make a generous contribution to the struggling school. "I said my hopes all centered in him, that if he would resolve to become the liberal and life-long supporter of the college, its enlarged usefulness would be assured." At the same time, Gwaltney must have also discussed the matter informally with various other persons in town. Weeks passed and Shorter made no overt response to Gwaltney's overture.

However, Shorter conferred with two of his friends, Charles G. Samuel and John W. Janes, both members of the Rome Baptist Church and trustees of the college. Years later Samuel recorded the events as he remembered them. Shorter expressed his intention to use some of

23

his wealth "toward helping an orphan asylum." They countered by suggesting that "a Baptist female college would be an ideal investment." He agreed to give the matter "serious consideration," to which Samuel responded: "Yes, Col. Shorter, make it your child." At this, Shorter "smiled approvingly." The next morning Shorter came to Samuel's office, "smoking a cob pipe." He shared his decision with Samuel, a decision made "while crossing the bridge this morning." He would give the college $20,000—selling three residences worth $9,000 through Samuel, who was to receive no commission, and adding the remainder in cash. His other condition was that Samuel would prevail upon each stockholder to transfer his stock to Shorter, who would thereupon pay off the note for the remainder of the original purchase price, have the land title made over to himself, and "hold it for the Baptists until they are ready to proceed." Samuel was sworn to secrecy until the business arrangements had been completed and Shorter was ready to make public the news of his gift.

Unaware of this activity, Gwaltney grew progressively despondent regarding the prospects of the college. Thus, in May when the trustees of Judson Institute, Marion, Alabama, offered him the presidency of that school for young ladies, he conveyed to them his tentative acceptance of the position, postponing a final answer until he visited the campus on June 22. Word of Gwaltney's probable move to Alabama reached Colonel Shorter. On the day that Gwaltney was scheduled to leave for his inspection of Judson, he was called to Shorter's office. There he was told: "Dr. Gwaltney, several months ago, I received a letter from you, asking me to devote a part of my wealth to the building of a college for women. I put your letter aside, but the suggestion took root in my mind and heart, and all through the months that have intervened since the reception of your letter, I have been thinking of how I could best carry out the great plan about which you wrote. I have asked you here to say that if you will give up the idea of leaving Rome and remain with us, I will start the building of a college with $20,000 cash." Gwaltney replied that his proposition had come too late, since he felt partially committed to the Judson trustees. He continued: "But let me say this: Whether I accept the Judson or not, you must make the Cherokee College your child. Do for it all that money can accomplish, and you will never regret it."

Shorter decided to act upon his intention, and Rome soon learned of it. On Monday, June 19, 1876, a called conference of the Rome Baptist Church was held, at which time resolutions were unanimously passed commending Shorter for his "most liberal donation" and requesting that Gwaltney stay in Rome. Earlier Shorter had expressed

24

objection to a suggestion that the name of the college be changed, but the citizens of Rome were of a different mind. Some in the conference wanted to call it Martha Shorter College—and while the Colonel came to favor this, Mrs. Shorter did not. Others proposed that its name become Alfred Shorter College. Charles G. Samuel later wrote: "I moved to lay each amendment on the table, because to name it either Martha or Alfred Shorter would imply the exclusion of the other, but if named Shorter College, would include both, and then it was more appropriate as it was a Shorter name." The Rome newspapers of the following week frequently mentioned his gift—and repeated the pun concerning the new name. The initial expectation in Rome was that Shorter would enlarge the present college building, improve the grounds, and arrange for a dormitory. Gwaltney privately had urged him to replace all existing structures, however, and this was the course which was eventually adopted.

Meantime the commencement exercises were held that June, and four graduates received their diplomas. Gwaltney then admitted that "this has been one of the most arduous years of my life; I have worked hard all the time, and have tried to make you do the same. . . . He then propounded the following problem: If it takes six teachers to keep seventy-five girls straight in school time, what will become of them in vacation?"

Early in July Gwaltney resigned as pastor of the Rome Baptist Church, to take effect the following September 1. A similar resignation must have been presented to the trustees of the college, but no records have been preserved. Commenting on his departure, a Rome newspaper stated: "The entire community deplore the idea of losing one who has been so eminently acceptable, not only to his own congregation, but all the others and the community at large." Of course no one could foresee the future. After six years as president of Judson Institute, Gwaltney was to resume his relationship with the college that he had helped to found—this time as its full-time president.

The Mallary Administration

Seeking a man to take Gwaltney's place, the trustees invited the Reverend Rollin Daniel Mallary, principal of the female school and pastor of the Baptist church at Albany, Georgia, to confer with them in mid-July. He spent a few days in Rome, was offered the position, and left town virtually certain that he would accept it. On July 29 the trustees formally elected him as president, professor of mental and moral philosophy, and head of the boarding department. His wife was

25

named associate in the boarding department and professor of mythology and history by mnemonics.

Mallary came to the college at the age of forty-eight, having previously spent twenty-five years as an educator. Son of the famous Baptist clergyman, Charles D. Mallary, he was born at Minervaville, South Carolina, in 1828. From Mercer University he received the Bachelor of Arts and Master of Arts degrees during the presidency of the venerable and eminent theologian, John L. Dagg. In 1853 he married one of Dagg's daughters, nineteen-year-old Mary Jane, and they had nine children, five of whom lived to adulthood. From 1851 to 1876 he served

President Rollin D. Mallary

preparatory schools in Columbus, Macon, and Albany, Georgia, was professor of belles lettres at Georgia Female College, Madison, and was president of Southwestern Baptist Female College, Cuthbert, Georgia, and of Union Female College, Eufaula, Alabama. During much of this time he was a deacon active in the life of nearby Baptist churches. In 1874 he was ordained to the Gospel ministry, but was initially pastor of only one or two churches. It was said that he had been offered the leadership of eleven other colleges since the war, and Rome felt fortunate to secure a person of his proven abilities. Actually, however, his wife was the more widely known of the two, having already achieved some national fame for writing two religious novels, *Horace Wilde* and *Elsie Lee*.

On September 4 the college opened with the smallest student body in its history—and its brightest prospects. About 80 were enrolled, of whom only about 8 were boarders. Extensive "chemical and philosophical apparatus" had been purchased for use. Shorter's gift of $20,-

000 had given the college a much-needed stimulus, but plans for his further philanthropies were still being confidentially discussed only with his wife. The young ladies soon found that the new president was a genial and informal individual who slipped food under the table, gave them his dessert, or winked when they unlawfully secreted biscuits in a napkin and removed them from the dining room "with a quick, guilty tread . . . ." They also soon found that his wife was stern and strict, always properly dressed, and not a little vain.

During the first two years of his administration, President Mallary was employed by the trustees at a specified, but now unknown, salary. After this, he agreed to a new contract by which he leased the college from the trustees for a period of three years. For twenty-seven years he and later presidents operated the school under the "lease-system," by which they paid for faculty salaries and other current expenses out of income from tuition, room, and board, and the trustees paid for capital improvements and scholarships out of income from the endowment which was soon established. The precise terms of the agreements varied from time to time, of course, and disagreements arose as to who should pay for certain items. The president was required to render a report to the trustees periodically—usually annually, and at times more frequently—regarding the size and condition of the student body, the persons on the faculty, and the expenditures that he had made on behalf of the school. Meantime, the trustees maintained a nominal control over the college through its executive committee and its buildings, grounds, and furniture committee, the members of which worked closely with the president and his associates.

Enrollment, Tuition, and Fees

During the six years that Mallary was president, student enrollment gradually increased from about 80 to 169—an average of about 137 each year. Approximately one-half were in the collegiate department. After the dormitory opened, the number of boarders reached a high of about 56 during his fifth year. The opening years of uncertainty were assuredly past; the college was prospering numerically as never before.

From the beginning a small number of boys had been accepted in the primary department, reaching a total of 16 in 1879. No reason was given when the catalogue of that year stated: "Boys will not be received in future."

One of the new students was fifteen-year-old Mollie Young of Cedartown, who much later recorded her memories: "I go to college! Not as

27

our mothers went, in family carriages and in silk attire, with Saratoga trunks, and often with a negro maid in attendance, for this was another day. We had shining zinc trunks, filled with bleached petticoats, long-sleeved gowns and other durable garments, but no silk, lacy lingerie nor toilet accessories. . . . What was my reaction to this great event in my life? At first, a dreadful nostalgia . . . . But these emotions could not long survive among kind and understanding teachers, and an aggregation of the finest girls that a benign providence ever brought together. . . . Of course, as yet, there were practically no professional fields opening up for women, unless marriages could be classed as a profession. To be candid, we must admit that we had dreams of success in such a field, and struggled on hopefully toward that goal."

Tuition and fees remained constant in the primary and preparatory departments and increased only slightly in the collegiate. For a minimum of $235 a boarder could attend Shorter for a full academic year, and the total would seldom exceed $365. Scholarships were continued for the daughters of active clergymen and for orphan children sponsored by benevolent institutions. Special terms were offered to those persons having several daughters enrolled in Shorter at one time. Briefly free tuition was given to the daughter of a deceased Confederate soldier to be selected by the local Fair Association. An important addition was made in 1879 when Alfred Shorter offered to advance up to $1,250 for the instruction of "beneficiaries," young ladies whose tuition would be waived. After he established a permanent endowment for the school, beneficiaries were provided out of the annual income from that source.

The New Building

After Gwaltney's departure, the Rome Baptist Church called Gustavus A. Nunnally to be pastor, and he assumed that position on November 19, 1876. Early the following year he was invited by the trustees of Mercer University to join the staff of that institution and devote his energies to fund-raising. Nunnally agreed and tendered his resignation to the Rome church. For the first time in his life, Alfred Shorter rose in church conference and made a speech. He asked Nunnally to withdraw his resignation until the two could confer. The surprised Nunnally acceded to this, and the next day Colonel Shorter came to his home. Nunnally recalled Shorter's words: "I am going to tell you something that I have never told anyone except my wife. Dr. Gwaltney talked to me about it, but I had not matured my plans before he left, but now I have fully determined to build a college. It may cost me

$100,000 or $200,000 or $300,000. I know nothing about a college. You do. I want you to remain here until the college has been built, completed, and in operation." After careful consideration, Nunnally decided to stay in Rome, and the two men developed their project. A. C. Bruce, an architect of Knoxville, Tennessee, presented plans which were accepted in May of 1877. C. M. Pennington, one of Shorter's best friends, was secured as superintendent of construction. Although Shorter had much more in mind, public announcement still indicated only that one building would be erected adjacent to the one already standing.

Construction was begun in August of 1877, as the contract was

Earliest known picture of the college, taken about October, 1877. Shorter Female College Academic Building and Chapel are on the left. Cherokee Baptist Female College Building is on the right.

awarded to J. A. Cooley, a local contractor. Concurrently he built the Masonic Temple still located at the corner of Broad Street and Fourth Avenue. Under Pennington, the work of removing the crest of the hill and terracing the property progressed rapidly. Some Romans considered this to be the real cause of a small outbreak of typhoid fever in the community, but the Rome *Weekly Courier* was careful to assert that this judgment was "erroneous, according to our medical opinion." Although Cooley lost over forty thousand bricks in an accident at his kiln, he was able to continue construction at a satisfactory rate. Every two or three days Shorter would be joined on campus by Mallary and Nunnally to inspect the building. One of the students later recalled his being "so gentle and amiable to the school-girls, but like a military General directing his forces, when it came to bossing men and building Colleges."

The cornerstone was laid at elaborate ceremonies held on October 18, 1877, beginning at 3:00 P.M. The editor of the *Weekly Courier* reported: "A wooden arch and a rostrum near the corner of the building were tastefully decorated with flowers, and there was also a raised platform opposite the rostrum, and it too was embellished with beauty, whence came sweet music from the joint choirs of our churches led by the tones of an organ placed there for the purpose. . . . Appropriate music from the Silver Cornet Band added greatly to the interest and pleasure of the occasion." The Masons of Oostanaula Lodge No. 113 laid the stone, and David E. Butler of Madison, a prominent Georgia Baptist clergyman and Most Worthy Grand Master of the Grand Lodge of Georgia, was the featured speaker. Just before the oration, someone asked for Colonel Shorter, but he was nowhere to be found. Later in the day he was seen coming into town from one of his nearby plantations. He explained his absence in these words: "I knew that those speakers would say something about me. I could not stand it, so I went where I could not hear it." The inscription on the cornerstone further indicated his modesty. Several suggestions had been submitted to him, some of which were loud in their praises of his virtues. Pastor Nunnally composed the one that was finally selected: "A GIFT TO OUR DAUGHTERS FROM ALFRED SHORTER." An iron box inside the stone contained numerous appropriate objects, including a short history of the college, annual catalogues, names of pupils and faculty members, and the "autograph signature of Rev. L. R. Gwaltney the first President and first friend of the College." Of this the newspaper editor remarked: "If ever a man deserved a warm place in the hearts of . . . the friends of education, he does, and such place we believe he has in the hearts of all who know him here. And we would wish him nothing worse than that the story of his labors for the building up of this school shall go down from generation to generation, until the marble of the cornerstone of the college building, disintegrated by the lapse of ages, shall expose his autograph to sight again." From Marion, Alabama, Gwaltney later wrote a letter expressing his appreciation that he had been remembered on that day. He concluded with words about Alfred Shorter: "Its generous friend has acted wisely and well. May he live many years to perfect the work so auspiciously begun."

Early in January, 1878, the roof was added to the structure, after which the interior of the building was completed. Thus, it was ready for use at the commencement held in June of 1878.

Numerous photographs, sketches, and word-pictures of the new building remain. Facing Elm Street (now East Third Avenue) it was 65 feet across the front, extending 90 feet deep along Alpine Street (now East Third Street). Officially designated the College Edifice, it was constructed of brick, with its windows and doors trimmed in marble. Thirteen rooms were provided for administrative and instructional purposes in the two- and three-story portion of the structure which was marked by a large corner tower. In the rear, an integral part of the building was the Memorial Chapel, measuring 40 by 60 feet and seating five to eight hundred. It was described in these words: "The walls and ceiling are adorned with paintings in fresco, and the windows are of stained glass. The Memorial Window, a rare specimen of art, is in memory of Mrs. Martha B. Shorter: on it are eight paintings, from Bible subjects, illustrating the life and reward of a good woman." Over the stage was a motto from Job 28:18: "The price of wisdom is above rubies." The campus was terraced; iron steps were installed containing the inscription, "Shorter College—1877"; and paths, trees, and shrubs were added. It has been estimated that Shorter expended approximately $30,000 on this first building.

According to President A. W. Van Hoose in 1910, this location was actually no more than a second choice for the Colonel—although all known contemporary records are entirely silent at this point. Both Gwaltney and Nunnally were in Rome as the plans developed to move the college to its present campus west of Thornwood, and either or both could have supplied Van Hoose with his information as he wrote: "Since 'Maplehurst' has been selected as the site for the 'Greater Shorter,' it has developed that this is the very site which Col. Shorter first selected for the College he wished to found, but certain influences were exerted which caused him to place it on its present location."

Mrs. Shorter did not live to see the completion of this first building, dying on March 22, 1877, at the age of seventy-eight. The faculty and students were present at the funeral, President Mallary led in prayer, and Pastor Nunnally delivered the eulogy. She was soon to be memorialized in the stained glass window already described and by the eventual forming of the Martha Shorter Missionary Society at the college. Before her death the pupils of the college had often eaten Thanksgiving dinner in her home; with her demise, they lost a grandmotherly friend.

At the completion of this first building, the involvement of Rome in a state-wide debate concerning the location of a proposed Georgia Baptist female university was brought to a close. It had been suggested to the Georgia Baptist Convention, meeting at Rome in April of 1873, that "a well-endowed institution of learning for the higher education of our daughters" be placed under the control of the convention—thus providing a counterpart for the all-male Mercer University. For the next four years the matter was discussed at great length, as more than a dozen Georgia communities expressed interest. At the height of the controversy, 1875 and 1876, the Rome newspapers frequently urged local action leading to the adoption of Cherokee Baptist Female College by the convention. At the meeting of the convention held in April of 1876, after an extended argument on the floor, the entire matter was tabled and the existing schools—at Forsyth, LaGrange, Perry, Madison,

Cuthbert, and Rome—were all commended. The Georgia Female Seminary (now Brenau College) was accepted the following April by the convention, which disclaimed any financial responsibility for the school and expressed readiness to accept any other school under the same terms. Nunnally appeared at the meeting "in behalf of the citizens of Rome, and asked for time to perfect and present a proposition." Alfred Shorter's contributions made such a proposition unnecessary, of course, and the end of this episode was marked by a statement composed by Nunnally and adopted at the meeting of the convention held in April of 1878:

We should feel grateful to God that he should put it into the heart of that devout servant of His, brother Alfred Shorter, to build and endow the college at Rome with such splendid and unrivaled facilities for the education of girls, and we commend the same to the Baptists of our country as in every respect worthy of their patronage and support.

Subsequently the convention often mentioned the college briefly but favorably and in 1886, when it met again in Rome, accepted an invitation to visit the campus.

The stockholders of the college had unofficially agreed to assign their stock to Alfred Shorter in June of 1876. This was done legally at a meeting of the group on February 13, 1877. Now that the property was entirely in Shorter's hands and his plans for a new building were public knowledge, the board of trustees sought for three amendments to the charter of the institution:

1st: That the name of said Institution be changed to "Shorter Female College."
2nd: That Alfred Shorter shall have the right and power to appoint the Board of Trustees.
3rd: That the Board of Trustees shall be seven instead of eleven Trustees, said Trustees to be members of regular Baptist Churches in good standing, said Trustees shall have the right to fill any vacancy in their Board that may occur by death, removal, resignation, or otherwise.

These requests were granted by the Superior Court of Floyd County on January 31, 1878, after which the new name, already regularly used in the local newspapers for five months, became entirely proper. The final legal step in the transaction was taken on July 22, 1878, when Shorter presented his college holdings to the board of trustees. The deed read in part:

Alfred Shorter . . . as "A Gift to our Daughters," appreciating the blessings of education, and desiring to benefit the community, and the world, in the instruction and elevation of the women of the land, and thereby the whole race of mankind, the said Shorter having expended at least Fifty Thousand

Dollars, to establish permanently said Institution in the City of Rome, does hereby transfer and convey . . . all the real estate . . . and all the buildings erected thereon, and all the furniture, apparatus and other outfit . . . to the Trustees aforesaid, upon the condition that said Trustees, and their successors in office, shall have no power, in any event, or under any circumstances, to involve in debt, the corpus of the property, of said Institution . . . .

Two Additional Structures

Apparently many in Rome initially had expected that the first academic building, which had once been a private residence, would be renovated and become a dormitory for boarding students. Shorter's plans were much more ambitious than this, however, and foundations for a dormitory were laid in May of 1878 and the old building was razed the following month. Nunnally reported that "a large force was put to work" and that the dormitory was "rapidly approaching completion" in August, but it is not known when it was first occupied. For five years the boarders—probably never more than 17 in any single year—had stayed in private homes off campus, and those who came on September 3, 1878, could have done likewise if the dormitory were not ready for them on opening day. Certainly it was completed no later than the summer of 1879: a datable photograph and description remain, and 41 boarders were enrolled that year. The structure was 114 by 50 feet in size and faced Elm Street (now East Third Avenue) to the right of the Academic Building as one climbed the steep steps from the street. The four-story, brick structure contained the president's office and apartment, kitchen, dining room, laundry and ironing room, parlors, music room, thirty-six bedrooms, and "bathing tubs and every other modern appliance for . . . comfort and convenience . . . ." It was lighted by gas and heated by steam—although coal grates were often used when the steam plant was inoperative. At the front were two towers and a veranda on which the girls could stroll; at the rear a porch extended the entire length of the building and led to the Academic Building and Chapel. Since very few schools for young women had as many as 100 boarders, these accommodations for 72 were thought to be entirely adequate for the future. The cost of this building has been estimated at approximately $30,000, and it was called Pennington Hall, in honor of the man who supervised its construction.

Soon thereafter the college catalogues began to mention the presence of Negro maids, the first of many who have served the school. "The bed-rooms are attended to by servants in every particular, not by the pupils; thus giving ample time for fresh airing every morning, and permitting the pupils to spend in exercise or study the time frequently devoted to domestic duties, which can be easily learned and practiced at home when necessary." In time a few servants' houses were erected on the campus, northeast of the dormitory and off the crest of the hill.

As the college experienced a steady growth, Colonel Shorter became increasingly aware that an additional building was highly desirable. Accordingly, by March of 1880 A. C. Bruce, who by then had moved to Atlanta, was preparing plans for this expansion. In August of that year a contract was signed with Messrs. Cooley and Patton for the erection of a three-story, brick building measuring 40 by 60 feet. Standing behind Pennington Hall and connected with it by a covered passageway, the structure was at first called the Music and Art Building. The first floor was divided into ten practice rooms, the second floor was furnished as a study hall, and the third floor became the art studio. It was completed early in the summer of 1881, costing perhaps $30,000.

The first possibility of taxation faced the college in the fall of 1881. The state constitution had earlier exempted all nonprofit colleges, but more recent legislation had led some to think that this provision had been removed. Hence, the Rome city council ordered all school and college property to be taxed. Letters in opposition by a member of the Shorter faculty, an anonymous trustee of the college, and President Mallary appeared quickly. The faculty member felt that the tax was legal but inexpedient, since it would in effect increase tuition and thereby be ultimately harmful to Rome. The other two defenders felt that the council action was illegal because the college had been a charitable institution from its beginning. Indeed, apart altogether from Alfred Shorter's large gifts, the college for several years had provided free tuition for about twenty Romans annually, thereby actually adding to the local economy. All three letters courteously invited the council members to reconsider their recent action, and since this was eventually done, the threat of taxation passed.

General Academic Matters

The courses of study were subject to gradual change. To the primary curriculum the faculty added drawing, calisthenics, and French, while they added drawing, natural history, and French to the preparatory curriculum. The collegiate department came to be subdivided into only four departments: natural science, modern language, music, and design. However, the overall course of study remained virtually the same as before, and the same seven areas were studied by the pupils. One innovation was introduced. The designation of classes was made —freshman, sophomore, sub-junior, junior, and senior—and the course of study for each was outlined. With the addition of the sub-junior year, a young lady might now be as much as nineteen years of age at graduation. By 1879 the two lesser collegiate awards had been dropped, and only the graduation diploma was given. In the first nine years of its existence, the college awarded 83 graduation diplomas, of which 78 came during the Mallary years. Of course examinations and report cards were retained. Five periods of testing were scheduled each year —in October, December, February, April, and June—and trustees and patrons were invited to witness both the written and oral aspects of them.

Within the Departments

The faculty expanded slightly in size. Ten persons were on the teaching staff one year, and the average was 8.

Faculty salaries were first made a matter of record in 1878. The president and his wife were guaranteed $2,000 annually, plus room and board, even though the lease-system was already in effect. Two full-time male professors received $1,400 each, while full-time female teachers were paid from $400 to $800 each. In most cases, room and board were also provided, adding substantially to the level of salaries.

ART. Under Miss L. Ella Leftwich the art department for nine years retained its excellence. Budding artists were given instruction in pencil and crayon drawing, water color and oil painting, and the theory of design. "Advanced pupils are taught Portrait Painting if desired, and are encouraged to sketch from nature, and reproduce the beautiful, unsurpassed scenery around College Hill." Later china painting and wax work were added to the offerings. The earliest known medal was awarded by A. C. Bruce, architect of Shorter College, to the most proficient art student of 1879–1880.

MUSIC. The department of music continued presenting concerts to which the public was invited, despite changes in personnel. For one year Carl Hintz, a native of Germany, was on the faculty. One of his students recalled that she had hitherto always studied under pianists who allowed her some choice of the selections she would learn. "But with the advent of Professor Hintz this system was changed. He arbitrarily made his own decisions. . . . He gave me a new 'piece' and didn't bother to find out whether I liked it or not. I worked on it some, but not very diligently, for I could seem to find nothing in it but movements, no tune at all. When time came for my next lesson I had made a decision, too, and innocently and nonchalantly informed him that I didn't believe I'd learn it. My! What had I said to arouse his ire? As he rose from his chair every hair on his partly bald head stood erect! He shook his finger in my face and thundered at me, 'Do you presume to criticize my friend, Gounod?' " At Hintz' departure William F. Clark, trained at the New England Conservatory of Music, headed the department for four years, being assisted by Miss Carrie Cowles. Under him, lessons were offered in piano, organ, violin, harp, guitar, cornet, and voice. Courses were devoted to "Notation, Musical Theory, Thorough-Bass and Harmony." During the fall of 1879 the Musical Association, apparently a civic music group, was reorganized by Clark and several other competent musicians of Rome, meeting each Thursday evening in the parlor of Pennington Hall and allowing the advanced music pupils of the college to become members. Soon thereafter a college choir was organized. Because Rome was seldom visited by outstanding artists, the students and faculty members went to Atlanta for performances.

MODERN LANGUAGES. The modern language department achieved regional renown starting in 1879 when Dr. J. C. Lynes, a graduate of universities in Paris and Berlin, introduced the then-unusual "natural method" in his instruction. "No grammar is studied in the commencement, but at the end, so to speak, when the pupils are familiar with the *spoken language*. Its peculiar character is to teach as a parent teaches, by ear, speaking only the language studied . . . ." Success was instantaneous according to the students themselves: "French at table—French on the terraces—French in the Halls—French in the Section rooms. The Natural System is working wonders in Shorter College." "Rose Geranium" wrote that "we always look forward with the greatest pleasure to our recitations, for it is quite a recreation from the hard studying and toiling over books . . . ." At once Lynes formed a French and German Society and scheduled frequent meetings. The first "Soiree Litteraire" featured advanced pupils who presented recitations, essays, and songs. "Col. Shorter, the generous founder of Shorter College, honored the evening with his presence, and must have felt convinced that his 'Gift to our daughters' was in safe keeping with such a faculty." The news reporter added: " 'La fortune est une bien bonne chose, mais l'education est meilleure': so thought one of the visitors assembled last Friday evening dans le salon spacieux du College Shorter. If he possessed the ready tongue of Professor Lynes' eleves, he might do justice to this, the most delightful soiree of the season . . . ." Lynes himself was described as being "idolized by his class, who look upon him as a philological wonder—a sort of linguistic phenomenon, which, indeed he is . . . ." Under the direction of Lynes and Clark the first session of the Southern Normal School of Languages and Music was held at Shorter for six weeks during July and August of 1881. An unknown number of teachers and other interested persons was present, some attending Lynes' classes on the natural method and others taking music lessons from Clark. The complete cost was about $40 for music and $50 for language, and this price included room and board at the college. A second session, under the sole leadership of Lynes, was held the following summer, at which time he also offered instruction in science. A third session, also under Lynes, was scheduled for the summer of 1883, but it is now uncertain whether it materialized. On a less ambitious level, Lynes also offered evening classes in French to interested townspeople. These were held three evenings a week for twenty-four weeks, at a cost of $30 per pupil.

NATURAL SCIENCES. The same Professor Lynes taught the natural sciences also. One student noted that his laboratory "has become one of the pleasantest, most instructive places wherein to spend profitably a leisure half hour." In providing for this, the industrious pupil felt, President Mallary "seems to realize that this is an age of progress, and that in order to meet with success he must keep pace with the progressive spirit in sciences as in all things else." Field trips formed a part of Lynes' instruction, as indicated by this observation: "Prof. Lynes escorted the Senior and Junior classes this week to see the telephone and telegraph. We enjoyed it exceedingly."

OTHER COLLEGIATE DEPARTMENTS. Other departments were active too. A public exhibition of the calisthentics class was held at the local skating rink, featuring interludes by various student musicians. Pastor Nunnally delivered an address in this connection, "highly spoken of" but not otherwise described. As a part of the senior year, Mrs. Mallary introduced courses titled "History by Mnemonics," in which she taught by the use of memory devices. Since no examples of her work have been preserved, it is now impossible to describe her technique with greater precision. Nevertheless it is true that the college attained local fame for this form of teaching. One of the graduates recorded her exposure, during her senior year, to a couple of notable books on Christian ethics and apologetics by the widely known John L. Dagg, father of Mrs. Mallary. Although these volumes had been used at the college from its beginning, she was the first to comment directly on them. "These books, having been written before the war, contained a chapter defending slavery, proving by the scripture that such a system was right. Of course we ignored those chapters because that question had been settled for us." Finally, a commercial department was organized in the fall of 1879 to acquaint the young ladies with bookkeeping and with business terms.

ALUMNAE TEACHERS. The first known Shorter graduate to serve on the faculty of her alma mater came during this period. Miss Marian Smith of the class of 1879 assisted in the preparatory department one year. Two others were student assistants with faculty standing. Miss Kate S. Winn of the class of 1881 was in the modern language department—and later married the professor! Miss Lola Milner of the class of 1882 was in the primary department and later returned to teach several subjects in the collegiate department for six additional years.

Organizing the Eunomian and Polymnian Societies

The Eunomian and Polymnian societies were formed in January of 1879. Two months earlier the R.O.K. Society had been reorganized after two years of decreasing vigor. At the suggestion of the president's wife, Mrs. Mallary, a change was decided upon, for reasons on which there was unanimous agreement: "1st. 'Competition is the life of trade.' For want of competition, the members of the R.O.K. society had grown lukewarm, and lost interest in their meetings &c. 2nd. Owing to the rapid growth of the college, the members of the society had become too numerous to be accommodated in any one room, which could be assigned to them." With the same unanimity, and again for two reasons, the former name was dropped: "1st. To avoid the appearance of dissension among the members—a faction withdrawing from the parent society. 2nd. To give each society an equal chance. Had one society retained the old name, it might have created a prejudice against it; or, on the other hand, enlisted the sympathy of former friends, to the injury of the new society." The property of the former society was equally divided between the two new ones, and the young ladies on campus were entirely satisfied with the new organizations. As a Macon newspaper commented: "The R.O.K. Society of the Shorter Female College, in Rome, has been divided into two, the Eunomian and the Polymnian, and the young ladies now think they r. o. k."

Signed "OLD MEMBERS," anonymous letters in the Rome newspaper indicated grave dissatisfaction on the part of others who had graduated earlier. They charged that the R.O.K. had suffered an "assassination." "It has been dissolved—annihilated—without the aid of judge or jury, and even denied the benefit of clergy." Concerning the division of property, it was asserted: "Surely, 'Dagg's Moral Science,' which was a text book of the College in our time, teaches no such monstrous doctrine, as that the right to the property of a deceased victim, necessarily belongs to those who effected its death." The former members had not been consulted in the matter—"we were not invited to be present at the obsequies." "In conclusion, we make a final appeal to those who have misused us: re-establish the R.O.K. Society in every feature as it was originally; we will work with you as heretofore in perfect harmony, otherwise we will always feel aggrieved." The "old members" held a reunion that spring, but the former organization was never reactivated in the collegiate department.

The names of the two new societies, recommended by Mrs. Mallary, indicated the classical bent of the institution. Eunomia was one of the Greek Horae, the goddess of moral law and order. Polymnia (Polyhymnia) was one of the Greek Muses, the goddess of poetry, music and dancing.

The groups doubtless composed rites of initiation, but only one pledge has been preserved: "You are now invested with the rights and privileges of membership in Eunomian Society. Cherish and maintain them and let the name you henceforth bear ever remind you that the fleeting hour ne'er returns to duties unperformed."

Each had a number of interests and functions. They were assigned "handsomely furnished rooms," and each attempted to build an excellent library for its own use. Periodically, meetings were held and papers on various literary subjects were presented and discussed. A "grand strawberry festival" was given at the Yeiser residence out in town, at which admission was 10¢ for the gentlemen and free for the ladies, the proceeds of which were used by the societies for their rooms.

Each of the groups had about fifty honorary members, including virtually all of the former graduates, Gwaltney and Townes, some members of the faculty, some trustees, business and professional men, and political leaders. Some were selected with an ulterior motive in mind, as one of the charter members later confessed: "We were as interested in furnishing our society halls as new housekeepers. Books and pictures were needed. These we acquired in a subtle and lady-like manner. We elected handsome and desirable young men as honorary members and notified them on perfumed notepaper and prayerfully awaited results, said results often taking the form of gifts of books and pictures." During commencement week the societies regularly had a reception for their honorary members.

Other social affairs were sponsored. In 1879 the Eunomian Society gave an oyster supper at Pennington Hall which "passed off pleasantly.

Quite a number of ladies and gentlemen came, not only to enjoy the good things set before them, but to encourage the young ladies in their efforts to improve their hall." They were especially flattered by the presence of Colonel Shorter. Later the societies proposed a joint entertainment, and it was reported that "the young men are on the qui vive to hear of the time" that it was scheduled. The only other word about it was this: "The rules of Shorter College were suspended last evening and the young ladies were allowed to entertain their gentlemen friends, which they did right royally."

Early in 1881 the Eunomian president was presented with a badge by a local merchant. It was described as follows: "Its centre is open-work, forming an exquisite monogram, E. S. This is surrounded by a heavy band, beautifully chased, on which is engraven the magic words, 'Eunomian,' 'Shorter College.' The design, in fact the whole workmanship, far surpasses anything of the kind we have ever seen." The badge for the Polymnian president is said to have originated at approximately the same time, but it was not mentioned on paper until the 1911 annual included a sketch of it.

Resulting from these two societies was the first student publication, the *Chimes*. Published monthly or bimonthly starting in February of 1879, for many years it was issued alternately under the direction of each society. At first it was a tabloid-size four-page newspaper, later becoming a pamphlet of twenty to forty smaller pages. Usually each one contained short stories, didactic essays, some poetry, news articles concerning the college, a few jokes, and advertisements from various Rome merchants. The subscription price was first set at 50¢ per year. Of course it preserved choice items that otherwise would have been forgotten long ago: "Have you seen the stationery of Shorter College? It is elegant." "O, how we do like to receive letters, and how eagerly do we listen for our names, when the list of letters, at noon, is called out." "A DANDY is generally supposed to be about one-fourth walking stick and the rest kid gloves and moustache." "At a certain store in Rome are three handsome, obliging clerks who never touch tobacco nor spirits in any form. Remember this, girls. Call on *Chimes* for the name of the store." "ANOTHER VICTIM.—For sometime Kittie had been suffering with heart disease, and under special medical treatment. Her case grew worse and worse daily, notwithstanding the skill and constant attention of her physician. Alas! Miss Kittie Jolly is no more. She—well, married Dr. Van Metre. Farewell, dear Kittie. The Polymnians will remember your many virtues, and will try to follow your illustrious example."

Rules affecting the behavior of boarding students were alluded to only generally in the catalogue of 1879. "This department is under the control of the President and his wife. Boarders are received as *members of their family*, and *governed as their children*." Parents were required to present written instructions covering numerous subjects relating to their daughter or ward: her course of study, her use of money, the name of the church that she was to attend on Sunday, and the extent of her social life. This system of control had been used in the South for fifty years; Shorter was not exceptional in this regard.

Many girls' schools of this period enforced on their pupils the wearing of uniforms, but this was not initially true at Shorter. The first clothing regulation came by action of the trustees in February of 1879: "Hereafter no pupil of Shorter College will be allowed to wear on Commencement or other public occasions, fabrics costing over 35 cents per yard, trimmings included. This rule is not to apply to clothing on hand." Prominently printed both in the *Chimes* and the annual catalogue, this limitation in price was considered by the administration to be "preferable to an established uniform."

Christianity on Campus

Religion played an important role in the life of the college. A "Beautiful sight" was described by one of the students—"the boarders in procession, on their way from Pennington Hall to the various churches, on Sabbath morning." According to the minutes of the Rome Baptist Church, "seats were assigned to Bro. Mallary for the use of the Young Ladies of Shorter College" who attended that church. Religious revivals were experienced occasionally at the college, and most boarders who had not already joined a church did so. Daily prayer meetings were held by the young ladies in the large parlor, where personal testimonies were given. A missionary society existed to which some of the students belonged, but little is now known about it. At least once young male visitors were admitted to a social affair that it sponsored. Unfortunately it rained on the important day, and one of the girls lamented: "As the Rome young men are so frail and delicate, few dared to venture out in such weather, nevertheless we had a real nice time, if we did have to divide forty girls between fifteen young men, which, according to my arithmetic, allowed each young man $2\frac{2}{3}$ girls." The boarding students participated in an infrequent Sunday school picnic held at Cave Spring. One such event was keenly anticipated: "Once there, under the shade of many trees and listening to the ripple of the limpid waters, we will drive away all thoughts of books for one day, and devote ourselves exclusively to the search of pleasure." At the picnic, the Cave Spring Baptist Church provided the food for President Mallary, the faculty, and the students; and the table "was covered with the choicest viands and delicacies, and filled to profusion."

Breaking the Routine

Special events added sparkle to the academic routine. As the Christmas of 1876 approached, a Rome newspaper recorded a rumble of discontent on the part of the students: "Some of the girls . . . say that President Mallary is very stingy, because he speaks of giving them only one week's vacation during the holidays. One week is enough, we think, young ladies. You will do enough mischief in that time, don't you think so?" Mallary did not repeat his "stinginess" the following year, for a vacation of two weeks' duration was announced. The majority of boarders would go home, of course, but every year a few would stay on campus. Hence, the newspaper observed one year: "The rules of Shorter College have been suspended for the holidays, and the young ladies appear to enjoy their freedom very much."

Undoubtedly the campus was a scene of excitement in 1878 when Mrs. Mallary gave birth to her ninth and last child, a son who was named Eugene Pennington. For the first four years of his life, while he was living on campus and sometimes entertaining the college girls with his antics, he went by the appropriate nickname, "Shorter" Mallary.

Classes were practically dismissed for an entire week in April of 1879 as the Georgia Teachers' Association held its thirteenth annual meeting at Shorter College. The members enjoyed the use of the chapel, inspected the buildings and grounds of the college, became acquainted with the faculty members, and heard the students present various musical numbers. The *Chimes* admitted that the girls had been looking forward to the event for several weeks and that "school books and all thoughts of them were banished to the vast realms of forgetfulness . . . . We thus had the opportunity to listen to profound essays and delightful lectures on subjects usually thought dull and wearisome to ardent youths . . . ." They expected to receive "inestimable benefits" from the speeches that they would hear—but honestly led them also to speak of the week as a "Celebration and Festival."

Before levees were built, Rome often experienced floods—sometimes of considerable proportions. During the spring of 1880 the Shorter pupils were almost marooned. "The view from College Hill was grand! Wherever we turned, nothing could we see but water, and we felt as though we were on some green island in mid-ocean. . . . It was strange to see hundreds of boats sailing up and down Broadway, and it was nice sport, too, for we enjoyed it ourself, thanks to a kind friend, who never forgets the College girls." Their pleasures were darkened somewhat, however, by one concomitant omission: "Next time it comes, the railroad, city or State authorities must build boats to bring our mail. Small matters like trade and commerce may stop; but we college girls *must* have our letters."

Commencement Week

Commencement ceremonies followed the familiar pattern already laid down in previous years. Late in June the baccalaureate sermon was delivered by a distinguished visitor at the Rome Baptist Church. Various literary and musical programs followed on the next two days in the college chapel. One such incident was comprised of a literary address by an Atlanta man and the reading of original compositions by the juniors. Commented one reporter: "We sat in the extreme rear part of the hall, and yet heard every syllable as distinctly as though the reader were sitting by our side (which—that is to say—a—that is—or rather which, we mean to say, we wish had been the case) ." The literary address prompted no such response. The formal graduation ceremony occurred on Wednesday, also in the chapel. A member of the class of 1879 later wrote about this event. The sixteen graduates endured the three-hour service "arrayed in beruffled white swiss, towing long trains, carrying white satin fans and essays tied with long white streamers." Referring to her composition, she recalled: "I was encouraged to believe that I could write a poetical essay, and there is a tradition that lingers yet about the time I climbed to the roof of Shorter to gaze on flying clouds, winding rivers, and distant mountains to invoke the poetic muse. . . . Fortunately, I knew doggeral from verse; consequently, I expressed my glowing thoughts in prose. My subject was 'Is a Thing of Beauty a Joy Forever?' " and her effort, according to the newspaper account, "received more applause than all her class combined." After all sixteen papers were read, President Mallary "delivered an able and feeling address . . . ." The diplomas were then awarded; a small choir presented the class song, "In the Sweet Bye and Bye"; the benediction was pronounced; "and the class of '79 were cast out on the stage of life to view the world no longer 'through the rainbow lenses of sanguine girlhood but henceforth as anxious women.' "

The graduates in the class of 1880 were the first to receive newly designed diplomas with a picture of Alfred Shorter, and one of them has been preserved—the earliest known. The diplomas were considered so desirable that members of previous senior classes were offered the privilege of receiving one for the low price of $2.

The Mallarys' Departure

The Mallarys remained busy in school and church affairs. At various times he was pastor of the Enon, Forrestville (now North Broad), and Cave Spring Baptist churches, preaching frequently throughout Northwest Georgia. She was organist at Rome Baptist Church and wrote her third religious novel, *New Fashioned Women*. However, the contract with President Mallary was renewed for only one year in 1881, suggesting that the trustees were not entirely satisfied with his administration. In March of 1882 they notified him that his contract would not again be renewed and that a successor was to be selected. At their June meeting they passed resolutions observing that he had conducted the institution "through the chaotic and formative condition incident to the transition from the old Cherokee Female College to the Shorter College . . . ." In doing so, they felt that he was worthy of commendation "as a gentleman of deep piety and strict integrity . . . as a thoroughly competent and efficient instructor . . . as a teacher of large and varied and successful experience, and as an organizer of great capacity and as a disciplinarian of unusual ability." "His excellent wife" was likewise recognized as "a woman of rare talent in the school room and of remarkable qualification for the management of the home life of girls committed to her care . . . ."

After leaving Shorter, Mallary spent five years as president of Shelby Female College in North Carolina, resigning because of ill health. For four years he was pastor of Baptist churches near Griffin, Georgia, after which he spent the remaining twenty-one years of his life in Macon, Georgia, where for three years he was the first pastor of Vineville Baptist Church. His wife wrote four more religious novels after leaving Rome and died at Macon in 1901. Eleven years later he died there at the age of eighty-four.

2
Years of Tranquillity

Gwaltney's Return to the College

For the second time, Luther Rice Gwaltney identified himself with the college which he had been so instrumental in founding—although, of course, its name had been changed while he was in Alabama as president of Judson Female Institute.

Early in 1882 Colonel Shorter urgently sent for him. Gwaltney later reported their conversation: "I found him in bed, very feeble, and much changed. We had a long and sad interview, though relieved with much that was cheering and precious. He asked me to return and take charge of the college . . . . I said, 'For what length of time?' He replied, 'For your lifetime, if you desire.' Tears filled his eyes and mine, as I said, 'I will do anything in my power for you. I will come back and take the college and do my best for it.'" He signed a contract dated March 20, 1882, agreeing to lease the college for ten years "as a first class institution, with a high grade and proper curriculum and a full corps of efficient and competent teachers in all and every department necessary for such an institution," the teachers to be selected by him with the approval of the trustees. No salary for him was specified; he was to receive the entire income from tuition, fees, room, and board— out of which were to come the salaries, the expenses of the boarding department, and the upkeep of buildings, equipment, and grounds. Gwaltney later wrote: "I never laid by a dollar from all the income of the college. I spent it for the liberal culture of the girls committed to my training—securing the best teachers I could command and reserving only a modest living for my family."

The Death of Alfred Shorter

Gwaltney returned to Rome at a time of mourning, for after months of declining health, Alfred Shorter died on July 18, 1882. Found in his wallet were these lines clipped from a newspaper: "I commend my soul into the hands of God my creator, hoping and assuredly believing, through the only merits of Jesus Christ my Saviour to be made partaker of life everlasting, and my body to the earth whereof it is made." He had regarded himself as a steward of God, telling Nunnally: "I can but wonder why the Lord allowed me, a poor boy, to make all this money. He must have intended that I use it for his glory, and I know of no better use to which I may put it than in building a school where God's name may be honored and where young women may be fitted to occupy stations of honor and usefulness, and thus make the college a blessing to humanity and a glory to God."

47

Shorter's estate was reliably estimated to be worth about $700,000. Among the many bequests in his will were two that related to the college: "I give and bequeath to the Trustees of Shorter Female College located in the City of Rome, Georgia, and to the successors in office $23,000 City of Rome bonds (known as 20 year bonds) and 100 shares of Rome Railroad Stock (making the nominal amount of $40,000), and this is my will that the corpus of said property as above mentioned be regarded as sacred and be forever set apart as a permanent endowment of the said . . . College . . . . Being satisfied that the . . . College is in present need of additional apparatus, furniture, instruments, etc. and that the grounds about the College buildings need improvement, I give to the Trustees of the said College an additional $5,000.00 to be used as soon as necessary under the direction of the President for the purpose above indicated . . . ." This portion of Shorter's will, in his own handwriting, was presented to the college in 1934 by Mrs. Shorter's niece, Mrs. D. B. Hamilton.

The trustees met, selected D. B. Hamilton as their new president, and unanimously adopted a resolution prepared chiefly by G. A. Nunnally. After recalling briefly Shorter's early life and financial abilities, it emphasized his years with Martha Shorter and his benevolences to the Rome Baptist Church and to his family. It continued: "And reaching beyond the home circle . . . his glowing heart was moved with a strong desire to benefit other children. Consequently he founded and built the Shorter College, upon which he spent his last days of toil and to which he gave his last hours of thought and care. He invested in buildings and furniture about one hundred and fifty thousand dollars during his lifetime, and intimated frequently in private conversation his determination to leave an endowment for the college . . . ." In view of his will, the resolution concluded: "Resolved: That we the trustees appointed by him to manage the Shorter College gratefully accept this trust confided to us and will faithfully endeavor to honor his memory by executing his wishes in dispensing his bounty to the beneficiaries of the college, that we will hold in last remembrance his noble virtue, spotless character and Christian life, and accept his example of diligence, piety and charity as a legacy worth preserving in the history of the institution and worthy of emulation in our individual lives."

Although these words undoubtedly were made public, rumors began to circulate around Rome that the trustees were dissatisfied with the provisions of the will. In order to squelch this false impression the trustees published a further resolution unanimously passed on May 30, 1883: "Be it resolved, that the noble spirit of benevolence and Christian philanthropy manifested in the erection of the college and the bequest by way of endowment are characteristic of the mind and character of the late Col. Alfred Shorter, and we hereby manifest our entire approval of the same, and although he may at some time have intended a bequest apparently more liberal, the expenditures afterwards made by him to a very great extent compensate any change he afterwards made."

An attempt to break the will was made by no less than twenty-three persons living as far away as Texas and the District of Columbia, and the case slowly moved through legal channels until the Georgia Supreme Court finally decided that the will could be executed. In July of 1884, two years after the death of Colonel Shorter, the trustees received the funds—$5,000 was immediately spent on improvements already made, and $40,000 was set apart as the first endowment of the college. In this way, Shorter College became the first institution for girls in the state of Georgia to have a permanent endowment.

The extent of Shorter's gifts to the college cannot be determined with accuracy. He liquidated the debts of the first three uncertain years and constructed and furnished three large buildings. Annually he supplemented the income of the college and paid the educational expenses for twenty to thirty young ladies. Finally, he provided a sizable endowment. An estimate by Van Hoose placed Shorter's total gifts at more than $165,000. The trustees in 1882 set the figure at $190,000. D. B. Hamilton publicly stated that "from first to last including the endowment Col. Shorter gave the college a quarter of a million dollars." Probably the truth lies somewhere between the extremes. He had doubtless contributed approximately $200,000.

The Gwaltney Administration

During his first year as president, Gwaltney made important additions to the life of the college. The Martha Shorter Missionary Society was organized on Sunday, February 4, 1883, holding its first meeting in the Memorial Chapel with its colorful stained glass window honoring the one for whom the society was named. Another day was added to the commencement program in 1883, as a memorial service for Colonel and Mrs. Shorter was introduced. The Alumnae Association was probably formed in 1883, holding its first reunion during commencement week, on June 28.

Other alterations were introduced as the Gwaltney administration continued. In the fall of 1883 arrangements were made for the first infirmary when a simple room was set aside for that purpose. The college catalogue soon noted: "Pleasant apartments are provided for the

49

sick. Meals will be served them *there* without extra charge, but will not be sent to private bed-rooms." A "College Depository" was also begun in the fall of 1883, the first book store on campus. Stationery, art materials, and sheet music were on sale, while textbooks could be rented. A small deposit was to be made for each student at the beginning of the term, thereby precluding the necessity of spending money for the girls. The trustees saw fit to enlarge the land holdings of the college three different times. In 1884 an adjoining lot was purchased for $1,200; in 1889 a house and lot, for $3,005; and in 1900 another lot, for $700. The brick house then called the Bayard House which stood a short distance from Pennington Hall soon became a dormitory for students and eventually was the residence of the college president.

Gwaltney felt the need for an associate in the growing school, and Archibald J. Battle, former president of Mercer University, became associate president in the fall of 1890. The trustees passed a resolution expressing "gratification at the prospect of Dr. Battle's association with our college." Each man had equal authority, exercised in different realms. Gwaltney supervised the financial dealings and the boarding department of the college; Battle directed its educational interests, exercised discipline, and lectured on mental and moral science and ancient languages. This arrangement existed for only one year—although apparently quite amicably—until Gwaltney resigned the following spring.

With a growing enrollment, it became imperative to provide more space for boarding students. This was effected by furnishing the Bayard House for student occupancy and by making renovations in the dormitory building. A contract was signed in August of 1890 for the erection of a three-story brick Kitchen Building that measured 24 by 52 feet, providing a kitchen and storeroom (that were soon turned to other uses) on the first floor, a laundry and ironing room on the second, and bathrooms, a linen room, and a servant's room on the third. The total cost of this building, plus repairing and painting the other existing buildings, was $4,715, and it was ready for use in February of 1891.

Having a son to educate in college and receiving an invitation to become pastor of the Baptist Church in Athens, Georgia, Gwaltney tendered his resignation to the trustees, effective June 10, 1891. After accepting it without comment, they agreed to purchase private property in the form of musical instruments, furniture, and the dining room outfit that he had been using at the college, and both parties expressed approval when fair valuation was set at $1,500.

The attitude of the community at large toward him was graphically shown at the graduation ceremony of 1891, which was his last as president. The large oil portrait of Gwaltney painted by Albert Guerry was given to the college by his friends in Rome. At the proper point in a presentation speech, two young ladies marched to the front, "all eyes were centered upon the picture, and as the features of the distinguished Doctor were revealed the audience burst into applause."

While in Rome Gwaltney had not departed altogether from the pastorate, having served the Cave Spring and DeSoto (now Fifth Avenue) Baptist churches for brief periods of time. Thus, his subsequent movements are not entirely surprising. For three years he remained at

President Archibald J. Battle

Athens, after which he spent eight years in a second pastorate at Edgefield, South Carolina. In 1902 he was for a third time to become associated with Shorter College.

The Battle Administration

The trustees had no difficulty in selecting a successor to Gwaltney, for Archibald John Battle was already on campus. A native Georgian, he was born at Powelton in 1826. After graduating in law from the University of Alabama, he spent twenty-five years in Alabama as a teacher, Baptist pastor, and president of Alabama Central Female College, East Alabama Female College, and Judson Female Institute. In Alabama he married Miss Mary E. Guild of Tuscaloosa, and they had five children. From 1872 to 1889 he was president of Mercer University, where he completed his regionally celebrated book, *A Treatise, Psychological and Theological, on the Human Will.* Four honorary doctor's

51

degrees were awarded to him, and for two years he was president of the Georgia Baptist Convention. Throughout his Mercer years he served as pastor of various churches and spoke widely over the state at religious and educational meetings. At the age of sixty-five, Battle was by far the oldest man ever to assume the presidency of Shorter.

He invited Ivy Walker Duggan, who for thirty years had successfully led preparatory schools in central Georgia, to become his associate. As the president, Battle was in charge of academic and disciplinary matters and was professor of psychology, ethics, and ancient languages. Duggan was the business manager, professor of mathematics, and steward of the dining room. Together they signed a contract for five years and two others for one year each, subject to the usual terms, with one major exception. For the first time in the history of the college, the new administration agreed to pay rent for the use of the buildings and equipment, varying from $250 to $1,250 annually. As a matter of fact, however, the trustees usually remitted the payments, and in seven years Battle and Duggan paid no more than $1,750, about thirty percent of the total.

The students found Battle to be tall, erect, courtly, and well dressed. His long white beard and hair were always carefully groomed. Although distinguished in manner and stern in discipline, he was genial, sympathetic, approachable, and beloved by his students. Mrs. Battle was a constant member of the embroidery class, but was physically unable to supervise the boarding department of the school. At her death in 1897 she was affectionately remembered by one of the students for her "sweet smiles," her "words of encouragement," and "the never-failing interest she manifested in all the girls."

Remarkably active for his years, President Battle was the founder and for eight years president of the Lanier Circle, a literary club in Rome, and lectured frequently before teachers' groups. As pastor of the Cave Spring Baptist Church for two or three years, he preached there and elsewhere with regularity. He even had time to give out the words at a spelling bee held for the benefit of the Methodist Church— as noted by a Rome newspaper editor who won the prize for missing every word, a dictionary! Nevertheless, as Battle approached his seventy-second birthday, the trustees were desirous of making a change in the administration of the college. In the spring of 1898 they signed a contract with Thomas J. Simmons to become the new president, after which they officially notified Battle and presented him with resolutions that said, in part: "Resolved, That our relations with Dr. Battle and Prof. Duggan have been pleasant and agreeable during the time of their association with us, and it gives us pleasure to say that their management of the college has been eminently successful and gratifying." This resolution was printed on page one of the Rome *Hustler-Commercial*, together with the news that Battle would "probably accept" a position that had already been offered to him on the new faculty.

Soon thereafter the paper noted that Battle had agreed to become president of a female college at Anniston, Alabama, while the Atlanta *Journal* reported that he and all of the teachers under him were "aggrieved" at the treatment they had received. The next day the trustees met and issued a response to the *Journal* article. In it they insisted that Battle and his staff had not been dismissed; the terms of the most recent one-year contract had simply run out. The contract required the serving of no notice, but in fact a notice of six months was being given. Certainly not all of the teachers were "aggrieved," because quite a number of them applied for positions under the new president—but it is true that Simmons retained only two of them. Representatives from all the classes in the collegiate department composed resolutions highly complimentary to Battle, Duggan, and Miss Eleanor Churchill Gibbs, professor of English, and these pleasantly surprised the honorees when they were printed in the Rome *Tribune* and the 1898 Shorter College annual.

Upon leaving Rome, Battle presided over the Anniston (Alabama) College for Young Ladies for four years. Several times during this period he came back to Rome and performed wedding ceremonies for his Shorter girls. Eventually he returned to Macon, Georgia, where he died in 1907. Indicating a continued affection and respect for him, a memorial service was held at the college and two years later the stained glass Battle Memorial Window was installed in the chapel by the ladies who had graduated during his administration.

Enrollment

During the nine years that Gwaltney was president, student enrollment varied from a low of about 170 to a high of about 220—the high coming the year after the Rome Female College closed. The yearly average was about 190, of whom probably about 120 were in the collegiate department. After 1883, when the first public schools opened in Rome, the number of primary and preparatory students decreased. The dormitory was filled to capacity most of the time, averaging about 70; and in 1885 it was declared: "Good board can be secured in private families, if any prefer it." For a few years "parlor boarders" were received, mature ladies not enrolled in classes who lived at the college. One year a male special student lived in the dormitory—apparently he was about twelve years old and lived with the president's family. Other males were also enrolled as special students in languages, music, and art, but they were allowed on campus only long enough to take their lessons.

During the Battle administration, student enrollment never exceeded approximately 200 in any one year, but the average rose to about 180. Figures are indecisive regarding the number of students in the collegiate department. Perhaps the number of boarding students averaged about 70, although the catalogues asserted that the capacity was 100.

One pupil recorded her earliest experiences related to the college. Miss Lucy Young of Cedartown entered Shorter in the fall of 1884. Since times were not so hard, "I had a huge trunk pressed just full— one dozen suits of 'spirit-of-the-loom' underwear, with lace, tucks, ruffling, all fluted; six calico dresses; twelve white aprons; one gray woolen uniform, with black velvet vest; and, Oh Boy! a blue silk dress! This did not quite fill my trunk so I swiped a few things from the family, among them Ma's white silk shawl. It took two mules to pull those clothes to the depot." As she boarded the train to Rockmart, "the crowning thing happened" when her father gave her a $5 bill "for pin money." After a layover of seven hours in Rockmart, she caught the train which arrived in Rome late that afternoon—a full day's journey from Cedartown to Rome! President Gwaltney met the train, inquiring: "Is there a young lady on board for Shorter College?" "I saw the passengers looking at me as I got up, and it made me feel very grand to be known as a young lady for Shorter!"

She found that Pennington Hall was a "modern up-to-date building" furnished with two bathtubs. "The rooms were lovely, each fitted out for four girls, two double beds, a dresser, with four drawers, one table, four chairs, one closet, and a nice little wash-stand."

The dining room also impressed her. "What did we have to eat? Plenty of good food,—nice country beef, rice, in fact every vegetable that grew under the ground and over the ground. And the dessert varied between hasty pudding, rice pudding, sweet pudding, poor man's pudding, and apple dumplings. When the old gong sounded we were ready to enjoy that nourishing food!"

That $5 bill did not last very long. "Ice cream was not sold down town and it was undignified for a woman to drink soda-water at the drug store." Hence, she soon saw "a gray cap-shaped hat, with a bill in front and a plume hanging off the back," and most of her money was left with the milliner as she wore that hat back up the hill.

Tuition, Fees, and Student Aid

The cost of attending Shorter College increased during the Gwaltney-Battle period of sixteen years. Under the former, while the term was still ten months in length, a boarder would usually be charged about $282 and seldom more than $422. When Gwaltney cut the term to nine months in 1887, these figures were reduced to $252 and $378 respectively, but the cost per month remained the same. Battle further reduced the fees to $237 and $372 respectively. The total income to the college from these fees was never officially stated in records that have been preserved and is usually a matter of conjecture. Duggan asserted that during his term as business manager, the students paid from $11,000 to $19,000 annually.

Scholarships were continued for the daughters of clergymen and for sisters, but discontinued for orphans sponsored by benevolent lodges. In 1893 free tuition was offered to the female graduate of the Rome public school who made the highest academic record. Others were also selected as beneficiaries, usually by the trustees, and the total apparently averaged about twenty per year.

Community Relations

It is evident that Shorter College was involved in the life of the wider community—the hill top location did not separate the school from the rest of the world. An entertainment of music and recitations was presented, with proceeds going to the Rome Baptist Church. Admission to a concert augmented the building fund of St. Peter's Episcopal Church. Profits from "A Midsummer Night's Dream" were given by the seniors to the women's department of the 1895 Cotton States and International Exposition in Atlanta. The operetta "Pinafore" was staged at the Nevin Opera House for the benefit of the Young Men's Library Association of Rome, and numerous Shorter professors and students were prominent in the production. A program was presented in Gadsden, Alabama, by members of the music and elocution faculty, and they were enthusiastically received. Often the Floyd County Teacher's Association met in the chapel, and faculty members participated. The Georgia Medical Association and the Georgia Federation of Women's Clubs met separately in Rome, where they were honored by concerts in the chapel. After the college girls were all safely home, a "grand levee" was held at Pennington Hall one summer in connection with a Fourth of July celebration. To these special occasions, of course, must be added the countless other programs open to the public that were regularly sponsored by the college, the evening classes offered in many subjects, the missionary activities of the Martha Shorter Missionary Society, and the religious and professional speeches made before many groups by the personnel of the college. Manufactured in Germany, ceramic items that publicized Shorter were available downtown—pickle dishes, decorative boots, and sugar and cream sets showing the main buildings.

General Academic Matters

Admissions requirements were specified in 1896—but little was really required. "Applicants for any class must give satisfactory proof of having pursued successfully the studies of the preceding classes." For the first time, some students were designated as "special"—those devoting themselves chiefly to music, art, or other optional studies and to at least one literary course.

Examinations were continued at intervals of four to six weeks, but evidently outside spectators were no longer invited. One student reflected her personal involvement as she wrote: "No one who has ever stood an examination can fail to appreciate a girl's anxiety and trepidation as she goes with her class to show how much she does or does not know; happy pupil, if she answers the questions intelligently and correctly; such a load, such an oppressing sensation is entirely removed; she feels 'almost too happy to live,' in her extravagant language! If, on the contrary, she shows that her acquaintance with the textbooks is not sufficiently thorough—ah! we can sympathize with her."

The two earliest report cards to be preserved come from the Battle era. One young lady in the senior class carried Original Composition, Trench on Words, Classics, Latin, Psychology, Physics, and Astronomy —averaging "V.G." (88) once and "Ex." (92) the other time. On individual courses she rated "Dis." (Distinguished, 99–95), but never as high as "Mx." (Maximum, 100)—and also "Md." (Medium, 85–80), but never as low as "T.," "Inf.," or "Def." (Tolerable, 79–70; Inferior, 69–60; Deficient, below 60). On both cards her grade for deportment was a commendable "Max."

A roll of honor was initiated in the fall of 1886, whereby a pupil would be listed if she made at least ninety percent in any one study for one session. At the graduation ceremony she was awarded a certificate of honor.

Gwaltney retained the sub-junior class that had been added during his absence but restored to the collegiate department the seven schools that he had originally formed in 1873, adding two others. These nine schools were as follows: English, history, moral philosophy, mathematics, ancient languages, modern languages, natural sciences, music, and art. A "Certificate of Proficiency" was provided for the successful completion of each school. Three grades of diplomas were provided for the graduates. The "Full Diploma" was awarded to those completing the seven schools of the collegiate department, one ancient and one modern language being required. Music and art were optional. The "English Diploma" was awarded to those completing the schools of English, history, mental and moral philosophy, and natural science and the schools of Latin and mathematics through the sub-junior class. Extra work in English was substituted for the omitted two years of Latin and mathematics. The "Eclectic Diploma" was awarded to those completing the schools of English, history, and natural science, the schools of Latin and mathematics through the sub-junior class, and the advanced course in music or art.

Gwaltney introduced a postgraduate course, providing for advanced study in music, art, languages, science, and general literature. "Handsome Gold Medals" were awarded to those successfully completing any one of these areas. Total charges for room, board, and tuition were $260 annually in one department, $300 in two, and $350 in three.

A "Normal Course" was offered by Gwaltney for the first time, providing "a systematic course in the Theory and Practice of Teaching." No details were given, and only two are known to have enrolled.

At the request of President Battle in 1892, the trustees authorized the faculty to confer degrees on the graduates. Henceforth the full graduates received the degree of A.B. or *Artium Baccalaura*; the graduates in the English course, the L.B. or *Litterarum Baccalaura*; and the postgraduates, the A.M. or *Artium Magistra*.

Some afternoon and evening classes had been offered earlier, but under Battle they were multiplied. Lessons were available for townspeople in French, music, art, embroidery, and elocution. No record remains of enrollment figures.

At the sixteen commencement ceremonies of this period, 231 young ladies were graduated from Shorter College, 93 under President Gwaltney and 138 under President Battle. Their awards were divided as follows: Full Diploma, 65; English Diploma, 14; Eclectic Diploma, 22; *Artium Baccalaura*, 40; *Litterarum Baccalaura*, 90. In 1930 the

57

trustees awarded a diploma to Mrs. A. H. Gibson (née Miss Annie Bruce), who was supposed to have graduated in 1891, thus raising the total to 232!

Within the Departments

As the student enrollment went up, the faculty and staff expanded in size. Ranging from 14 to 21, the number of faculty and staff members rose during this period to an average of 17 per year.

Salaries were reported for two successive years in the 1890s, and no annual increase was indicated! The president received $1,200 plus room and board for his family; the business manager, $800 plus room and board. Full-time male teachers were paid from $577 without room and board to $800 plus room and board; full-time female teachers, from $300 to $900 plus room and board.

ART. After studying in New York and Paris, Miss Anna M. Lester of Rome led the art department for five years, making use of many models which had recently been secured. Art embroidery was taught for nine years by a Shorter graduate, Miss Mattie Rowell.

ENGLISH. The English department enjoyed the services of two fine teachers, Miss Hattie A. Brown, a graduate of Shorter in the class of 1882, for five years and Miss Eleanor Churchill Gibbs for twelve. The latter was described as the queen of the queen's English, cultured, gracious, energetic, tenderhearted, and snowy-haired. She was very careful about the girls' behavior, feeling that it was bad manners to cross one's legs. Thus, when any pupil on the front row did so, Miss Gibbs would place a waste paper basket in front of her to obscure the ankles that might immodestly show. To meet such needs, she kept a supply of baskets in a convenient place. During one interview she suddenly said: "Here are my politics." "Where?" asked her companion. Miss Gibbs then pointed to a picture on the wall of Jefferson Davis holding the Confederate flag. More than simply a classroom teacher, she was said to have contributed essays and poems to the leading periodicals of the day.

MATHEMATICS AND NATURAL SCIENCES. Sometimes called "Mr. Jim" by the girls, James D. Gwaltney, a son of the president, taught mathematics and natural sciences for eight years. Apparently he was guilty of keeping his classes overtime, as is suggested by this item in the *Chimes*:

Hear the merry, merry chime
Say, the period is done!

58

And the pupils at one time,
"Mr. G. the bell has rung!"

He did not always make his classes unhappy, however. He took one senior class in geology on a field trip, principally to discover fossils. In the course of the hike, they came upon a bed of daisies, and though no daisy chain was made, they lost interest in fossils temporarily. When they had gone "what seemed to be at least four miles," they returned to the college by a different route. "We reached the river at twilight, and just in time to see one of the steamers land at the wharf." Back at the college, "a more tired crowd could hardly be found anywhere. But we had much fun, and will be glad for the time to come for us to go again."

For the use of the astronomy class, a telescope was ordered in 1883 and paid for the following year. Manufactured especially for the college in England and France, it finally arrived in 1888, five years after being ordered!

Widely appreciated by the girls was Ivy W. Duggan, professor of mathematics for seven years under President Battle. Genial, warm-hearted, and gentle, he was "dashed with the rich warm blood of the Emerald Isle" and possessed with a kindly sense of humor so that it could be said: "Every joke gives pleasure to everyone." Unlike Battle, he was sloppy in his attire, slouchy in appearance, often wearing baggy trousers. One of his pupils recalled: "In cold weather, Prof. Duggan would give us a cordial 'Good morning, young ladies. Come up to the fire and get warm, then take your places at the blackboard.'"

MUSIC. Although the department of music suffered from a rapid turnover of faculty persons during the Gwaltney years, the program of instruction was enlarged. By 1888 it was claimed that "a full conservatory course" was offered. Four full-time faculty members were provided, two of whom had been extensively trained in Germany. Instruction in piano, organ, violin, guitar, voice, and theory was emphasized—and was offered also in viola, banjo, mandolin, and harmonium. The new catalogue announced: "Pupils in every branch are required to practice a certain minimum of time fixed by the teacher, with a view to insure such improvement as can be expected; a maximum time is also fixed, in order to avoid the breaking down of industrious pupils."

Under President Battle, the department consistently called itself the Conservatory of Music, a usage which persisted for many years. Stability was achieved when for seven years three persons remained concurrently on the teaching staff. Charles A. Thompson, trained at the New England Conservatory of Music, was director, assisted by Miss Nellie Dustman in piano and organ and by Miss Annie Louise Griswold in voice. The school was advertised as being similar in character to "the best American conservatories."

It experienced competition after the Southern Conservatory of Music was founded in 1885. Located in the same block with Shorter, at the corner of Elm Street (now East Third Avenue) and Cherokee Street (now East Fourth Street), it was in operation for fifteen years. Providing highly specialized and competent musical training, it inevitably attracted some students who otherwise would have taken lessons at Shorter.

Periodic student recitals were thought to give the young ladies exceptional opportunities for improvement in their musical skills. At times the public was invited, but usually the performances were for college audiences only. A writer in the *Chimes* asserted: "We Would Like To See . . . A girl who takes part in the recitals on Friday nights who does not become desperately ill one half hour before the Recital." An occasional operetta was staged by the students, often in connection with commencement. Visiting artists presented recitals in the college chapel and at the local Nevin Opera House, and the girls were expected to attend.

One imaginative student good-naturedly poked fun at herself as she imagined looking back on her Shorter years from the vantage point of four decades later: She had come to Shorter "with a wild desire to become a musician and to rival Beethoven, Mozart, Liszt, and a few others." For her first few days at Shorter she saw the "music master" only at a distance, but "the 'great day' finally came, the all-important day on which I was to take my first music lesson, and begin my career. I entered the music room in fear and trembling, which was not lessened when a voice somewhere from behind the fierce moustache told me I might play something." For a year she regularly took lessons and diligently practiced. At the last lesson she asked the professor what part of her music she needed to cultivate most. "Ah, Madame, ze moosic was left out of your composition, it was not zere. I would advise madame to cultivate one market garden, or some zings." And now, after pondering his advice "long and earnestly," she has acted on it and "the fame of my early radishes and spring greens has gone forth throughout the land . . . ."

On March 30, 1887, the first known college music club, called the Euterpean Society, was formed, with Nannie Gwaltney as its first president. Monthly entertainments were planned for the college students and semiannual entertainments, for the general public. A separate music library was discussed, but was probably never established. Membership pins were worn, but none has been preserved. After a year the society faded from view, and no similar group was organized for the next ten years.

SPEECH AND PHYSICAL EDUCATION. Elocution and physical culture, as these subjects were then called, usually were taught by the same persons—including, among others, Miss James E. Selman, a Shorter College alumna. Instruction in elocution was offered both during the day and in the evening. Visiting elocutionists presented programs in the chapel, and recitals were given by the classes and by individual students as a part of the graduation requirements. One of the floors in the Music and Art Building was converted into a gymnasium about 1890, and much equipment was purchased. Tennis courts were installed nearby about three years later. For a time, students were charged extra for physical culture, but in 1896 this fee was removed.

ALUMNAE TEACHERS. Graduates of the college continued to be added to the faculty, as well as some who attended but received no degree. Of the fifteen graduates, three have already been named, and three others were notable: Miss Leola Selman, the presiding teacher in charge of the study hall for three or four years; Miss Mollie Boyd, art instructor for three years; and Miss Marie Celeste Ayer, also art instructor for three years. Five who did not graduate were accorded faculty standing, and five who received degrees were teaching assistants during their last year on campus. One alumna, Miss Mary Darlington, was offered the position as presiding teacher when Mrs. H. C. Cooper retired in 1887, but this first graduate of the college elected to remain as a teacher in her native state of South Carolina.

Administration and Staff

For eight years President and Mrs. Gwaltney supervised the boarding department. Because Mrs. Battle was physically unable to replace them when her husband assumed control of the school, Mrs. Eunice A. Cunningham was matron for ten years, with Miss Maggie McCauley as her assistant during half of that time. Mrs. Ivy W. Duggan was stewardess during the seven years that she and her husband were with the college.

In 1887 Gwaltney requested a "library room," proposing that the trustees appropriate $200 and the alumnae raise a like amount for furnishings, "thus getting a start towards a long desired object." The trustees and probably the alumnae complied, and the amount was made available "for the purchase of books as a nucleus for a library, a book case, and library table." Thus, three distinct libraries existed; each literary society maintained its own, and the college had a separate one. Its condition was so poor, however, that on November 13, 1891, the senior class held a meeting "for the purpose of establishing a library," as their minutes read. Inspired and guided by Miss Gibbs, they were able to accumulate a collection of 150 volumes, adding these to a dictionary and a set of the *American Encyclopedia* that Alfred Shorter had provided years before. Subsequent classes presented musical, elocutionary, and gymnastic entertainments, the proceeds from which went to purchase additional books. The 1894 catalogue contained the first description of the library: "One of the attractions of the school is the reading-room, which is fitted up with taste and comfort, and is a favorite place of resort for those who love reading. . . . The college reading-room is accessible at all times." The following year, it was claimed, 1,300 books were available to students: 600 in the college library, 400 in the societies' collections, and 300 in the home section, "kept in the dormitory for the use of boarding students." The class of 1897 was unusually active, contributing $110 to the college library. They sponsored teas on the terraces of the school in October and April, attended by many Rome persons, including young men. They also provided an entertainment in the chapel, for which they charged admission. Some money came from individual effort, such as sewing and hair dressing. One brave senior even killed a rat for Mrs. Battle, receiving 25¢! In June of 1897 the trustees directed that permanent book cases be installed "in a room to be selected" as the college library. Misses Cordelia Veal and Lutha Moss of the class of 1897 spent many hours that summer cataloguing the eleven-hundred-volume collection, producing a sixty-seven-page pamphlet entitled "Catalogue of Books Belonging to Shorter College Library." The Alumnae Association joined the seniors the following year in contributing money to the library fund.

A Consciously Christian College

The college was consciously Christian, but not denominational. President Gwaltney wrote: "There is no intention to render the college sectarian in its influence. Denominational preferences and associations are, in accordance with the wish of its founder, most carefully respected." Yet the Shorter girls attended the Rome Baptist Church in sufficient numbers to reserve pews for them, and their presence at the annual spring revivals was also noted. Twilight prayer meetings in the college chapel were held nightly or weekly, and briefly a chapter of King's Daughters was active on campus. First published in 1883, the *Baptist Hymnal* was soon purchased for use on campus. An optional Sunday evening service was initiated by President Battle, and infrequent lectures were given in the study hall during class hours by visiting pastors. All students were required to attend morning devotional exercises in the study hall and to answer their names at roll call. President Battle would enter with a stovepipe hat on his left arm, wearing a Prince Albert coat. He usually read the Bible, frequently selecting 1 Corinthians 13 or Isaiah 55. At a musical concert by the intermediate students one winter, "the exercises concluded with a sacred pantomime, illustrative of the sweet hymn 'Jesus Lover of my Soul.' . . . Twenty-five lovely maidens beautifully arrayed in white . . . illustrated by graceful attitude and gesture the successive pious sentiments of the hymn, as it was sung by the concealed quartette. As each line was sung the posture and movements were changed to suit the change of sentiment. The audience gazed and listened with a hushed awe and the tears streamed down from many eyes."

The Martha Shorter Missionary Society held regular meetings in the chapel on the first Sunday afternoon of each month, being composed of students, teachers, and a few citizens from Rome. Its members accepted an invitation to attend a missionary conference at the Methodist Church of Rome, since its interest was not restricted to Baptist work. Yearly the group raised from $50 to $75 for various missionary projects, including the education of one or two young girls in Mexico and Christmas gifts for the residents of the Baptist Orphan's Home in Hapeville, Georgia. Its size is not usually known; one year 58 of the 176 students held membership.

The Literary Societies

Each literary society met regularly each Friday evening. Two of these meetings every month were for the transaction of business, held in their respective halls. The other two were of a literary or musical nature, and some were presented in the chapel with the societies alternating in giving the program. When this occurred, it was decreed that "all pupils of the Collegiate Department, whether members of the societies or not, are required to be present at each meeting." More often, these literary programs were held separately in the two society halls. At one of them, which seems to be typical, the roll call was answered as every girl recited a poetical quotation. The vice-president read selected portions of Scripture, after which two papers were presented, "The New Church Organ" and "The Art of Book-keeping." After adjournment the members would usually remain for a time gaily chatting with their friends before returning to their rooms. Public entertainments were sponsored once or twice a year, and admission was often charged. The life and work of Longfellow was the subject of one such program, and another was comprised of musical numbers, recitations, and a debate on the topic, "Resolved, that Civilization Does Civilize."

By the mid-eighties, distinctive membership pins were popular in both societies. The Polymnians persisted in having honorary members, and this was probably true of both. Into the late eighties, both maintained separate libraries and rendered public thanks for assistance with them. The *Chimes* was published alternately by the two groups until about 1890, when the senior class took over that function. During the academic year 1897–1898 the Polymnian Society numbered thirty-two members and was by this time solely in charge of editing it. In the first college annual, published that year, the Eunomian Society was not included.

Indeed, it is highly probable that the Eunomian Society was not in existence from about 1893 to 1898. President Battle apparently felt that the competition between the societies was undesirable. Since the Polymnian Society was larger, it was allowed to live and the smaller one was merged with it.

During commencement week the reunion of the two societies was an increasingly important event. Engraved invitations were sent jointly, and the receptions were held at the same hour in the two halls. For a few years the anniversary of the societies was honored by a formal program consisting of musical selections and a literary address by an invited guest.

Although one year the Polymnians utilized the motto of the former R.O.K. Society, the earlier group was not reactivated by the college girls. However, in 1897 the name "Reapers of Knowledge" came to designate a newly formed literary society in the preparatory department.

Keeping—and Bending—the Rules

President Gwaltney rewrote the regulations regarding student activities. All students coming from a distance were required to board with his family. "Under no other arrangement can there be judicious watchcare." It was advertised that "a generous table will be kept at all times. The health of the pupils will be carefully guarded . . . . A bright, happy *home* school, with the faithful performance of duty, and yet with cheerful contentment on the part of pupils and teachers —this is the ideal constantly kept in view." "A close system of espionage is not enforced, but assiduous care is exercised over the manners, habits, and language of the pupils." Young men were not allowed to visit the students separately, but only in carefully supervised groups. "Extravagance in dress" was frowned upon, as was the practice of sending "spending money," which was considered altogether unnecessary. The girls were not permitted to leave campus without official approval, nor to open charge accounts without parental permission in writing.

For the first time in the fall of 1883 the students were required to wear uniforms on public occasions "to promote economy, and to avoid rivalry in dress . . . ." These were described as follows: "For Winter:—Dress of gray cashmere, medium shade; cuffs, vest and collar of black velvet. No silk or satin trimmings. Plain linen collar. Cloak of black cloth. Hat: drab felt, shade of dress, with gray velvet bands and two tips of the same color. No plumes. For Spring:—Dress of simple white. Hat: Leghorn, trimmed with white satin and one white plume, or with simple white flowers, if preferred." Although slight changes were made frequently in their style, uniforms were retained for many years.

Rules were expanded two years later. "The discipline of the school is firm, but kind. Parents must be willing to delegate their authority to the President, who administers discipline mainly by appealing to the honor and conscience, and confiding in the integrity of his pupils." Twenty-seven rules were then printed, most of them for the first time. All signal bells were to be obeyed promptly. Hours for study and rest were to be faithfully observed. Sunday school and church were to be attended with propriety. Nothing was to be sent or received through day pupils or servants. Communications of any kind from young men were prohibited without proper permission. Novels and newspapers were to be read only under the direction of the teacher of literature. Parents were requested not to send "boxes of eatables and confections," which "are a fruitful source of sickness and doctor's bills"—but "ripe fruits may be sent." All letters were to be addressed in care of the president, who would permit the delivery of mail only from persons whom the parents approved in advance. The reason for this was explained: "It is not the intention of the president to inspect letters, but simply to guard against devoting too much time to unprofitable correspondence." Parents were urged in the interests of "proper mental training" not to request that their daughters be allowed to leave campus in the evenings, on the Sabbath, or during Christmas (which was again being observed as a one-day holiday only). "Such privileges do much to dissatisfy pupils, to increase the difficulties of school discipline, and to defeat the important aims of school life." Finally, the president would positively refuse to allow pupils to leave for home until he had received instructions in writing directly from the parents "indicating the time, route, and persons in whose care they are to be placed."

President Battle issued a six-page leaflet, "Shorter College Rules and Regulations," that governed student life. General classroom rules included these: "If a teacher fails to meet a class, the pupils will wait quietly ten minutes and then report to the presiding teacher. . . . When not at recitations or piano practice, all pupils must be in the study hall. . . . Pupils must not go to the reading room or elsewhere without special permission from the presiding teacher. . . . Eat nothing in the study hall or recitation, music or art rooms during study hours." Residents in the dormitory were admonished: "Do not sit in windows, and do not gaze at visitors from doors or windows. . . . All cooking in bed-rooms is forbidden." They could have no visitors except with the approval of the matron or governess. "Do not sleep elsewhere than in your own room, except by permission of the matron." During evening study hours they were to be either in their room or in a music practice room. "Pupils must not leave the college grounds without a teacher, and even then, *permission must be obtained from the governess.* . . . Pupils who wish to make purchases must, by Friday evening, put in the Request Box a neatly written list of articles needed. . . . Pupils must not speak or make signals from any part of the building or from the grounds, to persons passing by." "No room may be entered without knocking, nor without the permission of the occupants. . . . After the servants have attended to the rooms the occupants must keep them in neat condition." "Pupils will not be allowed to have photographs taken without written instructions to the President from parent or guardian; and no pupil will be permitted to have her photograph taken with arms or neck bare, or with drapery in lieu of waist. The governess must accompany all who visit the photograph gallery." Rules relating to Sunday were precise: "All pupils are expected to attend church and Sunday school, unless excused by matron and governess. . . . Pupils who are excused must remain in the dormitory until the return of those who attend. . . . Pupils must remain quietly in their rooms from 2 to 4 P.M. on Sunday afternoon. They cannot receive visitors on the Sabbath. . . . Pianos must not be used on the Sabbath." Rules followed them into the dining room. Seats were assigned, and no changes could be made without authorization from the governess. All conversation was to be held "in an undertone, and only with those near. . . . No article of table furniture or food (except fruit) must be taken from the dining hall." The day students were not forgotten: "Day pupils must not enter the college home without permission. . . . Day pupils are expected to return home immediately on the close of school, unless special permission to remain for a definite purpose is given them by the governess, and even then they must confine themselves to study hall and reading room. . . . Lunch must be eaten at desks or in the yard between buildings. Leave no scraps on or under the desks. . . . Day pupils must not carry packages, notes or messages to or from boarders, except by permission of governess or President." Demerits were given for violations—if more than three were accumulated in any one month, the student's name would not appear on the roll of honor. The concluding section of the leaflet contained a blunt reminder: "Attendance at school is considered as a standing pledge of obedience to all College regulations. Those who purpose to disobey should at once withdraw from school."

A few of the rules were broken—or at least bent. The B.A.T.s (Back Alley Trotters) were the boys who tried to attract the girls to their windows, or to whom the girls called. Miss Dustman would come out of her studio and chase them away, reprimanding the girls for urging them on. Some young ladies kept on their lights after hours and secretly enjoyed delicious cakes and goodies sent from home—the first known midnight feasts! On the weekends one of the day students would often have some of the girls visiting at her home. President Battle gave approval only on one condition: "Promise they will not see any boys." She later admitted: "I always evaded this, for I knew quite well the boys would be there."

A "Typical" Day

The pattern of a "typical" day—if such a thing has ever existed in the life of a college student—emerged during these years. The "old historic triangle" was rung about 7:00, after which breakfast was served. While the smaller children gathered in their respective classrooms, the entire collegiate department was present in the study hall for roll call, announcements, and a brief religious service. The study hall had in its center a "mammoth stove," behind which all of the older students wished to sit, so that they could be farthest removed

67

from the presiding teacher who reigned up in front. A "little recess" came at mid-morning, when the girls would chatter with friends and share "Shorter's far famed and world renowned ginger-cakes and crackers . . . ." Students were called to the main desk to pick up their mail, and many a young lady dropped her eyes and blushed as she returned to her own desk with a letter from her young man. The town students regularly brought lunches to school—containing delicacies such as dill pickles, coconut cake, and preserved cherries—and ate them in the study hall, in music practice rooms, or on the playground. Of course the dormitory students had theirs in the dining room. Classes continued in the afternoon until about 3:30, when the town students left the campus and the boarding students had some time for relaxation. The long verandas on Pennington Hall were sources of much pleasure when the weather prevented the use of the terraces. Such freedom was short-lived, however, because the girls were expected to "dress" for dinner, to attend the twilight prayer service, and to heed the bell that signaled two more hours of school work. On Friday evening this routine was altered by the society meetings which were held in the parlors. A brief period of free time was permitted just before the bell called for lights to be turned out about 9:30 P.M.

When the Girls Were Not Studying

Life on campus was not all study and lectures—part of it was rest and relaxation. Halloween came to be celebrated with an evening of bobbing for apples, roasting chestnuts, and throwing apples through gilded horse shoes—all by the wavering lights of jack-o'-lanterns. Music, refreshments, and recitations rounded out the event. "What a pity that there is only one Hallow E'en in a year," bemoaned one participant. On Thanksgiving the president conducted a service of worship in the chapel, a "bountiful and delicious dinner" was served, and the college group attended the early evening union service held at one of the nearby churches.

The brief Christmas holiday was a time of diversion, even for those remaining on campus. One year selected young men of Rome were invited to the college, where they entertained the girls with a display of fireworks that was "one to be remembered with admiration and pleasure." A reception in the parlors of Pennington Hall concluded the evening. "The brightly lighted rooms, decorations of evergreen, holly and mistletoe, the dainty refreshments and the *smilingly conscious* dignity of the girls in serving them, mingled with the gay voices

68

and merry laughter of all, combined to make it the most animated and delightful scene imaginable." The next day was Christmas, and visitors came in such numbers "that *few* girls had time *to waste* on the turkey, mince pie and other requisites of the bountiful Christmas dinner." The vacation was soon concluded, however, for "the next morning school opened again . . . ."

The coming of snow was never overlooked: "On Tuesday morning . . . learning lessons was hard work, for our time was occupied in watching the falling snow and thinking how we would snowball each other at recess. But our hopes were blighted, for there was only enough snow for one duel." January 19 provided an annual celebration, on the birthday of "that tall exemplar of a grand historic race— Robert E. Lee." In the spring, Rome often experienced a "freshet" sufficient to affect the lives of the girls. One of them was notable: "During the flood the gas was cut off, and for a day or two we tried the virtues of kerosene and candles. The verdict in favor of gas was unanimous." Briefly the streets were covered, and the pupils amused themselves by watching people row their boats to the post office.

Practices on April Fools Day varied. One year it was recorded: "No holiday on the 1st for April fools. The girls April-fooled Dr. Gwaltney by going quietly to school. He kindly consented to let us spend the 15th in the woods"—probably at Mobley Park, where Darlington School is now located. On another, later occasion the seniors read humorous essays at a program in which they introduced "Sillie Gism and Major Premise" to the college family. Also present that night, according to report, was "laughter holding both his sides." On at least one Good Friday, "immediately after breakfast, Dr. Gwaltney was surrounded by the girls, who were eager for a holiday. After hearing their petitions and exacting many promises from them, Dr. Gwaltney kindly consented to give them a holiday. A more pleasant day has rarely ever been spent by the girls." The Memorial Day ceremony continued to be supported by the Shorter group. About 1890 the annual May excursion down the Coosa on a steamboat was initiated, a diversion that was popular for twenty years.

President Gwaltney and twenty-nine Shorter students attended the New Orleans Exposition, being away from March 27 to April 4, 1885. A lively student reported a week of visiting important buildings, getting lost in the French Market, holding a million dollars at the mint, attending services at the Second Baptist and First Presbyterian churches, lingering at two notable cemeteries, and wandering over the Exposition grounds for three days. "A pleasant surprise" was theirs when they discovered that President Battle and his seniors from

Mercer University had checked in at the hotel where they were staying. At Battle's suggestion and with Gwaltney's permission, they held a reception for the young men, and "all fatigue was quickly forgotten in that brilliant circle of wit and wisdom." Later they took a boat excursion with the Mercer boys, "in which all joyously participated." On the trip home, the girls were treated to fruit, flowers, candy, and chewing gum by the railroad officials in Atlanta. "Every young lady on board was industriously chewing gum" upon her arrival in Rome. Meanwhile, back on the hill "April the first was a red-letter day for the Shorter girls. Instead of worrying the teachers out of a holiday, they were presented with one free gratis, and in the afternoon the whole crowd turned out in carriages and took in the city."

The following spring the Georgia Baptist Convention met in Rome. Its secretary reported that on Friday afternoon "a motion to adjourn varied the monotony and gave us ample time to rest and 'brush up' before we should visit the College to see Dr. Gwaltney's girls." The messengers inspected the campus, heard some musical selections, were impressed with the art studio, and spoke a word of thanks for the invitation through President Battle of Mercer University.

At times the faculty permitted the pupils to attend performances at the local Nevin Opera House—"The Merchant of Venice," a Chinese wedding by a troupe of Chinese students, and "Herr Andre's Choir and Tyrolese Company."

At other times recreation was confined to the campus. One evening, as one of the girls described it, President Gwaltney "gave us permission to have any kind of fun which would not be too noisy. 'May we pop bags?' could be heard from all around. 'Yes, you may, if you will not pop any more after you are requested to stop.' We popped bags till we were tired, then made turkeys, had a comb concert, had a game of blind man's bluff, and as a crowning effort made the famous 'tall Betsy.' We heartily enjoyed all our devices to provoke laughter, and were ready to endorse the words of one of our teachers: 'Fun is the next best thing to religion.' "

Not a little merriment was afforded by one courageous letterwriter who was described in the *Chimes*: "One of our Seniors had the impudence to write to President Cleveland for his picture. Strange to say, impudence didn't get its reward, for the picture was sent. She is now thinking of writing for Queen Victoria's."

During the Battle era, Shorter College welcomed back one of its former students, Inez Grinnell Robins, who had finished the music course in 1889. Later she had studied two years in Berlin and two in Paris, had successfully toured Europe as Inez Grennelli, and was then touring the United States.

The Cotton States and International Exposition was held at Atlanta in 1895, and President Battle escorted many of his pupils, dressed in their black uniforms, to the exhibit one day. They were properly impressed and did not want to leave. One of them reported: "When the time came for us to go home, we had in a manner, returned to that unreasonable state of childhood, when 'the more you give a child, the more it wants.' Dr. Battle had to play the part of the stern parent, shake his head and say 'all gone.' All gone the 'Chutes,' all gone the 'Phoenix Wheel,' Buffalo Bill, the lake, the lights, the little boys selling the 'Official Guide,' the big boys, the melodious music in the Midway, and gone those insulting men who would 'sing out' to you, 'Just come this er way, ladies, and get a souvenir 'twont cost you a cent.' " That autumn, the Liberty Bell from Philadelphia was taken on a tour of the country, arriving in Rome at 10:40 A.M. on October 8. Classes were dismissed as the president, teachers, and pupils of the college joined the thirty-five hundred others who flocked to see it.

A year later a Rome newspaper reported an incident that must have stimulated the interest and sympathy of the nearby girls:

> JUMPED TOO LOW.
> A cow attempted to jump the iron fence that surrounds the grassy terraces of Shorter College yesterday afternoon but didn't go quite high enough. She fell on spikes amidships. She was carted away this morning.

For their own amusement, the sub-junior class organized a secret society called the T.P.E.S. Club, holding Friday evening meetings consisting of recitations, music, refreshments, and business sessions from which all but members were ejected. They revealed the meaning of their name, "The Pickle Eating Subs," only when they decided to adopt a new one, the C.C.C. Club. The significance of the new name remains one of the major mysteries of the century.

The first national sorority on the hill lived briefly in this period. During the Christmas holiday of 1897 Rome members of the Sigma Alpha Epsilon Sorority and Fraternity encouraged some members who were students at Shorter to form a chapter. Since President Battle had already joined the fraternity while a student at the University of

Alabama, he was undoubtedly instrumental in having the Alpha chapter established on March 15, 1898. The group was given quarters for a decorated sorority room, first in the tower and later on the first floor of the Academic Building. It apparently became inactive when Battle left.

Finally, it must be remembered that the coming of *any* young man to see *any* young lady was still a cause for excitement. One such event was made a matter of record. The brave visitor calmly ascended the iron steps to the main entrance, enduring the "quizzical eyes" of the strolling girls. After ringing the loud bell at the dormitory door, he was ushered into the parlor, "to face Dr. Battle, who was a gem without a flaw when it came to powers of inquisition relating to infrequent calls of a young man upon a young lady student." Eventually his beloved Bessie was allowed to sit with him in the parlor—as Mrs. Cunningham, the matron, read a book at the window seat and the doors were left wide open, providing an unobstructed view for the many students who decided that this was a splendid time to walk up and down the hallway.

The First Annual

The first Shorter College annual, the *Iris*, was published in the spring of 1898. A 144-page volume measuring 7 by 8 inches, it was sold for $1.75. Its binding was white and gold, the colors being chosen by the editors, Cordelia Veal, Elizabeth Harris, and Edith Hardy. This appears to be the origin of the college colors. Dedicated to "Dr. L. R. Gwaltney, Beloved friend of Alfred Shorter and former President of Shorter College," it contained photographs of and articles about the college, Martha and Alfred Shorter, and A. J. Battle. The faculty, seniors, juniors, sub-juniors, and various social and literary organizations were also pictured. The history of those three classes and a character analysis based on the handwriting of each senior appeared. Since it is probable that only one issue of the *Chimes* was printed during that year, this *Iris* included poetry, descriptive essays, short stories, and some humorous pieces. Some of the pictures were of bona fide organizations—but not quite all of them. The Merry Maids of Sparta, the Mystic Order of Old Maids, and the Country Maids were pseudoclubs organized solely to get their members' pictures in the annual! Described as "the only young man allowed on the campus" and "the college pet," Colcord Thompson, the son of the director of music, was honored with a picture—on a separate page.

By 1895 engraved invitations to the Shorter College commencement ceremonies were being sent. Of course the proceedings varied, extending from four to seven days and comprising an amazing variety of separate programs. The juvenile entertainment came first, consisting of recitations, individual musical numbers, calisthenics, and often a cantata. On Sunday morning the baccalaureate service was held at the Rome Baptist Church, while in the evening the visiting preacher usually delivered a missionary sermon before the Martha Shorter Missionary Society. The next two days were replete with an art exhibit, a physical culture drill, a play or recitations sponsored by the elocution classes, a French play, and two concerts prepared by the music department. The two societies and the alumnae enjoyed reunions, a part of which was sometimes an elaborate banquet given by the president.

The class of 1895 informally entertained in the study hall, "to which only a few spectators were admitted." "A Prophecy of the Future," "Retrospect," a history of the class, and the recitation of an original poem made up this first known Class Day of the college. This addition reflected a self-consciousness on the part of the senior class that grew during the 1890s. Each class adopted a motto such as "Aspiro," "Talitha Cumi," or "Ich Diene." A class author was named—Lanier, Milton, Tennyson, or others. Often a class flower and color were selected. The class of 1896 produced the first "cheer" on record:

> Shorter! Shorter! Here we are!
> Shorter! Shorter! Tra, la, la!

It also produced Miss Ruby Hightower, who later returned to teach mathematics for twenty-nine years at Shorter. She composed a poem, "Maiden, Arise," in keeping with the motto of her class, concluding it with these words:

> As you enter on life's pathway,
>   May your motto, shedding far
> Golden beams of truth and courage,
>   Ever be your guiding star.
>
> When the glow of life's last sunset
>   Slowly fades from evening skies,
> To the dawn of Heaven's bright morning,
>   May your spirits pure arise.

The actual graduation service was always lengthy. The stage in the chapel would be decorated with fragrant green pine boughs, smilax, and great clusters of magnolia blossoms. Original essays were read by each graduate until the late eighties when this practice was discontinued. While none of these has apparently survived, many of their titles are known: "Vim"; "Better Fifty Years of Europe than a Cycle of Cathay"; "Night Brings Out the Stars"; "O Tiber! Father Tiber! To whom the Romans pray!"; "The Stories that Rocks Tell"; "Great Art, the Type of Noble Life"; "The Secret of Creation"; "The Soul's Rialto Hath Its Merchandise"; "Harmonies Struck Out by a Master's Hand"; and others. In the nineties the graduates first appeared in white robes, usually carrying roses or carnations, and a formal academic procession was formed. Musical numbers, both instrumental and vocal, were rendered by students and faculty members. Visiting orators were unfailingly eloquent and/or long. One spoke in the midst of a storm, causing a reporter to comment: "The magnificent pyrotechnics produced by the incessant lightning flashing through the gorgeous memorial window of the chapel were scarcely more brilliant than the rhetorical kaleidoscopic pictures created by the genius of the orator," who spoke on "Eve." In a later year the Honorable John Temple Graves delivered a 2½-hour lecture on the topic, "The Twentieth Century Woman." Awards in the form of medals, certificates, or laurel wreaths were presented for excellence in art, embroidery, bookkeeping, penmanship, English composition, French, German, music, elocution, history, various postgraduate courses, and deportment. The service was made all the more impressive by President Battle as "the rich deep toned Latin, spoken with the Roman accent, fell from his lips in rounded sentences as he conferred the degree upon the full graduates . . . ." The memorial service came at the conclusion of the program. Portraits of the Shorters, usually hanging in the parlor, occupied the center of the stage. The graduates would read a specially prepared poem in unison or make an appropriate, simple statement, such as: "Alfred and Martha Shorter, your daughters rise up tonight and call you blessed." After this they would twine "garlands of beautiful flowers around the portraits of the sainted couple whose memory Romans will ever cherish and keep green." Later in the evening the president might give an informal reception for the young ladies, few of whom would bother to go to bed because the train to Atlanta left at 5:00 the next morning.

The First Alumnae Association

The Alumnae Association was probably organized in June of 1883, but its first two years are now in obscurity. The members held their third reunion on June 10, 1885, when the first known president, Miss Kate Winn (class of 1880; later Mrs. J. Colton Lynes), took part in the graduation program. She welcomed the graduates to the association and distributed to each an alumna badge inscribed with the motto, "The Price of Wisdom is above Rubies," found also over the stage on which she stood. During the next three years the group was heard from, usually in connection with commencement, and then it faded from view for eight years. The senior class wrote invitations to all the alumnae in Rome, requesting their presence at the Class Day exercises, June 1, 1896. At that time they were urged to reorganize the association, and this apparently was done. The following year it became the first such group in the state to gain membership in the Georgia Federation of Women's Clubs. Four meetings were devoted to musical and literary features, and members contributed money which was used to enlarge the college library. In addition, they sponsored a well-attended reunion during the commencement of 1898, hearing a speaker in the college chapel and holding a reception at the Armstrong Hotel that was described as "a most elegant one."

3
"The Vassar of the South"

The Coming of the Simmons

Soon after his arrival, the new president of Shorter College, Thomas J. Simmons, had a large advertisement printed in the Rome newspapers setting forth his intentions for the school. He began by asserting that "The New SHORTER COLLEGE will be 'The Vassar of The South.'" Although it would not imitate any "society school . . . worthy of contempt," it "will not neglect the proper social development of its students. Attention is asked to the elegance of the parlors and drawing rooms now being fitted up, as well as the handsome furnishings throughout the entire building." Instruction in music was to be emphasized, as evinced by "the large and able Musical Faculty" and "the splendid equipment of the musical department." Nevertheless, the advertisement concluded, "THE GREAT WORK of Shorter College will be in the LITERARY DEPARTMENT," provided with excellent laboratories and distinguished professors.

This statement of purpose was in harmony with the desires of the trustees "to place the college on a higher plane, a more advanced curriculum, more thorough and practical instruction, abreast of the age in modern teaching and progressive methods." After interviewing various persons early in 1898, they had signed a contract for five years with Simmons, in which the usual terms were agreed upon—with the single exception that he would pay the premiums on $30,000 worth of insurance on the buildings and equipment for the period of the contract.

Thomas Jackson Simmons was born in 1864, the son of a professor at Wake Forest College, North Carolina. From that school he received the Master of Arts degree in 1883, being honored by membership in Phi Beta Kappa. For ten years he was a public school teacher and administrator in North Carolina and Georgia. Assuming the presidency of Union Female College, Eufaula, Alabama, in 1893, he remained there for a very successful five years. In 1891 he married Miss Lessie Southgate, who was already a regionally famous musician. Born at Louisburg, North Carolina, in 1863, she received her training in Virginia, in the Grand Conservatory of Music, New York City, and under private voice instructors in Berlin and Paris. She later made the claim that one of them, E. Delle Sedie, was "the established authority for all that pertains to the culture of the human voice" and that he "held full sway for fifty years." She was director of a school of music in Durham, North Carolina, before her marriage and led the music department at Union Female College while there with her husband. No children were born to their union.

As the Simmons came to Shorter, he was president of the college and professor of psychology and ethics. She was director of music and professor of piano and voice. Together they supervised the boarding department. He became a member of the First Baptist Church, while she joined the First Methodist Church. At a public reception in honor of President and Mrs. Simmons and the new faculty, the "beautiful lawn and verandahs" of the college were lighted with Chinese lanterns, and it was a "brilliant" affair attended by Rome's "best people."

President Simmons was a husky man, handsome and dignified in his long-tailed coat. Quiet and modest—indeed, almost shy—he was

President and Mrs. Thomas J. Simmons

often preoccupied and absentminded. As a former student said of him, he "always recognized his wife as the real leader she was." Mrs. Simmons was a large, august, imposing, talented person. She was vice-president of the National Music Teachers' Association of America, member of the Cercle Artistique of Antwerp, honorary member of several other European music associations—and called "Lessie Southgate" behind her back by many of the girls who stood in awe and fear of her. She was a "dramatic soprano of great brilliancy," and her voice was "very highly cultured, of great power and finely modulated." The local newspaper lauded her appearance and abilities. At one concert, "Mrs. Simmons was superb. She looked a veritable queen of song in a long trained gown of heavy white satin with long angel sleeves of embroidered mousseline. Brilliant jewels gleamed on her neck and in her hair." Leading a program that was "high-toned, refined, up-to-date, artistic, and beautiful," she was held to be so famous that "there is not one in America that does not know her and recognize her as a final authority and a court of last resort in matters musical."

Enrollment and Charges

During the Simmons administration, the student body ranged from a low of about 155 in the first two years to a high of almost 270 in the tenth. The average number each year reached about 217, of whom about 107 were boarders. Although a few part-time students in the arts and languages were male, the *Chimes* quoted Ruth correctly:

> Old Lady—Is Shorter a sectarian school?
> Ruth Elgin—No'm, just girls go there.

During the summer of 1900 a vigorous canvass was conducted by the college as six of its representatives traveled through the Southeast. Immediate results were seen as the enrollment that fall jumped by 40 to a total of almost 200. In later summers, thousands of circulars and catalogues were sent out, and once more several teachers traveled in the interests of the college. Enrollment was able to increase sharply because Simmons rented and leased available houses in the immediate neighborhood, while filling to the limit the buildings owned by the college. During some years six girls occupied rooms designed for four. Had accommodations been adequate, Simmons reported one year, "the number of students could easily have been doubled"—and this would have been over 200 boarding students. After a peak enrollment of 268 in 1907–1908, it declined each of the two years thereafter. The students formed "The Shorter Three Hundred" in 1908, a club with the purpose of building "the best college in the world." Exuberantly they said, "We expect to have three hundred students at Shorter next year," but actually the figure dropped to 248 and then to 221 the following year. The fact must not be forgotten, however, that enrollment sharply increased in the first decade of the Simmons administration, leading to a prevailing spirit of optimism.

Parents were reminded early in Simmons' administration that, due to the gifts of Alfred Shorter, "students do not really pay the College *half* the cost of their education." The average student paid no more than about $225 for a nine months' course of study, and about $375 if the finest instruction in music and art were added. By 1910, though, prices were significantly above this average—$275 and $438, respectively. One year a five percent discount was offered for early registration and payment. As many as twenty-four girls in a single year were "beneficiaries"—that is, recipients of scholarships—chosen by the trustees. In 1902 it was claimed that 399 young ladies had by then received such assistance, at a value of $19,950. Total receipts of the college are known for five years, ranging from about $20,000 in 1900–1901 to about $43,000 in 1908–1909. The strength of the music program was shown by the fact that approximately thirty percent of the total was raised by tuition from that department alone.

An Improved and Enlarged Campus

The existing buildings had deteriorated, and the Simmons put them in excellent condition. Paint, wallpaper, rugs, and new furniture improved the dormitory area, while new pianos and other forms of equipment aided in instruction. In 1899, Senior Hall was arranged so that the entire class could sleep in one large room. The beds were a newly painted green, and each could be separated from the others with white curtains. The following year the chapel was renovated, becoming the new study hall. All of the stained glass windows except the Shorter Memorial Window were removed, new heating added, and desks installed. The former study hall on the second floor of the Music and Art Building was then altered and became the new gymnasium, being outfitted with $200 worth of new equipment. Later three bowling alleys were added. This became designated as the Gym and Art Building.

Of great importance to the college community was the installation of electric lights in January of 1900. The extension of telephone service to the campus in the summer of 1901 proved to be a talking point for gaining prospective students: "Parents will be interested in knowing that Rome is connected by long-distance telephone with all the important points in the South, thus making it possible for them to talk directly with the College in event of any emergency," by asking the operator for number 228. During the summer of 1903 the long-needed heating system was finally installed in Pennington Hall and the Academic Building at a cost of about $4,000.

Although the college constantly stressed the healthfulness of Rome, its leaders admitted that occasionally a student required medical attention. In the sumer of 1900 Alfred Shorter Hamilton of Trion, Georgia, provided a new infirmary, the Margaret Hamilton Room, in memory of his recently deceased wife. Starting that fall, Dr. H. H. Battey was listed in the catalogue as college physician, and provision was made whereby a dormitory student might receive all needed medical treatment after paying an annual fee of $5—an early form of medical insurance! Later Dr. Walker Curry shared the responsibility with Battey for five years, but both were relieved of their positions in 1907 without printed explanation.

Bayard House continued to be used as a dormitory but was renamed Bellevue by Mrs. Simmons. In the summer of 1902 it was renovated, becoming the Simmons' home. She moved her studio into one room of the house, and a few students lived in some of the extra rooms.

Meantime the studios and parlors of the college were achieving local fame for their furnishings. In Mrs. Simmons' studio was "a collection of busts, pictures and musical trophies which betoken the taste, travels, culture, and refinement of the owner." Included were musical instruments from all over the world, the most recent acquisitions being from India. The parlors—called at various times the Grand Salon, the Italian Parlor, the Dutch Room, the Curio Room, and the Chinese Room—were crowded with metal wall pieces, an antique spinning wheel, much statuary, a Muslim prayer rug, numerous framed photographs, many large divans and chairs, cabinets of exquisite Japanese and Chinese carving, an elaborate array of carved teakwood furniture, two tall menorahs, pianos, oil paintings of the Simmons, and a frieze in oil of a Venetian water scene executed by Miss Lula Ross, the instructor of art. The students enjoyed two contradictory jokes. One insisted that the iron fence around the campus kept out the microbes! The other observed that because the Simmons had brought so many items from foreign countries, one should be vaccinated before entering the parlors!

One small building was constructed on the campus early in the Simmons administration, but no indication remains of its cost or the date that it was first occupied. A one-story, two-room stucco structure measuring about 15 by 20 feet, it was variously utilized as piano studios, a meeting place for the Martha Shorter Missionary Society and Young Women's Christian Association, and living quarters for janitors.

Beginning in the fall of 1901, boarding facilities were expanded— some years almost doubled—when Simmons personally purchased or rented various structures in the neighborhood and converted them into dormitories. Over the next nine years he secured a total of six such houses, for periods of one to nine years each. To most of these, Mrs. Simmons attached names: The Gables, located next to Bellevue on East Third Avenue; Rosemont, located behind the chapel on East Third Street; Locust Cottage and Villa Graziani, located on East Fourth Street. Two others, the Fortin House, located on East Fourth Street, and the antebellum Brookes Mansion, located on East Third

Avenue across from the dormitory, retained their earlier names. Much to the displeasure of Simmons, the trustees refused to repair or furnish any of them, since they were not owned by the college itself, and Simmons spent a good deal of his own money for furniture and extensive renovations. In 1903 the trustees explored the possibility of buying all of the property and equipment that Simmons then owned, but when it was discovered that this would involve an expenditure of $20,000, the matter was quietly dropped.

In 1901 the Southern Conservatory of Music closed, and Simmons bought the building and expanded its facilities. It contained an auditorium seating about 250, music practice rooms, professors' studios, and some dormitory space. This acquisition proved to be very valuable, because hundreds of concerts open to the public were held in St. Cecilia Hall, as the auditorium was called, and because instruction in music was even further strengthened. At the end of his administration, then, Simmons personally owned this building, plus four homes used as dormitories, together with practically all of the musical instruments, furniture, and other equipment in them.

The Building Fund

For nine frustrating years a campaign was intermittently waged to secure funds for an ambitious building program. Several important consequences flowed from it—including the present campus—but the downtown site remained unaltered throughout all of the activity.

A new dormitory was suggested in 1900. Mrs. Ethel Hillyer Harris, an alumna and long-time friend of the college, reported: "Some of the professors have been relegated to some of the outbuildings in the yard, which have been put in shape. Some of the music teachers have had to convert their boudoirs into classrooms and resort to folding beds when they seek repose at night. . . . Now the time has come when a new dormitory must be had." In 1901 President Simmons proposed a $50,000 auditorium with additional space for the music and art departments and a new gymnasium. Upon the erection of this building, the twenty-year-old Music and Art Building would be converted into dormitory area. With the purchase of the Southern Conservatory of Music later in 1901, Simmons returned to the original recommendation, a dormitory. An architect's sketch of the new plant was drawn in 1906. The Academic Building was to be enlarged and renovated, the dormitory was to be renovated, and another structure the size of the Academic Building was to be added east of the dormitory. The mansard roofs were to be replaced by much lower hip roofs, and the many

Corinthian columns proposed for the three buildings tended to unify them.

Four conditions inhibited efforts at securing money for these improvements. The trustees felt that the lease-system of management had to be removed so that funds would unquestionably remain at their command. Accordingly, when the lease expired in 1905 they assumed direct control. President and Mrs. Simmons signed a contract to continue in their respective posts for an unlimited time at an annual salary of at least $2,000 each and perhaps $3,000 each if the income of the college warranted it. With the trustees in effective charge, they could face the public with fiscal confidence. Again, on December 19, 1905, R. L. Chidsey and others filed suit against the trustees, seeking to eject the college from its lands in order to recover one-eighth of the property which they claimed under the provisions of a will that had been probated in South Carolina in the year 1848. When the Floyd County Superior Court decided in favor of the college in 1907, the Chidseys carried their appeal to the Georgia Supreme Court. In 1908 the lower court was finally upheld, and this threat to the college was removed. Third, the entire nation experienced a financial depression in 1907, and Floyd County went through months of "stringency in money matters." Finally, Monroe Female (now Tift) College and Mercer University each conducted an extensive state-wide compaign for funds during a part of this period, thus reducing Shorter's appeal beyond Northwest Georgia.

Despite these obstacles, the trustees took major steps to raise funds. A local canvass for $50,000 occurred in 1901. Although subscriptions amounted to only one-fifth of the desired total, three men important to the eventual development of the college were first made aware of its needs: J. L. Bass, a merchant and real estate dealer in Rome; W. W. Brookes, a Rome lawyer; and J. P. Cooper, a businessman of Rome and Boston, Massachusetts.

Luther Rice Gwaltney was secured in 1902 as financial and soliciting agent with faculty standing as chaplain and professor of Christian morals. The newspaper reported that he "received much encouragement" during that spring and editorially supported his efforts to raise money. During March the *Tribune* carried a series of four articles by Gwaltney, expressing the conviction that adequate subscriptions "CAN BE ASSURED within fifty days" and a dormitory could be ready in the fall. His optimism was unjustified, however, and no construction resulted. Late in 1903 he again tried to revive the canvass. Six articles dealt principally with the economic benefits that Rome had realized because of Shorter. In the quarter-century since Alfred Shorter had taken over the college it had spent more than $1,000,000—mostly in Rome—which was an average of about $40,000 annually. Rome was being asked to raise $30,000 of the $50,000 which the college was then seeking, enabling the enrollment and income to be doubled. With help from some of his business friends, Gwaltney estimated that this would produce a $10,000 annual profit for the Rome economy, which after three years would be a clear profit. The articles did not achieve their purpose, though, and Gwaltney thereafter spent most of his time within the college walls as chaplain and professor.

The college was voluntarily placed under the control of the Georgia Baptist Convention with the hope that the new arrangement would quickly provide a marked increase in income. The charter having expired, the trustees passed a resolution asking for its extension at their meeting on May 5, 1902. They indicated a desire to change the name to "Shorter University" and to alter the terms so that the university might come under "the patronage and policy of the Georgia Baptist Convention." For several weeks the Rome newspapers publicly accorded the school university status in their various articles, but on November 27, 1902, the charter was granted for a term of twenty years without any change of name. Meantime, representatives of Shorter College met with the Education Commission of the convention, perfecting the terms of their agreement. Formal ratification occurred at a meeting of the convention on November 22, 1902. The board of trustees was to be increased from seven to fifteen; the current members were to retain their positions and the additional eight were to be elected by the convention. Since both Monroe and Shorter were then engaged in fund-raising campaigns, the convention commended Shorter, giving it "our moral support for one year" while the Monroe canvass was being concluded. Thereafter, Shorter was to get "our active and material support in the completion of their proposed effort to raise $50,000 for enlargement." The trustees next met on December 19, 1902, at which time "the officers of the old board tendered their resignations, which were accepted, and the old board as such adjourned *sine die*. The new board proceeded at once to organize"; D. B. Hamilton was reelected president and James B. Sullivan, secretary and treasurer. The trustees appointed a committee of five "to consider plans for obtaining the enlargement fund for Shorter College . . . ." This enlargement and endowment committee included two new trustees, J. L. Bass as chairman and J. P. Cooper as another of its members. At a meeting of the Georgia Baptist Convention in November of 1903, a damper was put on Shorter's hopes of immediate state-wide financial support. Because the drive by Monroe College had not been completed, the "active support of the Convention" was extended to July 1, 1904. After that date, it was agreed, "the active and material support of the Convention shall be given to Shorter College."

A fund-raising drive was discussed in June of 1904 with W. W. Brookes as the leader. A recently elected trustee of the college, he announced that the desired total was now $100,000, to be spent on new dormitories, classroom buildings, and equipment. When the drive was initiated in October, four men subscribed $5,000 each—Mark McDonald, J. L. Bass, J. P. Cooper, and W. W. Brookes. For the next month an almost daily solicitation was conducted, and the total grew by $2,000 to $5,000 each day. On November 23 the *Tribune* proudly announced that $50,000 from Rome was assured for the Greater Shorter movement. Two days later Editor T. P. Bell of the *Christian Index*, who was also a trustee of Shorter College, reported to the Georgia Baptist Convention, then in session at Columbus, that the sum had been raised. He reminded the group that, although the college had possessed the right to call for the convention's "active and material support" a year earlier, it had then waived that right. Now, however, the time had come for the college to claim its privilege as a child of the convention and ask for assistance in raising $150,000 more in the state at large. "We ask you to cordially endorse our plea to the State for this additional amount, give us the field to work in, and bid us Godspeed in our effort." A resolution pledging cooperation was adopted without opposition. That afternoon the Rome *Tribune* carried a jubilant, front-page, three-column headline, "SHORTER FUND IS NOW $250,000," that turned out to be exaggerated and premature. Although the convention had agreed to help in securing $150,000, the paper reported the figure at $200,000, including in its total $50,000 which it somehow expected John D. Rockefeller to contribute—presumably through the General Education Board, which was not mentioned. In the months that immediately followed, probably Brookes communicated privately with certain wealthy Baptists throughout the state, rather than conducting a public campaign. During the commencement week of 1905 the *Tribune* reported that one anonymous Georgia Baptist had promised $25,000 and that two others had promised $12,500 each. Rockefeller was not mentioned. A total of $100,000 had been subscribed—but no money was in hand. In November of that year the trustees expressed their pleasure to the Georgia Baptist Convention that Brookes had thus far succeeded in raising "in good and substantial pledges" from various Georgia givers a sum that had increased by then to $125,000. However, they pointed out: "Quite a considerable part of this $125,000 is in conditional pledges, the condition being that the full amount of $200,000 shall be raised." They asked that the convention continue to endorse their campaign at least until July 1, 1906, "when we are sure the whole sum will be raised." Of course their optimism was ill-founded.

Finally, a drive for $25,000 in cash was initiated in May, 1907. Construction on the first group of new buildings was expected to commence in July, and occupancy was hoped for one year hence. Although the *Tribune* supported the project and indicated that some donations were being received, actual construction was once again not forthcoming.

Within the next year several of the trustees concluded that the current site should be abandoned and a new one occupied. The first recorded statement came from the enlargement committee on May 24, 1908: "Quite a number of our trustees have expressed their judgment against placing any new buildings on our present grounds, claiming that they are too small for the future uses of the institution. Additional land in the neighborhood of the college property cannot be obtained, at this time—some parties refusing to sell at any prices, and others, only at most unreasonable figures." A proposal was then made that determined the future of the school: "Some of our trustees, among them, members of this committee, very strongly favor the removal of the College to the suburbs of Rome, and plans have been drawn for locating Shorter outside of the city, where large areas could be secured. It is desired on the part of this committee that the Board should consider this matter before further steps shall be taken." The report was signed by J. L. Bass, chairman of the committee, and was adopted by the board. The enlargement committee expressed this conviction before the full board again on May 31, 1909, insisting that "prompt action should be taken. The need is imperative and delay will jeopardize much of the subscription." Later in the day a committee was appointed to investigate the legality of selling their present property and relocating the college.

For nine years the trustees and the citizens of Rome had been involved in this proposed building program. As a consequence, the life of the college had been drastically altered. The external control of the institution had left the hands of a self-perpetuating board of trustees and had passed to a board containing a majority elected by the Georgia Baptist Convention. The internal control had left the hands of the president under the lease-system and had passed to the trustees. And now, it was being strongly insisted that the college be moved.

86

Other events in the life of the college were usually less far-reaching —and often less serious in nature. On November 2, 1898, a local newspaper came out with this article, quoted here in full:

> SHORTER COLLEGE PIGS.
> —This afternoon a colored servant of Shorter College herded a drove of pigs from the college terrace to Mayor Seay's office. The swineherder said the porkers had been playing havoc with the sod on the terraces. Mayor Seay had the rooters turned over to the police authorities and they were hustled into the city pound.

President and Mrs. Simmons toured Europe in the summer of 1900. He left Rome early in May, and the Shorter girls almost wept. The *Tribune* reported: "Mrs. Simmons says they were thinking of all the nice oyster suppers and ice cream treats he had given them lately." It added, "Yarrum, his Great Dane dog, is the picture of despair and grief"—but Mrs. Simmons did not attempt to explain this situation. After visiting Russia, he was joined by his wife, and they saw the Oberammergau Passion Play and the Paris Exposition. He returned to Shorter first, while she studied until September under her former teacher, Delle Sedie. They spoke of their trip to several groups in Rome—and for a time President Simmons attracted much attention by wearing a beard that he had grown while away. One of his stories concerned a runaway horse in Milan, Italy. Mrs. Simmons had become quite tired and had stayed in their carriage while he walked through a beautiful cemetery. During his absence the horse was stung by a bee and ran off, with Mrs. Simmons still in the carriage. For a mile it galloped, alarming—by Simmons' own estimation—ten thousand people. He gave chase, but a soldier was able to grasp the horse by the neck and finally drag it to a halt. Next morning the city officials came to Simmons, asking about the incident and wishing to have a banquet and tender the soldier a medal for bravery. Simmons gave them money with which to reward the man. The officials took it with the statement: "Give us your American address that we may return it to you in case of refusal." During the spring of 1904 President Simmons made a tour

87

of North Africa, Jerusalem (where he attended the World's Fourth Sunday School Convention), Athens, Italy, Gibraltar, and Spain. The local Rome paper carried a number of descriptive letters from him, and the college trustees were presented a gavel and inkstand made of olive wood which he brought back from the Holy Land.

"Devoted to the Interests of Female Education," the *Bulletin of Shorter College* was published about four times each year, beginning in June of 1901. Many issues were four-to-eight-page leaflets publicizing such news items as a recent commencement, new faculty members, and the purchase of the Southern Conservatory of Music. One pamph-

D. B. Hamilton   Charles M. Harper   W. W. Landrum

let was an eight-page miniature catalogue. Numerous photographs of the campus were prominent in three numbers. Annually, one number comprised the college catalogue.

After serving as president of the board for the longest period in the history of the college, twenty-two years, D. B. Hamilton resigned from that office—but not from the board—in 1904. The Shorter students observed the fiftieth wedding anniversary of Colonel and Mrs. Hamilton on November 26, 1906, by marching out to the residence, Thornwood, and extending congratulations and best wishes. The girls were not allowed to attend a reception that evening, but white chrysanthemums were sent on their behalf. From 1904 to 1909 W. W. Landrum, pastor of the First Baptist Church, Atlanta, Georgia, was president of the board. For a single year, 1909 to 1910, W. W. Brookes was president, although he held the office a second time from 1913 to 1917.

Charles M. Harper died in 1910 after twenty-five years on the board. The trustees estimated in 1903 that the total value of the college, including the endowment, was about $150,000. The endowment was a little more than $40,000 and was safely drawing from six to eight percent interest annually. The tax collector of Floyd County ruled that the endowment was liable to taxation, and taxes were paid from 1904 through 1906. By May 31, 1909, the trustees were already expressing doubts concerning the relationship of the college to the Georgia Baptist Convention. At that time they appointed a committee to investigate the right and authority of the board "to make the contract with the Georgia Baptist Convention." As will be seen in the next chapter, this action was culminated by the removal of convention control in 1914.

Mrs. Simmons' talent in the kitchen showed itself at least twice. In 1901 a Rome newspaper stated: "Mrs. T. J. Simmons, dean of the music faculty of Shorter College, is a wonderful woman. We have known her as a great vocalist, a great pianist, a great artist and a great elocutionist. In fact, she is a woman of extraordinary ability in every respect. . . . When the Negro servants could not be longer endured Mrs. Simmons took the helm in the kitchen, and put in sixteen white servants. These were mostly from the country, unused to domestic service, and had to be trained. Mrs. Simmons has succeeded admirably in this. But during the training she has been in the kitchen, made and cut out the 308 biscuits used for a meal, and demonstrated thereby that as great as she is in her other accomplishments she is equally as great as a cook." During the summer of 1906 she supervised a great deal of canning and preserving. Six hundred bushels of fruit were prepared, including huckleberries, quinces, peaches, apples, plums, pears, and scuppernongs. A two-story coop was erected in the back yard, where one thousand chickens and two hundred turkeys were kept briefly at various times during the year.

The first known wedding ceremony to occur on campus was held in the college parlors on June 3, 1908, as Miss Mildred Jones, who had been on the music faculty for nine years, was married to O. W. Baynes of Winston-Salem, North Carolina, by R. B. Headden of the First Baptist Church of Rome. The room was decorated in daisies, and afterwards an informal reception was held. Several graduates had stayed a week after commencement in order to attend the wedding. As one of them said, they had a most "brazilious" time, throwing just a little rice in spite of Mrs. Simmons' orders to the contrary.

An official college seal was finally designed in 1908–1909, first being used on the commencement invitations that year. Similar to the one now in use, it contained a cross, an open Bible, a glowing sun (doubtless symbolizing enlightenment and righteousness), and two Latin words, *lux* and *veritas* ("light" and "truth"). It carried the inscription, "Founded 1877 by Alfred Shorter," and the printed programs accordingly proclaimed that this was the thirty-second commencement. This seal was constantly used until 1923, when the present one was adopted.

Community Relations

Altogether apart from the fund-raising campaigns, Shorter College was often in the public eye as its personnel prominently related themselves to the community. The Lanier Circle lived an additional four years after Battle left, with Shorter persons usually serving as president and music director, giving numerous speeches and musical numbers, and attending meetings, many of which were in the college parlors. Receptions almost without number were held at the college—to honor the Association of Travelers, the grandmothers of Rome, the friends of various departments, members of the faculty, or visiting musicians, artists, or elocutionists. For years the second Monday in each month from 4:00 to 6:00 P.M. was the time for the regular public reception, after which it was changed to each Saturday from 3:00 to 5:00 P.M. The students appeared in their white frocks; Mrs. Simmons presided in a gown and jewelry that often attracted newspaper comment. She frequently spoke in Rome, Atlanta, and elsewhere, on topics such as music education, the voice, and the medical aspects of alcoholism. She, her music faculty, and her students were constantly presenting recitals —to the Georgia Federation of Women's Clubs meeting in Atlanta, a public assembly at the Cartersville Opera House, conferences of music teachers, Masonic meetings annually held in Rome, and conventions of the Daughters of the American Revolution and the United Daughters of the Confederacy. Musical programs were sponsored to benefit the Methodist Woman's Foreign Missionary Society, the Salvation Army, the DeSoto Park Baptist Church, and St. Peter's Episcopal Church tower fund. Faculty members appeared in concert at the Rome Opera House with regularity, and year by year they and the students purchased season tickets for the Rome lyceum programs that occasionally were held in St. Cecilia Hall. President Simmons led the Rome Teachers' Club one year, and it often met on the campus. One spring the school commissioners of Georgia convened at Shorter; faculty persons delivered addresses, a concert was given, and the inevitable reception was held. The girls were allowed a half-day holiday so that they might attend one of the sessions. J. H. Simmons, the professor of English, often participated in the Baptist Young People's Union of the First Baptist Church, making talks that were commented on for their clarity and religious content. He and Gwaltney delivered speeches at the annual birthday celebration honoring Robert E. Lee. In the early 1900s, items were on sale in town that reminded the community of Shorter: engraved stationery, colored postcards showing the main buildings, silver spoons with a view of the main buildings engraved in the bowl, and stick pins in the form of a white pennant bearing the word *Shorter* in gold letters.

Developing Social Graces

Although "Social Training" had not been ignored earlier, Mrs. Simmons laid emphasis on this aspect of college life. Tea was served daily at 4:00 P.M. in the parlors, and the girls were expected to be present. Of course the pupils "dressed" for the evening meal, after which they assembled with the faculty for "reading and social converse." Every Monday evening they gathered in the parlor for a lecture by Mrs. Simmons, who then would tell them how to conduct themselves properly in the presence of young men, teach them good table manners, suggest styles and colors of dresses, and instruct them in ladylike behavior on the train when a vacation was forthcoming. Occasionally on Saturday she held a convocation for all the day students in the chapel. Once she came on the stage rolling a wheeled tray loaded with china, silver, and glassware. She proceeded to place a table cloth on a table and lay a cover in the correct manner, telling the girls as she worked what she was doing and the reasons for it. She demonstrated the manner in which one was to pick up her doily and place it on her lap, how to use a knife and fork, and how to lift soup from a bowl with a spoon. "In fact, she became our 'Emily Post,'" commented one in her audience who recalled the event fifty years later. Such lectures were supplemented at mealtime by a crack on the hand with a ruler wielded by Mrs. Simmons when a young lady, after repeated warnings, failed to handle the silver properly. Regular receptions and musicales were held on Saturday evenings, open only to the college community. At intervals formal receptions, to which outside guests were invited, also allowed students to develop social graces.

Never one to lose an opportunity for instruction, "Your Other Mother," Mrs. Simmons, some years addressed an extended mimeographed letter just before Christmas to "My Dear Girls." In one of them she suggested ways in which they could improve their use of the coming holiday. Put aside "the Santa Claus idea" and cultivate the spirit of giving. Be thoughtful to your parents, grandparents, older persons, and "all people of all color." Avoid critical remarks and demands that will overburden your mother. "If anybody must have a rest, let it be the mother. . . . Entertain the children part of the day. . . . When father comes home, receive him with a smile, see that there are no cares and no worries that you could have adjusted before his arrival. . . . The custom of mother and daughter visiting together is a beautiful one. Prefer her society to that of your young friends this time. . . . Carry good cheer and peace into the home." To each of the graduates Mrs. Simmons also addressed a long letter, similar in form and spirit to the one sent at Christmas. She spent much time describing modest and becoming clothes, appropriate patterns of behavior both inside the home and in public, and the proper attitude to take regarding the year's work at Shorter.

General Academic Matters

Admissions policies remained academically indefinite. The young lady was expected to have a good character and good intentions—and to "possess an adequate knowledge of all subjects belonging to the preceding classes." "We will not knowingly receive any who have been dismissed from other colleges." Soon the faculty agreed to admit graduates of the Rome public schools to the freshman class without examination. By 1908 the various state universities in the South had compiled a list of preparatory schools whose graduates could be admitted without examination, and Shorter adopted it to govern admissions. Students wishing such consideration could secure forms—"furnished gratis," stated the catalogue—that principals could complete and return directly to the college. "Data on such certificates are confidential and must not be exhibited by the principal to the student." For the finest of results, Shorter began to recommend six years of primary preparation and four years of academic preparation. Indeed, full admission to the collegiate department was contingent upon completing the four-year prerequisite course of study, although a student who was no more than one semester short of this requirement was allowed to enter the freshman class and to make up the additional work during her first two years at Shorter.

A pattern of activities at the opening of school became visible during this period. Opening convocation was usually held in the chapel at 9:00 A.M. Large numbers of townspeople would attend, as would the trustees. The girls would sing several songs, a local pastor would lead in a devotional period, and announcements would follow. One evening President and Mrs. Simmons would entertain at a reception that enabled the students to meet each other. The next afternoon they might be given a trolley party that took them sight-seeing over the town, or they might attend a musical recital. Soon the students would meet with the teachers and arrange class schedules for the year—a brief and painless form of registration. Matriculation cards signed by the bursar certified that the student, "having paid the matriculation fee, is authorized to enter the appropriate classes and to have free use of the library of Shorter College during the present session." During the semester, she might receive other official cards reading: "As the President wishes to speak with you on business, you will please call at his office at your FIRST VACANT PERIOD, unless a specific hour for the call is written in the blank space which follows." Commented one of them: "You bet your life I went!!!" Concerning a similar card from the bursar she wrote: "I took my own sweet time."

Classes were held five days each week, Tuesday through Saturday. At 8:30 A.M. all students gathered for chapel service three days and Bible study the other two. Following this, classes began on the hour starting from 9:00 A.M. through 1:00 P.M. The average student was occupied with classes or laboratory sessions nineteen hours each week. Lunch was served at 12:00 for half of the students and at 1:00 for the remainder.

Periods of testing continued, although final examinations were waived for all those with a grade of 95 in any course and fewer than nine absences. Other students could not ignore them, as indicated by this comment: "Examinations, which always come in January, did not fail us this year, and it is to be hoped that we did not fail in them." The system of grading became more familiar:

A. Excellent—90–100
B. Good—80–90
C. Fair—75–80
D. Failed to Pass—below 75

For seven of the Simmons' twelve years, all the grades have been preserved, the first extensive records of this sort known to exist.

The Curricula

The curricula were changed with the coming of President Simmons. Although the sub-junior class was removed, a sub-freshman class was added for those whose preparation was considered inadequate. Separate courses within each of the various schools were described in greater detail, and the use of a classification very similar to the modern semester hour system was introduced. For graduation, a total of 142 s.h. was required, distributed approximately as follows: English language and literature, 24 s.h.; history and political science, 14 s.h.; Latin, 24 s.h.; psychology and ethics, 4 s.h.; Bible, 8 s.h.; mathematics, 22 s.h.; French or German, 10 s.h.; and natural sciences, 36 s.h. Other courses were offered in Greek, art, speech, and music. Two degrees were continued—the Bachelor of Arts, awarded to 69, and the Bachelor of Letters, awarded to 66—and a new one started, the Bachelor of Science, awarded to only 2. A further requirement was reintroduced, a thesis of not less than fifteen hundred words showing "careful reading and research on a subject approved by the Faculty . . . ," to be written during the senior year. For students completing satisfactorily any of the departments of the college, a special diploma was awarded. To the requirements for the Master of Arts degree was added the completion of another thesis, and one such degree was awarded.

In 1906 the college began to recognize two years of work by awarding an engraved certificate to those who were then given the title of College Associate. At the same time the Bachelor of Music degree was instituted, but only one was ever awarded by Simmons. The student was to complete the regular freshman and sophomore courses, taking such electives as prescribed by the music faculty, and two additional years altogether in music. Also, diplomas in voice, pianoforte, pipe organ, and violin were provided for those not wishing to complete a four-year course of study. The average age of the full graduate was about nineteen. As was true of Vassar and Wellesley graduates, they were accepted by the graduate school at Yale without further examination—a fact that provided President Simmons with much satisfaction.

Foreign travel was recognized to be both educational and pleasurable by the Shorter faculty, and five or six summers saw Mrs. Simmons and Miss Elizabeth Waddell lead student parties through various parts of Europe. No college credit was given for this travel, but the catalogue yearly encouraged the girls to avail themselves of these tours.

Within the Departments

The faculty and staff grew steadily in numbers from 21 to 37, with a yearly average of 31.

Music. The music department was always the largest. Mrs. Simmons assembled a very stable group of instructors that included Misses Bertha Patterson (a Shorter graduate) and Virginia Pell for eleven years each in piano, Miss Mildred Jones for nine years in piano, Benjamin F. Havens for eight years in piano, Dr. J. Fowler Richardson for nine years in organ, Miss Madeleine Petit for five year in violin and orchestral instruments, and Miss Anne C. Worrill for five years in voice. The latter had studied with Mrs. Simmons and later sang in the company of a large Berlin theater. Two other former students of Mrs. Simmons also taught under her: Mrs. Ida Nevin Patton for four years in voice and Vernon D'Arnalle for two years in voice and piano. The Villa Graziani was named for Madame Elise Graziani of Germany who gave lessons in voice for three years—and was almost legendary for her prowess on the sewing machine, as she skillfully altered the girls' clothing!

Members of the music faculty were sometimes suspected, sometimes critical, and sometimes affectionately businesslike. One was an organist and pianist from Germany who had a waxed mustache and was so short that he wore high heels. He carried a cane, which the girls imagined was a sword cane—but they never actually saw it turn into a sword! A music teacher sharply insisted that one girl with a lovely soprano voice had it as a gift from God, for she did not have a brain in her head with which to find or improve it. One of the piano professors and his wife were invited to visit in the home of a favorite student at Christmas. He penned a refusal with thanks, indicating that he had officiated over the campus party as Santa Claus and adding in a most professional fashion: "If you work at the op. 110 don't forget to use Von Bülous' fingering."

In 1900 this department officially came to be called "The College of Music," with schools of voice, piano, pipe organ, violin, and harmony and history of music. With the acquisition of the Southern Conservatory of Music the following year, the Rome *Tribune* exclaimed: "It is now generally acknowledged that Shorter College is the greatest music college in the south." Soon after purchasing the Conservatory, Simmons decided that a new organ was needed for its auditorium. Accordingly, the John Brown Organ Company of Wilmington, Delaware, was contracted to build an instrument especially for the college at a cost of $2,000. It was completed in the spring of 1902, and the first public use apparently came in a concert during commencement week.

With a large faculty and a separate building for instruction, the College of Music was always active. Public recitals were presented in the auditorium by students, faculty members, and guest artists, one year numbering about thirty. Once the operetta "Queen Esther" was staged—and all the parts were sung by students, including those of Haman and Mordecai. Trained by Mrs. Simmons, the chorus was said

95

to be "superb." Unfortunately, it was reported, the cultured audience should have been much larger than it was. Visitors to the college included moderately famous musicians of the day: Lillian Carllsmith, Heinrich Pfitzner, Laura Mehrtens, Angelo Patricola, Ernest Hutcheson, W. Waugh Lauder, and Vladimir DePachmann. The last, a very small man, involuntarily exclaimed when he was introduced to Mrs. Simmons: "What a great big lady!" To this she immediately responded: "And what a little bit of a man!" During one year eight faculty concerts were scheduled, and season tickets were sold for $1 each. Since only half that number were given then, the other four were faithfully presented the following year. The unusual act of charging admission occurred because the Simmons were then trying to pay for the new organ. The girls, who were required to attend all of these many concerts, usually went with "dates"—other girls.

The daring Mrs. Simmons attracted a great deal of attention to her students and herself by one concert that she sponsored on May 9, 1901, at the Grand Opera House of Atlanta which she rented for the occasion. A Rome newspaper observed: "This invasion of Atlanta is a noteworthy event in the history of Rome's celebrated college which truly ranks as 'The Vassar of the South.' " On the day of the concert the paper said: "It is a very ambitious undertaking—the most ambitious Shorter College has ever known—but under the direction of Mrs. T. J. Simmons all things are possible." Even the Atlanta newspapers observed the coming of the event, giving several extended notices of it. On that fateful Thursday evening the girls from Shorter covered themselves and Mrs. Simmons with glory. Dressed "in girlish white gowns of thin material, and all evidently happy and content with the world," they faced a large, critical, and enthusiastic audience. The program consisted of Chopin, Schubert, Liszt, MacDowell, Mendelssohn, and others; and each girl had one or more encores. As a special number, eight pianos were played in unison, and the artists were "rapturously applauded." One young lady received American Beauty roses with stems that were said to be two yards long, tied with about twenty yards of ribbon—but it is doubted that even Mrs. Simmons could have produced such a bouquet as that. A Rome paper observed the next day that the girls "acquitted themselves brilliantly" and that "all Atlanta is praising Shorter College." Again in 1904 the students performed at the Grand Opera House under similar conditions, and in 1907 the faculty presented a program there.

Although the young ladies were seldom permitted to attend programs at the Rome Opera House, at times the instructional value of the performance was sufficiently great to make exceptions. Hence, they heard the Dresden Philharmonic Orchestra, the Schubert Symphony, the Royal Hungarian Orchestra, the Pittsburgh Festival Orchestra, various operettas, the Clansmen, the Kilties' Band, the Vanderbilt University Glee Club, and John Philip Sousa's band.

Even more rare were their visits to Atlanta, where they heard Madame Patti and Madame Melba. Twice President and Mrs. Simmons and several Shorter girls attended a concert by the pianist Moritz Rosenthal. The first time the group went backstage afterwards and met the artist, presenting him with a gold-headed cane engraved: "To the Great Rosenthal, from Shorter College." He insisted upon being introduced to the young ladies and secured their addresses—"presumably for sending them an autograph letter of thanks," said a Rome reporter.

The great Paderewski played in Atlanta on the evening of February 22, 1900, and sixty Shorter students and faculty members were in his audience. Provided with a private car, they left Rome on the early morning train, arriving at their destination in mid-morning. After a day of sight-seeing and shopping, they occupied seats in the second balcony of the Grand Opera House and "with opera glasses had a splendid view of everything." The artist "held the immense audience spell-bound from start to finish," and one awed Shorter student refrained from a detailed description of his music because it would have been "an insult to the performer." After the sixth encore the recital was over, and the girls boarded their special car. At 2:30 A.M. they were back in Rome, "happy," "pretty well tired out," "thankful," and "rejoicing."

Among the more talented student pianists at Shorter, a degree of excitement was generated in the summer of 1900 when an anonymous friend offered a $2,000 Hallet and Davis grand piano to the student who would do "the most satisfactory work" between then and June of 1902. A committee of twelve persons was named to watch the progress of those pupils desiring to enter the competition. Finally in 1903 the prize piano was awarded to Rosalie Fenn of Cordele, Georgia. Since she was not a graduate, she made her way from the rear of the chapel to receive certification of her award. "The glad approval of the generous classmates was heard in the delighted hurrahs that were distinct even above the storm of applause of the house." A second piano was promptly offered for presentation two years hence, but none seems to have been awarded either then or later.

Younger children were also encouraged to take piano lessons at Shorter, even under Mrs. Simmons. One afternoon, without previous warning, she called upon her primary students, "wearing their little white aprons," to participate in an impromptu concert. When introduced, they "marched forward with a confident air and standing at the piano, played well their selections." Formal concerts with printed programs were also presented. Actively seeking younger students, Mrs. Simmons personally offered to instruct new piano pupils aged six to twelve for a period of time and then turn them over to one of her assistants. The price for this was to be $10 for the first semester, a considerable reduction from the regular fees that she charged. She also organized the primary music students into the Bach and Handel Club, which had regular meetings and provided some public concerts.

In the fall of 1898 Mrs. Simmons announced to the older music students that a musical society was to be organized. Called the St. Cecilia Society, its officers were elected and committees appointed. By the third meeting a constitution and by-laws had been drawn up and were then approved. Often its president was a member of the faculty, rather than a student. One young lady wrote: "Mrs. Simmons fondly calls it 'her society,' as indeed she may, since she is at once our guardian, instructor and entertainer. Whenever she is absent the meeting loses half its charm." Once she styled the members the great-grandchildren of Liszt, since she herself had studied under one of his pupils. Designated for their use in the dormitory building, a special hall was decorated with blue walls and hangings, several pieces of choice statuary, and a rosewood piano. When the Conservatory was purchased, of course, the meeting room was moved to St. Cecilia Hall. The group met on the first and third Mondays at either 3:30 or 8:00 P.M., enabling interested persons from the city to hold membership. Among the frequent concerts presented was one in 1907 to benefit the great American composer, Edward MacDowell, who was then gravely ill. A less serious concert was given one afternoon two years later at Berry School. The forty girls were taken out on the trolley car to the end of the line, where they were picked up by buggies, wagons, and carriages for the remainder of the journey.

ART. Under the guidance of Miss Lula M. Ross, professor of drawing and painting for eleven years, the art department held small, informal receptions in which student work was displayed, sometimes sponsored a formal exhibit in December, and always presented a commencement exhibit for the art graduates. The course in art embroidery was discontinued, while emphasis was placed on drawing, painting, and some ceramics and china painting. The Pen and Ink Club was formed in 1900, apparently the first such club in the history of the school. Five years later another group emerged, the Art Club, which was much more active. At its meetings the latest art journals and selections from appropriate books were read and discussed, to provide something of the history and philosophy of art as well as classroom techniques. A good time was always assured by the inclusion of salad courses and ice cream. In the studio were the familiar plaster casts, jugs, and baskets —as well as the traditional green teapot and red onion. Prior to one Christmas holiday the members sponsored an exhibit and sale. Pictures were auctioned off to the highest bidder—one item was "knocked down at $2.75"—followed by refreshments. In the spring, outdoor sketching became popular. One notable Monday picnic was spent on Mount Lavender, after which they visited the dining room of Berry School and were greeted with "enthusiastic applause." Another year the art class enjoyed a "frolic" at Barnsley Gardens, making the trip in a large band wagon.

MODERN LANGUAGES. French and German were taught each year, and by 1909 clubs devoted to those subjects were reestablished after a lengthy lapse. An anecdote involved one of the professors. While Theophile Dambach was instructing his class, a piece of plaster fell without warning from the ceiling, narrowly missing his head. Everyone quickly looked up, and there was a foot protruding from the floor above. A girl exclaimed: "I believe that is a little boy's foot." Dambach responded: "Oh no, I think it is that of a young girl. It is so small!" Of course his class speedily disappeared, and soon everyone on the hill was laughing—except, perhaps, the science teacher whose foot had caused the commotion.

RELIGION. R. B. Headden, pastor of the First Baptist Church, was part-time professor of Bible and Biblical literature throughout this entire period, teaching two mornings a week. The four-year course was divided as follows: Old Testament history, life of Christ, the apostolic church, and the poetic and prophetic books. For two years the catalogue stated that all Bible courses were nondenominational in content, adding: "All students are expected to take these courses, but may be excused therefrom at the written request of parents." In the third year the assurance of their nondenominational nature was omitted, while in the fourth year all of the foregoing was dropped in favor of this statement: "To thoughtful people, it is unnecessary to speak of the great importance of this department of study, or to give utterance to the opinion that unless based on the divine truths of revealed religion, all human knowledge is vain." For 8½ years Luther Rice Gwaltney was chaplain and professor of Christian morals, but the amount of his classroom instruction is now uncertain.

SPEECH. The School of Oratory, as this department was named, had as its "main design" the making of "good *readers*." The pupils and teacher took part in frequent recitals, and each graduate in oratory was required to give a public recital. Visiting elocutionists appeared, the most popular being Henry L. Southwick, dean of the Emerson School of Oratory, Boston, from which Shorter obtained several of its teachers. At times the students were permitted to view performances at the Rome Opera House, such as "King Richard III" and "As You Like It." The production of plays became more prominent during this period, and always the male roles were filled by the young ladies. The first student organization within this department, the Dramatic Club, was started early in 1907, but little was subsequently heard from it.

OTHER COLLEGIATE DEPARTMENTS. Four professors in as many departments were long-time favorites of the girls. The Waddell sisters, said by one of their students to have "brains as big as their hearts," taught for twelve years each—Miss Sallie N., in mathematics, and Miss Elizabeth F., in history and political science. "Miss Bessie," as she was called, "so vividly presented" history that "it was never dull. If we did not know our lesson we switched her off on the subject of Napoleon and the hour was enlivened and we did not have to confess we hadn't studied as we should." "Her smile was proverbial, and rarely was she out of patience with the most stupid ones of us." Both were housemothers in smaller dormitories; one student remembered "our Rosemont mother" calling out: "Mary, Bek, Susie—all my children, to bed, lights out, see about the fires, good night." Mrs. Irene M. Starke taught Latin for eleven years in a quiet and unobtrusive way that produced much affection but little comment. J. H. Simmons, brother of the president, was professor of English language and literature and secretary of the faculty (registrar) for twelve years. His classes in Shakespeare were so notable that many townspeople attended, along with the regular students.

One of the science teachers was a fine man who was not always aware of a young woman's interest. On a Saturday afternoon he required a student to remain after class in order to complete the dissection of a cat that could not be preserved until Monday because of the absence of refrigeration. Her young gentleman friend was home from college and paced up and down the alley until she finally emerged. Neither professor nor cat permanently got in the way of their romance, however, and she later became his wife.

PRIMARY AND ACADEMIC DEPARTMENTS. Shorter offered eight to ten years of instruction at the secondary level, finally providing six in the primary department and four in the academic department, as it came to be designated. In 1901 the primary department received renewed emphasis. An issue of the *Bulletin of Shorter College* entitled "What Shall We Do with the Children?" provided reasons for enrolling one's six-year-old daughter in the school. For six years Miss Pauline Ramsey was the remarkably successful principal, maintaining a full enrollment in various appealing ways. One September she entertained more than seventy children at a Mother Goose party on the terraces of the college. Humpty Dumpty, Mistress Mary, Little Red Riding Hood, Little Miss Muffett, Little Bo Peep, and Little Boy Blue were present, and each child recited the verse appropriate to her outfit. With Miss Ramsey's departure for the purpose of marriage, the future of the department was considered so uncertain by some persons in Rome that they issued a public statement in the press protesting its presumed closing. Both President Simmons and D. B. Hamilton of the board of trustees responded, insisting that the department would remain open if support warranted it. Soon thereafter an advertisement was run for three days calling for fifty primary pupils, and the department was opened on schedule in September. It was discontinued in 1910.

The academic department functioned satisfactorily without gaining undue publicity. The Round Table Club was composed of its students, and for a couple of years beginning in 1906 it functioned. Literary programs were held, but of course refreshments were served at some of their meetings—and in the spring of 1907 it was reported that they started "the picnic season" by a trip to Horseleg Creek.

OTHER ALUMNAE TEACHERS. As has already been observed, Shorter alumnae continued to remain on the hill in significant numbers as members of the faculty. In addition to those already named, sixteen other graduates served from one to three years. Of these, three were in the preparatory or primary departments for three years each: Misses Belle Comer, Annabel Rhodes, and Ethel Cowan. Four others who attended the college but did not graduate were also faculty members one or two years.

Administration and Staff

The library in Pennington Hall grew to about 5,000 volumes, eventually necessitating a full-time librarian. For two years Miss Susan T. Austin was the first "Superintendent of Library," while serving also as professor of oratory and physical culture. In October of 1898 the libraries of the two societies were turned over to the college and became a part of the general collection. The first full-time librarian, Miss Irene

Dabney Gallaway, joined the staff in September of 1900. She organized the books according to the Dewey Decimal System and prepared a card catalogue containing author and title cards. She was succeeded by a Shorter alumna, Miss May Fortenberry, who was librarian five years. Eventually the job went to Miss Linnie Hargrove, who spent eight years at Shorter, chiefly as a matron. Each student paid $2 annually for the purchase of books, and donations were encouraged. The seniors and alumnae combined forces to provide an oyster supper downtown one February, at which, they assured the public, oysters cooked in every style could be secured. Another time the seniors entertained at a tea on the Shorter terraces, probably for the *Iris* and the library. It was announced in the newspaper: "All ladies 'and married men,' (N.B.) are cordially invited, and they can depend on prompt service, and a sumptuous menu. The price for the full course is only twenty-five cents. Young men are debarred, for obvious reasons. Be sure to go and encourage these noble girls."

The administrative staff included two other persons who served five years each: Miss Cora Neal as executive clerk and principal of the business department and George A. Foote as bursar and assistant to the president.

The Two Societies

Eunomian and Polymnian meetings continued weekly, and while membership was not required, it was strongly recommended. Each society had a separate meeting hall, occasionally improved with new papering, paint, rugs, curtains, and pictures. Meetings usually dealt with figures such as Burns, Whittier, Lanier, Scott, Goldsmith, Shakespeare, Tennyson, Wordsworth, and Longfellow. Some debates were held within each society: "Resolved, That England is justified in her war on the Transvaal"; "Resolved, That Examinations Are Necessary to a Thorough Understanding of a Subject"; "Resolved, That it is better to have loved and lost than never to have loved at all." In each case, the decision favored the affirmative!

If the last topic seems less than serious, so also were the parties that the societies held. In anticipation of leap year, the Eunomians sponsored a Proposal Party late in 1903. According to the rules set up for the evening, twenty "demure and coy" young ladies were to resist the words of love addressed to them by twenty classmates dressed as men. At the ringing of a bell, "each man at once proved his fickle heart by changing his seat and pouring his tale of love into another fair maiden's ear." Prizes were awarded for the young lady who was "most successful in warding off the youthful effusions" and for two young "men" who were "so fascinating in their love-making . . . ." To celebrate their anniversary two years later, the Polymnian Society had a party at which each person was given the name of another girl in the society about which she was to compose a rhyme. First prize was awarded for this one:

> Dora Brown went to town
> Turned around and saw a clown
> And knocked him down.
> This Dora Brown, who weighs but a pound
> Is very solid and I dare say sound.

There is no record that the authoress was the featured literary figure at a subsequent society meeting.

To provide funds for decorating their halls, the girls were permitted to look both inside and outside the college fence for assistance. Once they gave a Christmas bazaar where various handmade items and delectable eatables—"Neapolitan ice cream, pineapple sherbet and stuffed dates"—were on sale. It was reported: "The light bell called us away from an evening of unmixed pleasure." They took charge of the Jervis Ice Cream Parlor once, and the newspaper obligingly asked for a liberal patronage. One May they sponsored a strawberry festival on the terraces of the college, where the invited public could purchase a plate of strawberries and cake for 10¢ or a plate of strawberry ice cream and cake for 15¢. This kind of activity finally led the editors of the *Chimes* to bemoan the conditions relating to the societies: "We are sorry to infer from what we have heard concerning the literary societies that there is very little life and enthusiasm shown in them. Instead of the enthusiasm growing in a literary way, we are afraid that it is assuming a greedier aspect, and probably there is more of a rush for the 'filthy lucre' than ever before in the histories of the societies." Later in the spring they happily reported: "It seems that they have been asleep with the trees and are now awakening with them."

For the first time, society colors were mentioned. The Eunomians started with violet and pink in 1899 but had settled on crimson and gold by 1901. The Polymnians adopted white and green in 1899, white and purple in 1901, and white and crimson in 1905.

Usually the societies cooperated in a fall reception for their new members. After 1905 they once more jointly published the *Chimes*. During commencement week they invited the alumnae to a reception, and at least once there were young men present, too.

In March of 1904, however, competition in the form of the first known intersociety debate was felt. Arguing the affirmative, the Polymnians were victorious on the topic, "Resolved, That unrestricted immigration is detrimental to the best interests of our country." Rivalry was present again when the societies played an exciting basketball game on April 1, 1905. "It was no April Fool joke to them . . . and their shouts of encouragement came from the bottom of hearts burdened with anxiety as to the final outcome." After eighty minutes of playing and resting, the Polymnians finally won by a score of 20 to 17.

With the passage of time there was "a growing tendency towards the 'Sorority feeling,'" and therefore it was reported in the fall of 1906 that "the college authorities have revised the Constitutions and established the Societies upon a purely literary basis." Each document was virtually identical, proclaiming that the object of the society was "the inculcation of a love of letters . . . and . . . the promotion of the interests of the college . . . ." "The name and character of this Society . . . shall remain forever unalterable. . . .The social or entertainment feature of the Society shall never become predominant, but if this feature exists, it shall be distinctly subordinated to the literary and culural features—the fundamental feature upon which the Society must forever be conducted." Nevertheless, according to the earliest extant minute books, not everything was of a serious nature. Punch and banana sandwiches appeared at one meeting, and several impromptu debates considered such weighty matters as these: "Resolved, That casing is detrimental to the welfare of a college girl"; "Resolved, Absence makes the heart grow fonder"; "Resolved, That co-educational schools are better than non-co-educational." Each society agreed to enlist no more than three-fifths of the eligible students as members.

In 1907 the Polymnians introduced a prophetic element, their use of the Greek letters Π Σ. Their membership pin for that year utilized them, as did pillows and pennants that were made then.

A request that the societies admit town girls came in 1909 from President Simmons and the board of trustees. The minutes contain the decision: "As this has always been against our rules and as our hall is too small for more members, the girls voted against taking in the town girls." Of course their first reason was not accurate, for at the turn of the century town girls had in fact been members, but at least their second one was correct. There is no record that their decision was overturned by those making the initial request.

The First Student Government

Under President Simmons, the public use of uniforms was continued. On the college grounds, of course, dresses were left to individual tastes, subject only to the dictates of simplicity and appropriateness. Uniforms for the winter were selected early in the fall—inexpensive, tailor-made suits that were usually brown, blue, or black. Before the uniforms were received, the girls wore a simple white dress for summer church wear and a black skirt with a shirtwaist for cooler church wear. Uniforms for warm weather continued to be a white pique skirt, white shirtwaist, and white sailor hat.

The long lists of rules regulating the lives of the students did not reappear in the catalogues after 1898. General statements indicated that obedience to authority and consideration of the rights and feelings of one's associates were expected. "Our aim is an atmosphere of love and helpfulness." If the rules did not appear in the catalogue, they existed just the same. Each student received a detailed one-page list with the heading, "Rules and Regulations for the Boarding Department." Although they contained little that Battle had not demanded fifteen years earlier, they made some additions and refinements: "Each student *must* exercise at least one hour daily. . . . Monday mornings must be devoted to a general cleaning. . . . The two amusements, card-playing and dancing, are not allowed. . . . The young ladies must furnish the President with a list of their correspondents in their parents' handwriting. Letters to young gentlemen on such lists may be written only once a month."

At times the rules were evaded. Although all packages were required to be delivered to members of the staff, in actuality the day students often brought boxes of candy and baskets of fruit from the Rome boys without usually getting caught. One girl preserved in her scrapbook a paper napkin obviously obtained during an unauthorized visit in town, inscribing above and below it: "We only stopped in from a walk, to rest a while. . . . If Miss Bessie knew where we got that cup of chocolate what would she say." On one occasion a young lady was discovered talking to her male admirer through the fence that surrounded the grounds. As punishment she was restricted to the campus for a time—but this did not deter the romance, and the two were later married. Lights were turned out at 9:45, but often the girls would sit on the floor in a closet, light a small candle, and enjoy a clandestine feast. Food for such banquets came from the maids, "who were well bribed to supply us," thus making the entire escapade against the college rules.

At times a rule was obeyed in unison. From 8:00 to 10:00 on Saturday evening the young ladies could receive their dates all together in the large Oriental Parlor. When the bell rang, all of the boys had to leave at once.

At times the girls were encouraged by merchants to be obedient. Advertisements one year told them, "Ask the Chaperone to take you to Fahy's," where a ten percent discount was offered.

When rules were broken too often, girls were expelled. After one name in the roll book kept by the secretary of the faculty was this notation: "Withdrew from College under the censure of the Faculty." One long-remembered young lady was excluded for "smoking and other things." She was always getting into trouble of some sort. In that period the girls were not allowed to lock their doors at night. Teachers could burst in upon them unannounced, trying to catch them in wrongdoing. This girl finally decided to give the teachers something to find. She stripped naked and calmly sat in her room until she was discovered by one of her elders. Soon she was fully clothed and on a train heading home. In 1909 Mrs. Simmons informed her seniors: "We have had a few misdemeanors and very few restrictions. Our girls have been lovable and law-abiding." She was pleased because for the first time in all her years at Shorter, no one had suffered expulsion.

Never a part of the official record was Mrs. Simmons' stipulation concerning what, to her, was the publicly unmentionable matter of underwear! Union suits were worn by the young ladies until she permitted their removal late in the spring. Composed by one unhappy lawbreaker, these lines tell a story of daring and dejection:

> April 26th in Rome was hot,
> And so were the girls at Shorter.
> But they couldn't pull off their shirts
> Until Mrs. T. J. gave the order.
>
> Some girls went to walk one day
> And not one of them wore her shirt.
> And on their return they stopped at Curry's
> Where some had a chance to flirt.
>
> That night those girls were summoned
> To the parlor; in haste they went.
> Mrs. Simmons was grossly insulted at those
> Who really no harm meant.
>
> And for five long weeks those poor girls
> On Shorter Hill did stay,
> Prohibited from going anywhere
> Until graduation day.

For a number of years the "Honor Roll System" was in effect at Shorter. The girls were instructed at the beginning of the year concerning the rules decided upon by the discipline committee of the faculty, after which they reported each week upon their honor whether or not they had violated any of them. If a girl reported "perfect" for twenty-seven weeks, she was placed on the self-governed list and given special privileges. Of these privileges only one is known: honor students could go downtown without a chaperone.

In 1908 fourteen students were selected—evidently by the faculty— to form a council called the Honor Board that would "supplement" the discipline committee and uplift all girls whose conduct or class work fell below the average. In this way, the girls were given a greater voice in their own discipline, which hopefully would improve conduct and scholarship. This was the first form of student government at Shorter, with Kittie Watson as president of the student body.

Religious Life

The Young Women's Christian Association became a part of campus life in 1898, while the following year the Martha Shorter Missionary Society was reactivated in order to emphasize world missions. The two groups thereupon functioned with virtually the same girls as members. Meetings occurred late on Sunday afternoon, with programs presented by the students themselves, various members of the faculty, and local clergymen. Occasionally a visitor would vary the routine: a missionary from India, the secretary of the Student Volunteer Movement, or national leaders of the Y.W.C.A. At different times the two groups provided clothing and books for a young lady enrolled in the Rome public schools, relief for several Rome families, funds for the education of two girls in China, $200 for relief work arising from the calamitous San Francisco earthquake of 1906, and Christmas parties for Rome youngsters who were given presents. The Shorter pupils frequently attended Y.W.C.A. conferences in Atlanta, Birmingham, Montgomery, or Asheville—usually accompanied by a chaperone.

A devotional period came at the beginning of each class day, together with required courses in Bible. On Wednesdays and Fridays the girls led twilight prayer meetings. "Unless . . . excused for good reason," all students were lined up and roll was called at 10:30 on Sunday morning. If inspection revealed that any had on rouge or lipstick, it was wiped off. Some always managed to replace a little on the walk down to the church, however. Shorter students furnished music for revival services at the First Baptist Church and were encouraged to attend with fidelity. Chaplain Gwaltney conducted a service of worship each Sunday evening in the chapel. A large congregation attended a program of music in St. Cecilia Hall one Easter Sunday afternoon.

"The stage, on which the choir of fifty girls were seated, was appropriately decorated in ferns, palms and many beautiful cut flowers, while the pulpit was one mass of Easter lilies." A special Christmas concert, "The Babe of Bethlehem," was presented later that year, comprised mostly of thirteen musical pieces by Mrs. Simmons, younger faculty members, and advanced students. The newspaper announcement urged promptness at the program, since the doors would be closed when the music began. In 1908 a new Martha Shorter prayer room was installed, and the following year men designated as "Preachers to the College" apparently delivered sermons at special services. The denominational affiliation of the boarding students can be determined for only one year, 1903–1904, when there were 59 Baptists, 28 Methodists, 16 Presbyterians, 13 Episcopalians, 1 Christian, and 1 Jew.

An Expanding Athletic Program

Intramural athletics flourished with the formation of the Athletic Association no later than 1899. The "Reds" and the "Blues" played basketball that year, while individuals participated in tennis, "golfette," archery, and gymnastics. The earliest athletic cheer emerged in 1900:

> Shorter! Shorter!
> Is our cry!!
> V-i-c-t-o-r-y.

Athletic clubs were pictured in the 1899 *Iris*: two basketball teams properly attired in ankle-length black dresses; the Tennis and Bicycle clubs resplendent in white blouses and skirts that swept the ground; and the P.C.C. Club, whose members held Indian clubs. In succeeding years several teams competed on the basketball court, and a Thanksgiving game became traditional. In 1906 the senior-sophomore team defeated the junior-freshman team by a score of 11 to 0, although generation names were not used. Gym suits were consistent with other forms of attire—black bloomers, black hose, and black or white blouses with long sleeves.

In 1904 the Athletic Association asked that Shorter engage in intercollegiate sports, partly to advertise the school. A petition was presented to the faculty, requesting permission to challenge Agnes Scott or Lucy Cobb to a game of basketball, but this was not granted. On November 25, 1909, a new age dawned when the college played its first athletic contest with a group from beyond its own campus. The girls of Miss Reynolds' gymnasium in Rome were the opponents at a basket-

108

ball game, but unfortunately it is not known whether Shorter had a winning season that year or not, because the score has disappeared.

When the Study Bell Did Not Ring

The amount of social life that the students enjoyed has a contemporary sound, even if there were very few young men around to share it with them. When all is considered, it must be admitted that the Shorter girls did not exactly study all of the time! Of course the fall circus was not on President Simmons' approved list, but one might accidentally be walking to a dental appointment just as the parade was noisily moving down Broad Street. In the fall and spring, students were often taken by the president and his wife on a trolley party, spending a pleasant Monday away from campus. One day the chartered trolley cars took them to Mobley Park, where they rowed on the lake and strolled through the woods. Later, they visited a blast furnace; "the molten metal was quite suggestive of Pluto's dominions." On the return trip they visited the powerhouse, which was then quite new. As they rode, they gave college and class yells, cheered President Simmons, and rendered familiar songs. Halloween continued to call forth elaborate preparations. This evening party in the gymnasium was sometimes supplemented by smaller festivities such as the Witch Walk given by five of the seniors in their "elegant apartments in Senior Hall." Thanksgiving Day always proved to be a busy one. The morning was marked by late breakfast, a basketball game, tennis matches, and attendance at church in "new and attractive uniforms." In the afternoon many enjoyed a five-mile hike, and all were impressed by an eight-course dinner from four to six that included roast turkey, Georgia corn pone, minced oysters, charlotte russe, mince pie, and much else. Many Thanksgiving menus printed in gold were preserved as souvenirs by the girls. In the evening a "phantom party" was customary. Some years President and Mrs. Simmons took groups on a visit to Mammoth Cave and Lookout Mountain.

During one Christmas shopping season, several stores remained open especially for the Shorter girls to make their purchases in privacy. The holiday was greeted with verse:

> 'Twas the week before Christmas
>   And all o'er the hill
> The students were restless;
>   Not one could be still.
> Few lessons were learned and no studying done
>   Because in each girl was the spirit of fun. . . .

Usually some of the pupils remained on campus throughout the vacation, and special activities were planned for them. At an "Advertisement Party" they identified many clippings from the then-current magazines and played numerous games while waiting for the prize to be awarded. New Year's eve was marked by a party at which all the guests appeared dressed as little children and played such games as "Drop the Handkerchief" and "Marching Round the Levee." Afterward the guests "went away to dream over the good time they had enjoyed and wake the next morning quite grown up."

George Washington's birthday developed into an annual celebration, complete with fancy invitations, sporting events, a skit by the seniors, and a party in the gymnasium at which the girls and invited young gentlemen would be attired in outfits appropriate for the eighteenth century. Almost every spring the University of Alabama Glee Club sang at St. Cecilia Hall. In 1908 the twenty-three Alabama girls enrolled in the college tendered them an afternoon Valentine party. One of the basses, French Craddock, was selected as "the lucky 'heart' and received an exquisite sofa pillow in yellow satin and white embroidery, carrying out the Shorter colors." The annual Memorial Day parade had lost its charm for the Simmons by 1903, and henceforth the girls did not participate.

With the coming of spring and the commencement season, activities moved out-of-doors. Picnics were numerous at Mount Lavender, Cave Spring, and DeSoto Park (as Mobley Park came to be called). After the day's work was done the girls might treat themselves to a progressive refreshment party. On a clear and warm March afternoon they enjoyed oysters at Satterfield's, peanuts at Kress', and sherbet at Hale-Jervis'. Another time several young men of Rome honored the seniors —accompanied by President and Mrs. Simmons—with two different trolley parties, followed by refreshments on the college terraces. "A most unusual enjoyment" was allowed the girls when they attended a baseball game between teams from the University of Georgia and the State Mutual Company of Rome.

The annual picnic on the Coosa River steamer came as close as possible to April 27, which was President Simmons' birthday, and was eagerly anticipated. "Everyone realizes that it is the last outing of the year, and knowing that 'after that, the deluge' of examinations soon begins, each tries to make it a red-letter day of the year." Every girl was at her prettiest as she wore her newest cotton dress.

The unexpected also afforded pleasure—as, for example, an hour at Curry-Arrington Drug Store in honor of a visitor or because of Mrs.

Simmons' generosity. Once an organ grinder and his begging monkey visited the campus, attracting a large crowd of students. A fragile photograph remains, showing Mrs. Simmons watching the situation intently from a nearby bench. The girls in one of the residential cottages were roused at 12:30 one morning when some of the shingles were ignited by sparks from a nearby chimney. Firemen quickly prevented a serious blaze, but doubtless sleep had fled from the cottage for the remainder of the night. A few months later at dusk the Conservatory roof caught fire, and the fire department was hastily called. "The clang of the alarm and the rush of the wagons aroused considerable excitement, and caused an exodus of crowds to the scene, but soon the signal 'fire out' quieted things down." Only a few shingles were destroyed, and damage was set at less than $10. One Saturday afternoon the sleet began to fall, and by evening it had turned to snow. An ecstatic girl rhapsodized: "The next morning, Sunday, we found everything covered with a pure white mantle. How calm and beautiful everything was, the stillness only broken by the breakfast-bell." In spite of the thermometer that read six below zero, "after breakfast we were allowed to have a snow battle. How thoroughly exhilarating it was! And what a beautiful picture was witnessed from the windows: the girls, their cheeks aglow with exercise, hats and cloaks covered with snow."

A three-state firemen's convention met periodically in Rome, calling forth a street parade with floral floats, carriages, brass bands, and excited spectators. During one convention, the unpredictable Mrs. Simmons and some of her girls occupied one of the decorated carriages. Since the girls had Monday off, the Mount Alto Golf Club voted to invite them and their professors to make free use of the links on that day from 8:00 A.M. to 2:00 P.M. Going even farther afield, the Simmons and some of the girls attended the Ivory Exposition in Charleston, South Carolina, in April of 1902. Later they visited the Louisiana Purchase Exposition at St. Louis. During the fall of 1907 they made an extensive tour that included Niagara Falls, New York, Philadelphia, and Washington, concluding with a number of days at the Jamestown Exposition. All of these longer excursions occurred during weeks that classes were meeting, and the travelers apparently lost no credit for being absent from campus! A less extensive journey in 1909 indicated that the college community was abreast of the times. One of the seniors entertained her class with an automobile trip the afternoon of May 11 —the first time that any Shorter persons are known to have joined "the honk colony," as a local newspaper designated it. Three large machines

111

were used to tour the best roads in and around town. The box of bon-bons that each girl received as a souvenir furnished a red and white ribbon for her scrapbook.

President Simmons was not a fraternity man, and sororities were prohibited because he felt that they tended to divert the students and cause jealousy. However, his attitude did not halt the proliferation of ephemeral social organizations. Often only the name is now known: the C.O.Y. Club, the Bachelorettes, the S.P.C. Club, the M.H.D.s, the Caldron Club, the Serenaders, the Jolly Seven, the Monday Afternoon Circle, the Do Right Society, the S.I. Club. The Beta Alpha Tau was said to have a limited membership, with 137 on the waiting list—but its very name suggests that the entire student body was interested in its noble purposes! The Alabama Club, Carolina Club, and Mississippi Circle were formed. The latter claimed to congregate "with and without permission. Theses and 'exams' were forgotten when dignified May and modest Bess would get out the chocolate pot. 'Nick' and 'Appie' would act as guard, while Katherine and Bess would 'twang' away on their mandolins as loud as possible so that any undue 'sizzing' of choco-late might not be heard beyond the four walls." Founded in 1908, the Kid Club had an existence that extended into the 1930s. Except for the last four, these apparently were constituted mostly for the purpose of getting one's face in the *Iris* or one's name in the *Chimes*.

The College Annual

The *Iris* was published in 1899 and 1900 by the senior class, and each annual was similar in size and content to the first one. One was dedicated to R. B. Headden, pastor of the First Baptist Church and the professor of Bible at Shorter, and the other, to President Simmons. Two of the pieces of fiction included descriptions of elaborate dances —social affairs that were not then allowed on campus, of course. One poem, "Shorter Bells," reflected much of the day-by-day routine on the hill:

> All the girls are sweetly sleeping,
>   Not a sound is anywhere—
> Suddenly a bell is ringing—
>   Wash your face and comb your hair.
>
> Girls are up and dressed for breakfast,
>   Rooms in order all around—
> Suddenly a bell is ringing—
>   It is not often that one frowns.
>
> Mail is called, and girls get letters;
>   After while the school-bell rings—

We have heard things that sound better—
Then to work for everything.

Next one is the bell for dinner;
We are as empty as a hat,
Rushing wildly for the table,
Think of neither this nor that.

Three o'clock does come so soon,
And we hear the same old tune,
Get to study and to practice
Every day until next June.

The trials of the advertising manager were reflected in one of them. A part of one page in the back of the volume was barren, except for this statement: "This space was reserved for H. B. Parks & Co. who now refuse to pay for it."

For the next six years no annual was printed. Then an editorial appeared in the *Chimes* for April, 1907, titled "Considerations for Renewing Publication of the College Annual." It was pointed out that an unpaid bill of $90 remained on the last *Iris*—issued seven years earlier! In the following issue there was a positive statement, "There will be an annual, next year," but of course there was not. That fall the question was raised in the *Chimes*: "Shall We Have a College Annual?" Answering her own question in the affirmative, the writer stated that the $90 debt had been paid and that there was nothing to stand in the way. However, the subject was again dropped; nothing more was heard of it during the remainder of that academic year. In the fall of 1908 two seniors were elected editors-in-chief, and other staff members were named. Once more silence prevailed, and no further annual was produced during the Simmons administration at Shorter.

Seniors and Commencement

Seniors continued to be feted by their schoolmates, the faculty—and themselves! The junior reception became an annual affair, making local history in 1903 when ice cream "in the shape of pink roses so perfect in form as to look as natural as a flower" was served. "This was the first time an order of ices frozen in shapes has been filled by a Rome firm." Doubtless the girls were more impressed with the young men in attendance who made it "a rarely pleasant evening." The reception given by the Simmons was often attended by as many as two hundred guests. Although simplicity of dress was enforced for the girls, one year "Mrs. Simmons was regal in a magnificent robe of white Brussels lace draped over corn colored satin. Her jewels were diamonds." In addition, the seniors enjoyed spring picnics sponsored by the sopho-

113

mores, juniors, and faculty. On a soggy day when "Miss Bessie" told them that May rains made people pretty, all cheerfully agreed that they should become beautiful indeed! Throughout the year, three seniors would join forces and give a party for the others of the class. "Christmas bells" was chosen as the theme for one of them. One of the hostesses had written her brother in Atlanta to see if Nunnally's would make them some candy bells to give as souvenirs. On the day of the party the express company delivered ten boxes, each thirty inches square, causing a great many questions on the hall. They had expected bells about an inch square—but instead they were eight by ten, "beautiful and delicious, red and green"! Another time the seniors gave a Salmagundi party for the rest of the school, charging each guest 10¢ for admission. Excitement mounted as the girls played games that involved tying knots in long strings, threading needles, fishing peanuts out of bowls, guessing anagrams and picture puzzles, and disposing of the "Old Maid." Waldorf salad, sherbet, and ice cream furnished the climax of the evening, cut short by the never-failing light bell that sent the girls to their rooms.

By 1908 some of the seniors were keeping bulky scrapbooks, "The Girl Graduate, Her Own Book." Containing snapshots, penned notes from classmates and faculty favorites, invitations to and souvenirs from dozens of parties, and printed programs and newspaper clippings concerning recitals and commencement, they vividly portrayed the college of that day.

Another literary project engaged the seniors—their theses. Only a few have actually survived the decades, but their titles were legion: "History of Ancient and Mediaeval Mathematics"; "Michelangelo's Conception of Art"; "An Ecological Classification of the Arborescent Flora in the Vicinity of Rome, Ga."; "Alarm Bells Rung by Modern Psychology"; "The Origin of Money"; "The Influence of Port Royal on French Theology"; "The State of Popular Education in Mexico"; "The Jew in Fiction"; "Dancing as Related to the Life and Religion of Primitive Peoples"; "The Effects of Child Labor on National Life"; "The United States Government and the Indian"; and many others. The single thesis for the Master of Arts degree was entitled "Index Raisonne sur Petit de Julleville."

The white robes of the seniors were discarded for the first five or six years of the Simmons administration, and the girls received their honors in white dresses. By 1907 black caps and gowns had been introduced, being worn at the first known Shorter Sunday held that fall at the First Baptist Church and again at the baccalaureate sermon and graduation ceremony the following spring.

Commencement week was customarily initiated with the Little Folks' Concert on Thursday or Friday afternoon. As usual, the baccalaureate sermon was delivered at the First Baptist Church by a guest clergyman, but by 1905 the memorial service for Colonel and Mrs. Shorter had been moved to Sunday at 5:00 or 8:00 P.M. Meeting in St. Cecilia Hall rather than the chapel, which by then had been converted into a study hall, this service usually contained much sacred music and a brief address, often by Luther Rice Gwaltney. The Simmons set aside all of Monday for the alumnae, entertaining them with an art exhibit and reception, a faculty concert, a formal reception at noon, and a literary address by a distinguished guest in the evening.

The seniors shone at the Tuesday morning Class Day exercise. The class of 1899 was the first to plant an ivy vine next to the chapel and to erect nearby a small stone inscribed with its class year. Both of these customs persisted until the new campus was occupied. In 1905 one of the seniors "conveyed to the juniors a much beribboned hatchet that with blood-stains as evidence had seen hard service as a noble weapon of defense. . . . A pipe bearing the colors of the class was held and lighted by Miss Ermin Pitts, who drew a great whiff first from the 'pipe of peace' then down it passed for all to do likewise." "Miss Eloise Simmons touched the torch to the pile of manuscripts laid before the class and as the blue wreaths of smoke curled heavenward the class breathed a sigh that their theses should have had so warm an end." The following year it was carefully noted that only "mock theses" were burned, while some years later textbooks received that treatment. In 1907 the Rome *Tribune* related, "As the junior class sang the Farewell Song, the seniors still surrounded by the garland of daisies, marched to the music"—the birth of the daisy chain! However, a picture of the 1908 exercise plainly shows an ivy chain, with no daisies in sight, and a newspaper account called it "a chain of magnolia blooms." The seniors first presented their robes to the juniors in 1907 and last burned their books or theses in 1908, substituting "class hates" thereafter. On Tuesday evening the Grand Concert was the center of attention, for those who had not become sick smoking the peace pipe.

The music graduates' recital was scheduled on Wednesday morning, followed by the actual graduation ceremony at 3:00 P.M. in the chapel. For several years President Simmons urged people not to attend—hoping thereby to publicize the inadequate size of the chapel and to gain support for the new auditorium that he wanted built. On June 1, 1909, an oil portrait of Alfred Shorter with a full beard, painted by the New York artist A. Edmonds, was presented to the college by Alfred Shorter Hamilton of Trion, Georgia, son of Mrs. Shorter's niece. Both Luther

115

Rice Gwaltney and D. B. Hamilton eulogized Shorter as a part of the ceremony.

When graduation came on Wednesday evening, as it did during the earlier Simmons years, Professor J. H. Simmons often spent a sleepless night, checking trunks, buying tickets, and otherwise caring for the departing graduates, most of whom left on trains at 1:30 and 2:30 Thursday morning. In 1901 Mrs. Simmons decreed that no one could leave on the late evening or early morning train and thus be kept up all night. A news reporter termed this "a wise decision"; the student appraisal was not recorded. Her rule was stretched somewhat later when a *special* car left Rome at 5:00 A.M. taking girls to Atlanta. After graduation was moved to the afternoon, of course, she found other topics for her decrees.

The Reactivated Alumnae Association

After the Alumnae Association was officially reorganized in September of 1897, its members supported the college with their interest and their money. Meetings were always held at commencement, and often, three to seven additional times a year. While the social element was important, many of the programs were of a cultural nature. Each year the alumnae provided free tuition for a student at the college, and during the various campaigns for the building fund, they added at least $450. Such gifts were made possible from annual dues of $1 and from admission charged for various public entertainments. Among other things, they sponsored comedies entitled "A Box of Monkeys" and "Professor Napoleon," six lecture-recitals on Wagner, a series of lyceum attractions, and a sale of fancywork, punch, and cake on Broad Street. Twice the ladies named a visiting committee to inspect the campus and make recommendations to the trustees. According to one of their reports, the needs were so plentiful that the committee hardly knew where to start! The trustees received it with thanks—and tabled it. In 1900 the association adopted a new constitution and by-laws, revising them five years later. The classes of 1899, 1900, and 1901 contributed $167.30 to the endowment, the first additions since Alfred Shorter had established it almost a generation earlier. By 1910 this "alumnae fund" amounted to almost $300, mainly due to interest that had accrued. A book of minutes begun in 1901 has been inadvertently destroyed, but the newspapers revealed three notable presidents: Mrs. J. P. Cooper (née Miss Alice Allgood, class of 1884); Miss Cordelia Veal (class of 1897); and Miss Joy Harper (class of 1895), daughter of Mrs. Shorter's nephew. In the summer of 1901 the first *Alumnae Bulle-*

tin was issued, a four-page leaflet edited by Mrs. Ethel Hillyer Harris (class of 1877). "Our motto" was printed prominently on page one: *Haec olim meminisse juvabit*. In keeping with this, the editor suggested a new project for the Alumnae Association, "a bust of the noble founder, Alfred Shorter, to be built in the niche built for that purpose."

Mounting Problems

Unfortunately the closing years of the Simmons administration were not happy ones. Controversy had been developing between the trustees and the Simmons for several years, resulting in suspicion and distrust. In 1905 Wake Forest College had awarded him the Doctor of Letters degree, but many felt that he was merely an absentminded figurehead. A person recalled: "It was said that Mrs. Simmons put a high hat and long-tailed coat on him and made him president." Again, many were wearying of Mrs. Simmons' claims to excellence. An admirer later admitted: "She spread the word that she was more brilliant than she really was." Further, Simmons' system of bookkeeping was not satisfactory to the trustees. The employment of an accountant to represent them in their dealings with him was seriously discussed, finally being rejected only because they could not afford one. Lastly, rumors were widespread that Simmons was receiving rebates from purchases made downtown by the girls. The owners of the Rome Opera House and Sam Powers' dry goods store printed affidavits in the newspapers specifically denying the charges. Indeed, the former complained because Simmons had not allowed the girls to attend his programs often enough!

During the academic year 1908–1909, two additional developments produced a great deal of unfavorable publicity for Shorter and undermined further the Simmons' effectiveness as leaders.

L. Reic Schocei

Late in the summer of 1908 the college employed L. Reic Schocei, who claimed to be a native of Germany and most recently the head of a music school in Iowa. His competence as a pianist was recognized, and he was hired without investigation. At about the same time, but entirely separately, Mrs. Joyce Barrington-Waters of Australia was also secured to teach piano. They assisted in several recitals during the year, performing satisfactorily in every respect.

The sad truth was reported during April and May in a series of news stories prominently featured on page one of the Rome *Tribune-Herald*. Schocei's real name was Luther R. Shockey, and he was from Davenport, Iowa, and Decatur, Illinois. The college authorities had discovered these facts back in October, deciding not to dismiss him because of the widespread use of professional or stage names among musicians. He and Mrs. Barrington-Waters had secretly agreed on February 6, 1909, to start a new conservatory of music in Rome, of which they would be co-directors, and she had advanced him $150 for this purpose. When Simmons learned of this scheme, he discharged Shockey on April 24—the day following a concert featuring him and Mrs. Barrington-Waters—for action "prejudicial to the discipline of the college." Shockey employed a lawyer, threatened to sue Simmons for breach of contract, and asserted that he would remain in Rome until his good name had been vindicated. On April 30, the day after the story first appeared in the *Tribune-Herald,* he decided to beat a hasty retreat. Purchasing a ticket for Decatur, Illinois, he boarded the next train without informing Mrs. Barrington-Waters, who that evening played in a recital. She took out a warrant charging him with being a "common cheat and swindler," but offered to drop the entire matter if he would return her $150. Shockey was arrested in Decatur, Illinois, on May 6 and taken to the county jail. Papers were secured to have him brought back to Georgia, and a police officer from Rome was readied for the trip to Illinois. At this point the newspaper account breaks off, and the remainder of the story is largely shrouded in darkness. Mrs. Barrington-Waters shared in three additional concerts during May, and Simmons expected her to return in the fall, apparently feeling that she was loyal to the school. However, neither she nor Shockey was on the Shorter faculty when September came.

The affair was said to have received publicity in almost every Southern newspaper. The Chicago *Tribune* carried "a very lively and somewhat exaggerated account of the matter," according to a Rome paper. Certainly it subjected the college and its administrators to widespread ridicule and embarrassment and contributed significantly to the trustees' loss of confidence in President and Mrs. Simmons.

The American College of Fine Arts

At the same time, events related to the newly founded American College of Fine Arts in Florence, Italy, were adding to the Simmons' already mounting problems. On January 28, 1908, President Simmons sailed for Florence, where he proposed to complete plans for opening the following October what he then called the American College of

118

Aesthetics. Although the trustees had taken no action on it and later disclaimed responsibility for it, the institution was widely referred to as a branch of Shorter College, and its only catalogue appeared with the name of Shorter prominently attached. Simmons surveyed about fifty homes in Florence before selecting the one in which the girls were to be housed, and he secured many part-time instructors. Within a week of his return to Rome the name had been changed to the American College of Fine Arts, and before the end of the spring Mrs. Caroline Whitmire, a matron on the Rome campus, had been sent out to recruit students for the new school. President Simmons limited the enrollment to sixty, but its ultimate size cannot now be determined.

In May a separate twenty-four-page "Preliminary Announcement" of the school appeared with two small pictures, followed the next month by the annual Shorter College catalogue containing the same printed materials and twenty-seven pages of larger pictures. The Simmons insisted that the school would be both reputable in the quality of its instruction and guarded in the social life that it would provide. Several American ladies—one of whom had lived for many years in Florence—had been employed as resident directors and as instructors in European history and literature, while almost thirty local persons had agreed to give instruction in their own studios. The institution was described as a graduate school for "those holding diplomas from any reputable American college, or non-graduate students of sufficient education or maturity to profit by the courses." Room, board, and tuition for those carrying a normal course of study was $1,000; additional charges were made for additional instruction and for all chaperoned travel to and from Florence and during the Christmas vacation. Supervised sight-seeing in and around Florence was furnished without further charge throughout the year.

In mid-September a number of persons made their way to Florence. Two were resident directors, Mrs. Kate R. Beckwith, who was the wife of a cousin of President Simmons, and Mrs. Whitmire. Three were students from North Carolina: Gladys Beckwith, who had been enrolled at Shorter since 1905, and two sisters, Essie and Fayette Morgan, who had not previously attended the college. The names of other possible participants are not known.

One of those students, eighteen-year-old Fayette Morgan, was an unwilling member of the group. Earlier in the summer a young man, W. Prescott Craig, had asked for her hand in marriage, but her father, J. L. Morgan of Marion, North Carolina, had abruptly refused him. To remove his daughter from Craig's influence, Morgan had enrolled his two daughters in the Florence school. The persistent Craig, however, secured funds from his mother, who had recently come into an inheritance, and followed his beloved to Florence. Early in October he persuaded her to elope with him, and Mrs. Whitmire felt it her duty to accompany them until the marriage vows had been exchanged. To Canterbury, England, the three went, where they remained through a two-week waiting period and where the wedding occurred. Mrs. Whitmire then took leave of them, writing to the bride's father that the deportment of his daughter had been "absolutely perfect" throughout the entire period that they were together. Since she still considered herself associated with the Florence school, she returned to that city.

Meantime, news of the elopement had reached Morgan, who urgently and repeatedly requested President Simmons to proceed to Europe on his behalf. Simmons "very resolutely and persistently declined," but went to New York City, where he was able to aid Morgan in a way that was mutually satisfactory. Morgan sailed for Europe in an unsuccessful effort to forestall the marriage. He met his daughter in Paris for a short time just before the end of October, several days after the ceremony in Canterbury. He was unable to convince her of what he thought were the errors of her ways; she remained in Europe with her husband for several weeks before returning to America. Morgan cabled and wrote Simmons, who was still in New York City, charging that "Mrs. Whitmire was more than guilty" and that she had "sold out to Craig"—charges that he repeated in a letter to the editor of the Rome Tribune-Herald in December. He also wired his other daughter remaining in Florence: "Shun Mrs. Whitmire forever." Because Simmons sided with Morgan, Mrs. Whitmire discovered upon her return to Florence about November 1 that she had already been discharged. She and Simmons had agreed to a contract that began: "This special engagement is strictly on a monthly basis, continuing only during mutual pleasure, either party being free to terminate the engagement, without notice and without forfeiture." Thus, Simmons was within his legal rights to take such speedy action. According to Morgan's later statement printed in a Rome newspaper, Mrs. Whitmire threatened to blackmail him and made the Florence villa "a hell" until she finally departed.

By the middle of December, Mrs. Whitmire was once more in Rome, claiming innocence of wrongdoing and ignorance as to why Simmons had discharged her. The Shorter trustees refused to become involved because of their insistence that the Florence school was an institution entirely separate from their college. Technically they were correct, for they had taken no recorded action on the Florence venture, but in the

120

public mind it was widely understood that the two schools were connected. President Simmons would not see Mrs. Whitmire, making two brief statements to a *Tribune-Herald* reporter indicating that in his opinion she had proved herself to be incompetent. She presented her case in three front-page news stories and left town insisting: "I have no apologies and no regrets for what I did."

A week after Mrs. Whitmire departed, the editor printed prominently on page one a long letter from Morgan. In it he made the numerous allegations against Mrs. Whitmire that have already been enumerated, while also lavishly complimenting Simmons and describing Mrs. Beckwith as "good and true . . . . long-suffering and patient to a remarkable degree." Neither Mrs. Whitmire nor Simmons is known to have made a public response to his letter, and the truth or falsity of these and other charges and countercharges cannot now be determined with any accuracy.

One undeniable fact remains. For two months newspapers all over the country were carrying stories that were sources of suffering and chagrin to the Morgans, Mrs. Whitmire, the Simmons, and the trustees and friends of Shorter College. It is not really surprising that on May 31, 1909, the trustees passed this action: "On motion the secretary was directed to notify President Simmons that the advertisements of the Florence School must not be published jointly or in the same connection with those of Shorter College, and that care must be taken not to permit the impression in any quarter that there is any connection between Shorter College and the Florence establishment, or that Shorter College assumes any responsibility in the premises."

The final outcome of the Florence school has not been positively determined. It has been said in Rome that the school existed one year, in one bed, in one hotel room—obviously referring to Mrs. Beckwith and her daughter Gladys. Furthermore, the Rome newspapers in 1909–1910 were silent concerning it. On the other hand, the trustees apparently expected the school to continue past that date. Sixty years later the daughter stated that she had been a student there for two years, but she provided no other details. The school lived for one or two years in precarious condition and was never revived.

The Simmons' Last Year at Shorter College

These numerous abrasive factors reinforced each other, leading the trustees on May 5, 1909, to offer the Simmons a new contract which included a reduction in salary. It was reported to the board on May

31 that the contract had been accepted, but at this time the trustees took steps to notify the Simmons of their dismissal effective June 1, 1910.

During the year 1909–1910 the trustees hired a firm to audit the college accounts for the years 1906 to 1909, and a new form of book-keeping was installed. President and Mrs. Simmons were no longer permitted to write checks for the college or to receive payments except upon specific authority of the trustees. Looking toward the following year, the trustees also ordered an inventory of college property.

Operating under the shadow of his impending departure, which was not yet publicly known, Simmons was defensive. In November of 1909 he issued a fifty-six-page *College Bulletin* entitled "Shorter College and its Faculty, Their Work and Influence." The introduction said: "Only a faculty devoted heart and soul to the mental and spiritual uplift of a student-body could accomplish the results which have marked the work of this College during the dozen years in which its gratifying reputation has been made." This was followed by no fewer than 114 letters from businessmen, political leaders, educators, physicians, attorneys, ministers, alumnae, parents, and former faculty members, in which the writers said much more about the Simmons than about the remainder of the faculty. One letter concerning President Simmons included a paragraph that unwittingly expressed the purpose of the bulletin: "Naturally, a gentleman of his large responsibilities and with so many people of various types and nationalities working under him should occasionally receive some adverse criticism . . . and it is only fair that an opportunity should be given the admirers of Dr. Simmons and his administration to pay their respects and give their appreciation to a man who has labored so hard and faithfully to live up to the trust imposed in him."

Sometime after his dismissal had been made known, he and Mrs. Simmons were extolled in a forty-page pamphlet compiled by Miss Mary Rosser, who for three years had been principal of the primary department at Shorter. Biographical materials were included, as well as numerous complimentary excerpts from newspaper articles and letters of commendation. This was apparently not an official college publication, but there is no indication of its financial backers.

From May 27 to 30, an abbreviated commencement program was held. The climax came at the graduation exercise which started at 11:00 A.M. on Monday. After the literary address by Luther Rice Gwaltney, degrees were conferred by "the retiring president of the institution." The newspaper account of the incident continued: "At the close of the presentation Dr. Simmons announced that the board of trustees had certain announcements, and that these would be made after the benediction, for which the audience were requested to remain. After the benediction the audience resumed their seats and then occurred an incident that created much comment. Former President Simmons left the room, followed by [almost] all the members of the old faculty . . . . Their exit was made while Col. L. A. Dean, of the board of trustees, was introducing Prof. A. W. Van Hoose, the new president. Under these circumstances President Van Hoose made a most graceful and tactful talk. He was greeted by storms of applause, both before and after his speech."

Soon thereafter the Simmons vacated the campus, taking with them practically all of the furniture, equipment, and books, and being joined by a large number of the former faculty members. It has been frequently said that much of this property belonged to the college and should have remained in Rome, but subsequent court action strongly supports the position that it was theirs to take because it was personal property.

On the day after graduation, the board of trustees initiated legal action against Simmons that was finally settled four years later. A complex series of claims and counterclaims emerged on page one of the Rome newspapers, the details of which can no longer be recovered with any certainty. Simmons claimed the right to collect money due the college and to retain it for himself, after leaving Rome. He further claimed ownership of the organ and chairs in St. Cecilia Hall which he proposed to move to Brenau College and of the Conservatory Building and the Gables which he proposed to raze. The trustees disputed each of these items and further sought to recover from him nearly $11,000 which they alleged he had overcharged them on salaries and rentals. While continuing to affirm the legality of his initial contentions, Simmons repudiated the trustees' charge that he owed them money and insisted that they owed him about $19,000 for teachers' salaries, food bills, and other things not now clear. At a hearing before the Floyd County Superior Court on June 4, Simmons' title to the property was affirmed, and he was given the right to collect money for his own use up to $1,000. The trustees accepted the former decision and agreed on July 3 to pay him $1,500 for possession of the organ and one year's rental on the Conservatory Building and the Gables. All other matters were contested, and the court appointed a special auditor to hear the complicated testimony supporting each case. These hearings dragged on into 1913, and finally the contending parties negotiated a settlement which the court approved. By its terms, Simmons and the trustees withdrew most of the claims that each had made. Simmons was awarded much of the money in a disputed bank account. He was also given the right to attempt the collection of "all unpaid notes and accounts" from his administration, amounting to about $10,000. This agreement was made final on April 13, 1914, concluding an extended period of rancor and bitterness that reduced further the esteem in which the Simmons were held in Rome.

This discontent did not follow them away from Rome, however. In 1910 they moved to Gainesville, Georgia, where he was co-president of Brenau College until 1913 and she was director of music until her death in 1914. After his retirement in 1913, he remained there as professor emeritus of philosophy, teaching occasionally as his health permitted until his death in 1942. Late in life he founded the Simmons Art Museum at Wake Forest College, where much of the remarkable furniture once located in the parlors of Shorter College may still be seen.

The Death of Luther Rice Gwaltney

On May 30, 1910, the seventy-nine-year-old Gwaltney had been vigorous enough to deliver the principal address at graduation with little advance notice. This was consistent with his practice of preaching with frequency in and near Rome—even during his declining years. In fact, for a brief time he served as pastor of the Mobley Park (now DeSoto Park) Baptist Church. Following a Sunday sermon and dinner he would often tell his host: "I'm going to be selfish for a while." Then he would occupy a chair, cover his face with his handkerchief, and take a nap. For the last two years of his life he taught Bible and ethics at the Rome High and Industrial School for Negroes, in spite of widespread public disapproval, while also retaining his ties with Shorter. On Monday afternoon, July 18, 1910, he quietly died. Northwest Georgia reacted with obvious grief. The funeral was held at First Baptist Church on Wednesday afternoon, with the college community in attendance. Several organizations scheduled memorial services: two groups of Masons, the DeSoto Park Baptist Church, and Negro and white Baptist Sunday school conventions. A Rome newspaper commented: "It is to him more than any other one person, except Alfred Shorter himself, that Rome owes her great educational institution. . . . He fostered and encouraged the great impulse in Alfred Shorter." At one memorial service the pastor of the Thankful Baptist Church of Rome was actually more accurate when he paid tribute by suggesting that the name of the institution be changed to

Gwaltney Memorial College. Of course his recommendation was not followed, but it appropriately indicated Gwaltney's stature and significance. The last of the founders was now gone, at a time when the college which he had served for almost twenty-one years was in the process of being moved from the campus which he had known so long.

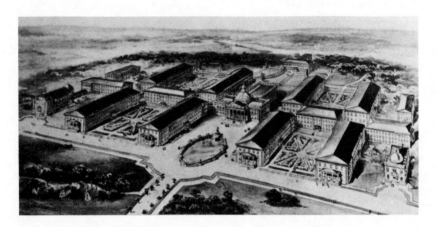

Greater Shorter as visualized by President Van Hoose

PART TWO

ON SHORTER HILL

1910-1973

4
"Greater Shorter"

The Coming of Van Hoose

Uncertainty surrounded the college for several months as a new president was being selected. Early in November of 1909 members of the prudential committee of the trustees were authorized to negotiate with M. L. Brittain about the position, although they had no power to make him a definite offer. At that time superintendent of schools in Fulton County, Brittain was the son of a Baptist minister and an active Baptist layman. Later to become president of Georgia Institute of Technology, his greatest fame lay before him. On November 29 the trustees formally appointed a committee consisting of T. P. Bell, editor of the *Christian Index*, W. W. Brookes, a Rome lawyer, and J. P. Cooper, a Rome businessman, with authority to employ a president. In mid-January of 1910 Simmons' resignation was received, dated six months earlier, and accepted to take effect on June 1, 1910. For two weeks nothing public was said, and then on January 23 a front-page *Tribune-Herald* headline broke the news: "Prof. M. L. Brittain to Be Next President of Shorter. Dr. and Mrs. Simmons to Leave For Brenau College." Brittain's acceptance was officially conveyed to the entire board a week later. The trustees recorded the next unexpected act in these words: "Mr. Brittain then addressed the board, and requested that his resignation be accepted, urging personal reasons. On motion, his resignation was accepted with affectionate regret." Each of Fulton County's ninety-five teachers had signed a petition urging him not to leave, and this convinced him that he should withdraw from the new post.

Soon page one of the Rome paper was providing its readers with an interesting rumor, carried under a headline that read: "Will Van Hoose Head Shorter?" It was reported that he and his wife visited in town and that Mrs. Van Hoose was honored at a reception attended by the wives of the trustees. The question was answered by a headline carried in the issue of March 31: "Professor Van Hoose is Shorter President; College to be Removed." A week earlier he had signed a

129

five-year contract, effective June 1, 1910, guaranteeing that the college would be moved to the Bass site by the fall of 1911, that $50,000 to $100,000 would be sought in Rome and vicinity, and that the old campus would be sold and the proceeds used for the new building. An editorial hailed the new appointment and the decision to move: "It is a splendid achievement to weave raw cotton into a finished product, or to link distant points by rails of steel. It is a greater achievement to work with the heart, the mind and the soul. There is no labor more exalted than the training of the south's young women for lives of Christian usefulness."

President Azor W. Van Hoose

With the coming of its new president, the college gained one of the greatest optimists in its history. Azor Warner Van Hoose was born at Griffin, Georgia, in 1860, where his father was pastor of the Baptist Church. After receiving the Bachelor of Arts degree as the first honor graduate of the University of Georgia in 1882, he taught briefly at three colleges in Alabama and Georgia. From 1886 to 1909 he was president or co-president of the Georgia Baptist Female Seminary (later Brenau College), Gainesville, Georgia, and a leading Baptist layman in the state. In 1887 he married Miss Lucy Rucker of Thomaston, Georgia; their four children died in infancy. Leaving Brenau, he and his wife traveled extensively in Europe, after which he intended to embark upon a business career. The offer from Shorter halted those plans and evidently contributed to the fact that Mercer University awarded him the honorary Doctor of Laws degree in 1911.

Once in Rome he proved to be all that the trustees had expected, a man of superb executive ability, faithful and efficient, with great intellectual strength. Handsome, dignified, and always well dressed, he was proud, yet humble, charming in social converse, firm but not formidable. Possessed of great conviction and determination, he had almost endless stamina. His interest in and devotion to the college and its students were widely known and appreciated. During his rare moments of anger, his face became very red and his eyes spoke a language all their own. Occasionally filled with gloom, he usually radiated happiness and courage.

The girls discovered that he was sometimes absentminded and forgetful. Often he gave the prayer of thanks at the noon meal in the dining room. Once after a morning of steady dictation he was reported to have said: "We thank Thee for these blessings. Very truly yours, A. W. Van Hoose, President." The girls dared not to laugh right then, but the dormitories were soon full of merriment over his conclusion. At another time he had planned to leave from his office to catch a train early in the afternoon. During lunch he glanced up at the clock on the wall and exclaimed: "Oh, I've left my watch at home." He then pulled it out of his pocket and asked: "I wonder if I'll have time to go home and get it?" Unable at first to recall students' names, he frequently called them by the name of their home town. Hence, Hazel became "Chipley" to him, even though she sat at his table in the dining room three times a day, and Susie became "Miss Talbotton." The girls also discovered that he was far from being childless, since he considered each of them to be his daughter. He wrote them a note that said in part: "My home, my office, my heart are always open to each and every one of you, and I wish you to remember that my time is yours and that I am never too busy to see you when I can serve you." On the bulletin board he would place a notice reading, "Will the following girls please see me as soon as possible," in order that he might inquire of their health and happiness. At least once each year every girl enjoyed lunch or dinner at Maplehurst, and daily Van Hoose visited those in the infirmary, taking flowers if possible. Every Mother's Day he brought red and white roses for each girl to wear to church.

The First—and Last—Year

The first year that Van Hoose led Shorter was the last year spent at the East Third Avenue location. Throughout the spring and summer of 1910, he was regaining public confidence for the college, gathering a new faculty, recruiting students, and supervising the renovation and refurnishing of the buildings left almost vacant by the Simmons. "There was left at Shorter nothing but prejudice and a loyal board

131

of trustees," he recalled ten years later. Several times he traveled over the state seeking support for the college. Returning for graduation, as has already been observed, he spoke briefly and met the alumnae at a reception held for him the next day. Thereafter he moved his wife and her mother to Rome and took active charge of the institution. The faculty and staff of 36 whom he assembled included several who significantly contributed to his administration: J. W. Gaines, dean and professor of mathematics for eight years; L. R. Hogan, professor of classical languages and Bible for six years; Miss Imogen Coulter, professor of art for thirteen years; Miss Anne W. Raynor, professor of modern languages, and Misses Annie Denmark and Grace Cronkhite, professors of music, for six years each; Miss Nannie M. Kennedy, bursar for fourteen years; and the beloved Miss Margaret L. Jacobs, resident nurse for twenty-eight years. Commenting on Van Hoose, Gaines, and Hogan, W. D. Upshaw, a Georgia political and religious leader, punned: "With this genial trio of gentlemen as their leaders the youth of classic Rome are Shor—ter win." The latter two canvassed for students during the summer, and their success was marked. By mid-August Van Hoose had called them back to Rome, for dormitory facilities were rapidly reaching their capacity. A month later there were late applicants in town for whom the college was trying to find living quarters.

On opening day, 142 boarders and 63 day students were reported— one of the largest groups in the history of the institution up to this time—and the yearly total reached 231, ten more than the year before. Every available room was used in the dormitory, The Gables (a new student called it "The Gabriels"), Bellevue, Brookes House, and Hiles House, a newly leased residence on East Third Street. Van Hoose boasted that three hundred could have been admitted if space had been sufficient. At the opening assembly, Bass exuded confidence as he predicted five hundred students on the new campus the following fall and a thousand within a few years. A Rome newspaper editorially commented: "It would not have been surprising, all circumstances considered, had the attendance during the present session been small. Romans had expected this to be a year of transition and preparation. Instead of that they realize that Greater Shorter dates from yesterday." Furniture and other equipment for the college had been purchased when necessary—including thirty-three pianos for the rented Conservatory Building—and under its new president Shorter was experiencing fresh vigor.

Life at the college did not radically change. The social culture of the students was promoted by the continuation of weekly musicales

132

and receptions, but it was carefully pointed out that these would not be allowed to interfere with anyone's regular work. Morning and evening prayers were held daily. Regulations concerning proper wearing apparel were not immediately altered.

Soon after school started a new girl was found weeping near the small marble slabs erected close to the chapel by several of the graduating classes. When asked about the cause of her tears she answered: "Isn't it awful to think of all these little dead babies?" On Saturday, October 8, Theodore Roosevelt visited Rome, giving rise to what was called "the Roosevelt sundae" to which Curry-Arrington Drug Company treated the Shorter girls at a special entertainment. They were to greet Roosevelt at the Fifth Avenue bridge, where they were to wave goldenrods and the public school boys were to flourish "big sticks." Roosevelt was late in arriving, the rain came down steadily, and the Shorter students and faculty stood drenched for two hours just to see him pass! The first Thanksgiving under Van Hoose was both sober and gala. After attending services at the Methodist Church, the girls spent two full hours in the dining room, enjoying Nixon's Orchestra, drinking toasts of black coffee to everyone "from Thomas the cook to President Van Hoose," hearing "bright and clever" speeches and responses, and singing college songs "with great spirit."

Of course a service in memory of Alfred and Martha Shorter had been held regularly since 1883 at commencement, but the time was altered by Van Hoose. In the spring of 1910 Mrs. Irene Tisinger, professor of English, suggested that a Founders' Day be set aside, and Shorter's birthday was selected. Accordingly, on November 23, at 7:30 P.M. the ceremony occurred in the Memorial Chapel. "Owing to the rain which came up just at the hour for beginning the exercises, the attendance from the city was small, but the students and faculty were all out." The Reverend G. A. Nunnally, who had been the first speaker twenty-seven years earlier, brought an address regarding the life of Colonel Shorter, and the college choir presented music. The reporter concluded: "It is intended to make Founder's Day a feature of each year at Shorter, and that it will grow in interest and importance was easily seen by all who were present at the exercises."

The Christmas spirit came early to Shorter this year—some trunks were reported packed and ready to go three weeks beforehand. Much against the rules, caroling broke out in one of the living areas at 4:30 A.M. the day before they left. Van Hoose and the faculty gave the Negro employees a Christmas tree in the chapel, when they were "remembered with gifts and were treated to a musical program by the

133

faculty members. Many of the servants have been with Mr. Van Hoose for years, and know what to expect, as this is an annual custom of his."

A tale of persistence and courage had its beginning during this Christmas season. Professor and Mrs. Alexander von Skibinski remained on campus during the holiday, their first in this country. Of course they felt that the season had to be celebrated in American fashion, so he secured what he thought were Roman candles to use on Christmas eve. Unfortunately a careless clerk sold him large firecrackers instead. One of them exploded in his left hand, blowing off the first finger and seriously mangling and burning the remainder of the hand. His career as a violinist seemed ruined, except as a nonperforming instructor. With determination the Russian obtained expert medical treatment, persisted in a strenuous regimen of physical therapy, and invented an artificial finger to take the place of the lost one. His story went all over the United States, and he received hundreds of messages of sympathy and goodwill. All of this took many weary months, after which he had to teach himself how to play again. He was "wildly applauded and encored" when he publicly performed on his beloved violin for the first time after the accident at the opening ceremony on the new campus. Louise Bennet, who was then a student, observed: "And today, with pride Shorter points to him— Alexander von Skibinski—her real twentieth century wonder."

On the Saturday evening after examinations in January, 1911, the students staged an "appropriate" entertainment. One of them wrote: "The most celebrated visitors were the three witches from Macbeth whose gruesome groans and frightful faces depicted too well the agonies to which the past week had subjected us." The first Stunt Night was held on February 4 of that year, with the 25¢ admission going to the fund for the college annual. Many townspeople attended, joining the students in buying candy on sale in the vestibule of the chapel. The program included vocal music, clog dances, a whistling solo, college yells, and a mock wedding.

With all of its success, however, this first year under Van Hoose was one of anticipation. When the societies just before Christmas debated the proposition, "Resolved, Men of thought have been more beneficial to the world than men of action," a Polymnian speaker arguing for the negative pointed out: "Just think for how long we have merely dreamed of a 'Greater Shorter,' and now through the effort and splendid ability of a man of action this great plan will be a reality. This shows what great good a man of action can do." That the judges decided in favor of the Polymnians is hardly surprising! The new annual was issued, prominently displaying a sketch of Greater Shorter on its cover and on virtually every page within. One of its editors spoke for all except the seniors: "Even the best of friends must part. Here's to a happy vacation and a glorious meeting next fall at the castle of our dreams—Greater Shorter."

After the college moved to its present location, the former campus was quickly renovated for use as a public high school. In 1924 the former Academic and Chapel Building was destroyed by fire, but the present structure was soon erected in its stead. The towers, front porch, mansard roof, and top story were removed from what was once called Pennington Hall; the rest of that building remains. The brick dwelling formerly designated Bellevue, long occupied by the super-intendent of the Rome school system, is now vacant. All other struc-tures have been destroyed by fire or otherwise razed over a long period of time, although the basement of the Kitchen Building has been covered and may still be seen.

Soon after the 1924 fire, the cornerstone and its contents were moved to the present campus. The stone is located in the quadrangle facing the Library-Administration Building; some of its contents are on display in the Memorabilia Room. The small class stones near the chapel were transferred to the Alumni Garden, and more recently inadvertently lost. Six months before the fire, the trustees voted to move the Martha Shorter Memorial Window, but they did not act fast enough to prevent its destruction. Two colored sketches of the window are all that remain of it. In 1967 the front steps, inscribed "Shorter College 1877," were installed in the parking lot near the present Fine Arts Building.

Funds for Greater Shorter

What was the origin of the dream for a Greater Shorter? Of course the Simmons had frequently spoken of expanding the campus at its first location. However, it was some of the trustees who in 1908 suggested moving the campus to a new site, doubtlessly receiving their initial stimulus from J. L. Bass. A local resident for twenty years, he was a merchant and real estate developer who, in Van Hoose's words, led Rome "from a straggling village into a live, progressive city . . . ." Married to a Shorter graduate of 1884, the former Miss Mattie Simpson, he was a most active trustee from 1902 to 1913 and president of the board for the last three years.

Although it is evident that the idea had been maturing in his mind for many months, it is not known precisely when Bass made his offer to the other trustees. Certainly by November of 1909 and probably by May of 1908, he had informed them of his willingness to give them his home, Maplehurst, and the surrounding thirty acres, estimated to be worth $40,000. At that time the trustees made a proposal to the Georgia Baptist Convention, promising that Rome would provide $50,000 in cash plus a $30,000 campus if the convention would endorse their private personal appeals for $50,000 from donors over the state. Feeling that the request of Bessie Tift College for $60,000 was more urgent, the convention took no action on the request from the Shorter trustees, and they were again thrown back upon local support.

The public was not informed of further developments until Van

J. L. Bass

Hoose's employment was announced on March 31, 1910. In that connection the trustees stated that Bass had made his gift, indicating that the total site had been increased to 155 acres by purchases of adjacent land. It was acknowledged that the additional land had been bought from Bass, who agreed upon a price of $25,000 and actually received only $15,000 for it. In this way the board of trustees calculated his total gifts to be $50,000—$40,000 worth of property and $10,000 rebate on additional property. The local paper exclaimed, "No wonder Captain Bass' friends declare that he is the 'noblest Roman of them all'" and ran a picture of him on page one. Predictably the college annual was dedicated to him in 1912, "in grateful appreciation of his generous gifts that first made possible a Greater Shorter and in loving recognition of his constant interest in all that pertains to the upbuilding of the college . . . ." More recently, the residence occupied by the president and later the dean of the college has been designated Bass House.

136

Through its Board of Education, the Georgia Baptist Convention reversed itself on April 23, 1910, by authorizing the secretary of the board, G. A. Nunnally, to direct a campaign in which Bessie Tift was to get $300,000 and Shorter, $75,000. Although Nunnally had a personal interest in Shorter—he had been Colonel Shorter's pastor-adviser when the first campus was constructed in the 1870s—the college received virtually nothing from his efforts.

In Rome, the Manufacturers' and Merchants' Association passed resolutions endorsing the efforts of the board of trustees to raise $100,000 in Rome, calling for the appointment of a committee of

W. W. Brookes

fifteen to assist in the canvass. Gifts and pledges began to be received early in May.

Without fanfare, J. P. Cooper and W. W. Brookes each contributed $25,000. For many years Cooper had lived in Boston as head of a large cotton concern, while also retaining his home and interests in Rome. He returned permanently in 1907 as a semiretired man of forty-nine, anxious to make a substantial contribution to the community. Elected to the Shorter board of trustees in 1902, he was currently secretary-treasurer of the board and was eventually to be its president for a decade. An early annual was dedicated to him, describing him as a man who has "in behalf of our Alma Mater rendered services that claim for him the abiding trust and gratitude of all who look to the realization of her promised growth and usefulness . . . ." W. W. Brookes was an attorney who had practiced in Rome for thirty years, becoming quite wealthy through his careful investments. A generous friend of foreign missions, he was named a Shorter trustee in 1903 and immediately became an active supporter of the college. For five years he was president of the board. During the financial canvasses relating to Greater Shorter, he gained a reputation among his associates as a highly successful fund-raiser. When asked the secret of his success, he responded: "I hit them so hard with the amount that I asked that they were willing to settle for half."

A fourth Roman, L. A. Dean, made a significant contribution to the college in time and ability, if not in large financial gifts. This successful attorney and political leader served as trustee longer than any other person, from 1890 to 1934. An active Baptist churchman, he

L. A. Dean

gave a great deal of his time to the school as its legal adviser and as a fund-raiser. "The best thing I ever did for Shorter College was to interest Cooper and Brookes," he was reported to have said. The father of eight children, he saw all five of his daughters graduate from Shorter College—another indication of his esteem for the school, and a record of patronage only once equaled and never surpassed!

The substantial gifts from Cooper and Brookes were not immediately reported in the newspapers, although presumably they were widely discussed by word of mouth. In order to increase public interest, Bass invited two hundred friends to Maplehurst for speeches and a meal of Brunswick stew and barbecue. G. A. Nunnally told the group that Colonel Shorter had never dreamed of more than ninety students, the limit for which he provided, since no woman's college in the South exceeded one hundred in 1877. Nunnally continued: "None of us need have any fear that the move would displease Col. Shorter.

If he were living today he would say: 'Go ahead, boys, move the school, do whatever is necessary to make it a great institution.' " Van Hoose predicted that in five years the college would enroll one thousand young ladies, adding: "Here and now I reverently pledge my earnest, my untiring, my zealous devotion to the cause of Shorter College." Soon thereafter he wrote: "Since 'Maplehurst' has been selected as the site for the 'Greater Shorter,' it has developed that this is the very site which Col. Shorter first selected for the College he wished to found, but certain influences were exerted which caused him to place it on its present location."

Mr. and Mrs. J. P. Cooper

Throughout the summer of 1910, the campaign for funds continued, with J. P. Cooper as general chairman. His wife led the alumnae, who made yellow and white rosettes for each contributor to wear until the total had been raised. For a time the ladies served a luncheon to the canvassers in the temporary headquarters at the M. and M. office. Across Second Avenue they had erected a sign that the newspaper said could be read for a mile: "$150,000 for Greater Shorter." Business establishments were decorated in the Shorter colors—the reporter was evidently a bit color-blind who insisted that Broad Street was a mass of orange and white!

In the midst of the drive, a traveling man came in on the train asking: "What is all this I hear about the Greater Shorter?" The Rome newspaper commented: "A friend, an enthusiastic Roman, proceeded to enlighten the drummer, and wound up by asking him for $1,000 for Shorter." Two different couples stopped by the headquarters to make their contributions, telling the workers that each had expected to buy an automobile during the summer. Instead, they gave their money to the college, since they could not afford to do both.

That fall a remarkable assembly in the Shorter chapel occurred. Van Hoose told the students of the campaign that had thus far been waged. Verbal subscriptions started coming in so fast that Professors Gaines and Hogan were unable to keep up with them. An eyewitness wrote: "Girls cheered and yelled as the subscriptions were announced; girls gave of the money with which they were to enjoy the many pleasures that usually delight the students of colleges for girls. They gave gladly, cheerfully, willingly, notwithstanding the fact that President Van Hoose urged them not to give unless they felt willing to make the sacrifice that the giving would entail." When the total of $3,319 was announced, "cheer after cheer came up from more than 200 happy girls and teachers, while tears of gratitude and joy came from the eyes of many."

After a lull, renewed vitality came on December 6, 1910, when the voters of Rome approved a school bond issue, a part of which was to be used for purchasing the East Third Avenue property and converting it into a city high school. The day of the election turned out to be "one of the bitterest blizzards of recent years." When the bonds had passed by 866 to 56, the newspaper commented: "It was not a landslide, but a snow slide for bonds." The trustees negotiated with the city council about the purchase price, and $71,000 was the final compromise figure.

The spring of 1911 saw another canvass, complete with a mass meeting at the Rome Opera House and cartoons drawn by Shorter art students appearing on the front page of the newspaper. Captioned "They Are All Busy Helping Shorter," one showed doors marked "doctor," "lawyer," "banker," and "merchant," with signs announcing that the occupant was out working for a greater Shorter. To the district meeting of the Masons held in Rome during that spring, Van Hoose made an address on the contributions of Masonry to world peace. He prefaced his remarks by admitting that he had dreamed of this engagement. In his dream he had forgotten his speech—and had started to take a collection for Shorter instead!

In approximately one year almost $225,000 had been raised in property, cash, and subscriptions: $50,000 from Bass, $25,000 each from Cooper and Brookes, $53,000 from other contributors, and

$71,000 from the city of Rome. Virtually the entire amount came from local citizens, at a time when the city had only about twelve thousand residents.

The Construction of Greater Shorter

Before an architect was employed, President and Mrs. Van Hoose visited Sweet Briar, Bryn Mawr, Wellesley, Vassar, and others, returning with many ideas for a superior campus. In their absence, the area near Maplehurst—where Bass House is presently located—was surveyed. Architect W. T. Downing of Atlanta was commissioned in September of 1910 to draw plans for an extensive physical plant. Meantime Van Hoose recommended that the buildings be erected on the crest of the hill beyond Maplehurst. Called Orchard Hill because of its peach trees, this eminence was surveyed and a new set of plans was ready by December 1. Downing was paid an additional $1,000 to prepare a schedule showing how much work would have to be completed each day in order for the college to open on time.

On Thursday, January 12, 1911, Van Hoose and the superintendent of construction, John A. Pierce, staked out the location of the different buildings. Grading was done by W. H. Mitchell, who during March employed nearly a hundred men using forty or fifty teams and a traction engine. The Rome Railway and Light Company added a trolley car line that ran up the hill to the construction site, branching off the main line at the corner of Shorter Avenue and what was eventually called Sherwood Road. At no cost to the college, the Central of Georgia added a spur from its main track to the trolley car line. The college purchased a thirty-five-ton locomotive, leading a newspaper reporter to comment: "It is doubtless the only educational institution in the south possessing such a pet. Since engines are always referred to as 'she' doubtless this one will be named, hazed, and initiated into a fraternity." Placed in service late in April, it enabled all freight to be delivered in the cars in which it reached Rome. It was estimated that twelve to fifteen hundred cars of materials would be used—including about six thousand barrels of cement, a million pounds of steel, and 1,750,000 bricks. Preliminary grading and stockpiling of materials were sufficiently advanced by the first Sunday afternoon of May that trolley cars left for the new campus every fifteen minutes, allowing the citizenry to see the work for themselves.

Of the Shorter students, the local paper observed: "They are immensely interested in the work and watch it from their windows.

Construction of Greater Shorter, summer of 1911

Often they inspect it at close range, and glory in the prospect." Van Hoose was the first Shorter president to own a car; the newspaper reported that he "purchased a handsome E.M.F. automobile, which he is learning to drive himself . . . ." Almost every afternoon he would go to the building site, taking a few of the girls along.

The Industrial and Engineering Company of New York and Atlanta began concrete and steel work early in June. On Friday, June 23, the first brick was laid. No delay was experienced even when the Shorter engine was wrecked in a runaway down the steep track. Apparently the engineer was hurt, although not seriously, and by the next day the Southern Railway Company had loaned an engine to the college until the wrecked one could be repaired.

In August the concrete and plastering were completed, fifty hours ahead of schedule. Branham Brothers plastered the walls and ceilings; J. F. Dupree and Sons bricked the buildings and did the inside carpentry; wiring and electrical equipment were installed by the Walker Electric Company; the plumbing and heating were added by the Rome Supply Company; and the roofs were placed by the Chattanooga Roofing Company. McDonald Furniture Company of Rome secured the contract to provide furniture, rugs, and window shades.

Van Hoose later wrote: "The weather was propitious; from the day that work was commenced, until it was finished, there was no rain except at night and on Sunday and the work was not halted until the buildings were completed."

The campus was comprised of five fireproof structures, each measuring 50 by 200 feet. The many exterior columns were bare red brick—the white plaster was not added for many months. The Academic Building (now Rome Hall) contained the president's office, bursar's office, book store, post office, bank, library, two society halls, the Y.W.C.A. room, and all recitation halls, each with a private faculty office adjoining. The Music Building (now the Alice Allgood Cooper Fine Arts Building) provided fourteen studios for the music faculty, fifty-two practice rooms, an auditorium seating six hundred, rooms for the department of expression, and a large gymnasium on the third floor. The Domestic Science and Art Building (now Alumni Hall) included accommodations for instruction in those two departments, a large kitchen and dining room, an infirmary, and some faculty living quarters. Each dormitory—Hall One (now Cooper Hall) and Hall Two (now Van Hoose Hall)—had rooms for ninety-six students and six teachers, with a large sitting room on each floor. The arrangement of suites gave rise to Van Hoose's comment: "If any other southern college combines all these points of excellence, it is not known to the writer of this article." One happy occupant soon wrote: "The college proper, from the standpoint of a girl, is just ideal. The rooms are arranged in suites for four, two bedrooms with a study between and a bath. And we have a lavatory with plenty of hot and cold water, in our bedrooms, and here, too, each girl has her own closet and single bed and individual dresser. It's such a relief to have things of your own—not to have your roommate's shoes on top of your best hat in the closet, and not to be forced to peek over her shoulder in the mirror to see how to powder your nose, or have your hair pins appropriated or your toilet water spilled. And in the study . . . we have a good, big study table and bookshelf. And with our private bath, what more could a girl wish?" So confident were the trustees concerning the safety of their buildings that they proudly advertised the absence of insurance on them!

Behind the main buildings stood the steam plant, first stoked manually with coal and later operated by gas. Down the hill a filter plant was erected near the stream (soon to become Rotary Lake) which at first furnished water for the college. This and a nearby frame dwelling were abandoned when the school was later placed on the city water system. In addition to the new buildings, the campus contained Maplehurst, the president's home, and several Negro servants'

Maplehurst

houses nearby. As many as four mules, twenty cows, and twenty-five hogs were kept, and a barn and pen were maintained for them. Also on campus were farm plots on which vegetables were raised for use by the college and an orchard that was continued for a number of years.

The total cost of the new plant was frequently stated by Van Hoose, who acted as treasurer of the building fund, to be approximately $300,000. In 1914 he reported that exactly $274,208.84 had been spent up to that time—the figure included furniture and equipment, but apparently not the value of the land itself. Six years later he calculated that the new plant had cost $285,041.51 in actual cash, to which he added $50,000 for the property that had come as a gift. Almost half of the money spent on the project was acquired from J. P. Cooper, who came to the rescue when the subscriptions were slow in being received. His initial gift was $25,000, "to which," said Van Hoose, "he added a large amount, no one knows how much, during the time that the new buildings were being erected." The addition was in excess of $100,000—an "advance," most of which became a gift because the college was never able to repay it. It is for this reason that Van Hoose described him as "the most potent factor in building Greater Shorter."

144

The Opening of Greater Shorter

Throughout the summer of 1911, Gaines and Hogan ranged widely over Georgia seeking students to occupy the buildings then under construction. Their chief difficulty lay in the fact that prospective patrons could not believe the campus would be ready for use on the projected day. In spite of this, a full house was reported in the fall, 228 students and 37 faculty members, and a third dormitory could have been filled if it had been available. The total for the year was 300, the largest such figure reached up to that time.

Girls of all ages arrived on campus in mid-October. To welcome them, the merchants downtown decorated their stores in yellow and white. A number of students came in on Monday, October 16, and regular trolley car service was initiated then. The next morning Mrs. J. W. Gaines, wife of the dean, gave birth to a daughter in their dormitory apartment. Said the newspaper: "Reports are to the effect that she can give the college yell with great vim and vigor. She has not yet decided upon exactly what courses she will take—but vocal will be one of them and English another." The freshmen immediately adopted her as their mascot, her picture appeared in the 1912 annual, and a poem was composed in her honor that read, in part:

> You the young matriculate, registered we're told
> In the great new Shorter when one hour old! . . .
> Yes, you rule the college,—that is plainly seen,
> Faculty and students, for you rule the dean.

The opening convocation was held in the auditorium of the Music Building, dominated by oil portraits of the co-founders, Alfred Shorter centered behind the pulpit and Luther Rice Gwaltney to the left of it. The invocation was given by G. A. Nunnally, followed by a brief speech by J. L. Bass, whom Van Hoose introduced as "the great benefactor of the college, the man who had given much time to the movement in addition to the site." Bass said, in part: "We may count this day a Thanksgiving Day for Shorter College, and invite future generations to look back to October 19, 1911, as a time of our great rejoicing. It was as yesterday when this entire peach orchard hill, with bloom and blossom unmolested, pledged its usual contribution to the year's inventory of soil products. Today, instead of peach trees there are great finished structures, clustering here—comprising one of the best built colleges in all the world—a college destined, so we believe, to take place and hold place in the front rank, among leading institutions of learning for all coming time."

145

Other participants included John S. Perkins, presiding elder of the Rome District of the Methodist Church, who "urged the young ladies that they . . . not spend too much time in ice cream parlors and moving picture shows . . . ." The mayor of Rome, J. W. Hancock, presented the keys of the city to the students, "so that they might do as they wished, and 'put the young men in jail if they do not treat you right.' " President S. Y. Jameson of Mercer University recommended that the girls "frown upon cigarette smoking and not allow the young men to do so in their presence." Describing the *Tribune-Herald* as "almost the best friend Shorter College has," Van Hoose presented its managing editor, J. D. McCartney, "who told of the interest all of the people of Rome felt in the college and its students."

The last speaker was the president of the Baptist World Alliance, Robert S. Mac Arthur of New York City. Impressed by the beauty of the surroundings, he suggested a Psalm that Van Hoose frequently quoted thereafter: "Beautiful for situation, the joy of the whole earth."

Georgia Baptists took note of the newly opened campus in several ways. The state convention of the Woman's Missionary Union met in Rome that fall, and on November 9 the delegates took special trolley cars, autos, and carriages to the college. Girls dressed in white ushered them to the auditorium for a program, showed them through the buildings, and guided them to the dining room where Mrs. Van Hoose held a reception for them. The November 16 *Christian Index* devoted the first five pages entirely to the college. Pictures were included of Bass, Cooper, Brookes, and Dean, as well as of Van Hoose, Gaines, and the proposed Greater Shorter. An optimistic article was printed purporting to describe the institution in 1921—with eighteen great buildings, twelve hundred students, and its "ever resourceful president, Dr. Van Hoose." The Georgia Baptist Convention also met in Rome that month, utilizing the college auditorium on November 21. Bass was invited to make some remarks, but he insisted that the buildings spoke more eloquently than he could. He added, "Although the peach orchard has been cleared away, we have peaches here still"—and lifted his eyes to the balcony occupied by the Shorter girls. The messengers were given a tour of the premises—"the last and best place being the immense dining room where refreshments were served," remarked one of them—and were favorably impressed with what they saw. At a later session in the week a serious suggestion was made on the floor of the convention to move Mercer University to Rome, but after extended discussion the matter was postponed for one year. Of course the Rome newspaper endorsed the proposal, as did the Shorter girls. One young lady was moved to poetry:

146

> Oh! gladsome day when Mercer boys
> With Shorter girls will share their joys;
> Oh, fortune to our Roman town
> With Mercer and Shorter her hills to crown.

However, as it later developed, it was only the young lady who was moved, not Mercer.

Additions to the Campus

Van Hoose and those whom he inspired looked forward to a truly magnificent campus that would ultimately accommodate one thousand students. In the not-too-distant future he intended to erect thirteen additional structures, including a central administration building topped by a massive dome. Architect's sketches of the ambitious project were publicized for the next fifteen years, but no detailed plans are known to exist. The girls were not above teasing their beloved president concerning his hopes; the last will and testament in 1914 included this item: "Realizing the vastness of Greater Shorter and the strain on our President's voice to address the entire student body, we will to him a megaphone."

Reality, however, was not as rosy. General statements were made at various times about the need for a separate gymnasium building, an infirmary building, one or two additional dormitories, a literary hall, a science hall, much faculty housing, a dining room building, and a separate chapel.

Four other structures were discussed in detail, two of which were erected after Van Hoose's death. A building for the alumnae and the two societies was suggested in 1913, pictures and plans were drawn and displayed around town, and almost $17,0000 was pledged. A domestic science building was projected in 1914, pictures and plans were made public, and the lumber necessary for its construction was offered as a gift to the college. In both cases, however, the proposals were forgotten when actual cash was not forthcoming.

A central administration building became a distinct possibility in 1916 when $3,000 was subscribed for it. Van Hoose urged in the 1918 catalogue that a drive for $100,000 be conducted, and in 1919 he expressed hope that the building might be completed within the next year. Almost half a century elapsed before his hope was realized.

More immediately successful was an extended and frustrating campaign for a swimming pool. As early as 1913 Van Hoose proudly displayed on the bulletin board plans that called for a pool 30 by 70 feet, with a depth of from 4 to 7 feet. Unfortunately a gift of $10,000 did not materialize, and the matter lapsed. In 1918 he was able to accumulate that amount, excavation was begun, and then the government commandeered all cement for the war effort. The following summer bricks were ordered and the excavation was continued, but apparently the bricks did not arrive. Van Hoose challenged the trustees in 1921 to build the pool, "so often hoped for, so long delayed." The graduating class of that year sadly recorded in its last will and testament, "To the Class of 1940 we will Shorter's swimming pool," presumably feeling that it might be completed by then. The pool was ready in the spring of 1923, but Van Hoose did not live to see it.

Meantime, the campus became a place of beauty. There was much room for improvement! The workmen had been intent on constructing five buildings, and the grounds were left in deplorable condition, presenting a stark and barren look. "When the rains came, and they came in great abundance, the students, looking out upon the grounds could see only a smooth expanse of Georgia clay, in its pristine redness and stickiness, relieved only by a few necessary and temporary board walks, and they fully realized that whatever may be said of the virtues of this same Georgia clay, it does not add to the desirableness of a promenade ground." In the spring the wild flowers appeared and "the five thousand peach trees skirting the foot of the hill burst into simultaneous blossom," but the campus was still in great need of attention. Grass soon replaced the mud, and the makeshift planks temporarily connecting the buildings eventually gave way to gravel walkways. Lombardy poplars were set out on front campus between the Academic Building and Hall One, giving the area its name, Lombardy Walk. Little by little shrubbery was planted, and ivy began to creep up the sides of the buildings. Contributed by the students of 1910 to 1912, a sun dial was installed in the center of the court between the dormitories, and in 1917 it was shifted to its present location so that the pond and fountain could be added.

Less evident to the casual visitor were the improvements inside the buildings. Mr. and Mrs. Frank Pidcock of Moultrie, Georgia, gave an organ valued at more than $5,000 in 1913—it was first played in public by their niece, Rebekah Clark, a music student at the college —and this was in constant use for more than forty years. (It was said that a new girl entered the auditorium and asked: "Why are the radiator pipes so much bigger in this room?") New pianos were added in 1917, and soon thereafter the auditorium was fitted with new stage curtains. Laboratories for biology, chemistry, and physics were equipped at a cost of $28,000 on the third floor of the Academic Building, where some teachers had previously been living. (Some of the less scientific students would stray from their experiments to the windows, where they could look out into the distance. At times the remark would be made: "There's Old Shorter—that's the past. Here we are—this is the present. There's Myrtle Hill—that's the future.")

Smaller buildings were added. Between 1914 and 1919 four homes were made available for the use of faculty persons—one, no longer existing, at the right of the Shorter Avenue entrance; two not now owned by the college on Sherwood Road; and another—then called Sunset Cottage—that is still retained, 21 Sherwood Road.

J. B. Sullivan   A. W. Ledbetter

Trustees

The trustees supervised the college, informally through individual members of the board who spent countless hours with Van Hoose, and formally through its committees: faculty and curriculum, grounds and buildings, audit, investment, legal counsel, beneficiaries, and prudential. J. L. Bass was president for three years, 1910 to 1913, and W. W. Brookes for four, 1913 to 1917. J. P. Cooper began a ten-year term in 1917 that ended only at his death. Two men who had long been identified with the board died during this administration: David Blount Hamilton, after thirty-eight years of service, and J. B. Sullivan, after twenty-eight. A. W. Ledbetter became a trustee emeritus after twenty-six years on the board. Five men were added who were

149

to be active more than twenty years each: the Reverend Luther Rice Christie of Columbus and Savannah, Dr. L. G. Hardman of Commerce, A. S. Bradley of Swainsboro, and T. B. Owens and Dr. W. P. Harbin of Rome.

In 1916 Van Hoose suggested that the board elect members from all over the South, but this was not done during his administration. The following year he recommended the election of women to the board— or at least a board of visitors composed of women. His smile still shows through the words that he addressed to the trustees: "Personally I am not very much in favor of such a step, for I am sure that the affairs of the college would be much more closely investigated and possibly, more severely criticised and that my position might not be so pleasant as now, but I really believe that a few members elected part by the board of trustees and part by the Alumnae Association, would bring strength and influence to the college and probably make its work more efficient." Once again he prophesied the shape of the future, but ladies were not added to the board until 1924.

Expanding Endowment

Recognizing the necessity of a strong endowment, Van Hoose quickly called for $160,000 that could be added to Colonel Shorter's original gift, increasing the total to $200,000. An anonymous individual offered to give $50,000 for endowment in 1912 if Rome would raise $50,000 and the Baptists of the state, $200,000 for endowment and enlargement, but this was not done.

Usually a full-time financial agent traveled over Georgia in search of outright gifts and pledges, but as Van Hoose ruefully observed: "It's hard to separate a man from his money." Almost $35,000 had been subscribed by mid-1913, but apparently little of this was ever received. On April 23, 1914, an educational rally was held at the college, with many of the 150 visitors coming from out of town. The main speaker was a trustee of the college who was then making a successful bid for the governorship of the state, Dr. L. G. Hardman of Commerce—his address was carefully advertised as being nonpolitical in nature! The visitors viewed a busy campus, heard encouraging news of subscriptions that had recently been made, ate their fill of barbecue, and left with an invitation to attend another such rally the following year. None was held, however.

In 1919 Van Hoose recommended a campaign for $350,000, and he was able to stir his associates to action. That June the trustees authorized him to lead a drive for $200,000 in additional endowment. During the summer and fall plans were laid, although the goal was reduced to a more realistic $100,000. A banquet for 150 civic leaders on November 6 launched the effort. The infirm W. W. Brookes came from Atlanta, where he had moved five years earlier, making a short speech containing a motto used in newspaper advertisements: "One of the best investments any city ever had." Saturday afternoon a truckload of Shorter girls came through the downtown section, making the streets "ring with their spirited college songs and yells." A great public meeting was scheduled for the following afternoon at the city auditorium, the entire student body sat on the stage as a giant choir, and the trustees' plans were fully explained to the assembled crowd. Approximately forty men, including all of the local trustees, participated in the public canvass, and the usual noon meals were provided for them by the alumnae. Posters drawn by the Shorter girls urged liberality, contributing to a campaign that was termed a success. Subscriptions were received from J. P. Cooper for $12,500, from W. W. Brookes for $10,000, from J. B. Sullivan for $5,000, from the students for $16,000, and from many others. The total finally reached almost $95,000, not all of which was ultimately collected, of course. By May of 1920 almost $33,000 had come in from the recent campaign and $5,000 from other sources, raising the total endowment to $79,822.76. Just prior to his death, Van Hoose reported that it had grown to about $100,000, a small portion evidently coming from Shorter's involvement in the Seventy-Five Million Campaign, yet to be described. Van Hoose addressed the trustees: "The great need of the college is endowment, endowment, endowment. . . . If I had a single fault to find with the student body of Shorter it would be that our girls come from the better families financially; we want some poor girls, girls of fine character and a yearning for real learning that is not often found among the girls of the well-to-do; a few poor girls would have a wonderful leavening effect upon our entire student body . . . ."

Negotiations were opened in 1911 with the General Education Board, funded by the Rockefeller Foundation, "looking to cooperation by that board in securing an adequate endowment." Application was made for $400,000—$110,000 for endowment and $290,000 for new buildings and equipment. This was soon refused, as well as a similar one in 1915. Shorter officials visited the New York office many times, Van Hoose sadly reporting that "questionnaires of almost interminable length have been answered." E. C. Sage, a representative of the board, spent April 28, 1921, on the campus, "and after examining the college

151

in every detail expressed the highest satisfaction with what he saw and promised to bring the merits of the institution to the attention of the board at its May meeting." For two years the board granted $5,000 annually to supplement faculty salaries. In 1923 it offered to add $100,000 to the endowment, but of course Van Hoose did not live to see that day for which he had so diligently worked.

The Georgia Baptist Convention

When Van Hoose was selected as president, the college had been under the control of the Georgia Baptist Convention for eight years, annually having several of its trustees named by that body. Most of those who had elected Van Hoose had approved a report in 1909 expressing mild disapproval of their treatment at the hands of the convention, feeling that the needs of Bessie Tift College had too long been given preference over those of Shorter. "It had been necessary to wait, but the Board earnestly hopes that the time has come." The request was made that Georgia Baptists aid the college in raising $50,000 outside of Rome by endorsing its drive and authorizing it to secure this sum by private personal appeals to various persons throughout the state. No such endorsement was given.

Widespread uncertainty existed among many Georgia Baptists concerning the ownership by the convention of Shorter College. At the time of Van Hoose's election, only four of the trustees had not been named by the convention, since they had been on the board prior to 1902 and had been allowed to retain their position until removed by death or voluntary retirement. Late in 1910 the Georgia Baptist Board of Education formally investigated the matter of legal control, submitting the relevant papers to a group of lawyers including Judge Beverly D. Evans of the Supreme Court of Georgia. The affirmative decision reached at that time was repeated by the Board of Education again in 1913. The following April Van Hoose answered in the *Christian Index* yet another inquiry questioning the status of the college, affirming that by then only two trustees had not been elected by the convention, L. A. Dean and Harper Hamilton.

Nevertheless, the convention continued to express itself favorably concerning Shorter. It was reported in 1910 that about $240,000 had been secured in bequests, donations, and subscriptions by the convention for Bessie Tift and Shorter, but evidently little or none of this was earmarked for Shorter. When informed that Rome had raised in excess of $225,000, the convention went on record as saying: "We think it only fair and just that the Baptists of the State at large contribute at least one hundred thousand dollars towards the completion of the magnificent plant during the coming year." Two years later it stated, "The generosity of our Baptist brethren in the city of Rome is unparalleled," erring only in restricting the generosity to the Baptists. It continued by admitting that "this remarkable and self-sacrificing generosity was largely inspired by the implied expectation that the Baptists of Georgia would carry on to triumph the splendid consecration of the Baptists in Rome." However, no financial assistance from the convention was immediately forthcoming.

To complicate matters further, the convention observed in 1912 that "while our woman's colleges . . . are both doing excellent work and have elicited enthusiasm and large gifts from individuals and are at present generously patronized by our Baptist people, . . . in curriculum both are directing their ideals to similar ends. It is impossible, therefore, to avoid their competition with each other . . . ." A committee was appointed to secure "a plan of adjustment in their courses of study" which would direct one of them toward "Normal and Industrial Training of the most thorough technical type . . . in order to fit those desiring it for efficient service as teachers and workers." One year later this committee reported absolutely no progress in modifying the curriculum of either school, and the convention accepted the impasse by approving a report which read in part: "We believe the Georgia Baptist Board of Education has acted wisely in leaving Shorter and Bessie Tift to work out their own destinies and note with pleasure that these institutions are equal before the Convention as schools of higher education for women."

At the same time, a serious and unpleasant reality faced the convention: Bessie Tift College was experiencing a decline in student enrollment because entrance requirements had been raised and a financial strain because of a growing debt. In 1914 the Board of Education described the situation in these words: "Bessie Tift College is in grave peril at this time and its extrication will tax the resources of the Convention to save it." By then the debt had risen to $90,000.

Tensions were relaxed that year when Shorter College withdrew from convention control. John E. White, chairman of the Board of Education, initiated the movement by suggesting a separation to Van Hoose. In a resolution passed on October 21, 1914, the trustees of the college favored this action. Hence, on November 18, after an afternoon of heated discussion by several messengers, the convention allowed the college to withdraw from the agreement made in 1902 and requested the trustees to take legal steps to recover their original powers. A further resolution announced that the convention looked with favor upon "the continued and enlarging usefulness" of the college, commending it "to the sympathy of the Baptist people of Georgia at large and throughout the South, as an institution guaranteed to the Baptists and capable of becoming a Baptist Woman's College prepared to serve the highest interests of the Baptist denomination as a woman's college of the highest grade." Immediately following the passage of these resolutions, Bessie Tift was instructed "to appeal to the churches for $100,000 . . . at once." Thereafter persons connected with Shorter attended each session and usually appeared briefly on the program.

With the advent of the Seventy-Five Million Campaign, the college again came to the attention of the Georgia Baptist Convention. The Southern Baptist Convention proposed to raise $75,000,000 in five years, 1919 to 1924, for foreign, home, and state missions, Christian education, ministerial relief, orphanages, and hospitals. Since each state convention was allowed to distribute funds allotted to it from the campaign, representatives from Shorter asked the Board of Education during the summer and fall of 1919 for its proper share. An agreement was reached that had to be presented to the convention for formal ratification: Shorter would once again come under convention control and would receive $185,000 for its endowment. Trustees were to be named for terms of three years each; the convention would nominate three men for each position, from whom the Shorter board would elect one. All endowment funds derived from the campaign would remain the property of the convention, Shorter receiving only the annual proceeds from the interest so long as the college remained under convention control. Either party was given the privilege of dissolving the relationship after a notice of twelve months.

Opposition was expressed by a minority group within the Board of Education. These members doubted that the convention would have any real power under such an agreement and questioned "the wisdom of the convention's investing large sums in institutions over which it has no legal control." They felt that the money could better be placed in those schools which the convention unquestionably owned and which were still in dire need of additional funds. Insisting that the leaders of the college desired the renewed relationship solely "in order to secure a large sum of money which they cannot get so readily otherwise," they openly charged that "the president of Shorter frankly admits that it is simply a question of the money, and if it were not for that, the college would not consider surrendering even this privilege [of nominating trustees] to the convention."

Opposition was further expressed by the Mercer Baptist Association, centering in Quitman, and by Dr. S. S. Gaulden, a physician of that area. Gaulden addressed correspondence to the Board of Education containing aspersions against Shorter and Van Hoose that were expressed in resolutions passed by the association.

Recognizing that the issues were too complex to be solved on the floor of the Georgia Baptist Convention and that their disruptive nature would shift the attention of the convention from the Seventy-Five Million Campaign itself, leaders of the convention suggested the appointment of an impartial committee to deal with the problems at open hearings and to formulate a solution that would then automatically be accepted by the convention without further vote. The motion was passed without discussion and the committee was named. While other business was being handled by the messengers at the regular session of the convention, the special committee conducted a stormy hearing that lasted almost twenty-four hours with very few recesses. Toward the close of the hearing, Van Hoose made a quietly positive, ten-minute statement that turned the tide in his direction. Gaulden thereupon affirmed "in the presence of the committee and those present that he was satisfied as to the orthodoxy of Dr. Van Hoose and the teachings at Shorter College, and extended to Dr. Van Hoose the right hand of fellowship." Hence, when the report came to the convention —presumably as information only and not as a topic for discussion— it began by stating that "Shorter College is an orthodox Baptist institution and its teachings and those of its president are in accordance with belief of orthodox Baptists." Holding that the admission of Shorter to convention control was "inadvisable," it agreed that as an "affiliating institution" of the convention the college should participate in the Seventy-Five Million Campaign to the extent originally recommended by the Board of Education.

The opposition was not ready to concede defeat, however. A spirited two-hour discussion ensued on the floor of the convention, finally resulting in a motion to postpone action on the report for twelve months. Someone offered an amendment suggesting "twelve minutes" instead—but this was defeated!—and the prior motion was eventually approved. Attention was then called to those statements relating to the orthodoxy of Shorter and Van Hoose, and the presiding officer ruled that action on these matters was not to be postponed because it had been fully settled by the special committee! But what of funds received from the campaign during the next twelve months? After further lively debate, the convention agreed to hold separately the money which "may accrue to Shorter . . . awaiting instructions from the convention" in 1920.

Meantime, back in Rome the daily newspaper carried on page one full accounts of the proceedings. The Alumnae Association wired its support to Van Hoose, as did numerous individuals. J. P. Cooper issued a statement backing Van Hoose. At the conclusion of the convention a three-column headline heralded the good news: "SHORTER COLLEGE VICTORIOUS AND DR. VAN HOOSE VINDICATED IN STATE BAPTIST CONVENTION." The accompanying article insisted that "Shorter College has received a wonderful amount of invaluable publicity, on account of the dignified attitude of its active supporters and of Dr. Van Hoose before the convention, and the further record made known to the convention of the result of the recent effort in Rome toward supplying the college with funds by the citizens and students there."

In the months before the meeting of the convention held late in 1920, Van Hoose made public his views respecting the ownership of Shorter College. To the trustees he said, "We would be untrue to the trust imposed upon us by the great spirit that founded the college if we should attempt to enter the Mercer System"—that is, come under convention control. Yet because we are a Baptist school, fully willing to cooperate with the convention, "we claim our share in any funds that the Baptists of Georgia may raise for general educational purposes . . . ." To the readers of the *Christian Index* he spoke concerning the trustees in these terms: "It is that . . . feeling of stewardship, of fidelity to a trust, that has caused these men . . . to feel that neither, under the law governing the will of Col. Shorter and the charter of the college, nor under the moral obligation which they assumed when they became trustees, have they the right to deed the property of the college to any other body."

After the year's postponement, the convention again took up Shorter's request and quietly passed an approving motion with little discussion. "In recognition of Shorter College as a valuable Baptist asset and of the co-operation of Shorter College and her friends in making the Baptist 75 Million Campaign a success," it was agreed that Shorter should receive the $185,000, if and when it was raised. "In the interest of harmony," it was also agreed that Shorter would withdraw her previous application for convention control—"with the understanding that at any future time negotiations may be opened either by the convention or Shorter College, without embarrassment or prejudice to either party."

Unfortunately the Seventy-Five Million Campaign was not an unqualified success, and many in Rome were—rather unfairly, it would now seem—dissatisfied with the share that Shorter finally received. During the five-year campaign a disappointing total of about

156

$58,000,000 was realized, which was only seventy-seven percent of the amount that had been expected. According to figures published by the Georgia Baptist Convention, Shorter seems to have gotten a total of $134,395.87, which was also only seventy-seven percent of the amount that had been expected. In view of the total situation, this would indicate that Shorter had indeed been treated equitably.

Over the years, the total value of the college markedly increased. Van Hoose estimated its worth to be about $111,000 when he first arrived in Rome. Two years later, after the new campus had been occupied, the figure had risen to about $415,000. By 1916 the total was $450,000. He presented an itemized statement in 1921, indicating that the value had reached $608,500: land, $75,000; buildings, $345,000; furniture and equipment, $88,500; endowment, $100,000. During a period of twelve years, assets had grown by nearly half a million dollars, more than five times their original level.

Enrollment

Shorter College prospered numerically under Van Hoose. In the summers he dispatched traveling representatives, wrote large numbers of letters, mailed hundred of bulletins and catalogues, and ran advertisements in various papers. All of this activity yielded results, and during his twelve years an average of 263 students was enrolled annually. The smallest number was 230, when the academy was first abolished, and the largest was 300, when the new campus was first occupied. Each fall except one the dormitories were filled to capacity, and at least twice a few professors and students were housed in Maplehurst. In 1918 the president declared that he could fill another dormitory in ten days, while the following year he insisted that he could have used two additional dormitories. Admission requirements were raised in the fall of 1921, and some applicants were refused because they could not meet the standards. Hence, the dormitories opened with 202 occupants, a reduction of 20 from the prior year.

Full-time college students ranged in number from about 120 to 246, comprising slightly more than half the student body during the first year and in excess of ninety-two percent during the last year. Receiving instruction in art, music, and speech, part-time students annually averaged about 30. For six years the institution continued to operate its academy, with as many as 68 enrolled one year. For the first two years after it closed, 40 or 50 were refused admission to the college annually because of insufficient preparation.

Male students were usually present only on a part-time basis, with

157

as many as 11 one year. It is not widely remembered that Harold M. Gaines, a son of the dean, was enrolled as a full-time student in 1916–1917, the first young man to enjoy that status in the history of the school.

While students occasionally came from places as distant as Honduras, New Mexico, Texas, Oklahoma, or Missouri, most of them were from the Southeast. Alabama, Tennessee, and Florida provided the largest numbers—except for Georgia, which accounted for about seventy percent of the student body. As yet no foreign students were on campus; the young lady from Honduras was American.

Never actually enrolled at Shorter, one of the most famous girls associated with the school was Midge, the heroine of a novel bearing that name and written by Miss Mary Frances Shuford, a graduate of 1917. At Oakdale Seminary, the president of which was Dr. Robert Adair ("Old Ajax," the girls called him), Midge and her class were humiliatingly hazed in the dormitory basement storeroom, emerged victorious over the hated sophomores in a contest to add books to the library, and were immensely honored when Midge located the crook hanging on Maplehurst while Class Day was taking place there. Later they located the enemies' midnight feast (Dr. Adair campused them for six weeks for being out of their rooms without permission) and almost held their own in secret—until Dr. Adair himself appeared. Eventually "their" sophomores made a daisy chain for them and they unmistakably proved their "senior superiority" when Midge removed the crook from high atop the campus clock tower.

Tuition, Fees, and Student Aid

During the years that Van Hoose was president, the cost of attending Shorter rose steadily, as did prices in general throughout the country. As soon as the school occupied its present location, the basic fees were set at $310 for nine months of room, board, and tuition. Art, expression, and music were subject to extra charge, but seldom would a student's expenditure exceed $410. Ten years later the basic fees were $508 for the entire academic year, with extra charges that would usually not go beyond $634. Since the school was still using mules to pull its wagons around town, one satisfied patron with more daughters than ready cash was allowed to pay for some tuition with hay, but this was not the usual medium of exchange.

Some discounts from the catalogue rates were given to individual students, when two or more came from the same family, when one was a clergyman's daughter, or when one was considered otherwise quite desirable by college officials. Ten scholarships were provided annually from the endowment, and numerous small gifts furnished funds for brief periods of time. The college regularly awarded full tuition to the best student in voice, piano, and art. In 1920 a gift of almost $10,000 established the Dr. and Mrs. W. B. J. Hardman and the Woman's Missionary Union of the Sarepta Baptist Association Loan and Memorial Scholarship Fund. Supplemented regularly through the years, the fund has by now more than tripled in value. Work grants were provided—as, for example, to a young lady who was employed in the college book store, ordering and selling books and other supplies.

Beginning in 1917 the college offered two fellowships annually to members of the senior class who wished to continue their studies for another year. Usually the students devoted two or three hours each day to tutoring or rendering assistance in the laboratories or library. Providing all expenses of room, board, and tuition, the award was made by Van Hoose to at least eight young ladies.

As enrollment and fees increased, the annual income of the college also increased—from $50,418.85 in Van Hoose's first year to $137,030.41 in his last full one. The college showed a twelve-year operating profit of $102,834.03, much of which helped to defray the costs of constructing Greater Shorter. In 1915 Van Hoose secured a professional audit of the operating funds for the first five years of his administration, after which an audit was made every year or two.

World War I

Early in the decade the *Chimes* showed that the Shorter girls were becoming increasingly conscious of national and international affairs. Essays appeared about England, France, Germany, and Italy—which might be expected because of courses then being offered—and also about Panama, China, and India. Woodrow Wilson was strongly supported in 1912, admiration for him simply growing as the years passed. Of course, his popularity with the girls was enhanced by his first wife, the former Miss Ellen Axson of Rome.

Before the United States actively entered World War I, the Shorter students were quite aware of the conflict. They told a story relating to one of their music instructors. A new girl asked: "Can you tell me the quickest way to the infirmary?" The answer came from one of the older girls: "Yes; stand in front of Mr. Pfitzner and say, 'Long live the French.'" The causes of the war were discussed in an issue of the

Chimes, and a later article favored selling arms to England. The French Club contributed $5 a month to a hospital caring for blinded soldiers.

In 1917 a chapter of the Red Cross was formed on campus, and every girl was said to be a member. A banner was awarded each week to the dormitory producing the greater number of items for the war effort, resulting in a prodigious output: 64,325 surgical dressings, 150 knitted sweaters, 10 pairs of knitted sox, and one box of wool clothing collected from various sources. Approximately $2,000 was given by students and faculty members to the Red Cross and the Y.W.C.A., and about $8,000 was invested in Liberty Bonds. A bootblack stand in the Glass Corridor was a profitable means of making money. Dressed as an organ grinder and monkey, two girls took up a collection. (The "monkey" gave "such a convincing impersonation that one wondered why he had not always believed in evolution.") Pictured with serious faces and busy knitting needles, the class of 1918 had a photograph taken in their Red Cross uniforms. They issued no *Argo,* voting instead to give that money to the Red Cross. As juniors the class of 1919 won a silver loving cup for making the largest subscription to a Liberty Bond drive and then as seniors also agreed to support the Red Cross rather than to publish an annual.

Organized "to create and foster a stronger feeling of patriotism throughout Shorter, and to keep information at hand in regard to the progress of the great war," the Shorter College War Council maintained its headquarters in the library, which contained many relevant bulletins and publications, and posted items of interest on the War Bulletin Board. Each Tuesday evening patriotic meetings were scheduled, often with visiting speakers, and after a motion picture projector was purchased, patriotic films were often shown. One Thanksgiving program depicted generous America who heard the pleas of the Allies and sent her harvest to them. A sophomore operetta was produced in order to raise money. At a Stunt Night the freshman skit was entitled "The Voice of Belgium." Uncle Sam and Liberty were married at an annual George Washington party. The students of drama planned a play, "War Brides." To promote physical fitness in case the girls were needed for active service, a hiking club was formed. Of course the dining room was not left unaffected: one young lady wrote of "the wheatless, eggless, sugarless, meatless, and at times almost eatless meals of now-a-days . . . ."

Even the academic program was influenced. For many years courses in German language and literature had been taught and a German

160

Club had been active. According to college catalogues, both of these activities were quietly dropped in 1919, to be resumed seven years later.

At least seven members of the staff and faculty left to enter various forms of war work. Two of the men served as chaplains in the Y.M.C.A., and one became a member of the armed forces. Although the activities of the others is now uncertain, some of the ladies expected to work in France through the Y.W.C.A.

In 2½-inch letters the Rome newspaper trumpeted the glad news: "WAR OVER." On November 11, 1918, "Rome went wild with patriotic fervor . . . . From the gray dawn of morning when the people were awakened by the shrieking sirens of the fire wagons, until midnight it was one long riotous jubilee of victory." The stores and schools were closed, a parade was set for 11:00 A.M. in which the Shorter girls marched, and a mass meeting followed in the city auditorium. Together with much oratory by their elders, "the Darlington boys with their yells and the Shorter girls with their songs enlivened the proceeding."

Of course influenza still hung over the city, and the rejoicing Romans disregarded all sane rules of health. When an upturn in the epidemic resulted, Shorter merely applied its rule more carefully: "All town students must be examined each morning before attending classes." Soon fourteen cases were reported on the hill, and as a consequence the college closed two weeks early in December. Those who were ill remained on campus until they recovered, and during second semester no recurrence was experienced.

Community Relations

Now that Shorter was located two miles from the center of the city, the college increased its efforts to attract the residents of Rome to its campus. Initially the new facilities were the object of frequent inspection, and for a time the ladies of the school had a monthly "At Home," which their friends were cordially invited to attend. Some of the college ladies belonged to the Woman's Club and the more exclusive Nibelung Club, both of which were entertained occasionally at Maplehurst.

Visiting performers, numbering about five each year, were featured in an annual artists' course. Over the years programs were presented by a wide variety of persons and groups: the London Concert Company, a female reformer, the Royal Welsh Choir, the Russian Symphony Orchestra, lecturers on the Grand Canyon and Alaska, a magician, an archaeologist, an impersonator, a Japanese lecturer on "Relations Between the United States and Japan," and numerous solo musicians. Of these, Ellison Van Hoose attracted most attention—both as a noted operatic singer of the period and as the brother of the president.

Shorter enjoyed a cordial relationship with the Rome Rotary Club which sometimes met in the dining room. To the tune of "America" the members sang:

> Oh Shorter, 'tis of thee,
> Best school in all Dixie,
>   Of thee I sing.
> School where old Van doth preach,
> School of the frequent peach,
> School of the classy teach'
>   To thee I cling.

Honoring Van Hoose at one of its meetings, the president of the club called him up for a presentation. As a large, delicate, glass punch bowl was being handed to Van Hoose, it slipped and smashed into a million pieces. Everyone was aghast at the accident, except the Rotary president who was laughing at them and at Van Hoose. Playing a prank on Van Hoose, he had deliberately allowed the bowl to drop, after which he had a silver one brought out!

Another close relationship was developed with the Rome Music Lovers' Club. Various Shorter musicians spoke and performed at its regular meetings. When it was hostess for the annual convention of the Georgia Federation of Music Clubs in 1921, Shorter College entertained with a reception. The following year the club sponsored the first observance of National Music Week ever held in Georgia, and the college provided a concert of sacred music.

Finding that many townspeople would not seek part-time instruction at Shorter because of its location, Van Hoose proposed in the fall of 1915 to open the Shorter College Musical Studio at 207 East Third Street. Professors in violin, voice, and piano were to offer lessons at that location, but apparently the demand was not sufficient to merit its opening. The indomitable Van Hoose recommended a similar venture in the fall of 1916, and the Broad Street Conservatory operated for nine months. Located over Johnston Hardware Company at 307–311 Broad Street, the facility included a large auditorium, several studios, an office for Van Hoose, a reception room often used by the alumnae, and a sitting room where students waited for the trolley car back to the main campus. A total of 61 persons enrolled for lessons in music and expression, and Van Hoose reported a profit of $1,247.37. It was not reopened in the fall, but the reasons are not known.

The bridges on Second and Fifth avenues were rebuilt in 1915 and 1916, and the temporary "swinging bridges" made the trip to the school hazardous. By the time the new bridges were opened, however, many Romans had lost the habit of visiting the campus. Hence, Van Hoose considered it necessary in 1918 to call attention through the newspapers to the many convenient trolley cars that made the trip in only fifteen or twenty minutes.

A year later he had to warn against too many visitors—of a certain kind. Young men began driving through the grounds "at breakneck speed" on Sunday afternoon and late at night. In some cases they parked their cars, brazenly entered the Sun Dial Court, and tried to peep in the bedroom windows. The distressed Van Hoose called attention on page one of the local newspaper to the presence on campus of a night watchman. He concluded: "I do not wish to make any threat, but I wish to warn those who have been giving us trouble that a shotgun will be brought into use if necessary . . . ."

Of course the college personnel constantly contributed to community life by their off-campus activities. The district meeting of the Masons continued to be held each spring in Rome; Van Hoose often addressed the group and the Shorter choir usually sang. Founded in 1912, the famous Scrap Iron Bible Class at First Baptist Church was taught by Gaines, Hogan, and Van Hoose. A city-wide Baptist Woman's Missionary Union meeting included a speech by Mrs. Van Hoose and music by a Shorter group, while many local churches were supported by students and faculty members.

In the spring of 1920 the Georgia State Baseball League opened its season with a game between Rome and Lindale, and the Shorter girls were allowed to participate in a parade down Broad Street to celebrate the occasion. Whether they witnessed the lopsided 16 to 0 victory by the local team is not recorded. The following spring Rome had a "Home-Coming Day," with an even more elaborate parade, in order to publicize local industries. Shorter entered a float—an "Argo" covered with yellow and white chrysanthemums and carrying eight coeds chic in their middy blouses and long skirts—which won first prize.

General Academic Matters

Admissions regulations were made more complex by Van Hoose. Shorter accepted any student upon her certification as a graduate of a school on the accredited list of the Southern Association of Colleges and Schools. Other students were accepted only after passing examinations prepared by the association or by members of the Shorter faculty. For unconditional admission to the freshman class, a student had to offer fifteen high school courses. Those who had not taken all of this preparatory work were admitted as "conditioned," at first in as many as four courses and later in no more than two. These conditions were removed by additional work done after entering college. After 1919 no junior was allowed to have such conditional work uncompleted; after 1920 no sophomore was allowed any; after 1921 no conditional freshman was admitted at all. By faculty action, a conditional student was not permitted to hold office or to represent her class in any public capacity.

Transfer students appeared before the classification committee to determine class standing. Examinations were given for those young ladies coming from schools not recognized by Shorter as being of equal rank, while others were accepted upon receipt of proper certification from an acceptable school.

President Van Hoose's connection with the Rome Rotary Club worked in favor of the college; after 1915 the Rotarians met all trains on which students and faculty members were expected, providing them with automobile transportation to the campus.

After moving into their rooms, the students were subjected to classification, a process of registration for courses that could not be changed except with permission of the professor or a physician. An opening exercise was held in the auditorium, often with a speaker from Atlanta, and always with local speakers including Van Hoose. Following one of these assemblies, a Rome judge and his niece left the campus in his electric runabout. The steering mechanism broke, and they found themselves coasting down the front road at "a pretty good rate of speed. . . . He immediately put on the brakes and threw in the reverse current, but was unable to stop the car." Leaving the road at one of the curves, it was "partially demolished." Neither occupant was badly hurt, the niece attending classes the next morning. A "matriculation sermon" was preached at the First Baptist Church on the first Sunday of each session, as had been the practice since 1907.

Classes met from Tuesday through Saturday, although for a few years they were held also on Monday. The rising bell was at 6:30. Chapel came at 8:30 or 12:30. Classes or laboratories met until 3:30 or 4:00, after which physical training was held. Dinner was at 6:00, often followed by an evening prayer service, and invariably followed by study until the "rec" bell rang at 9:45 and the retiring bell at 10:15

(11:00 on Saturday). Of course this bell was not invariably followed by sleep. It was reported that two girls spent thirty minutes after light bell softly talking about a teacher who lived right above them. One of them wondered: "Do you suppose she's alive enough to hear what we've said?" "No," came the tired reply. "Let's go to sleep." When they were almost asleep, a shoe hit the floor, followed by the words: "She who hath ears to hear, let her hear."

Because absences and poor grades were not unknown, legislation was passed to deal with them. One year a zero was given for each absence, regardless of the cause. Since most of the girls felt that this practice was unfair, the custom soon prevailed of allowing three unexcused absences per semester and of reducing the final grade by two percent for each additional unexcused absence. Fifteen absences for any reason resulted in automatic exclusion from a course, with faculty vote required for reinstatement. The grading system was eased slightly:

> 90—A—excellent
> 80—B—good
> 70—C—average
> 60—D—conditional, becoming an E if not raised
>   in the next semester
> under 60—E—failure

A formal policy of academic expulsion was adopted in 1920: a student was not permitted to return if she had failed to pass more than half of her work for the current year. Students failing individual courses were placed on a kind of academic probation which restricted their social activities.

Examinations continued to be administered at the end of each semester, and for the first time it was specified that they must cover the work of the entire semester. Grades were sent home after each semester—and at mid-semester for those students failing a course at that time—on separate report cards signed personally by each instructor.

With respect to the Southern Association of Colleges and Schools, Van Hoose initiated a movement that once more bore fruit after his death. In October of 1915 he made application for membership, which was turned down mainly because of the small endowment and library collection. Six years passed before he again applied, and this time his request was deferred, not rejected. As before, the endowment and library were largely responsible. During the Blocker administration, in 1923, the application was finally approved.

Although the college was not yet accredited by the Southern Association, its graduates were being accepted by a growing number of graduate schools. Among these were Columbia, Chicago, Johns Hopkins, and state universities in Georgia, New York, Missouri, Illinois, Ohio, and Wisconsin.

The Curricula

Three different degrees and eight different diplomas and certificates were awarded to 310 graduates during the Van Hoose years, but by the end of his administration all degrees and diplomas had been abolished except the Bachelor of Arts and the Bachelor of Arts in Music degrees. Certificates in piano and art were given to 9 for three years of study and a brief recital or small exhibition. Diplomas were provided to 70 for four years of study in piano, voice, organ, expression, or art, each requiring more than half of the work to be done in major and minor courses and a satisfactory recital or exhibition. The Bachelor of Science degree, given to 41, required 120 s.h. of study, with majors possible in mathematics, science, or domestic science.

The Bachelor of Arts degree, given to 189 persons, specified 120 to 125 s.h. of study, of which about two-thirds were in courses required of all graduates. Majors of 24 s.h. and minors of 18 s.h. were introduced in the 1918 catalogue. Thereafter, majors were always allowed in biology, chemistry, English, French, history and political science, Latin, mathematics, and speech. Majors were sometimes allowed in German, philosophy, physics, and Spanish. Minors were allowed in any of these fields, plus education, religion, and sociology. The Bachelor of Arts in Music degree, given to only one person in the last year, specified the same general outline of study, except that the major and minor courses were in music.

Within the Departments

The size of the faculty and staff remained fairly stable during this period, ranging from 34 to 38. Of these, 24 to 26 were classroom teachers and 10 to 12 occupied supporting positions. The average salary rose almost threefold: a full professor received $2,500 in 1921–1922. Salaries were sometimes supplemented by free room and nominal or free board. Standing committees of the faculty were named for the first time. Although they varied from year to year, some were constant: admissions; curriculum; library; catalogue, schedule, and diploma; public lectures and recitals.

Approximately 153 faculty members were employed by Van Hoose, of whom about 83 remained one year or less. Among the 45 nonmusicians associated with Shorter two or more years, the highest earned degrees were distributed as follows: bachelor's, 16 (seven of these claimed additional work on the next degree); master's, 14 (nine of these claimed additional work on the next degree); doctor's, 10. The remaining 5 persons in this category had no degree listed in the catalogue. Graduate schools most frequently attended by the nonmusicians were at the universities of Chicago and Virginia, Columbia University, Southern Baptist Theological Seminary, and the Women's Medical College of Pennsylvania.

Among the 25 musicians teaching at Shorter at least two years, the highest earned degrees were distributed as follows: bachelor's or diploma, 3; master's, 4; doctor's, 1. Six were graduates of various conservatories, and 11 had no degree listed in the catalogue. Conservatories most often attended were in Boston, Cincinnati, Oberlin, Germany, and the Netherlands. Because of the high esteem in which this department was held, it must be noted that formal degrees were subordinated to personal proficiency.

ART. Under Miss Imogen A. Coulter, who took some of her early training at Shorter College and later returned to teach there for thirteen years, the art department offered 10 s.h. of instruction in history and appreciation, plus four years of practical techniques in the studio located on the second floor of the Domestic Science and Art Building. Twenty-one certificates and diplomas were earned from this department, but by the close of the Van Hoose administration art courses were permitted only as electives. Often with printed guidebooks, a student exhibition was invariably shown at commencement. The Art Lovers Club was formed in 1910, meeting weekly in order chiefly to study the history of art. The same year the Sketch Club was organized, and when the girls were not drawing scenes from the Shorter forest and the seven hills of Rome, field trips were taken to Mount Alto, Cave Spring, Mount Lavender, and Barnsley Gardens. For several years an honor roll was maintained for the young lady producing the best drawing each week. Student artists were active in the preparation of the college annual, one of which was dedicated to Miss Coulter, "who has contributed much toward the success of all the *Argos* . . . ."

ENGLISH. The department of English language and literature was organically separated from the school of expression until 1919, after which they were united as the department of English language, literature, and speech, with courses totaling 70 s.h. in English and 34 s.h. in speech. For ten years the popular Miss Anne Wynne Stevens was in the department, and an annual was dedicated to her not long before she left. Because she was a confirmed bird watcher, the girls sometimes insisted that one had to join her in that endeavor in order to make an A in English under her! Her enthusiasm in this extracurricular activity was indicated by a speech that she made to the Woman's Club, "The Contributions of Birds to the War Effort." After 1915 the department was significantly strengthened by the coming of Paul M. Cousins who was a full-time professor for fifteen years and also president of the college for another fifteen. Voted "most considerate" by the graduates of 1921, he was also honored when the *Argo* was dedicated to him by the next class—from which his future wife was to come! A Scribbler's Club lived for a few months in 1917; more successful in terms of size and longevity was the Phi Kappa Alpha Literary Club, formed in 1921 and soon including over forty members.

FOREIGN LANGUAGES. The department of classical languages was first led by L. R. Hogan and later by Dr. Clara L. Thompson, who re mained at that post for thirty-four years. Instruction grew to 20 s.h. in Greek and 35 in Latin. One course was introduced especially for students expecting to teach Latin in high school. In the fall of 1921 a Classical Club was organized, and meetings were characterized by discussions, readings, games, puzzles, and refreshments.

Four modern languages were taught at varying times during this administration. About 30 s.h. were offered in French. Spanish was introduced in 1913, eventually providing 40 s.h. of instruction. Italian was inserted for one year only, 1913–1914. German was dropped after the war, but 36 s.h. were available prior to that time. Miss Anne W. Raynor instructed in German and Spanish for six years, while two Shorter graduates were assistants in French for one year each, Misses Velma Osborne and Elma Dominick. The French Club met twice monthly, becoming "L'Alliance Francaise au College Shorter à Rome, Georgie," in 1914 and publishing its "Statuts et Annuaire" which proclaimed that the group "a pour object d'encourager et stimuler l'etude du francais . . . ." Occasionally the members presented a French play. The German Club was a casualty of the war, while the Spanish Club was not started until 1921.

HISTORY AND POLITICAL SCIENCE. The curriculum in history and political science expanded from 20 to 55 s.h. Included in this department were courses in economics and sociology, the nuclei of later departments. A. M. Arnett taught for five years, being named "most intellectual" by the students during his last year at Shorter. His successor in 1917 was Miss Clara L. Kellogg, whose connection with the college extended to the time of her death in 1958. She was instrumental in organizing the International Relations Club in 1921.

MATHEMATICS AND SCIENCE. The mathematics department remained stable, providing approximately 30 s.h. each year. J. W. Gaines taught for eight years, amusing his students by frequent, glowing references in class to "my son Karl." Unknown to either Gaines or his beloved son, a funeral occurred on campus for a doll that had fallen to the floor and shattered. The mourners secured a casket, flowers, and an enterprising classmate who acted as the officiating clergyman. She eulogized the deceased doll, likening her in character to the greatest person known to any of them, "my son Karl." Warmly admired by the girls, Gaines and his wife would often notice a lonely student and invite her for a ride around town in their automobile. In 1919 a Shorter graduate in the class of 1896 returned to teach in this department, Miss Ruby Hightower. Soon voted "sweetest" by the students, she eventually became the first Shorter alumna to earn the Doctor of Philosophy degree.

The number of courses in the sciences more than tripled. At first the department of natural sciences offered work in astronomy, biology, chemistry, physics, and geology, for a total of 32 s.h. Emphasis was given in 1918 to the expansion of the laboratories, which were estimated to contain $28,000 worth of equipment three years later. Astronomy and geology were dropped, while the other three areas became separate departments. Instruction in biology was raised to 34 s.h., in chemistry to 45 s.h., and in physics to 35 s.h. Before the division, Oakley M. Bishop was professor of natural science for five years; after the division, Miss Susie Earnest, a Shorter graduate who became Mrs. Aubrey Matthews, was instructor in chemistry for six years, and Everett E. Porter began an illustrious career as professor of chemistry extending thirty-three years. Several Shorter alumnae returned as instructors for brief periods of time: Miss Susie Smith in chemistry for one year; Misses Laura Belle Brewster and Mary Frances Shuford in biology for one year each; and Miss Mary Alice Tingley in biology for three years. A Nature Study Club and a Chemistry Club existed for a few months in 1916, while in the spring of 1922 a Science Club, encompassing all three departments plus mathematics, was at last organized.

MUSIC. The Conservatory of Music that the Simmons had developed was not continued by Van Hoose, and music no longer dominated the school. Courses in history, appreciation, and theory totaled 30 s.h., to which were added four full years of individual instruction in piano, organ, violin, and voice. With five full-time professors, however, this

169

was still the largest department in the college. Misses Grace Cronkhite and Annie Denmark taught for six years each, and Miss Edith Hall, for five. Several Shorter graduates assisted in the department: Misses Marjorie Bush, Martha Galt, and Phosa Durden for two years each and Misses Rebekah Clark, Glennis Hancock, and Ida Holloway for one year each. Miss Louise Bennet became professor of voice in 1921, remaining with the school in several capacities for twenty-five years.

A particularly slow piano student finally learned to play one piece, "Believe Me If All Those Enduring Young Charms." At length her honest teacher told her: "Honey, I'm glad you're taking music, but you're wasting your father's money. I don't believe I'd waste it, if I were you." Another pupil in obvious difficulty was reported to have left a voice lesson exclaiming: "Oh, I can't do those old archipelagoes which Madame wants me to do!" A third young lady was impressed by her piano instructor, a native of Germany who wore a waxed mustache and goatee and was usually dressed in a long-tailed coat and stovepipe hat. He and his wife took his students to "Camp Pfitzner" on Mount Lavender for a weekend camping trip, and this time he wore knickers and a soft crowned hat. The girls "boldly" went wading in knee-length bloomers and middy blouses.

"Rules Governing Conservatory Practice" were laid down by a playful student: "Do not throw metronomes through the glass doors. If you insist on doing so, please sweep up the pieces. Students must not sit on the radiator while practicing. . . . No metronome solos allowed without accompaniments. Voice students having a cold may induce the frog in their throat to sing for them. . . . Students upon leaving practice rooms at 9:30 P.M., will close the lights, put out the piano and kiss the radiator goodnight. They will proceed to the dormitory on tiptoes . . . ."

Dozens of musicians performed in the auditorium, some of whom were advertised in superlative terms—"the greatest organist that America has yet produced," "one of the world's greatest pianists," "the famous German pianist," and others. Apparently each professor gave a recital at least once each year, as did every junior and senior student. (One uneasy student recitalist received a telegram saying: "Hope you can beat Padew-esky.") Beginning in 1913 the Shorter Glee Club, accompanied by guitars, mandolins, and harp, presented occasional programs. For five years the St. Cecilia Society was active, but after 1915 it was gradually supplanted by the MacDowell Choral Club. Easter and Christmas concerts and an infrequent operetta comprised its chief public offerings. A college orchestra was formed about 1917, holding weekly rehearsals and giving concerts each year.

One Shorter performance attracted unusual notice because it was presented at the Blackstone Theater in Chicago, Illinois, on April 23, 1916! Misses Marjorie Bush and Martha Galt gave a two-piano recital attended by a small but appreciative audience. One Chicago critic observed: "Their attacks synchronized well, their tones were well equalized, and were of good quality."

PHILOSOPHY, EDUCATION, AND PSYCHOLOGY. Voted "most intellectual" by the class of 1921, Dr. W. D. Furry was at first the professor of philosophy and education, although later he became dean and then president of the college. Two courses in psychology and one each in logic and ethics were offered early in the Van Hoose administration. In 1915 offerings were enlarged and eventually included 20 s.h. in education, 15 s.h. in philosophy, and 12 s.h. in psychology. Certification by the Georgia Board of Education was available beginning in 1916 to the student successfully completing 18 s.h. of study in professional education, and as many as sixteen are known to have received such certification in a single year. Practice teaching at the West Rome elementary school was introduced in 1921, with the promise of a higher level upon demand. Provided for the first time in 1920 was a "Bureau of Appointments" which aided Shorter graduates in securing teaching positions.

PHYSICAL EDUCATION. Two hours of physical education were required of all students each week, although later this was waived for seniors. A total of 8 s.h. was available in the department, the completion of which entitled the student to a certificate for teaching physical training in the public schools. The various instructors also supervised all extracurricular athletics, to be described later in this chapter.

RELIGION. The department of Biblical literature and religious education was led by several men, one of whom—L. R. Hogan—remained six years. Called "Cousin Luther" by some of the girls when he was not around, he also made many friends by frequently taking groups of them on rides in his new car. Dedicating their annual to him as "our friend, counsellor, and teacher," the seniors of 1916 pledged this popular bachelor their "confidence and devotion." He expanded the offerings of the department, adding religious education, the history of religions, and the history of Christianity. Courses in theology and missions were later introduced, raising the total to 24 s.h. Requirements for graduation always included courses in Bible, but this department was allowed to offer only a minor. For a time the notable *Outline of Christian Theology* by William Newton Clarke was in use as a textbook.

171

SPEECH. Frequently seen by the general public were the teachers and students in speech. After a number of ladies remained only a year or two, Mrs. Allie Hayes Richardson joined the faculty in 1918, being associated with the college as an active or emeritus professor until her death in 1966. Assisting her during her second year was Miss Margaret Davison, a recent Shorter graduate.

Recitals were constantly being sponsored by this department, sometimes by visitors, but more often by junior and senior students and by the instructor. Special programs were presented at Christmas and at least once on the birthday of Robert E. Lee. The Story Teller's League was comprised of speech students who each Sunday went to various mission points in town and told stories to the underprivileged children (and adults!) who eagerly attended.

Each year numerous plays were staged, once reaching a total of fifteen. In the earlier years the absence of stage curtains was made obvious by the ingenuity of the girls who stretched a taut wire across the stage and suspended clean sheets on it by safety pins. The annual expression program in the spring was soon accompanied by a Shakespearean drama, often presented on Lombardy Walk. Thus, elaborate productions of "The Taming of the Shrew," "Twelfth Night," "As You Like It," "The Merchant of Venice," and others were captured by visiting photographers whose pictures remain. Student organizations were active: the Oratory Club for one year, the Dramatic Club for nine, and the Shorter Players founded by Mrs. Richardson in 1919 and still existing.

DOMESTIC SCIENCE. From 1911 to 1921 domestic science was a part of the Shorter course of study, offering instruction in cooking, sewing, home nursing, sanitation, and hygiene. A resident physician for several years taught in some of these areas and afforded the girls excellent health treatment, facts which were widely publicized. The cooking classes sometimes displayed their skills by inviting trustees or faculty members to a banquet. Once or twice a year the sewing classes sponsored exhibits of their dressmaking, embroidery, and millinery work. Each student kept a notebook containing examples and explanations of various types of needlework, some of which have been preserved. Facilities for home economics were located on the second floor of the Domestic Science and Art Building; a separate building was long desired but never constructed.

THE ACADEMY. At first Van Hoose returned the academy to direct college control, and as many as 68 girls aged thirteen to seventeen were enrolled. The *Shorter Academy Bulletin*, bound in the 1911 *Argo*, contained poems, stories, essays, jokes, and personal items of academy and college life. The Van Hoose Literary Society was formed; at the modest president's request the name was soon changed to honor Luther Rice Gwaltney. Housed in suites with older college girls, many of them joined the Eunomians or Polymnians. One recalled her dormitory life by admitting: "I learned a lot that first year that I probably shouldn't have." Another remembered how homesick she was, adding, "My father came to see me and brought a Shorter pin for me"—a tiny replica of the college seal. As early as 1913 Van Hoose was ready to abolish the academy, but this was not done until 1916.

Administration and Staff

The library was on the first floor of the Academic Building, where it remained until it was moved to the second floor in 1935. Virtually nonexistent when Van Hoose assumed control, the collection had grown to 3,000 volumes in 1916. In order to meet a requirement of the Southern Association, the number of books was doubled that year by means of a drive among alumnae and students. At the victory celebration on Washington's birthday, it was announced that the juniors and freshmen had secured the greatest number of additions and had won a silver loving cup. Annual expenditures ranging from $500 to $3,000 provided expansion to 8,500 volumes in 1922. For the most part, the library was staffed with students and recent graduates. Misses Opal Hall, Sallie Geiger, and Sarah Moore each worked there for a single year. Miss Ethel Stephens was librarian and director of religious activities for four years—long enough to find that books even then had a way of disappearing. The class of 1914 bequeathed to her "a stout padlock and key in order that she may keep James, *Psychology*, and Joseph Jastrow's *Fact and Fable* in the Library." Vividly described on a full page in the 1916 annual, her marriage to Professor A. M. Arnett was the first to be held on the new campus.

Other staff members also left their marks on the institution. Miss Virginia Wendell was dean of women for nine years, long remembered as being very strict with her girls. Once voted "most dignified" by the students, Miss Nannie M. Kennedy was bursar for fourteen years. Mrs. K. E. Parker was matron for six, and Mrs. N. B. King was housekeeper and supervisor of the dormitories for fifteen. Starting about 1916, "Mr. Mac" MacDurmont was night watchman for a decade.

The infirmary was located on the third floor of the Domestic Science and Art Building, being in charge of "Sister Maggie"—Miss Margaret L. Jacobs—from 1910 to 1938. Over the years she nursed, doctored, and mothered the hundreds who came to her, doing as much for her patients with "her wonderful cheery disposition" as with the medicine she gave. One admirer described her this way: "In case of serious illness she has been known to go night after night without sleep. In cases of homesickness she can think of dozens of things to do to chase away the blues. . . . Her religion is one of service, of tolerance, of kindness, and of cheerfulness, and she lives her religion daily." For the first time in the history of the school, death visited the student body while the college was in session; in 1914 a young lady was discovered to have died of "heart failure" in her sleep. Once a pupil leaned too far out of a second story dormitory window and landed temporarily in the infirmary. Soon thereafter another girl fell down a chute in the dormitory leading to the basement, and her injuries were much more serious but not fatal. Ordinarily, however, Sister Maggie's patients were not as spectacularly incapacitated as these.

The college dining room and kitchen occupied the entire first floor of the Domestic Science and Art Building. In announcing a new dietician, Van Hoose found it necessary to admit: "I hope that the food will hereafter be not only more palatable, but more nutritious." Needing an old hound for a skit, two students late in this period borrowed one named "Minnie" and kept her hidden in their room for a few days. She disappeared while they were absent briefly. When the origin of the meat at dinner that evening could not be positively identified, the girls suspected that it was "Minnie-meat"—a designation that persisted thirty years for such morsels.

"The Shorter Shadows," as they were called, were given a full page in one annual; nine servants were pictured, but no names were recorded. Doubtless one of them was Victoria (Mrs. John Anderson), who spent twenty-seven years on the hill, chiefly as maid in the entrance hall of the Academic Building. There she received visitors, handled packages, and did "a thousand things for the Shorter girls and faculty." Cheerful, quiet, and efficient, she learned how to read and write with Dean Wendell as her teacher, read the newspaper each day, and wrote telephone messages for the girls. Probably another was Steve Graham, the headwaiter in the dining room for more than sixteen years. Expressing disgust at the girls who rushed in just as the door was being closed, he possessed an "eagle eye" that carefully scrutinized them when they left to be sure they carried out no food. His jolly nature came to the fore when visiting orchestras played on special occasions; he would almost be dancing as he served table.

174

Starting as the Honor Board in 1908, student government expanded during the Van Hoose administration. The Student Government Association of Shorter College was formed "to preserve the student honor, to regulate the conduct of resident students, and to enforce such regulations of the College as do not fall exclusively within the province of the Faculty." That the faculty still furnished the regulations was made clear by a student speaker in 1910 who urged her audience "to keep the rules as they are laid down for us." As time passed, at least some of the rules were made by joint faculty-student action. Membership was secured in the newly formed Southern Intercollegiate Association of Student Government in 1917.

Officers and class representatives of the Student Government Association were elected each spring and installed at a special program in the auditorium. In some years each dormitory had a house council, made up of the dormitory president and the student proctors named by the Student Council. (These girls were labeled the "Hoo Doos" by some who did not appreciate their investigations.) Legislative and judicial power rested in these student organizations, although the faculty executive committee and the president of the college always retained final authority.

One student officer was much in evidence when "Pay Day" was held several times a year. Making it easier to pay dues for the various organizations, the student treasurer was stationed in the Academic Building. Each principal group levied a charge, ranging from 75¢ to $1 for the Student Government Association, the Athletic Association, the Y.W.C.A., the Choral Club, or the Shorter Players. The literary societies set their dues at $2 to $6. Students were required to join only two organizations, the S.G.A. and one of the societies.

Residential students were expected to remain on campus most of the time, and special rules governed their departure for shopping, visiting in private homes, and going home on weekends. Each girl was provided a page in the large sign-out book on which she was to record her movements, even for a very short trip into town. The page was sometimes bypassed. President Van Hoose strictly forbade attendance at the occasional visiting circus, but two young ladies sneaked out dressed as old women, just the same. Any other such infractions have not been openly admitted. Of course, proper dress was regularly emphasized. Therefore, President Van Hoose must have been greatly discomfited the day he read a news article in the Rome paper captioned: "Shorter Girl Wears Green Stockings on Streets of Rome."

175

While on campus, the students had an abundance of rules to obey. They were to dress modestly, but uniforms were not required. For formal affairs, no "décolleté gowns" were permitted. "Victrolas are not to be played on Sunday. . . . Students are asked not to entertain callers on Sunday." "Students must never spend a night out of their own rooms without permission. . . . Students must not stand, talk nor loiter in the corridors during recitation or study hours . . . and all students not engaged in recitations must remain in their own rooms. Students must not entertain day students or other visitors in their rooms. All visitors must be received in the first floor sitting rooms. . . . The telephone is not to be used by students. Permission to send messages may be obtained from the Lady Principal at her office hours. These messages must be written. . . . Cooking in their rooms is permitted to students only on Saturdays from three to ten P.M., and on Mondays from eight A.M. to seven P.M. Students are not permitted to buy or use canned meats. Students may not wear hats, caps, or basketball sweaters to any meals. Middy blouses may not be worn to dinner nor to Sunday night suppers."

Dean Wendell took seriously the rule that read: "Students are held responsible for the neatness and order of their rooms, which must be ready for inspection by eight-thirty every morning." She left many "reminders" on little slips of paper as she went from suite to suite: "Too much dust." "Flyspecks on mirror." "A piece of wearing apparel left on bed—where is your closet?" "Destroy old newspapers." "Where is your broom?" "Do you feel better bathing in a tub with dirty rings?"

In addition to these and other formal rules, numerous "hints" were urged: "Do not make a noise in eating soup, crackers, celery, etc. Remember, the principal differences between the savage and the civilized man is in his manner of eating. . . . Neither a borrower nor a lender be. Do not visit your friends oftener than they visit you. Your visits may become tiresome. Do not allow your room to become untidy during the day. The slovenly girl makes the slovenly woman. . . . Do not use slang nor begin your sentence with 'Say!' Leave those habits to the girl who chews gum and paints her face. Do not talk loudly nor laugh shrilly. 'The loud laugh bespeaks the vacant mind.' . . . Do not slam the doors nor run up and down the corridors; save your strength for better use. . . . Do not save your best manners for special occasions. The oftener they are used the more natural they become."

To assist the girls with some of their purchases, "the College's little store" was located on the first floor of Hall One. "The usual grocery supplies may be bought here in small quantities. Fresh fruits and candy can be purchased any time in the day until 7 P.M."

Not all of the rules related to campus activities were obeyed. During study hours the young ladies circumspectly exercised their cooking skills or slipped out of their rooms to visit friends elsewhere in the dormitory, usually without getting caught. Two girls were sent home "for having an extended conversation with two soldiers on that part of the college grounds near the river road." The president explained further: "They did this not once, but twice. . . . There was nothing particularly wrong in what they did, except it is a general rule of the college that young ladies are not to meet or talk with young men on the grounds except when the meeting takes place in the college parlors." Long after the 10:15 retiring bell had rung, a girl might be lowered through the shaft leading from each floor to the basement where the college stored its extra food. She would then be pulled back up to her floor, usually bearing various sorts of canned goods—"sheer thievery," as one of them later admitted. One girl brought back a cocoa can and tipped it up to determine its contents. The cocoa covered her, and she and her co-conspirators had to scrub her very carefully so that the odor would not betray any of them. Yet another young lady returned from Christmas holiday with a package of violet-scented cigarettes. She gathered a group in her bathroom and each took a puff or two. In her excitement at such forbidden pleasures, one girl knocked over a soap dish and they were all discovered. Restriction was their fate. One of them tried to climb through a loophole in the rules and made things even worse for herself. Up to this time the rules had allowed a restricted girl to go home. Since she was a Rome resident, she accordingly signed out—and then went shopping in town. Unfortunately she met one of the teachers. Soon thereafter the rule about restricted girls was changed, and their actions were more severely restrained. In those years there was no railing on the roof which was so accessible from the second floor of Halls One and Two, and rules strictly prohibited crawling through the windows and occupying that area. During the day the girls would slip out and sunbathe, and on hot, stuffy nights they would pull out their mattresses and sleep there. For some inexplicable reason they were not often apprehended, nor did they ever seem to fall off and hurt themselves. An editorial in the *Chimes* commented knowingly: "One of the great flaws in the system of student government is the failure of girls to report what they see and hear that is wrong. Not until every girl realizes that the greater wrong is in not reporting, and co-operates with those in authority in truly working for self government, can we say we have it."

In 1915 the "point system" was introduced, attempting "to develop competent leaders among the girls, by distributing the offices more evenly and by centering energy upon the phase of work undertaken." Each office on campus was designated a value, and the maximum number of points first allowed was 12. Some of these were: president of the Y.W.C.A. or Student Government Association, 12; president of either society, 8; debater for either society, 6; editor or business manager of *Chimes* or *Argo*, 8; class president, 5; class playwright, 4; president of Athletic Association, 5; president of Dramatic Club, 3; president of Art Lovers Club, language clubs, or Choral Club, 2. Later the value of some offices was modified, and the maximum was raised to 14.

Religion on the Hill

The college encouraged its students in their religious life by several means. Five or six mornings a week required chapel services were conducted, usually by faculty members or the students themselves. "Poor conduct" and "dull programs" were occasionally claimed in the *Chimes*, along with some expressions of pleasure because of interesting presentations. The girls were expected to be in attendance at Sunday school and morning worship service each Sunday, although Sister Maggie reported that the only epidemics on campus were of "Sunday headaches" which not even her ever-present bottle of castor oil could cure. In 1919 the policy was changed, making morning attendance optional. Van Hoose reported that "under the old method, the infirmary was usually full of sick (?) girls every Sunday morning" but that under the new system thirty-five to fifty percent of the pupils voluntarily attended church, almost as many as before. A Sunday vesper service was made mandatory for all residential students, a requirement that was not lifted for almost forty years. Van Hoose urged a chapel building and Sunday school and church services on campus, but he elicited no support for either project. Under the auspices of the college, religious speakers were brought to the campus. The first Religious Focus Week seems to have been held in the spring of 1912 with Emmet Stephens, a Baptist missionary from China, as the guest. Other notable visitors included Dean Shailer Mathews of the University of Chicago Divinity School, Professors A. T. Robertson and W. O. Carver, both of the Southern Baptist Theological Seminary, and several leading pastors from Georgia: L. R. Christie, Charles W. Daniel, Ashby Jones, and John E. White. The professor of religion usually provided instruction in teacher training using manuals supplied by the Sunday School Board of the Southern Baptist Convention, and diplomas were awarded at graduation to as many as thirty girls completing the course.

The young ladies displayed other evidence of their religious devotion. The Martha Shorter Missionary Society faded from view in 1910, leaving only the Y.W.C.A. This was replaced by the Martha Shorter chapter of the Baptist Young Woman's Auxiliary in 1911, but returned in 1914. It developed three circles honoring Mrs. Martha Shorter, Mrs. Harriet Cooper (mother of J. P. Cooper), and Mrs. Wilda Hardman Poteat (a Shorter alumna who was then in China as a missionary). Regardless of the formal organization, however, membership was held by virtually all students and the programs varied but little as the girls met in the room set apart for this use. An opening reception for the new students came early each fall. Morning watch and evening vespers were held three to five days a week, with the average attendance one year reported as 25 and 114 respectively. Voluntary classes dealt with such topics as Japan, Burma, the American Negro, the social teachings of Jesus, China, and South America, enrolling as many as 180. During one January week of prayer, Miss Edna Earle Teal, a missionary in China who had attended Shorter in 1899–1900, received special attention. Voluntary offerings were made supporting various Southern Baptist missionary enterprises, as much as $575 in one year. Clothes were gathered for a young lady in the Baptist Orphan's Home at Hapeville, money was raised for a school girl in China, and musical instruments were obtained for a boys' school in China.

Provided for at least five years, the *Y.W.C.A. Hand Book* was a small booklet containing detailed information about the religious work on campus. In addition, there were brief notices about other student organizations, a greeting from Van Hoose, space to record one's daily schedule, and several advertisements that helped to pay for the publication. Some years it was combined with the student handbook, being published jointly with the Student Government Association.

Van Hoose expressed his conviction "that the college . . . should touch elbows with the common people; that it should use the consecration of its teachers and the enthusiasm of its students in doing what it can for the development of those who are less fortunate," and he was able to secure the agreement of others. Each year twenty-five to seventy-five students and faculty members taught Sunday school classes in town, while many others conducted domestic science and art classes for local girls. At Christmas time a party was held in the gymnasium for West Rome children, who had been asked to write brief notes expressing their hearts' desire. One youngster laboriously penciled these words: "To the Ladies of Shorter College. I would like very mutch to have a Doll." Another said: "Dear Santa Clause. Please send me a little train." By 1921 the girls were also providing Thanksgiving baskets for the needy.

179

Shorter students attended Y.W.C.A. conferences at Blue Ridge, North Carolina, in such numbers that they joined with the Y.M.C.A. of the University of Georgia and had a cottage built that the two groups owned together. (The Shorter girls received much assistance in paying for it from Rome merchants who made donations.) The Georgia-Shorter cottage was ready in 1915 and held about twelve young ladies who attended the two weeks' meeting.

As the Georgia Baptist Convention showed greater interest in the Baptist Young People's Union, so also did the Shorter students. In the fall of 1916 forty of them took a training class and organized a union that ran parallel to the work of the more inclusive Y.W.C.A.

The First Baptist Church occasionally held a reception for the students and faculty early in the year, and many of them regularly attended that church. When the governor proclaimed a "Go To Sunday School Day" in Georgia, twenty-five Shorter girls formed a special choir for the observance. At local churches the male professors often preached and the girls conducted classes or provided other programs. Each fall several Shorter pupils participated in the state convention of the Woman's Missionary Union.

Composed of girls interested in becoming missionaries, a Student Volunteer Band was soon formed that maintained a rather constant membership of about six. Shorter was hostess to the annual convention of the Georgia Students' Missionary League in 1912, at which six girls volunteered. Two years later Van Hoose and a few pupils attended the national meeting of the Student Volunteer Movement in Kansas City, Missouri. Eventually Shorter joined with Bessie Tift and Mercer to organize the Georgia Baptist Student Volunteer Movement. Of the students attending Shorter during these years, seven eventually served on foreign fields: Mary Goethius, Wilda Hardman, Lucy Wright, Lucia Rodwell, Agnes Rowland, Sadie Wilson, and Mary Tennant.

With regularity students expressed their interest in religious matters by means of articles printed in the *Chimes*. Walter Rauschenbusch was approvingly cited, and a definite espousal of social Christianity was evident. Governmental housing regulations, woman's suffrage, the improvement of movies, compulsory education laws, labor unions, and control of trusts and corporations were all advocated. Other essays appeared concerning the Bible, the theories of atonement, heathenism in American colleges, religious education, and Hinduism.

Denominational statistics contain no startling revelations. The Baptists numbered about sixty-three percent, the Methodists about nineteen, the Presbyterians about ten, and the Episcopalians about four. All others were usually much lower, although in some years Jews,

Roman Catholics, or members of the Christian Church exceeded one percent.

Publications

In May of 1911 the college annual was again published after a lapse of eleven years. Named the *Argo* and bound in brown leather, this 225-page issue was dedicated to Van Hoose. Of course its new name recalled the famous ship of Greek mythology, and the introductory poem assumed a knowledge of the ancient story. In a later issue, the tale of Jason and the Argo was properly told.

The editors sometimes called themselves or all of the seniors the Argonauts, but this name did not take on its present meaning for many years to come. One year they recorded: "February 21—Annual goes to press. Editors collapse." Later they calculated that the *Argo* had been produced in 15,275,000 seconds! In addition to materials usually found in such publications now, earlier issues contained articles concerning the alumnae, Halloween and Thanksgiving, and numerous original poems, stories, and drawings by Shorter students. Cash prizes were offered in some years for such original productions. The class of 1918 substituted a thirty-one-page *Our Senior Book*, containing their history, poem, prophecy, last will and testament, and the text of their play. Resumed in 1920, the *Argo* has subsequently been issued without interruption. Its price was first $3.00 and later, $3.50.

In its absence, the *Periscope* was initiated by the class in journalism in December of 1919. Described as containing four pages, each with six columns eighteen inches long, it was first edited by Rosa Smith, a senior biology major from Claxton, Georgia. This newspaper was issued semimonthly and sold for 15¢ per copy or $1.50 per year.

Two other student publications are described elsewhere in this chapter as the sponsoring organizations are discussed, the *Y.W.C.A. Hand Book* and the *Chimes*.

Under the direction of Van Hoose, the college catalogue was published annually in March or June. The *Shorter College Bulletin* continued to be issued quarterly, providing information about the school and advancing the cause of education generally. Most of the issues display numerous photographs of the campus, by which one can trace its scenic development. Other discreet forms of advertising included a colored postcard showing the proposed Greater Shorter and two others with views of the Sun Dial Court. A "Shorter Book of Views at Christmas" appeared in 1912, in which Van Hoose wrote: "As you turn the pages remember that on each one is not only the picture, but written there, in invisible ink, is my Christmas wish for you and the burden of it is, *Good will to you in the Spirit of Christmas."* At least two years were marked with calendars showing scenes of the college—the new buildings, Maplehurst, Rotary Lake, student groups, and Van Hoose himself.

The College Creed and Songs

The Shorter Girls' Creed first appeared in the *Chimes* for December, 1911, and was probably written by several members of the 1912 *Argo* staff.

I believe in girls, in the women of a great tomorrow, and that whatsoever the girl soweth the woman shall reap.

I believe in the curse of ignorance, in the dignity of learning, and the joy of serving others.

I believe in wisdom as revealed in human lives as well as in the pages of printed books, in lessons taught not so much by precept as by example, in ability to work with the hands as well as to think with the head, in everything that makes life large and lovely.

I believe in beauty in the home, in the class room, in the work room, and in the influence of God's great out of doors.

I believe in laughter, in love, in faith, in all distant hopes that lure us on.

I believe in the present and its opportunities, in the future and its obligations, and in the divine joy of living, here and hereafter.

At least six songs were entitled "Alma Mater," only one of which is now heard. Initially printed in the *Chimes* for April, 1915, were these words by Mary K. Bruner, who would be a graduate in the class of 1917:

> Far above the winding Coosa
>   'Bove its waters clear,
> Stands forever Alma Mater,
>   Shorter, loved and dear.
>
>   CHORUS—
> Lift your voices, send them upward,
>   Loud her honor sing,
> Hail to thee, O Alma Mater!
>   Wide thy praises ring.
>
> Far above the mountains azure,
>   And the town of Rome,
> In our mem'ry cherished ever,
>   Stands our college home.
>
> Stand forever throned in beauty,
>   Hold thy purpose high,
> And thy fame, O Alma Mater!
>   May it never die.

As the seniors marched toward Maplehurst for the Class Day exercise on June 10, 1912, the first known use of "Hail, Dear Old Shorter" occurred. The identity of its author has not been discovered.

Hail, dear old Shorter—
    Noble and strong,
To thee with loyal hearts
    We raise our song.
Swelling to heaven loud,
    Our praises ring;
Hail, dear old Shorter—
    To thee we sing.

Majesty as a crown
    Rests on thy brow,
Pride, honor, glory, love
    Before thee bow.
Ne'er shall thy spirit die,
    Thy walls decay.
Hail, dear old Shorter;
    For thee we pray.

Hail, dear old Shorter,
    Pride of our youth,
Lead thou thy children on
    To light and truth.
Then when death summons us
    Others shall raise,
Hail, dear old Shorter,
    Through endless days.

At the suggestion of President Van Hoose, Miss Louise Bennet composed "The White and Gold" in 1918. The students at once began to sing it, but it was written particularly for the alumnae who first used it at their Monday evening banquet during the commencement of 1919.

The white and gold of memories dear,
Enshrine we in our hearts.
The teachings of these colors clear,
Will ne'er from us depart.
The white shall stand for purity,
The gold for worth untold.
We'll prove Shorter's worth
In the world's great strife,
We'll uphold the white and gold.
Our Alma Mater's standards true
We'll bear where e'er we go
That others seeing our lives
Her glories too may know.
Our lives shall stand for purity,
Our hearts for worth untold,
We'll prove Shorter's worth

In the world of men,
We'll uphold the white and gold.

In a vastly different vein, "Nothing's a Cinch at Shorter," sung to
the tune of "Took My Girl to a Restaurant," was so popular that each
new student was told to learn its words before coming in September:

Took myself to Shorter Hill
  For a little rest and ease,
Thought I'd get nothing but A's,
  I'm thankful now for C's.

Thought I'd take a history course
  But they had too many tests.
Then I took up literature,
  Mr. Cousins knows the rest.

Turned my attention then to Math,
  Hoping for a cinch,
Dropped that subject in three days
  And then I took up French.

Finding Latin was too hard
  I decided on B. S.
But when I entered that German class
  I flunked out like the rest.

Chemistry lab, three times a week,
  Biology as well.
But speaking of geology,
  Oh, that's too sad to tell.

By this time, to my mind,
  Came this little thought:
Shorter is a grand old place,
  But it ain't no winter resort.

The First Intercollegiate Athletics

The absence of athletic facilities on the new campus led one writer
to moan: "How can we be athletic without anything but Georgia
mud?" But then she brightened: "Why only think how many courts
we can get on one hundred and fifty acres . . . ." With no outdoor
fields, all basketball was played in the gymnasium—"although," it was
admitted, "concrete floors and plastered walls are not especially conducive to ease and comfort." Nor was the gymnasium conducive to
high, arching shots; 9½-foot rafters loomed scarcely a foot above the
baskets! Soon, however, an athletic area was provided, furnishing
three unpaved tennis courts, one basketball court, and one large general playing field, all located near the Music Building. In the summer
of 1915 a short golf course was placed on the gentle slope between the

Academic Building and Maplehurst as a gift from J. P. Cooper, but a combination of poor usage and scarcity of labor contributed to its closing three years later. Although promises to reopen it were made for several years, most of the golf was played at the Coosa Country Club. Providing swimming and boating, Rotary Lake was available in 1916 after the Rome Rotary Club had a dam constructed across the creek running through the rear of the campus. Approved attire usually consisted of white middy blouses, dark bloomers, and dark hose. Tennis and golf called for the same blouses and white skirts reaching almost to the ankles. For swimming, black suits revealing bare arms were permitted.

Physical training was emphasized by Van Hoose, who instructed the teacher to take various measurements of the girls at the beginning of the semester. Just before Christmas the same measurements were again taken, showing that the average weight had jumped from 116.4 to 126.9 pounds and the average capacity for chest expansion had increased from 3.4 to 6.3 inches. The latter part of each afternoon was set aside for athletics, although many of the young ladies spent more than the allotted one hour in such activities.

The Athletic Association continued to function, annually electing officers and involving 150 to 200 participants. Basketball, volley ball, baseball, tennis, golf, field hockey, track and field events, soccer, fencing, hiking, boating, and swimming were most popular, but some years bowling and riding were also available. The inevitable clubs sprang up, some with names that were something less than prosaic. The Water Babies had their motto: "Sink or swim." Many of them were also in the Minnehaha Club for boating enthusiasts. The Walking Stick eventually became the Pilgrims' Chorus, claiming to meet at 5:30 A.M. Wednesday and Saturday on "the open road." The Racquet Raisers, whose test of membership was the "ability to raise a racquet of your own," produced their own motto: "Serve others as you would *not* be served." The "F-Rs" was a jogging club for a few months, but the meaning of its mysterious initials remained a secret. Some opined "Fast Runners" or "Fat Racers" or "Flesh Reducers," but the members were said to be too out-of-breath ever to explain.

Annual tournaments between teams representing the various classes aroused much excitement and rivalry, for a silver loving cup and class honor were both at stake. Basketball, volley ball, baseball, and tennis produced the greatest interest, but the classes competed also in golf, field hockey, and soccer. Much to the dismay of the older girls, some years the academy team won the school championship in one sport or another.

Individual athletic awards were presented for this intramural competition. Members of class teams in basketball, volley ball, baseball, and tennis were given armbands. When a girl accumulated three of these, she then was eligible for a white sweater with a large S prominently displayed. Soon the rule was changed to require six armbands before a sweater could be secured, and finally the number became eight.

During the spring for several years a school-wide Field Day elicited much cheering as the classes engaged in contests such as the barrel race, potato race, fat race, lean race, walking race, wheelbarrow race, three-legged race, various relays, and a tug-of-war. One time the event was called the Fool Meet—"which," wrote one of the victorious freshmen, "was no reflection on our ability, although the Sophs thought it quite appropriate."

Although basketball games were scheduled with the Rome Athletic Club or the Rome High School girls' team, a varsity team was not permitted to play against teams coming from outside of Rome. On Washington's birthday of 1919, however, Shorter was hostess to the Atlanta Y.W.C.A. team, said to be the state champions who had not suffered defeat in six seasons. The college gymnasium was packed to its low-hanging rafters, and Shorter unexpectedly won by a score of 45 to 16. An Atlanta paper later jokingly charged that the Shorter girls had fed their visitors so many bonbons prior to the game that they were "weighed . . . down and their pep left them."

Hardly had the losing team departed before President Van Hoose was presented with a perplexing ethical issue. Should he allow his girls to face the dangers of Atlanta for a mere sporting contest? After "much discussion" he and the faculty agreed that the risk should be taken. He issued an ultimatum allowing only four men to be present—representatives of the three Atlanta newspapers and himself—and the three journalists were required to wear smoked glasses. Morgan Blake, sports editor of the *Journal* and active Baptist layman, commented: "We don't know whether Prof. Van Hoose compels his girls to wear veils on the streets and in the theaters, but we presume he does. Prof. Van Hoose's philosophy on the seclusion of the female doubtless springs from the quaint Turkish custom which was discarded by Anglo-Saxon countries a century or so ago." Blake then proceeded to secure a picture of the Shorter team sitting on the balustrade and wearing middy blouses, black bloomers, and black hose. Spread across five columns, the photograph appeared the day before the contest. Continuing his good-natured teasing of Van Hoose, Blake directed his staff artist to produce a large cartoon which was printed on the day of the game. It portrays several related events: When a man dressed as a woman is kicked out by the censor, he flies through the air contentedly saying: "A good look is worth a hard kick." Four males are crowded around one small window, having knocked out a pane of glass for clearer vision. A man waiting his turn for the binoculars with which his friend is looking down the chimney of the gymnasium complains: "You got an eyeful. It's my turn." His entranced companion can only exclaim: "Oh boy!" The game itself is shown, together with the three properly equipped reporters—and three large windows full of faces! "Fully a thousand daughters of Eve" packed the Wesley Memorial Gymnasium on that Saturday evening, March 8, including fifty from Shorter. The *Constitution* writer observed that about twice every minute the college girls would sing "Shorter," which was "a whirl of words." Because they were "a Chinese puzzle of words," he could not finally decide whether they were Greek or Hebrew! The match was much closer than the first one, but when Shorter won it 25 to 20, "those rooters from the college nearly went wild." At a banquet tendered by the Atlanta girls afterwards, "toasts were drunk to the fame of the victors and the endeavor of the losers, and all agreed with an Atlanta reporter that, 'if there is any girl's team in the land that can beat that Shorter Six, we would like for somebody to trot 'em out.'" Four months later the *Shorter College Bulletin* contained an account of the contests, primly adding: "Nothing unladylike occurred; everything at both games was carried out in the best manner possible. . . . Just what the attitude of the Faculty of Shorter will be towards future games cannot be foretold, but those in charge of the *Bulletin* hope that many other games may be played between representatives of Shorter and other institutions." Apparently the widespread publicity distressed Van Hoose, however, and Shorter rested on her laurels during the following year. In 1921 the two teams met again; Shorter lost in Atlanta and won at home. On March 21 of that year Shorter entered its first intercollegiate contest, suffering defeat from the girls of Stetson College, 26 to 11. Two games were scheduled the following year with the State Normal School at Jacksonville, Alabama, but that brief season ended with two losses for the Shorter lasses.

The first faculty-student athletic contest to be recorded took place in 1915. "The line-up for the faculty was composed largely of faculty members, but through the kindness of 'Associated Charities,' it was aided by some members of the junior and freshmen classes." Their opponents were the seniors, who proved their prowess with a whopping 26 to 10 victory. The feminine "Nifties" and the masculine "Bulldogs"

—both faculty baseball teams—later clashed in a game that was "a scream from start to finish." Male superiority was established when the ungallant Bulldogs won 10 to 9.

The Two Societies

As school opened, the older girls diligently sought out the newer ones, attempting to influence their choice of a society. Letters were often written during the summer, but under no circumstances could a pledge be made then. On alternate Saturday evenings, each society held a big party in the gymnasium, with a skit portraying the ideals of the group. By 1920 an enthroned Polymnia introduced a little "boy" (first called Peter Pan in 1922) to true happiness through music after his world-wide search had proved unsuccessful. This was followed by music and dancing that included no real boys and with elaborate refreshments. All new girls were required to attend both of these functions. Much squealing, shouting, laughing, and singing accompanied the actual process of pledging, regardless of the system employed. At the ringing of a 6:00 A.M. bell on the Monday following the second party, the girls rushed from the dormitories to the vestibule of the Academic Building where they were to sign the desired society roll. The great pushing and shoving would have suggested to an outsider that they were trying to hurt each other—but actually the society whose roll was signed first was thought to gain the greater honor, and the pledges were simply trying to bring credit to their own group. In later years the hour of the morning remained the same, but the process became a bit more sedate. The pledges lined up in the dormitory hallway, wrote their choice on a slip of paper, and placed it in an envelope. They then marched to the vestibule where a locked box was provided for the selections to be placed—after which the tumult began as they ran with great fervor to the society hall of their choice. Following this the girls could wear the colors and pin of their society and were not permitted to alter their selection. As the school grew, the size of the societies increased to an average of about 92 for the Eunomians and about 103 for the Polymnians. After 1916 the practice of having honorary members fell into disuse for about twenty years.

The proposed new society and alumnae hall produced friendly rivalry and cooperation on the part of the two groups. The building was suggested in 1913, and for three years money was raised for it. Christmas bazaars featured Indian wigwams for fortune-telling, Japanese tea rooms, and festively decorated booths with useful and attractive items for sale. An Oriental operetta produced additional revenue.

"Buy a Bale of Cotton" was the motto in Rome one fall, and the societies responded. "In went the big college wagon one day, and, when it started back to the hill, the people of Rome looked on with staring eyes. Within the wagon were two bales of cotton, and on top of these were five girls, wearing pennants and banners. The driver was a tall, stately gentleman whom some town people recognize as the man whom the college girls all love and honor." The cotton was held for a year, at a profit of only $20. All of these efforts were ultimately in vain, of course, and the girls' hopes were not realized.

Four times each year the societies joined forces to publish the *Chimes*. Each group provided an editor, associate editor, and business manager, the six young ladies working in union. The annual subscription price remained at $1 throughout these years. For four years during and after the war, the periodical was discontinued, and when it was revived in 1922 the societies no longer sponsored it.

Society meetings came regularly each Saturday evening. Everyone dressed for dinner, after which each went to the appropriate hall. Occasional outdoor bonfires and marshmallow roasts near Rotary Lake varied the locale and required somewhat different attire. The literary element of the meetings was reduced, but not forgotten. Hence, programs were given on J. M. Barrie, Bernard Shaw, William Butler Yeats, Ibsen, Tolstoy, Paul Lawrence Dunbar, William D. Howells, Henry Van Dyke, and others. Current events were at times discussed: trusts, civic improvement, child labor, municipal reforms, and woman's suffrage. The Bible, music, and sculpture also became topics of study. Impromptu debates within each society continued: "Resolved, that a Maxwell car is superior to a Buick"; "Resolved, Christmas vacation shall begin on November 12 on account of the coal shortage"; "Resolved, that love is more painful than a toothache"; "Resolved, that woman's suffrage would be beneficial." Regarding that last one, the secretary commented: "The judges gave their decision in favor of the negative. And all of us said, 'A—man' to Miss Aunspaugh's remark 'that it was better to have a voter than a vote.' " One might also wonder how serious everyone remained when a program was concluded with a "Community Sneeze."

Other recreational activities were recorded in the minute books: "We spent a jolly hour together punching peanuts," and "We had a jolly good time playing the game of Old Maid." Prior to Christmas, many programs consisted chiefly of sewing for the bazaar. After the new girls gave their society a victrola, "we just naturally bubbled over with Eunomian religion . . . ." In 1918 a society orchestra became prominent in the meetings: "The orchestra played the best loved tunes and we got regular Polymnian religion." At intervals one society would entertain the other at the Country Club, providing sports, refreshments, and dancing, or at similar functions in the more mundane gymnasium. When a society celebrated its anniversary, the other would gather out in the courtyard and give a yell in its honor.

Each society hall received special attention as to furniture and decorations; a newly purchased baby grand piano for one of them was proudly christened "Little Eunomian." Late in the period a formal installation of officers was begun, with an inaugural address by the new president and finally with a formal banquet in their honor at the General Forrest Hotel. Leaders of each society formed honorary service clubs, the Thugs for the Eunomians and the H.O.T.s for the Polymnians. By 1911 the Polymnian colors were changed for the last time, becoming red, white, and green. The Eunomians retained crimson and old gold until 1915, when the light green and dark green were finally selected.

Three long-lived Polymnian songs emerged. Appearing first in the 1916 annual were these words:

> My mammy told me
> Long time ago,
> Says, child don't you join
> Any other club you know.
> You lose all your honor
> 'Crease all your woe,
> What in this world would become of you
> Nobody knows.

No indication of authorship accompanied them. Miss Wilda Hardman, a Polymnian graduate in 1916, married Edwin McNeill Poteat, Jr., and went with her husband as a foreign missionary. Four years later she announced the arrival of their first daughter in a letter to President Van Hoose: "I write to ask you to reserve my old room (Room 200, Hall II) for Miss Harriet Alden Poteat, for September, 1937. She arrived . . . on July 5, and gives promise of being a fine vocal student at Shorter some years hence." Later to become a world-famous college professor, Baptist pastor, seminary president, and author, the scholarly father of little Harriet playfully penned lines in Kaifeng, Honan, China, that he dedicated to his daughter. Although the child died in infancy, the song lives on:

> When Peter Pan Polymnia lost
> He laid his pipes aside;
> No heart had he for melody,
> He hung his head and cried.

190

But ages later one spring morn
   Upon the Shorter Hill
Within a hundred hearts he found
   Polymnia living still.
He grasped his pipe in ecstacy
   And thrilled the woods again;
And if you listen, you can hear
   Him trill the sweet refrain.

I love the name of Polymnian
   It's the sweetest of music to me.
I love the girls of Polymnian,
   They're the girls that the world loves to see.
I love the past of Polymnian,
   Though the best is the last with Polymnian
And the red, white, and green of Polymnian
   Is the certain sign of victory.

"Polymnian Blues" was written by 1921:

Now if you want my heart to bust wide open,
Mention Polymnian Days,
Start me thinking of my friends at Shorter
And Polymnian ways. . . .

The earliest known Eunomian song was composed by 1918, but its
writer cannot be determined:

We are Eunomians, we are Eunomians,
   Well, we are Eunomians as you see.
We are Eunomians, we are Eunomians,
   Well, we are Eunomians as you see.

We run the college, we run the college,
   Well, we run the college as you see.
We run the college, we run the college,
   Well, we run the college as you see.

So you must be a wearer of the green
   If you want to be the only one that's seen
      on the campus.
Oh, you must be a wearer of the green
   If you want to be the only one that's seen.

At about the same time, two others appeared. One declared:

Oh, you don't know how nice you have to be
   In order to be a Eunomian;
Never say or think you know it all—
   Stop, look, listen, keep mum, lay low.
Girls, as a rule, stick to lessons and to school
   And never yet have they broken a rushing rule.
Oh, you don't know how nice you have to be
   In order to be a Eunomian.

191

> Eunomian born, Eunomian bred,
>   And when we die we'll be Eunomian dead.
> So rah, rah, Eunomians, rah, rah, Eunomians,
>   Rah, rah, rah, Eunomians, rah, rah, Eunomians,
> Rah, rah, Eunomians, rah, rah, rah!

The other admitted:

> We love new Shorter,
> Polymnians with the rest.
> We love every sunbeam
> That shimmers on your breast.
> But bless you people—
> We love Eunomians best.

Competition between the societies was expressed in three annual events, the basketball game, the spelling match, and the debate. Held on Thanksgiving Day, the basketball game required decorations, songs, and yells by each side, and committees were appointed weeks in advance to prepare them. A silver loving cup was offered to the victor, which added to the intensity of feeling. Although the custom was broken in 1918 at the request of the faculty and president—evidently the spirit was too keen—it was renewed in 1921 without the loving cup as a prize.

Soon after the Christmas vacation there was for a few years an intersociety spelling match. Held in the auditorium on Saturday evening, it pitted fifty girls from each group against each other. President Van Hoose gave out the words from the *Blue Back Speller*, and the two matches whose results are known found a Eunomian standing with him at the end.

Said to be "*the* great event of the college year," the annual debate was reintroduced in 1910. Just before Christmas of that year an animated group filled the auditorium with bright banners and pennants, with "cute songs," and with "happy hurrahs." The question for debate was "Resolved, Men of thought have been more beneficial to the world than men of action." The jubilant Polymnian victors, who had argued the negative, received many congratulations and consumed much "delicious punch" in Eunomian hall afterwards. During commencement week the next May, the tables were turned. Professor L. R. Hogan offered a silver trophy to the winner of a debate on the topic, "Resolved, that immigration is detrimental to the United States." Once more a carnival spirit prevailed, and this time the Eunomians, who argued the affirmative, won. Since the year had ended with a tie, it was decided that henceforth only one championship debate would be held annually near the time of commencement.

On the new campus the practice persisted with renewed force. Each society elected its two strongest debaters who spent months investigating the question. One young lady resigned as society president in order to devote more time to her preparation—to be a debater was more important in her estimation than being president! Highly respected by their societies, the debaters received flowers and jewelry and eventually were honored at banquets held in a downtown dining room. The librarian once announced that they could check out books at any time. Committees spent many hours writing songs and yells—which were commercially printed in little leaflets—and planning for the decoration of the auditorium. As the debate grew closer, society meetings and the nightly "rec" periods were devoted to practicing these songs and yells under the direction of the cheerleaders.

The interest was intense as the groups marched in, the Eunomians occupying one side of the auditorium and the Polymnians the other. Society banners were everywhere in evidence. For half an hour the songs and yells foretold victory. After the audience assembled, the speakers and judges, headed by President Van Hoose, took seats on the stage. The debaters marshalled their arguments, the judges rendered their decision, and the air was filled with the cheers of the triumphant side.

Topics for debate varied widely from year to year: the superiority of coeducational schools, international arbitration, the power of the press to shape public opinion, American neutrality regarding the war, government ownership of railroads, immigration laws regarding Orientals, Philippine independence by 1927, and others. The previous losers selected the topic for several years, but finally it was proposed by the faculty.

Eunomian success was indicated by the fact that the Hogan trophy became their permanent property when they won it four years in a row, 1914 to 1917. Thereafter the loving cup was provided by Van Hoose, but no succession of victories was forthcoming.

Classes, Generations, and the Crook

An official pronouncement quite plainly said, "Hazing shall not be permitted"—but the girls did not always observe it. At times hazing was quiet and gentle. Accepting the suggestion of a seemingly sympathetic sophomore, some of the unsuspecting freshmen decided to show their superiority by occupying a Senior Table one meal. They laid their plans carefully, arriving at the dining room door well before meal time. Much to their delight, they were invited to stand just inside the door, rather than out in the hall. When the bell rang, they immediately rushed for the coveted table and exultantly took possession. Strangely enough, no one contested their claim. As the waiters distributed the food, they became increasingly aware that their table was not being served. Eventually their growing uneasiness was dispelled when Garnett, the headwaiter, came out of the kitchen, with his tray high in the air. When it was lowered and its contents placed before them, they discovered that they had been served—baby bottles with nipples.

At other times hazing was boisterous and rough. In January of 1912 the commandment was published: "All Freshmen are expected to wear their hair in two plaits down their backs for three days. No curls or kinks." All went smoothly until the second day, when the freshman president appeared with "puffs, curls and rats." A fight broke out in the dining room as the sophomores attempted to take down her hair and the freshmen attempted to protect their comrade. The dean and the lady principal halted the affray with a stern warning, and "to this day the Freshmen and Sophomores have been on friendly terms"—but only for that year! About 5:00 A.M. a later group of sophomores decorated each sleeping freshman with a green F on her cheek, and those who bravely wiped it off soon had another one in its place. Another year the five freshmen officers were taken to the gymnasium about 4:00 A.M., "where they performed for us," after which they and all the others received green and black Fs on their faces. "The 'Discipline Committee' and Dr. Van Hoose were scandalized. . . . We learned ere long that our fun with the Freshies was considered 'quite a serious offense,' but, after keeping us in suspense over a month, the faculty decided to let us remain at Shorter." A "Hunt For Shoes Party" was the feature once as the sophomores invaded the freshmen's rooms and removed every shoe that could be found. "These were all carried to a safe hiding place and next morning the Freshmen were invited to select their shoes from the huge pile in the court"—some four or five hundred. By 1921 the placards, the clothes worn inside out, the mismatched shoes, and the bowing to sophomores appeared.

Each class quickly organized itself with officers who led in various exploits. Cloth class banners were soon produced with the year of graduation proudly displayed. Each class staged a Stunt Night: a freshman circus, a sophomore rendition of the "average" faculty meeting, a junior showing of moving pictures borrowed from the Bonita Theater with their own skits between reels (including one entitled "Reveries of a Bachelor"), a senior vaudeville show, and many others. Some of the traditional events came to be sponsored by the classes:

194

the freshmen were responsible for the George Washington birthday party; the sophomores, for the Valentine party; the juniors, for the Thanksgiving program; and the seniors, for the Halloween festivities. It became a matter of class pride to arrange a better program than any earlier one. To paint one's class numerals on the water tower brought glory to that class, and disagreements between classes on and about the tower would often bring President Van Hoose out, roaring like a lion and ordering them to stop. Of course the classes vied constantly for sports championships and in many money-raising ventures. Even before the senior year, other events occurred that gave the classes a sense of identity—a freshman picnic, a sophomore fudge party, or a junior play called "Hiawatha," for example.

The two generations emerged during the year 1915–1916, although the origin of their names remains unknown. As freshmen and sophomores, the class of 1917 had won the basketball cup. In their zeal to retain it a third year, they held many pep rallies to fire up their team. They became the first to call themselves High-Minded, composing a little song that they often used:

> Junior Class is high-minded,
> Believe to my soul they're double-jinted,
> They can work and don't mind it—all day long.

Apparently the song possessed the desired power, for they won that coveted cup two more times before leaving Shorter undefeated. In subsequent years the words necessarily were altered slightly and were handed down in the spring. The sophomores that year (the class of 1918) were the first to call themselves Whoop-Em-Ups and the first to issue a class paper, the *Blazer*. Full of now-obscure personal references, it was initially printed when one of the generation classes had a midnight feast that went undetected by the other generation. Their musical skills were evident in a long song that concluded: "And when at last we come to sit with chillun round the door, we'll teach them that the thing to do is Whoop-Em-Up some more." Other competition between generations involved generation flags and the water tower. One Whoop-Em-Up flag was removed from the tower, whereupon the High-Mindeds held mock burnings and funerals for it, finally returning it on Class Day.

Within each generation there were festivities. The juniors gave the freshmen a Mother Goose party, while another year the freshmen gave the juniors a Christmas party, complete with a Santa Claus, dancing, and a program by the hostesses. The senior-sophomore relationship was stronger and will be described later.

A combination of class and generation rivalry was abundantly evident in two Shorter institutions that emerged in this period, the midnight feast and the crook. Each class planned a feast late at night—in a dormitory basement, behind the Music Building, in the gymnasium, in the power house, down the hill on front campus, or any other place that could be kept a secret. As the night approached, food would be accumulated and carefully hidden from the other generation. At the appointed time the adventure would begin. One junior wrote: "Doors open, coated figures appear along the corridors. There is a rustling of soft silks, a patter of slipper-clad feet, excited whispers, a gathering of the clan in the vestibule, and then out into the cold night air they go. Across a boardwalk and into the sheltering darkness of another building. Up dark stairs and then—the goal of their desires! A room, dimly lighted by candles and a table literally groaning under its weight of good things." When the feast was not discovered, the gloating participants would issue a *Blazer*, if they belonged to the Whoop-Em-Up generation, or perhaps sing of it in the courtyard, even before breakfast. One year they revealed their success for the first time on their class page in the *Argo*. The opposition might get wind of an impending feast and "imprison" the class president in her room by watching the door. Since a feast could not be held without her, at least once she made her exit through a third story window, fashioning a rope out of sheets. Of course the feasts were often discovered—one class declared that "we had to whip half the school before we got into the gym to our food." In these cases, the feast was held as scheduled, but with a decided reduction of fervor, and the other generation might distribute a poem at breakfast next morning boasting of its detective work. The greater honor came when the opposing generation slept through the event, but in any case the food was not left unconsumed.

The crook was given to the class of 1914 by a Rome businessman, Elmer Grant, who was a son-in-law of D. B. Hamilton. Made from a single two-foot oak plank, it was initially marked only by a metallic ring reading "Shorter College 1914." At first only a few simple rules governed the seniors as they hid it and the juniors as they sought it:

1. At least $1\frac{1}{2}$" of the crook must show.
2. The crook may not be taken by a junior when a senior is touching it.
3. No force may be used when its location has been discovered.

For two years the seniors avoided disgrace as the juniors vainly combed the attics, the organ loft, the rafters of the gymnasium, the basements, and the space under the board walk leading from the Music Building to the dormitories.

Then came Saturday evening, May 27, 1916! Earlier on that fateful day the seniors had moved the crook from the ventilation shaft in one of the bathrooms on the third floor of Hall Two because of a rumor that the juniors suspected its location. The senior guarding the newly hidden crook was visited by a junior friend who wearily sat down on her bed and leaned back against the wall. She could feel the crook, but because the first rule had been violated, could not see it! Trying to remain nonchalant, but fearful lest her expression betray her, she soon left the room. Eight juniors were quietly alerted, and during the Grand Concert that evening slipped back to their rooms and changed from their formal gowns into middy blouses and bloomers. Two of them immediately went to the room where the crook was hidden, while the others occupied a position on the ground under the window. Abandoning subtlety and the third rule, one of the juniors grabbed the senior who was allowed to be standing guard. The smaller senior bit her attacker hard enough for scars still to show more than fifty years later! The other junior could not extricate the crook, so she pulled the whole mattress across the room and pushed it out the window. The girls on the ground quickly disappeared with their prize, hiding it in the woods at the rear of the campus. When the struggling senior was freed, she frantically rushed down the corridor screaming at the top of her voice: "Seniors, seniors, the crook, the crook!" The chorus in the auditorium was in the midst of a song, which was somehow brought to a proper conclusion. The seniors then scrambled from the stage, out the door, down the steps, and over to their hapless comrade. The class president recalled that in her haste she lost the heel of her shoe. President Van Hoose tried to restore some semblance of order in the auditorium, but the uproar was too great and the concert ended precipitately. The usually calm Van Hoose quickly learned the names of the juniors involved in the escapade and called them into his office. One of them later remarked, "He jumped us good," as he refused to credit them with innocence when they insisted that *they* had not made the noise that broke up the concert. The seniors were so incensed at what they considered an unfair departure from the rules that on Class Day their president firmly announced: "It is now time for the capping ceremony. We will omit it today, for reasons that the public is not interested in. The college people know the circumstances quite well." Many students were so opposed to the juniors' behavior that the eight were soon being called the "Reprobates"! Undaunted by opposition, they cheerfully accepted the name and posed for a picture that occupied an entire page of the 1917 annual. While not expelling the juniors, President Van Hoose was so annoyed that he confiscated the crook until every student then at Shorter had left. Thus, it was not again hidden until the spring of 1921.

When the crook was concealed in the gymnasium in 1922, two versions of the story apparently resulted. One says: "A word dropped by a senior was enough to give the juniors a clue and in less than no time the juniors were in the gym. Grace Marie started out on a search with the thoroughness of Hawkshaw himself and she almost found it but the seniors came tumbling in and a scrap ensued. Was violence used? The question was never settled in the heated debate that took place afterward." The other says: "Another free-for-all happened when a chance shot with a basket-ball dislodged it from the rafters in the gym. That was the one and only time [except for 1916] that the Crook was ever captured by the Juniors—and they had to give it up as a penalty for the following scrap." In either case, the juniors were permitted no claim of success.

Other Forms of Recreation

For two years recreation was afforded to about one hundred girls by the five national sororities that Van Hoose permitted, Phi Mu, Sigma Iota Chi, Phi Mu Gamma, Alpha Kappa Psi, and Alpha Sigma Alpha. At first he expressed the feeling that they were "exceedingly helpful in aiding in the maintenance of a high standard of scholarship and a fine spirit of discipline in the college." One of them contributed a one-year scholarship at Shorter and pledged $75 in the Greater Shorter campaign. Each was given a room on the second floor of the Music Building, and the members purchased furniture, rugs, and draperies to furnish them. However, in the spring of 1912 Emmet Stephens, a missionary on furlough from China, preached on campus and expressed opposition to them. For some months Van Hoose and the faculty had been harboring suspicions concerning their utility, and Stephens' eloquence simply hastened a decision. The girls were consulted individually and collectively as the new policy was explained to them. Even though many quietly objected to the ban, they agreed not to voice objection. When he received outside criticism, Van Hoose found it necessary to write an extended defense that was carried in the Atlanta *Journal*.

Purely local in nature, other social clubs proliferated, many of which flourished briefly and then silently withered away. Some were restricted to girls coming from one state (the Mississippi Crusaders, the Alligators of Florida, the Texas Club, and others), from individual localities (the Seven Roman Geese, the Atlanta Boosters, That Commerce Crowd), or from a former school (the Locust Grove Institute Club). Some were named for a characteristic common to the members: the Carrot Tops, the Sisters' Club, the Mary Club, the Preachers' Daughters' Club (their aim was "To prove that we are real human beings"), the Old Shorter Club, the Kat Club (made up of six Katherines and Kathleens), or the Doctors' Daughters' Club. Formed about 1915, the Granddaughters of Shorter was comprised of girls whose mothers or aunts had attended Shorter before them. Coming from an earlier day, the Kid Club persisted. Other groups suggested amorous interests: the Diamond Seekers' Club, the Maidens All Forlorn Club, the True Loves, the Disappointed Lovers' Club, the Might Have Beens, or the Why Knots. Ominous names abounded: the Black Hand Club, the Kann-Ables, the Snakes, the Mummy Club, the Imps, and the Flashlight Club. The Susie Dahms soon became the Several Dahms, and inexpensive club rings were purchased by some of the members. Other groups are preserved only in now-meaningless names and a few smiling faces captured in annual photographs.

The girls eagerly anticipated numerous events that had become traditional on the hill. October 31 was President Van Hoose's birthday, and the evening meal was always a banquet in his honor where the girls presented him a gift. Directed by the seniors, the Halloween party that followed was elaborately executed. Colorful invitations were sent—perhaps a red pasteboard devil with news of a trip to Hades. Through the eerie darkness of the Music Building the girls were led, hearing clanking chains, the rattle of bones, muffled screams, and "horrible screechy music." Entering the black gymnasium they might be greeted by a clammy hand, or even by the Prince of Darkness himself. One year a fiery furnace loomed before them, and each was consigned to its flames. On the other side were corn, vines, leaves, jack-o'-lanterns, bats, and black cats. Palm readers, fortune-tellers, and Egyptian soothsayers were present, as well as nuts and fruit for those still hungry. The program might include ghost stories—and four departed spirits who had come back to tell their doleful stories: senior privilege had died because of being abused; a senior of twelve years earlier, because of dissipation in the dance hall ("She seemed satisfied with her fate," one spectator noted); a senior of today, because of overwork; and the spirit of the swimming pool, because of this unhappy condition:

199

Oh! long drawn out my life has been,
I did deserve a pension.
A slow and horrible death I died,
I died of good intention.

On this particular occasion the girls had been led through the woods behind the college, with ghosts standing behind trees and bodies hanging from branches. Through the covered bridge near Rotary Lake they passed, "which, too, was inhabited by ghosts and demons, who uttered shrieks of delight as they spattered the poor victims with blood, worms and other disagreeable and horrible things." The ultimate destination was a clearing and a large fire, surrounded by shadows and darkness from which emerged the quartet of ghouls.

Because Thanksgiving was a one-day holiday, the dormitory girls all remained on campus. A chapel service was always held before the main meal that began at 2:00 P.M. The dining room would be decorated by the juniors with a carpet of gaily colored leaves, cardboard birds flitting everywhere from invisible wires, and make-believe trees. In the center of each table might be a brown sugar turkey surrounded with mints. The printed menu showed an abundance of roast turkey, cranberry sauce, oyster dressing, candied yams, Neopolitan ice cream, and other delicacies. Toasts were offered from different tables to Sir Gobbler, Miss Grammar (who was a housemother, not a course of study), the juniors, the faculty and trustees, and to "ourselves." Often a skit was presented, as well as music by Nixon's or Rhodes' orchestra. At times an evening program would be given in the auditorium, an original play or motion pictures.

Christmas was a time of sponsoring the tree for the West Rome children, of packing one's bags, and of catching the "Shorter Special" to Atlanta. In the midst of such preparations, the annual Christmas dinner did not seem to impress the girls as much as other banquets. On every table might stand a miniature tree, "gloriously bedecked with tinsel and lighted tapers. But in the center of the dining room stood the big tree, the cynosure of all eyes." A multi-course meal would be pleasantly interrupted by toasts and concluded by Santa Claus and his well-filled sack. For several years the girls of the German class greeted him with "O Tannenbaum, O Tannenbaum." The dormitories closed during the vacation; a few girls might stay at Maplehurst. One faculty member opened a present on Christmas morning, later writing to the student who had given it to her: "I hope you are having a merry Christmas. It is *dull* enough on Shorter Hill without our girls. But we try to enjoy the dullness with quiet content of spirit."

Dan Cupid was never a stranger on campus, but the sophomores made sure that none forgot him on Valentine Day. Even though young men were conspicuous by their absence, the evening meal was attended by the girls in all their finery. Hearts and Kewpies covered the walls and hung from the ceiling; each table was splendid with flowers or a large china Kewpie. While the meal was in progress, sophomore Fairies distributed valentines and gifts to "their" seniors, and later to others in the room. An original skit might feature Prince Charming as he wooed and won Princess Winsome; their wedding day was portrayed with the King and Queen of Hearts, the attendants, the nymphs, and Cupid. In later years the entire assemblage would gather in the gymnasium for an evening of dancing to the strains of a visiting orchestra.

Giving rise to a student's note in her scrapbook, "Don't we wish we had more George Washingtons, though, so we would have more holidays and big dinners," the fourth traditional celebration came on February 22, under the auspices of the freshmen. At times the gymnasium was a colorful red, white, and blue, as bunting and flags were everywhere. The Virginia reel and the minuet were danced by chivalrous "gentlemen" adorned with buckles and frills and their stately damsels with powdered hair and voluminous skirts. In the year "MIXCXV," as the printed program proclaimed, "Ye doors will be open at early candle light and ye play will begin at eight o'clock by ye Academic clock." After this performance in the auditorium, "Good folks will join ye actors in ye academic building" for a reception. Eventually the center of attention came to be the dinner, where decorations would feature Mount Vernon, colonial dames, spring flowers, and perhaps a liberty bell. Following one meal a skit pictured a very skeptical little Jimmy and Mary Jane who soon were convinced by Uncle Sam and Columbia that the man of the hour was indeed without guile.

The first May Day festival came in 1913 with Louise Bennet as the queen elected by the student body. Held on the tennis court and directed by the departments of physical training, expression, and music, it consisted of a coronation, choral music, a grand march, dances from Denmark, Russia, Ireland, and Scotland, a Maypole dance, and a concluding song by the assembled crowd, "Hail, Dear Old Shorter." The pagentry was soon moved to a clearing near Maplehurst, reached by a lengthy procession down the winding road. One participant was Richard the Lion-Hearted, whose horse was so frightened by the commotion that it had to be led by a servant. She later admitted that she was even more frightened than her steed and not at all lionhearted! Later the production was moved back up to the quadrangle between

201

the Academic and Music buildings. One year the May queen had fallen asleep, to be awakened only by some fortunate prince. The Prince of Gooseland, Mother Hubbard, Red Riding Hood, Jack Horner, various freshman fairies, junior troubadours, and others tried in vain to rouse her with singing and dancing. At length the Prince of Love and his followers, portrayed by the sophomores, were successful. Taken to the throne, she and her prince were crowned, after which they presided over the Maypole dance. In the early twenties, a village green "in Merrie England" during the time of George III was the scene of a visit by the princess of a nearby castle. The program included several national dances, a gypsy fortune-teller, a charming strolling violinist, a dainty minuet, the gayest of madrigals, and the winding of the huge Maypole.

Other events on campus provided diversion for the girls. Annually a glee club from Alabama, Mercer, Emory, Chicago, or Vanderbilt would sing in the auditorium—precipitating a mad rush for the front seats—and would be honored by a reception in the parlors. Of one such affair, it was written: "So enjoyable did it prove that when the bell rang for departure, the boys lingered until it was truly said of them:—'It's not their fault if they didn't turn to salt!' " On other evenings the auditorium was equipped for movies that were considered to be thrilling and entertaining, including "Ragamuffin," "David Crockett," "Going Straight," and "The Dark Silence." "As they must pass the 'College Board of Censors,' they are always good." Back in the dormitory rooms some of the girls dared to play cards (even though the handbook was temporarily silent on the matter, the administration's attitude was largely negative), and mock weddings might be performed for the amusement of those on the floor.

Young men were allowed on campus under careful surveillance by the girls *and* the faculty, albeit for different reasons. With written permission from her parent or guardian, a student could receive a young man two evenings a month. If she were a senior, this privilege extended to any evening of the week. What this usually meant in fact was that the two could sit in the parlor and talk. When chaperoned by a member of the faculty or staff, she could have dinner, go to ride, or attend the theater with a young man. Sunday visitors were discouraged.

The coming of soft feathery flakes of snow made happy the hearts of the Shorter pupils, some of whom had never seen snow before. Building snowmen, engaging in snow battles, and rolling each other in the snow, the girls became hilarious. One Florida girl gleefully exclaimed: "Why is this course not in the catalogue? Of course it is an elective, but if it were put in the catalogue and required, I believe more girls would come to Shorter." The picture of one faculty sculptor and his creation was included in an annual: the seven-foot-tall, bald-headed snowman wore a coat and vest, and his right hand reached into a pocket. Under General Gaines and Captain Hogan a decisive battle on the "Plain of Snow" was savagely fought. "Girls rolled as cannon in the snow, snow balls rained as shot and shell, panic and confusion followed, down went Captain Hogan's army in defeat, while the victorious army marched off singing." The slopes were ideal for sledding, and college dustpans made suitable sleds—even though the girls would arouse the displeasure of the maids and the lady principal for "ruining college property" and would get blistered when they accidentally slid off.

Although Van Hoose preferred that his girls remain on campus as much as possible, they utilized manifold methods of transportation when they did leave. Walking down "a beautiful path through woods" to the J. J. Conn and Son store in West Rome that advertised itself as the "Shorter Girls' Store," they could obtain "everything for feasts." Others left in a large, green, fourteen-passenger automobile that might take them to Cave Spring, Chickamauga Park, or Lookout Mountain and the Table Rock for a day's outing. At least one group departed in a mule-drawn wagon with a large Eunomian banner draped over the side—of the mule.

The method of departure most frequently used, however, was the trolley car. Steps that were at first wooden and later brick led down the hill near Hall One to the car stop, which eventually was a tiny frame structure. A spur from Shorter Avenue to this spot had been constructed in 1911 to facilitate the building of the campus; thereafter Car No. 121, holding about fourteen passengers, plied back and forth all day long between the college and the transfer station on the main line that extended from Broad Street, across the Fifth Avenue bridge, and down Shorter Avenue to Pop Skull (Burnett Ferry Road). When the girls wanted the genial Ivan R. Carlson and his conveyance to come up the hill from its waiting position near Shorter Avenue, they pushed a button on the post at the foot of the steps and soon he would be seen slowly making the ascent. If the weather were threatening, he would warn his passengers: "You'd better go back and get your storm sticks." Often he would loan the girls their fare, 5¢ from the college to Broad Street, and always he would carefully look up the steps before starting the descent. Once as the car was pulling away, a rather large matron at the college hastened down the steps shouting: "Mr. Carlson, hold the car." Soon thereafter the amused girls were calling out: "Oh, Mr. Kyarlson, please hold that kyar while I put on my kyarset to go to

203

Kyartersville." Only once did the trolley car come down the hill so fast that it jumped the track. Unknown to Mr. Carlson, a company employee had added grease to a curve on the route, but fortunately no girls were in the car and the kindly driver escaped with only a few scratches.

One could always tell the Shorter girls on Broad Street, for they carefully dressed up to leave campus. Always in groups of at least two, except for seniors who could go alone, they went to town only one afternoon a week during their freshman year, two afternoons a week during their sophomore year, and any afternoon except Saturday thereafter. Of course there was virtually no thought of their leaving campus in the evening. Once in town they might visit the Shropshire Book Store for the purchase of Shorter stationery, pennants, and banners. They were invited to "wait for your car here." At the Griffin Hardware Company they picked up athletic goods and chafing dishes, while at McWilliams and Company they could secure canned goods, coffee and tea, and bread that was already sliced. "Our new Shorter jewelry" was on display at Wyatt Jewelry Company, and "just the kind of hats the Shorter girls like" could be found at Miss King and Company Millinery. A special invitation brought the girls to Taylor and Norton Drug Store, where the guests were served free ice cream amidst a gold and white color scheme. The ever-popular Hale-Jervis Company advertised: "The best to be had at a Soda Fount—always on tap for the Shorter girls." Public movies were still questioned by the college authorities, but the freshmen were permitted to attend the Amuzu, the Elite, the Bonita, and the Strand twice monthly, while the upperclassmen could attend once weekly. In 1916 "The Birth of a Nation" came to Rome; one young lady preserved the twelve-page printed brochure that was produced especially for the local showing. On Sunday any student—even a freshman—could spend the entire day with a friend in Rome, with the lady principal's permission, of course.

The new campus could hardly be reached by the flood waters that visited Rome, but what of the girls who came to class from their homes in town or the dormitory girls who wanted to go downtown? The levees had not yet been erected, and a wooden railroad trestle stretched from the intersection of Shorter and Second avenues all the way to Broad Street, paralleling Second Avenue. During a flood all trolley car service was suspended west of the rivers. The more energetic town students could walk the trestle or take a canoe or bateau and then trudge through the mud and rain for the last uphill mile. Many of them just did not bother to attend classes when such an unexceptionable "excused absence" presented itself. The hardier souls living on campus might also walk the trestle, although others waited at the intersection and hailed the incoming train that would carry them to the Broad Street station. A group of students had to catch the morning train in order to attend a meeting of the College Press Association in Gainesville. Wrote one of them: "No streetcars were running because of the high water, and we couldn't walk the trestle with all our luggage. The solution was that the four of us, with our suitcases, were loaded into one of the wagons used for hauling coal, and Dr. Van Hoose sat with us, on improvised seats while the two mules nearly swam through the muddy water, which came up to the bed of the wagon."

Seniors and Commencement

"The torment of the flowing robe and choker which braced the head at the proper angle to balance the cap with the tassel that just would stay in my eye" was one of the darker elements in an otherwise thrilling year. The seniors were formally invested with their caps and gowns at the Class Day exercises held at the close of their junior year or at a chapel ceremony conducted by President Van Hoose at the start of their final year. Shorter Sunday at First Baptist Church continued to be observed; one girl claimed that "everyone . . . almost choked to death before they got back," but no fatality was ever publicized. Starting in 1914 they had their own Senior Hall, where they constantly partied each other, and Senior Tables in the dining room.

Seniors were accorded special privileges that varied from year to year. They could leave the campus without companion or chaperone. Permitted to sit up until 11:00 P.M., they had to be in their own rooms and completely quiet. Cooking could be done any day of the week—either in their rooms or in the kitchenette on their floor—and they were not required to attend any meals. "Young men callers" could be received any evening in the week. The lower classes were instructed: "Remember to show seniors deference; let them pass in and out of doors and streetcars first; be considerate of the rights that are justly theirs."

Late in her junior year each girl selected a freshman who became "her sophomore" the following fall. One wrote: "That night we asked our Sophomores! The thrill that comes once in a life time and all that! Why, I was positively ill until mine accepted." This was sometimes followed by early breakfast the next morning at the Busy Bee Cafe. Eventually it became customary for each senior to allow her

205

sophomore to wear her class ring, usually making the presentation in an unexpected way. In the fall of 1917 each robed senior entered her sophomore's room at midnight and "in a sepulchral voice" commanded: "Get up and come with me!" Assembling in the gymnasium, the two classes were made one by a mock wedding in which the rings were properly given and received—the precursor of the later Whoop-Em-Up Wedding! In another year the sleeping sophomores were ordered to dress and go immediately to a given society hall, ostensibly to attend a special meeting of the Student Council. Met at the hall without a light, each was told to enter the darkened room without speaking to a soul. The frightened sophomores "tried to think of everything they had done since entering Shorter and wondered whether or not any of the list was a shipping offense. Suddenly the lights flashed on and the Seniors, robed in caps and gowns, marched in singing . . . . In a very few minutes each Senior had her Sophomore fitting her Senior ring on her finger."

The two classes feted each other throughout the year. At times the sophomores held a reception at the Country Club, a Valentine party in the gymnasium where hearts and blue birds were profuse, or a May banquet at a downtown dining room. One year the seniors were presented a victrola for their sitting room. Another time the sophomores entertained with a possum hunt that succeeded in treeing two possums, but concluded with a wiener roast. Usually the seniors treated the sophomores; one year it was a hike that culminated in a huge bonfire and toasted marshmallows, pickles, coffee, and mincemeat pie.

Individual seniors kept scrapbooks; the class of 1916 had a "Shorter College Memory Book" prepared with a college seal engraved on the brown leather cover. Some classes selected a mascot, Frances Marion Gaines, who had been born on campus just before school started in 1911, or Mary Elizabeth Van Hoose, whom the president and his wife adopted in 1920. For the first time the 1913 *Argo* printed a list of "Hoo's Hoo at Shorter"—Sweetest, Cutest, Smartest, Best Musician, Best All-Around, Faculty Pet, Most Indifferent, and others—and many of the girls were seniors. Four years later the use of pictures was initiated, but still not all were seniors. In 1920 the seniors excitedly found a photograph of their class in the rotogravure section of the Atlanta *Journal.* Several years the seniors presented a gift to their alma mater, the entrance posts at Shorter Avenue, the lamps atop them, and contributions of $1,000 and $1,050. As yet, the average graduate was about twenty years of age.

Commencement exercises extended from Friday through the following Tuesday, and the hours were busy. Beginning in 1913 the department of expression presented on Friday afternoon a play by Shakespeare, "As You Like It," "A Midsummer Night's Dream," "The Merchant of Venice," or "Twelfth Night." At the first out-of-door program "a small-sized panic was caused . . . when a section of the temporary grandstand built on the campus collapsed . . . ." The planks were only a foot or two from the ground, but "for a brief period commotion reigned." There were "a few slight bruises" and "considerable nervous shock" that caused a couple of ladies to faint. The area near the long balustrade between the Academic Building and Hall One was usually reserved for this performance.

Saturday was devoted to the annual art exhibit and reception, a domestic science exhibition, and the evening Grand Concert. Normally a painfully staid affair, the 1916 concert came to an abrupt conclusion, as has already been noted.

The baccalaureate sermon on Sunday morning was moved from the First Baptist Church to the college auditorium, while the early evening service was held in the auditorium or on the lawn. Most of the graduates would doubtless have agreed with one of their number who stated: "It is insufferably hot, as all Commencement Sundays are, and the advice falls on unhearing ears. Our thoughts are all of the future." The entire faculty marched in caps and gowns with the seniors for the first time in 1921. Speakers for this and the Tuesday ceremony were always visitors of some eminence, including Professor John R. Sampey of Southern Baptist Theological Seminary, Professor W. L. Poteat of Wake Forest College, and President Rufus W. Weaver of Mercer University.

Over the weekend many of the students in the lower classes were expected to leave Rome so that the alumnae could occupy their rooms in connection with the annual reunion on Monday. In addition to the business meeting, this usually included a banquet at Maplehurst, in the school dining room, or at the General Forrest Hotel.

Surrounded by the sophomores singing "Hail, Dear Old Shorter" and carrying the daisy chain, the robed seniors marched down the hill late Monday afternoon to occupy the front porch of Maplehurst for their Class Day program. One of the less ambitious sophomores commented concerning the daisies, "How it hurt to have to get up so early for two weeks before commencement until we finally picked twenty tubs of the abominable things"—in those days the flowers grew in such abundance near Rotary Lake that the girls did not have to leave the college grounds to find them. No class stones were placed and no books or theses were burned. Amidst both laughter and tears, the class history, poem, prophecy, and last will and testament were read.

In a ring ceremony the sophomores returned those prized possessions, and some years each senior gave her sophomore a silver ring showing the college seal. Usually the senior president presented a cap and gown to the junior president and the crook was passed down to the junior class. Singing the "Alma Mater" concluded the program.

The tempestuous Eunomian-Polymnian debate occupied the center of attention on Monday evening until 1914, after which it was scheduled earlier in the spring. Taking its place was the senior play, always an original production written by two or three class playwrights and always kept a dark secret until curtain time. Printed in the 1915 annual, the first script was titled "Jean's Quest for the Jewel" and was an allegorical drama depicting the heroine's four years at college. Facing opposition from such terrors as Classification Committee, Discipline Committee, Sophomore, Mathematics, History, Bible, Chemistry, Psychology, French, and Economics, she nevertheless relished pleasant times with Basketball, Feast, and Privileges. Much to Jean's delight, Commencement finally appeared, saying: "Come, let me lead you to the Kingdom of Happiness." She was then wed to Prince Charming, who rather incongruously symbolized the benefits of the bachelor's degree.

The presentation of the 1917 play, "See It Through," posed a moral problem to the strict President Van Hoose. How could male characters be properly portrayed if only females were members of the cast? In the past he had permitted a young lady playing such a part to wear male attire—with a long skirt instead of trousers. Finally one senior decided that this should be changed, introducing trousers into the rehearsals. When Van Hoose got wind of it, he placed a brief note on the bulletin board: "Dr. Van Hoose desires to see Miss Massengill." Their heated discussion was concluded by his decree: "I will not allow this. You cannot give it." Soon the seniors voted to go on with the play, trousers and all. When their committee informed him of their intention, they found him as adamant as before. After threatening to take the matter to court, they departed, an angry and tearful group of girls. The next day Van Hoose countered in a surprising fashion as he again called for Polly: "Well, you've won your point—go on and let your men characters wear trousers!" However, a general rule was soon passed: "Students are not allowed to wear men's apparel except when taking part in a program authorized and directed by the head of the school of expression and approved by the Lady Principal."

Starting in 1919, the production was moved to the city auditorium on Saturday evening, and a wider audience was reached. That year the play concerned Catholic-Protestant relations, being titled "The Mid-

Wall of Partition" and producing quite a furor in the community. After viewing the dress rehearsal Van Hoose commented to a newspaper reporter: "I'd rather be the president of Shorter with this senior class than the president of the United States."

The stately graduation service on Tuesday morning provided the climax. During the organ prelude the graduates, faculty members, and stage party marched to their places. After the invocation, several musical selections were rendered by the MacDowell Choral Club and instrumentalists. Of the main address that followed, an honest young lady wrote: "Someone speaks, but we do not hear it." Van Hoose then conferred the degrees, whereupon the diplomas were awarded, the hoods adjusted, and the tassels changed. During his brief talk to the seniors, Van Hoose could become affectionately blunt. A member of the class of 1917 remembered his saying: "Young ladies,—you are my dearest possession in life. You have been my naughty child, you have demanded my closest attention and care. But even as parents love their mischievous children, and must punish them most, you have been on my mind and heart for four years and I am loath to let you go. There have been many stormy passages to brave with you, but it was all a labor of love. I congratulate you, my beloved and mischievous class, as you go forth from your Alma Mater. May you carry on as nobly as you have begun." A hymn, the "Alma Mater," and the benediction concluded the morning. No doubt many a senior's ring still seemed large on her finger, although perhaps not as large as the lump in her throat.

In the course of commencement week, several special awards were made for meritorious work in general scholarship, religion, and art. The Phi Sigma Alpha Honor Society was organized in the spring of 1917, composed of girls possessing superior character, scholarship, and leadership abilities. Four seniors were selected—Martha Galt, Annevic Greene, Annie Blount Moseley, and Susie Smith—as well as one junior, Ida Bell Ray. Soon its membership was restricted only to those seniors who had achieved a grade of at least ninety percent during the last three years at Shorter and who had received no failing grade. For an essay regarding Sunday school work, the Sarah A. Faust Medal was first given in 1915 to Reba Pitman by George M. Faust of Crawford, Georgia, in honor of his mother, the former Miss Sarah Ann Raines. This endowed award continues to be made annually, but now it is in cash and is for an essay on any religious subject. For five years after 1915, J. C. Massee, an influential Baptist pastor from Dayton, Ohio, presented a medal to the student who wrote the best essay on some Biblical topic, but none of the winners is now known. Named for

Miss Susie Buttolph of Marietta, a Shorter graduate in 1881, the Buttolph Medal for excellence in art was first given in 1914, with Louise
Moultrie as the recipient. After being discontinued in 1922, it was
again awarded from 1934 to 1958.

The Alumnae Association

With a total membership of about two hundred, the Alumnae Association eventually developed branches in Atlanta and Columbus, in
addition to the one in Rome. Comprising half of the total, the latter
was by far the most active. About fifteen ladies provided significant
leadership in Rome, including Miss Elizabeth Harris (class of 1898),
Miss Alida Printup (class of 1893), Mrs. Robert Wyatt (née Miss
Elizabeth Betts, class of 1916), Mrs. A. D. Moore (née Miss Jessie
Hine, class of 1909), and Mrs. Mark A. Cooper (née Miss Sarah Joyce
King, class of 1917). After 1917 Mrs. J. P. Cooper (née Miss Alice
Allgood, class of 1884) was also elected as honorary president. Miss
Cordelia Veal (class of 1897) furnished constant enthusiasm and
ability as president, treasurer of the building fund, and corresponding
secretary. A business meeting and banquet were held at commencement time, with monthly or bimonthly business and social gatherings
scheduled some years. Receptions in honor of Van Hoose and the
faculty were occasionally planned. Although much energy was expended, the ladies failed to erect a hall for the alumnae and societies,
a statue of Colonel Shorter, or a memorial to President Gwaltney. In
1910 and 1919 the association tastefully supported the financial campaigns by providing lunches for the canvassers.

The publication in 1915 of a booklet, *Sweets and Savouries*, was a
financial success and a means of giving new life to the association. A
collection of recipes compiled from the membership, it had a title page
containing a quotation from "Antony and Cleopatra": "We'll feast
each other ere we part; your fine Egyptian cookery shall have the
fame." Forty pages were devoted to salads, sandwiches, beverages,
breads, creams and jellies, and novelties. The professor of art suggested
a "Shorter Salad": "Use the hearts of crisp lettuce. Sprinkle with English walnuts, and serve with mayonnaise. This suggests the Shorter
colors."

For several years a Christmas bazaar occupied much of their attention, enabling them to raise additional funds. Held on Broad Street
or in the Music Building on campus, it featured items contributed by
local members, out-of-town alumnae, and students, netting as much as
$500 some years.

On September 16, 1920, the Martha Shorter Tea Room was opened on the second floor of the Music Building and overlooked the scenic Coosa River. Mrs. Mark A. Cooper conceived of the venture, leading in its operation. It contained twelve "white enameled tables and chairs and draperies in blue and white checked gingham. A tiny bud vase centers each table and menu cards are in unique designs." Tomato aspic on lettuce, cheese mousse on pineapple and lettuce, tomato and cheese-olive sandwiches, lime ice, angel food cake, cookies, and iced tea were on the opening day menu. Each Wednesday, Thursday, and Friday from 3:00 to 6:00 P.M. ladies from Rome and the students enjoyed congregating there. In the spring of 1921 the Alumnae Association used its facilities in entertaining the seniors.

The ladies raised in excess of $5,000 during these years for projects usually associated with the college. A contribution of about $2,000 was made to the Greater Shorter campaign. To help in the expansion of the library, the group gave about $900. The Shorter Alumnae Endowment Fund was launched in 1919 under the direction of Mrs. J. P. Cooper, securing about $500. Scholarship assistance amounted to less than $500, since this aspect of their work was no longer emphasized. During the war an unknown amount was sent for Red Cross work, and briefly the association "adopted" a French war orphan. Commenting on one of the school colors, a president insisted: "Gold is a jolly color, and a great good. . . . Our Alma Mater likes it. Dr. Van Hoose will accept it for the endowment fund, and our treasurer of the Alumnae Building Fund would risk her best hat, if by passing it around, she could get it back gold-crowned and gold-filled."

Occasionally after 1915 the *Chimes* carried a page or two of alumnae news, and the first separate *Shorter Alumnae Bulletin* was issued in June of 1919. Early that year a questionnaire was sent to every known alumna, of whom about half replied. The thirty-page booklet contained the names and locations of the 585 respondents, together with news items relating to some of them.

As early as 1915 the suggestion was made that branches of the association should be formed, and "one of the strongest graduates" was chosen by the college to visit Atlanta, Macon, and "other cities where old Shorter girls are leaders in civic, social, and philanthropic life, and form them into chapters." However, not until December 1, 1920, was the Atlanta chapter organized, with about seventy-five charter members. The first president was Mrs. H. N. Cooledge (née Miss Rebekah Clark, class of 1915) , in whose home the first meeting was held. Soon thereafter the Columbus chapter was initiated, with Mrs. George Cox (née Miss Ophelia Davis, class of 1916) as first president.

The Death of Van Hoose

For a crucial decade Van Hoose was president of Shorter College. In addition to his monumental labors for the school, he was active as a Mason and as a member of the board of examiners for the University of Georgia. Serving extensively within the Baptist denomination, he was a trustee of Hearn Academy, Cave Spring, and a member of the executive boards of the Layman's Association of the Georgia Baptist Convention and of the Floyd County Baptist Association. At the First Baptist Church of Rome, he was a deacon and a Sunday school superintendent and teacher.

His unceasing efforts gradually undermined his health, and conditions took an ominous turn in July of 1921 when the ailing Van Hoose wired Dr. W. D. Furry, dean and professor of philosophy and education, to return from his vacation at once. Together they were able to prepare for classes, and the college opened without delay. Two notes written that fall reflected diverse sides of Van Hoose's state of mind. To one parent he was cheerful: "Hazel sang beautifully in recital last night. Wish you could have heard her. Fine girl. A great pleasure to have her. She seems well and happy." Shortly thereafter he addressed a recent graduate in more somber words: "I am getting my affairs in order, preparing to make that last journey from which no traveler ever returns."

Following a comparatively brief illness, Van Hoose died in the Harbin Hospital on Sunday, December 11, 1921, about ten days after an operation for an abscess on the liver. Conducted by J. Ellis Sammons, pastor of the First Baptist Church of Rome, the funeral was held the next day at Maplehurst. Most of the undergraduates dressed in white middy blouses with yellow ties, "carrying out the college colors," as the newspaper observed. The senior class historian described the event: "And then—can you ever forget the second time we wore our caps and gowns? How we stood on the porch at Maplehurst and heard once more the words of the funeral service read, and the words of the song so beloved by him, 'Abide with Me.' Even after you saw him lying so gray and still, alone in that flower-filled room, did you realize that our Dr. Van Hoose was gone? That he couldn't ever talk to his girls anymore and never would we see his beloved face at Chapel. . . . All that put a different meaning into our caps and gowns for us all, I think. And after Christmas we had to go on as if nothing had happened." Among the flowers was a large white and gold wreath sent by the students. Accompanied by Professors Allie Hayes Richardson, W. D. Furry, and Paul M. Cousins, representing the college, and by J. P. Cooper and T. W. Lipscomb, representing the trustees, the body was taken to Gainesville where it was interred.

A memorial service was held in the college auditorium on Sunday afternoon, December 18, 1921. Opening music included solos by Miss Louise Bennet, professor of voice, and Caroline Gray, a violin major in the class of 1924. Professor Cousins read the Scripture lesson, Romans 8:18–39. President Cooper of the trustees alluded to Van Hoose's generosity, faithfulness, courage, and gentleness. Mrs. Mark A. Cooper of the alumnae described his unfailing sympathy, courtesy, and spirit of cooperation. The president of the student body, Ada Belle Patrick, spoke of "his fatherly attitude to the students, his sympathy and concern for their happiness and welfare."

Of the numerous published statements about Van Hoose, the one adopted by the college trustees received wide notice. A part of it said:

In Dr. Van Hoose God gave to us a most delightful friend and fellow-worker;

In him God gave to Shorter College, at a time of great need, a wise and most successful leader;

In him God gave to Shorter College, for eleven years, a mind, a soul, a character,—made broad, deep, strong and gentle by Divine inspiration, that our Daughters might be led into larger fields of usefulness;

In him God gave to education and the uplift of humanity, forty years of glorious service.

The Rome *Tribune-Herald* commented: "He fell in the midst of an active and useful career, when hope beat high, at the noontide of life, when his powers both mental and physical, were at meridian." The editor of the Atlanta *Constitution* concluded: "He was a man of high refinement of character, a scholar of rare attainments, a school and religious executive of marked ability; and above all he possessed a degree of fineness of personality that made friends and admirers of all with whom he came into contact." The *Christian Index* soon devoted its front page to his picture and several other pages to brief tributes: "He was human, yet he ever sought to bear in his life the reflection of the divine. . . . He was a great soul, a Christian gentleman, a sincere friend, a chivalrous opponent, a fair fighter, a generous winner, a philosophical loser, a real manly, Godly gentleman" (Arch C. Cree, executive secretary-treasurer of the executive committee of the Georgia Baptist Convention, Atlanta). "A delightful comrade, a loyal friend, a personal inspiration, has gone out of my life. . . . Two words have ever been married in my thought of him—sweetness and strength. . . . I have seen him in those supreme moments of testing when that institution, into which he had translated ideals and convictions, was

213

assailed, stand with unyielding courage and unembittered kindliness of spirit" (Ashby Jones, pastor of Ponce de Leon Avenue Baptist Church, Atlanta). "In him the elements of good breeding, real culture, and the grace of God combined to make one of the most splendid men I have ever known" (Charles W. Daniel, pastor of First Baptist Church, Atlanta). "Shorter College, rising from a mountain height, beautiful for situation, will stand for all time as his monument" (President Rufus W. Weaver, Mercer University). "The hundreds of girls who have gone out from the college shall reincarnate his spirit and carry his message to the world. We are all richer because he has lived" (J. C. Wilkinson, pastor of First Baptist Church, Athens).

The vacuum that Van Hoose left was partially filled by Dean Furry and J. P. Cooper. The trustees authorized Furry "to assume direction of the College and to do such acts as may become necessary in the conduct of its affairs until further notice." Working closely with the trustees' prudential committee and with Cooper in particular, Furry was acting president for a full year. Mrs. Van Hoose was provided housing and her late husband's salary during the remainder of the academic year, after which she was college librarian for another year before leaving Rome. Cooper appointed a committee to seek a new president and directed that a circular letter be sent to all alumnae asking for their support "at this critical period of the college." Clearly this was a trying time of transition for the institution, because, as Furry remarked, "in the higher sense of the word Shorter was President Van Hoose and President Van Hoose was Shorter College."

5
The Recognition of Academic Excellence

Months of groping followed the death of President Van Hoose. Directed by Dr. W. D. Furry, dean and acting president of the college, and J. P. Cooper, president of the board of trustees, Shorter enrolled a total of 245 students in 1921–1922. In April of 1922 the trustees offered the presidency to Dr. William J. McGlothlin, president of Furman University, Greenville, South Carolina, a distinguished church historian and research scholar. The following month the position was tendered to Louie D. Newton, editor of the *Christian Index*, Atlanta, Georgia. Dr. Harry C. Wayman, professor of Old Testament and Hebrew at Southern Baptist Theological Seminary, Louisville, Kentucky, was elected in July. That each man refused undoubtedly contributed to a fifteen percent decrease in enrollment during 1922–1923.

On November 28, 1922, the trustees were finally successful in their selection, and a front-page, seven-column headline in the Rome newspaper announced: "Dr. Blocker Accepts Presidency Shorter College." Born in Starke, Florida, exactly one week after the Cherokee Baptist Female College first opened in 1873, Daniel James Blocker earned the Bachelor of Arts degree from Stetson University, the Master of Arts and Bachelor of Divinity degrees from the University of Chicago, and membership in Phi Beta Kappa. For two years he was pastor of the Irving Park Baptist Church in Chicago, after which he returned to his alma mater as professor of psychology and education and dean of the department of education for eight years. Stetson awarded him the Doctor of Divinity degree in 1918, while he was still associated with that institution. In 1921 he moved to Williamsburg, Virginia, where he was professor of philosophy and Bible at the College of William and Mary and pastor of the First Baptist Church. He had married Miss Florence Evelyn Jackson of Williamsport, Louisiana, in 1917; to their union was born Daniel James, Jr., who became a favorite Shorter mascot.

Described as "a man of robust health . . . . rather stout of build," with "blue eyes, light hair, and . . . genial disposition," Blocker did "not display the austere mannerism so frequently characteristic of men of learning and literary pursuits." His inauguration was a formal, 2½-hour ceremony held in the Shorter auditorium on January 4, 1923. On the journey from Virginia, he had caught a cold and was still quite hoarse—unlike any of the other sixteen speakers. Included in the program were J. P. Cooper; Miss Louise Bennet of the class of 1913, acting for the alumnae; Florre Jo Everett, president of the student body; Rufus W. Weaver, president of Mercer University; D. C. Barrow, chancellor of the University of Georgia; John D. Mell and Arch C. Cree, representing the Georgia Baptist Convention; and Louie D. Newton, who could have been the honoree had he chosen. The main address was given by Clifford J. Walker, governor-elect of Georgia and a Shorter trustee under Van Hoose.

The installation was publicized in the *Christian Index*, along with a picture of President Blocker. He and his wife soon joined the First Baptist Church of Rome and were given a reception by the Rome chapter of the Alumnae Association at the home of its president, Mrs.

President Daniel J. Blocker

John Glover (née Miss Mattie Wall), with seventy-five guests present.

President Blocker's entire five-semester administration was dominated by the memory of his masterful predecessor. He arrived in Rome just in time to participate in the formal opening of the swimming pool so long desired by Van Hoose. Utilizing funds advanced by his father, F. S. Cooper was authorized by the trustees and alumnae to be the "inspector" in charge of construction. The architect finished his design in July of 1922, and work proceeded rapidly. The completed tile pool was 20 by 80 feet, with a depth of 4 to 8 feet. Plans called for a second story to be added to the building where a permanent gymnasium would be located. Meantime, however, on January 30, 1923, a gathering in the college auditorium heard short speeches by Mrs. J. P. Cooper (née Miss Alice Allgood, class of 1884), who paid tribute to Van Hoose while presenting the pool to the school, and by President Blocker, who accepted the gift on behalf of the college. The applause that followed merged into "enthusiastic college yells given by the student body." Moving to pool-side, the audience enjoyed "acquatic stunts"—a relay race, a candle race, a "follow-the-leader" race, and others—after which the Martha Shorter Tea Room was opened for several small parties. A graduating senior later toasted the new pool in these words:

> On one of Rome's most lofty hills,
> Outlined against the sky,
> The first school in all the land
> For years stood, high and dry.
> There was water, water everywhere
> Around this school for women,
> Water, water everywhere,
> But not a drop to swim in.
> Then Shorter's fine big sisters said,
> "Oh, this will never do,
> If other schools have swimming pools,
> Why, Shorter'll have one too."
> And when alumnae all around
> Began to work and plan,
> Old Shorter Hill quite suddenly
> Ceased to be just dry land.
> So here tonight we give a toast
> To the finest place we've found,
> "Here's to the Alumnae Swimming Pool"
> (We'll omit the "Drink it Down").

A photograph of five grinning students enjoying the pool was included in the *National Geographic Magazine* for September of 1926, giving it wide publicity. It was considered a gift of the alumnae because of their diligence and J. P. Cooper's generosity. During a six-year period after it was opened they raised $15,000, while he contributed an additional $2,000 and financed the entire loan without charge.

Although the college seal steadfastly insisted that the institution had been founded in 1877 and the 1922 commencement had been numbered the forty-seventh, Dr. Furry announced in the fall of 1922 that the college was beginning its fiftieth year. Soon the seal was altered to include a more accurate date of founding, 1873, and to omit the name of Alfred Shorter. A fiftieth anniversary number of the *Chimes* was issued in June, 1923, which included pictures of Colonel Shorter, Gwaltney, Van Hoose, and Blocker, a ten-page article, "The Origin and Development of Shorter," by Paul M. Cousins, essays by Blocker, Furry, Mrs. J. P. Cooper, and others, and an advertisement reading: "To Shorter College, established 1873, The Fahy Store, established 1873, extends heartiest congratulations." The Fiftieth Anniversary Banquet occurred on June 3, when almost three hundred guests and students squeezed into the college dining room. Presided over by Mrs. Mark Cooper (née Miss Sarah Joyce King, class of 1917) and President Blocker, the affair featured a class roll call, to which more than half of the classes responded. Mrs. Elmer Grant, the great-niece of Mrs. Alfred Shorter, gave a piece of wood from Thornwood that was soon fashioned into a gavel still used by the Shorter College Alumni Association. Affectionately recalling Van Hoose, the group formally decided to present the college with an oil portrait of him, a decision that was actualized seven years later. The editor of the Rome newspaper commented: "The college has grown within a period of fifty years from a small school for girls to the proportions of a magnificent educational institution. . . . [that] ranks with the best in the land. . . . The people of Rome are proud of Shorter College; they have observed its constant progress and improvement, and they gladly lend encouragement in every movement tending towards the enlargement of its activities."

An important sign of progress and improvement came later in 1923 when Shorter at last attained membership in the Southern Association of Colleges and Secondary Schools. Under the inspiration of Van Hoose, application had been made several times, but each was deferred because of insufficient endowment. After assistance came from the General Education Board and the Georgia Baptist Convention, application was renewed in 1923, when Blocker, Furry, and J. P. Cooper attended the annual meeting of the Southern Association in Richmond. Blocker wired the results—in an economical night letter!

> 4X BY 10 NITE
>   RICHMOND VA DEC 6 1923
> PROF COUSINS
>   ROME GA
> ANNOUNCE TO STUDENTS AND FACULTY THAT
> SHORTER HAS BEEN ADMITTED
>   D J BLOCKER
>   714A DEC 7

About 8:25 on Friday morning, December 7, according to one student, "Miss Kennedy rushed from her office as few of us had ever seen her do before and wrote hurriedly and nervously on the bulletin board: 'Shorter has been admitted.' That was enough to call forth yells of rejoicing from the on-lookers. The news spread like wild fire over the school and every student was in the hall singing . . . ." The first two classes were halfheartedly met, after which Cousins announced a holi-

220

day voted by the faculty. A song was soon composed and learned by the students. That evening the Davidson Glee Club sang in the college auditorium before an almost ecstatic audience. Saturday a two-page "Special Extra" of the *Periscope* appeared with a reproduction of the telegram and pictures of Blocker and Furry. In the evening the Shorter Players went ahead with the staging of two one-act plays, followed by "almost a whole night of hallelujahs and rejoicing, manifested by torchlights, parades, bonfires, songs, and yells." Asserted one young lady: "Dr. Furry commanded our love and esteem, for it was largely through his efforts that Shorter was recognized as a standard college." Late that night—9:30—a torchlight parade of screaming girls wound down the hill to Maplehurst. The climax came on the following Tuesday evening when the seniors honored the triumphant Blocker and Furry at a special dinner. No similar celebration occurred in 1924 when the school was admitted to the Association of American Colleges. By then it was also a member of the Association of Georgia Colleges and the Association of Baptist Colleges of the Southern Baptist Convention.

In the early twenties, oil portraits of an almost clean-shaven Alfred Shorter and of Martha Shorter were removed from Thornwood and loaned to the college by the Hamilton family. Both were given outright to the school in the next decade and eventually restored.

At the close of his first full year as president, Blocker had expressed to the trustees his personal happiness and his wish to remain permanently at Shorter. "So far as I know at the present time I am ready to give my life to the institution . . . ." In June of 1924 he accepted election for an indefinite term. Somewhat unexpectedly he addressed a letter of resignation to the trustees on February 19, 1925, agreeing to work energetically for students and endowment until his departure the following summer. The trustees passed resolutions that affirmed, in part: "This committee deeply regrets that this occasion has arisen, and appreciates the expression of friendly interest embodied in Dr. Blocker's letter of resignation. . . . This committee is sensible of its kindly goodwill toward him, and its earnest desire that he may find increasing usefulness in whatever field of endeavor he may enter." Appreciated also by the girls, he had the 1925 *Argo* dedicated to him "as a college father, a kind Christian friend ever ready to help, and a sympathetic executive . . . ." After leaving Shorter, he spent five years as professor of philosophy at Furman University, Greenville, South Carolina, and the remainder of his active years as head of the department of sociology at the College of William and Mary, Williamsburg, Virginia, where he died in 1957.

The New President, W. D. Furry

A new president was close at hand: William Davis Furry, was unanimously elected on March 17, 1925. A native of Cumberland, Maryland, he was born in 1874 and was reared in the Brethren church, which had originated among German Baptists. While a Brethren pastor in and near South Bend, Indiana, he earned the Bachelor and Master of Arts degrees from Notre Dame University and membership in Phi Beta Kappa. After studying briefly at the University of Chicago, he attended Johns Hopkins University, Baltimore, Maryland, which

President William D. Furry

awarded him the Doctor of Philosophy degree. From 1911 to 1919 he was president of Ashland College, an important Brethren institution in Ohio, where he published several essays in philosophy. In 1895 he had married Miss Nina Smith of Sharpsburg, Maryland, but they had no children. Joining the Shorter faculty in 1919, Furry was professor of psychology, education, and philosophy, later also dean of the college, and for one year acting president. Possessing a clipped English accent, small of stature, and wiry, he was fastidious, immaculate, a bundle of nervous energy. To some he seemed distant and cold, devoid of humor, cutting, unable to mix socially, and somewhat vain. To others, however, he appeared courteous, capable, a fascinating teacher, and a fine educational administrator. He and his wife joined the First Baptist Church of Rome upon the transfer of their letters in 1922. Often his exact opposite, Mrs. Furry was stout of body and placid of disposition—and fondly remembered as always being ready to eat!

Under President Furry, enrollment quickly peaked and then slowly declined. For three years, 1925 to 1928, the dormitories were filled to their capacity, and the total enrollment averaged 287. During two of these years, Furry taught off-campus extension classes in psychology to about thirty teachers in Dalton and Rome, contributing to an average figure that suggested greater prosperity than was actually being experienced. Additional rooms were provided in the fall of 1926 when the second floor of the Dining Hall Building was converted to that purpose. Unfortunately they were not long needed. The occupancy of the dormitories in this period averaged about eighty percent. As the depression continued, the size of the student body fell to an all-time low on the present campus of 162 full- and part-time students in 1931–1932. During his eight years of leadership, Furry enrolled an average of 223. College students numbered from 147 to 246, annually averaging about 203. Eleven to 29 each year were special students, of whom never more than 5 were young men. About eighty percent of all students were from Georgia, with smaller numbers coming from Alabama, Mississippi, Tennessee, and Florida. Two young ladies were from Brazil and one was from Japan, but all three were daughters of American missionaries, not international students.

Numerous efforts were made to increase the enrollment. Letters to prospective students were written, advertising was placed in various periodicals, and several persons traveled on behalf of the college at different times. Said to be the first institution in the state to do so, Shorter sponsored at least three College Day programs for senior girls who attended classes, utilized recreational facilities, met the students and faculty, and enjoyed a meal in the dining room. A separate booklet showing many views of the campus was widely used, being revised a number of times, and a series of folders that included "The Book of Shorter College Advantages" also appeared.

Tuition, Fees, and Student Aid

Not unexpectedly, tuition and other fees increased as the years passed—but, as Furry pointed out many times, the students were paying only twenty-seven percent of the real cost of their education. A charge of $515 was made for nine months of basic instruction and room and board, a charge that finally reached $600. Additional fees for laboratory sciences, speech, and music raised the total at first to no more than $685 and later to $810. Appropriately enough, the 1929 *Argo* was dedicated to "Our Mothers and Fathers."

The costs of receiving an education were reduced for some by occupying student positions in the library, post office, laboratories, offices, or music department. Scholarships and loans were continued, as were discounts for the daughters of clergymen and for two or more girls from the same family, usually benefiting ten to twenty young ladies each year. At the depth of the depression some scholarships were authorized for which willing recipients could not be found! Until 1926 two fellowships were awarded to graduating seniors who returned for a fifth year of education without charge while rendering assistance in the library or laboratories.

Trustees

The self-perpetuating board of trustees continued to exercise control over the college through its committees: prudential, grounds and buildings, investment, legal counsel, endowment, and audit. Over the years it grew in size from fifteen members to twenty-five, two of whom, L. A. Dean and Harper Hamilton, were designated life trustees. Beginning in 1925 persons were elected for a four-year term, after which they might be reelected immediately without an intervening period of time.

The board named a committee in 1924 to consult with the General Alumnae Association about electing "a lady trustee." Three recommendations were forthcoming, and the following year these were duly named: Mrs. A. W. Van Hoose of Atlanta, who served twenty-five years; Mrs. John Wright of Augusta (née Miss Alice Louise Hicks, class of 1907), who served twenty-nine years; and Mrs. W. A. Steed of Newnan (née Miss Sallie Pinson, class of 1881), who resigned after seven years. Mrs. J. P. Cooper of Rome was a trustee from 1928 to her death in 1938, being first elected to fill the unexpired term of her deceased husband.

Death robbed the board of three notable members during this period. Called "this great friend of humanity and of education," William Walker Brookes of Atlanta was memorialized in 1924 after twenty-one years of service in resolutions that spoke of "his generosity, liberality and activity, devoted to the Christian Education of young women to the Glory of God, to the spread of the truth of Christianity, and to the extension of the Kingdom of God throughout the Earth." Seventeen years later Brookes Chapel was named in his honor.

After thirty-eight years as a trustee, Judge Harper Hamilton of

Rome died in 1930, "a kind, a courteous and a lovable man . . . held in the highest esteem by every member of the board . . . ."

The president of the trustees, J. P. Cooper, suffered a heart attack that caused his immediate death on December 17, 1927. Words of appreciation for his twenty-five openhanded years on the board were expressed by the Rome newspaper, the *Christian Index*, President Furry, the Shorter General Alumnae Association, the faculty, the students, and the trustees. Editor Newton of the *Index* quoted a statement that Cooper had made to him: "You know, the wonderful thing about this sort of work is the assurance you have that you are making

Harper Hamilton

an abiding investment when you put your money and your thought and your time in the betterment of youth." The trustees stated: "The records show that during the years he made contributions to the college totalling $165,568.15. Without disparagement to many of the other fine friends of this great institution, it will not be extravagant to say that he has been the most valuable and vital friend the institution has known since the days of the great Alfred Shorter, and will take his place in the life of the college alongside the immortal founder." A memorial number of the *Chimes* was issued, one of the residence halls was named for him in 1930, and the J. P. Cooper Memorial Loan Fund was initiated by the alumnae in 1930.

At Cooper's death, the governor of Georgia, Dr. L. G. Hardman of Commerce, who had been a trustee since 1911 and vice-president for three years, automatically became acting president. On January 27, 1928, he was formally elected president, thus becoming the only person to occupy both positions at the same time. Four Romans who were to be active more than twenty years each were added to the board: Aubrey Matthews, F. S. Cooper, Claire J. Wyatt, Sr., and W. F. Barron.

Since the college charter had expired, the trustees applied for a renewal, asking "That the word 'Female' be striken from the name of the corporation, so that its name after the granting of this petition shall be 'Shorter College.' " The new name became official on March 26, 1923, when the Superior Court of Floyd County gave its approval.

Ostensibly at the initiative of the students, a Homecoming Day to honor the trustees was held on February 23, 1932. A busy day was scheduled: lunch with the students; an afternoon meeting of trustees and heads of student organizations; tea at five for trustees, students, and faculty; dinner with the students; and a one-act play in the evening. Hope was expressed that this might become an annual event, but it was soon discontinued.

Increased Financial Assets

The permanent endowment grew during the Blocker-Furry years from approximately $100,000 to $350,523.06. As early as 1911 Van Hoose had requested assistance from the General Education Board of New York, but the college was not considered sufficiently strong to merit a grant. Subsequently the library holdings increased, faculty salaries rose, and the only debt was removed when J. P. Cooper released the college from an obligation to him of $47,500. From 1921 to 1924 the General Education Board contributed $15,000 for operating expenses. On November 13, 1922, the trustees signed an agreement with the board, specifying that Shorter College would receive $100,000 in endowment as rapidly as it raised $200,000 from other sources for the same purpose. Payments to the college were to be made quarterly, and the deadline, which was extended several times, was finally set at March 31, 1928. Apparently funds were applied to this purpose from the Baptist Seventy-Five Million Campaign, from the small, annual appropriation from the Georgia Baptist Convention, and from the Greater Shorter campaign still being carried on without fanfare in Rome. By mid-1927 the college had claimed almost $75,000 of the total, requiring $51,263.76 in order to get the remaining $25,631.88.

Plans were announced early in 1928 by a newspaper article carrying an eight-column, page-one headline: "CAMPAIGN TO BE LAUNCHED TO RAISE $60,000 FOR SHORTER." Supporting the drive, the editor observed: "Shorter College stands at the dividing of the way. . . . It must either slip back from its high position or, if it is to maintain its present standing, it must enlarge its endowment." Before the canvass began, many articles and advertisements appeared in the paper, sermons and speeches were delivered at the churches and service clubs, and an informative pamphlet, "Why Shorter?" was distributed to every home by the alumnae and mailed to every business establishment by the trustees. The campaign was made all the more crucial by the recognition that the Southern Association was requiring for continued accreditation an annual income of $25,000 from sources other than student fees, implying an endowment of at least $500,000. Hence, it was promised, after the current drive the state at large would be asked for the additional amount. Led by W. S. Cothran, O. P. Willingham, and G. E. Maddox, seventy-two men fanned out over Rome on February 21 to 23, reporting only $42,803. Facing what they called "dismal failure," the leaders resumed the effort, announcing that they were still "plugging away." On March 15 a total of $50,738 in cash and pledges was revealed. Although the goal had not been reached, Furry publicly pronounced the campaign a success, and the trustees formally thanked all who had participated in it. The pledges were soon converted into cash by being sold to a local bank, the General Education Board sent the remainder of its promised amount, and later in the year the endowment was $344,264.82. Once again the Cooper family showed its support of the college. The three sons—Frederick, Mark, and Andrew—guaranteed the bank that it would not suffer any loss by purchasing the pledges and eventually paid it about $3,700 when sufficient collections could not be made.

Meantime, the college continued to be "affiliated" with the Georgia Baptist Convention, electing its own trustees, making annual reports to the convention, and receiving goodwill and financial assistance from it. Because the published figures are incomplete, question must attend any effort to determine denominational support during these years. From 1919 to 1925 the convention made its first financial contribution to the college, probably giving $134,395.87 through the Seventy-Five Million Campaign. Of this, at least $21,070.07 came during the Blocker years. Although the convention made a strenuous effort to continue that level of giving, the college reported receipts of only $13,709.38 during the period from 1925 to 1929. A state-wide campaign for endowment was launched in cooperation with Mercer University and Bessie Tift College in 1926, but evidently little except publicity was realized from it.

In 1928 the proposal was made that the convention issue debenture bonds worth $1,500,000 for the various Georgia Baptist enterprises, a proposal that was coolly received by the trustees. Nevertheless, the college was allotted $141,404.63 of them. The proposal was to pay the entire face value of the bonds to the college by 1939, together with five percent interest ($7,070.23 annually) starting in 1929—the entire enterprise to be funded from the receipts of the Georgia Baptist Convention through the Cooperative Program. Unfortunately the great depression crippled these ambitious plans, and the convention labored mightily in a vain effort to carry out its promises. By 1932 some of the more pessimistic Baptists were suggesting that the debentures be repudiated and that all of the Georgia Baptist colleges except Mercer be removed from the convention budget. Neither of these suggestions was acted upon during the Furry years, although the debentures were to be surrendered in 1935. Shorter apparently received from the convention $22,622.44 as interest from the debentures during the years 1929 to 1933. Thus, the convention provided a total of $57,401.89 to the college while Blocker and Furry led it.

Meantime, the annual income of the college fluctuated. Because of the uncertainty following Van Hoose's death and a great drought over much of the state, the college accumulated debts of $20,590.28, operating on an annual income of about $120,000. For the next five years, however, the annual income gradually grew to a high of $154,700.80, the debts were easily paid, and a small profit was finally shown. Income abruptly began to decline in 1930, reaching a low of $94,863.16 in 1932–1933, and the college again operated at a deficit. The entire budget for 1931–1932 was cut by ten percent, and this included faculty salaries. The following year salaries were reduced by another thirty percent. Dr. L. G. Hardman, president of the board of trustees, offered to give the college a large farm in South Georgia, conditioned upon the immediate erection of an administration building. Because of "the economic condition at this time" and the "severe task of operating the college," the trustees found it necessary to refuse his offer. Within a year they were faced with an even more unpleasant necessity, that of dealing with a $25,000 deficit which could not be covered by current receipts. The General Education Board recommended that the trustees secure permission from the Floyd County Superior Court to encroach upon the endowment. In May of 1933 a court order was secured, with the understanding that restoration would be made as soon as possible, the notes were paid off, and the school was given at least another year of life.

The total assets of the college, which had amounted to $608,500 in 1921, slowly grew to a figure just under one million dollars. The auditor's report for 1933 showed that the endowment was $491,927.69, of which $141,404.63 was in debentures soon to be withdrawn. The land, buildings, and equipment were worth $484,011.47—including $1,407.15 in livestock and farm equipment which were finally sold that fall. (Prior to 1928 the trustees had boasted that fire insurance was unnecessary; in that year $342,350 worth was finally taken out on the buildings and equipment!) Current funds totaled $12,712.72. Thus, the assets reached $988,651.88, an increase of about $380,000 in twelve years.

The Campus

Throughout the Blocker-Furry period, the trustees continued to visualize expansion. In 1924 they passed resolutions proposing a five-year project to raise one million dollars for endowment and buildings. The familiar picture of Greater Shorter was used the following year, apparently for the last time. Plans to construct a $150,000 administration building and dining room were actually announced in the newspaper, and a sketch of it was carried in the *Chimes* for March, 1927. It was to house administrative offices on the first floor, the library and classrooms on the second, and dormitory rooms on the third. In the rear of this building was to be the dining room that would accommodate 350 students. After the construction of this, the old dining room was to be converted to additional residence space for students. In 1930 application was made to the Presser Foundation for a new music building and to the Carnegie Corporation for a new library. The following year Furry stated that "the college has been placed on the approved list of institutions to receive library support," but the amount is not known. At the same time the trustees proposed hiring a fund-raising company to secure $500,000 for salaries, buildings, and endowment, but general conditions made such a move impossible.

Of course some alterations and improvements were made on the campus. The last of the wooden walkways was removed, and the round pool between the Academic and Music buildings was converted into a flower bed. The grounds were carefully maintained, and each spring the beauty of the campus was once more noted. During the summer of 1927 all of the buildings were renovated, and later new furniture was placed in the entrance halls and the Glass Corridor. An unsolved problem perplexing the school was its water supply, but the digging of an artesian well was rejected. One of the workers observed in exasperation: "Why of course we're going to have trouble with the water system. Those girls up there take a bath *every* day, and each one

229

uses a *different* tub of water!" Due to the generosity of Floyd County, the drive from Shorter Avenue to the college buildings was paved in 1930. The names of the dormitories were changed in June of 1930 by joint action of the General Alumnae Association and the trustees: Hall One became Cooper Hall and Hall Two, Van Hoose Hall. Passing from the scene was Ivan Carlson's familiar "Toonerville Trolley" as the track was removed and bus service was provided by the Georgia Power Company from about 1930 to 1937.

Community Relations

Honoring a long-standing relationship, the editors of the 1924 *Argo* dedicated their publication "to the people of Rome, to whose unselfish interest Shorter largely owes her present foundation, and to whose kindly spirit of cooperation Shorter girls owe much of the happiness of their college life . . . ."

A constant flow of visitors came to the campus. Members of the Rotary and Kiwanis clubs enjoyed banquets in the dining room, their own skits which poked fun at the college faculty or the annual May Day celebration, and programs staged by the girls. On Shrine Day the fun-filled men invaded some schools in the city, kidnapped the teachers, dismissed classes, and invited the students to attend a parade and program downtown. "Woe for the restricted girls," bewailed the *Argo* that year.

The lyceum series provided a more serious type of guest on the hill, as over the years some distinguished persons appeared in the Shorter auditorium: Wilfred Grenfell of Labrador; Richard Halliburton, traveler and writer; Lothrop Stoddard, historian; Hugh Walpole, English novelist; Count A. N. Tolstoy, Russian novelist; Mme. Wanda Landowska, harpsichordist; and Carl Sandburg, poet. Many others were also heard, including a member of the Royal Canadian Mounted Police, the first woman governor in the United States, and lecturers from India, China, and Germany. Musicians performed with frequency, and in 1928 the practice of mailing announcements concerning recitals was initiated.

Although a school of music at a downtown location did not materialize when it was proposed in 1931, college musicians constantly displayed their talents off campus. The Rome Music Lovers' Club and the Rome Symphony Orchestra both received the assistance of Shorter persons, and conventions of the Masons and American Association of University Women heard the college choir or individual artists. In 1928 the Georgia Federation of Music Clubs, meeting in

230

Rome, was addressed by President Furry and was entertained with a program and reception on campus. The choir presented programs in Rome, Cartersville, Atlanta, and Macon. Including numbers by the Shorter Syncopators and the Shorter Trio, radio station WFDV of Rome was formally opened on the evening of March 5, 1930. When WSB of Atlanta offered thirty minutes each month for a musical broadcast, the invitation was eagerly accepted, and the program was aired for a couple of years. Of course the churches of Rome benefited by the inclusion of Shorter vocalists in their choirs, and Miss Louise Bennet was director of music at First Baptist Church. For several years Wilbur Rowand was organist there and Mrs. Dora Ware, at St. Peter's Episcopal Church. Others on the staff and faculty spoke at many service and women's clubs, while several were active in the churches as pastors, supply preachers, deacons, missionary leaders, and Sunday school officers and teachers.

In Pursuit of Academic Excellence

As dean and as president, Dr. Furry exalted the ideal of academic excellence. Observing a general indifference toward spiritual values, he laid part of the blame on education. "Both in the lower schools and in our institutions of higher learning religion is too frequently treated with disregard if not with contempt. With due respect for the work of our institutions of higher learning, the fact remains that the mass effect of contemporary teaching tends powerfully toward skepticism." To combat this growing feeling, he felt that denominational schools should be continued and that state schools should be led to recognize their responsibilities in the area of religion. "Our problem, therefore, is not simply the supporting of a few schools as denominational propaganda but the larger problem of so organizing and conducting our institutions of higher learning that the spirit of God may blow through the bones of our national life already withered and dry because of lack of that vital breath." "It has been said that the Church taught the State to educate its youth. It is historically true that education was born at the altar and the Church has been for all time the chief friend of education. The next great task before the Church is to teach the State that while sectarian instruction is properly excluded, religious education is absolutely essential to the accomplishment of the aim which the State has in view in expending vast and increasing sums for the support of its schools—the creation of citizens of the highest moral character." Because his interest was not primarily in state-supported education, Furry did not provide practical guidance for

231

achieving these suggestions. He concentrated on the purposes and programs of the denominational college.

In defining the purposes of a Christian college, he insisted that it was not intended to be a high school with preparatory courses, a university or professional school adding to the sum total of human knowledge by active research, or a vocational or trade school where mechanical skills were taught. Instead, this kind of college "owes its students sympathetic understanding of the civilization in which they live." It must develop "the power to think, consistently, effectively and fruitfully." It ought to "provide for and guarantee the development of moral character." Finally, it must assist in "the development of the religious consciousness of the students committed to it." Furry held that "education without religion is atheism, while religion without education is superstition." "Believing that Christianity is a vital part of the warp and woof of our Western civilization we must also believe that any neglect of the Christian view of the world makes for a defective view of education. . . . To produce moral personalities who in individual character and social life are like Jesus Christ, this is the goal of Christian education and the function of the denominational college." "Essentially and fundamentally the field and function of the church college appear in this: The significance for the individual and the world at large of the Christian approach to all truth and the Christian way of life in all relationships. For state and private colleges and universities this may be incidental only; for church colleges it must be primary and controlling." "Our colleges founded under Christian auspicies will never justify their right to existence and be worth our support until the enlightenment of the soul is given the primacy. . . . While not a theological seminary the college must nevertheless bring its students to know that you cannot have a sociology without religion, an economics without religion, a science of government without religion, or a science without religion."

Furry vigorously supported the traditional goal of the liberal arts. The college "should seek to prepare individuals to live rightly rather than make a living. Its task is not to prepare any man or woman for a specific purpose, not to qualify its students to accumulate money or achieve success in business. In fine, the college should not seek the exclusive development of the particular powers of the individual but rather the fullest possible development of the fundamental powers and interests which underlie and give force and meaning to the specific powers of particular individuals." Hence, he felt, "vocational courses if at all introduced should be admitted into curriculum with caution and moderation." "The main business of the college is . . .

232

to create personalities, capable of large participation in life and of making large and original contributions to life."

Attempting to put his concepts into practice, Furry tried to enlist religiously sensitive faculty members with "enthusiastic, contagious interest" in their subject matter and their students. "No teacher is long retained unless he is an actively working scholar, a lady or gentleman, an effective teacher, a ready friend of the individual student and a Christian." Again, he advocated and announced a selective policy of admissions, insisting that "ability to pay tuition is no longer sufficient criterion for admission to college." Finally, he introduced a separation in the curriculum of the first two from the last two years. The Years of Orientation provided "a complete survey of . . . modern civilization," involving the successful completion of required courses in Bible, science, English, a modern foreign language, history, Latin or mathematics, psychology, and social science. The Years of Concentration permitted the completion of a major sequence of at least 18 s.h. (reduced from 25 s.h.) and a minor sequence of at least 9 s.h. (reduced from 15 s.h.), together with numerous elective courses. Superior students were encouraged to apply for the privilege of reading for honors in the subject of their major interest, and Furry looked toward the day when serious and competent students "will be released from details of class-attendance and permitted to pursue their particular work according to their own plans." In light of his academic attitudes, it is not surprising to find him saying: "The atmosphere of the college should be one of work. Certainly a college course should not mean four years of laziness and luxury. Every college ought to demand serious, honest and persistent work of every student."

The recognition of students who attained academic excellence was also a part of Dr. Furry's purpose. In 1924 grades were assigned values: A, 3 points; B, 2 points; C, 1 point; D, 0 point. (Soon another was added: F, −1 point.) Based on this scale, honor graduates were accorded special notice: *cum laude*, 2.5; *magna cum laude*, 2.75; and *summa cum laude*, 2.875. On March 10, 1931, the first Honors Day program was held; Dr. W. D. Hooper, head of the department of classics at the University of Georgia, was the main speaker; and students were named to Phi Sigma Alpha and the honor roll.

The fact that agencies and organizations apart from the college paid attention to Shorter's growing academic excellence added to Furry's pleasure and dedication. Periodic reports were made to the Southern Association, and its accreditation has been continued to the present. Membership in the Association of American Colleges was secured in 1924. The college was elected to the American Council on Education in 1925, joining Agnes Scott and Emory and becoming the third Georgia institution to gain membership. Four years later the American Association of University Women first opened its organization to those graduates of Shorter College holding an academic degree, making its action retroactive. In 1931 the school was placed on the approved list of the Association of American Universities, which Furry claimed was the last and highest recognition open to a college offering only undergraduate instruction. One girl later recalled "Dr. Furry, in ecstasy as were we all over Shorter's admission . . . ." The boards of education in Georgia and Texas granted professional certificates to those Shorter graduates who had taken the requisite courses. Other graduates were regularly accepted by graduate schools of American universities without further examination, as well as by similar schools in France.

General Academic Matters

Students were admitted as freshmen by certification from accredited high schools or by examination at the hands of the Shorter faculty, after the successful completion of fifteen satisfactory units in high school and the receipt of letters certifying good health and character. Transfer students were awarded advanced standing if they came from accredited colleges or after a semester of acceptable work if they did not. Some special students were allowed to reside in the dormitories, but most came from town to receive part-time instruction in art, music, or speech.

As students arrived in Rome, members of the Rotary and Kiwanis clubs met them at the train station and transported them and their baggage to the campus. Arriving well in advance of the proper time, one young lady told the president: "If I'm too early I'm sorry. All the other girls were leaving the village, so I left too."

A three-day period of freshman orientation each fall was initiated in an effort to introduce the new girls to the complexities and perplexities of their surroundings. Lectures by Dr. Furry and Dean Mildred Mell, the administering of intelligence tests, counseling and registration by the faculty, and classes in Shorter customs and traditions by the leaders of the Student Goverment Association comprised the serious part of the program. Tours of Rome and environs, a picnic by the Rome alumnae, a reception by the Y.W.C.A., and other entertainment by the S.G.A. comprised the remainder of it.

A faculty adviser was formally designated for each pupil. Registration for classes was completed as the students secured faculty approval by trudging wearily from office to office; as yet there was no centralized process. Classes normally began on Friday or Saturday, with opening convocation coming at 10:30. Guest speakers were sometimes featured —William Russell Owen of the First Baptist Church of Macon or Louie D. Newton of the Druid Hills Baptist Church of Atlanta— although often President Furry made the formal address. Shorter Sunday at the First Baptist Church of Rome came early in the fall— made more memorable one year "when the street car on which the whole Freshman class was crowded and wedged left the rail and parked, as it seemed, for half the day."

Classes continued to run from Tuesday through Saturday, with bells to regulate almost every moment of the waking day: rising bell, 7:00; breakfast bell, 7:30; seven class bells; chapel bell, 10:30; lunch bell, 1:00; dinner bell, 6:00; study bell, 7:00; recreation bell, 8:30; room bell, 8:45; retiring bell, 10:30 (11:30 on Saturday). Regular attendance at all classes, chapels, and vespers was expected. A young lady was excluded when she passed less than half of her work in any year—or when she married. In the latter case, she might be readmitted upon vote of the faculty. The inevitable semester examinations were given as scheduled by the administration, and no professor was allowed to alter that time. The equally inevitable report cards were sent home to the parents, with a neat "L.T." penned at the bottom by the registrar to validate them.

The Curricula

The Bachelor of Arts degree was the only one awarded during most of these years, and a total of 406 persons received it. English proved to be the most popular major, being selected by about one-third of the students. About fifteen percent of them chose history as their major; twelve percent, music; ten percent, speech; and nine percent, mathematics or French. Majors were also taken in biology, chemistry, Latin, physics, and Spanish (which was dropped in 1932).

While retaining the Bachelor of Arts degree with a major in music, the college reinstated the Bachelor of Music degree in 1933 and awarded it that year to one young lady. About one-fourth of the courses required for it were allowed to be in the liberal arts; all others were in theoretical and applied music.

All graduates were encouraged to make use of a vocational placement bureau that the college operated through the alumnae secretary.

During a time of curtailed student enrollment and severe economic strain, the size of the staff and faculty never exceeded 35, of whom no more than 25 were full- or part-time classroom professors. Faculty salaries slowly rose from a high of $2,500 to $3,500, while the low ranged from $900 to $1,300. Room was often furnished in addition to this, but a nominal charge was usually made for board. In the early thirties, salaries were cut first by ten percent and then by an additional thirty; but, in order to protect the professional standing of the faculty, contracts continued to show the predepression figures, together with a clause providing for the emergency measure. The faculty maintained standing committees dealing with the curriculum, registration, admissions, lectures and concerts, other public functions, student health, chapel services, the library, the daily schedule, and the catalogue. Mrs. Allie Hayes Richardson served as secretary to the faculty throughout the entire period. Of course an undetermined number of other persons was on campus as maintenance workers, maids, and kitchen employees.

President Blocker and Furry employed about 85 faculty members, of whom one-third remained only one year and 20, no more than two. Among the 54 associated with the college for two or more years, the highest earned degrees were distributed as follows: bachelor's, 23 (thirteen of these claimed additional work on the next degree); master's, 17 (eleven of these claimed additional work on the next degree); doctor's, 14. Among the nonmusicians holding an advanced degree, the graduate schools frequently attended were at Columbia and Johns Hopkins universities, the Southern Baptist Theological Seminary, and the universities of Chicago, Georgia, Illinois, and Indiana. The musicians at Shorter two or more years had most often received their professional education at Oberlin Conservatory, Shorter College, and various schools in Europe, including frequently the Conservatoire Fontainebleau of France.

ART. The once-vigorous art department declined after 1923 when Miss Imogen Coulter retired. Leaving with her were the two groups that she had fostered, the Art Lovers Club and the Sketch Club. For two years only the course in art appreciation was taught by part-time teachers, after which art was completely removed from the curriculum and the Buttolph Medal was no longer awarded. The vacant studio was converted into dormitory rooms, and the aged equipment was thrown away or stored in the basement of Cooper Hall. In 1930 Miss Martha Griffin became instructor in art, occupying as her studio a room on the first floor of the Music Building that quickly proved most inadequate. Understandably the 31 s.h. that she offered at first had very little studio work included! Nevertheless, an annual art exhibit at commencement was initiated in 1931.

ENGLISH. Composition, literature, and speech continued to be administered within the department of English, but in practice a major was offered by each division. Courses in composition and literature, reduced during this period from 70 to 58 s.h., were taught by the same persons, including Paul M. Cousins and Miss Jeanette Foster, who for six years was associate professor of English. Dedicated to Cousins, the 1928 *Argo* described him as one "who has been content to stand behind the scenes, whose slight gesture of disapproval, quiet word of encouragement and slow smile of confidence have inspired in us the desire to put into the playing of our roles the richness of beauty and truth . . . ." In the *Harper's Magazine* for October of 1927, Miss Foster published a short story, "Lucky Star," set in a quiet Southern town and including details suggestive of Colonel Shorter and Thornwood, Mount Alto, and the Coosa River. The Phi Kappa Alpha Study Club presented biweekly literary programs as the societies gradually lost interest in that sort of thing. For those concerned with creative writing, the Shorter Scribes was formed in 1922, becoming Chi Delta Phi in 1925 and Rho Delta in 1928.

FOREIGN LANGUAGES. Five classical and modern languages were taught during this period: 20 s.h. of Greek, as much as 51 s.h. of Latin, 36 s.h. each of French and Spanish, and 12 s.h. of German, which was resumed in 1926. Dr. Clara Thompson greatly expanded the offerings in Latin; Dr. and Mrs. John N. Ware provided instruction in modern languages for many years; Miss Sara Woodruff, a Shorter alumna who later earned the Doctor of Philosophy degree, was associate professor of French for six years; Paul McConnell was associate professor of Spanish for six years; and Miss Ida Vandiver, a graduate of the college, returned for one year as assistant in French.

The Classical Club met monthly for study and annually produced a Latin play. A French honorary fraternity, Beta Pi Theta, lived briefly in the late twenties. The French Club one year claimed nearly one hundred members, becoming a division of the Modern Language Club about 1929. The other division was devoted to the study of German but was not yet particularly popular with the girls. The Spanish Club became the Hispanic Society about 1927, sponsoring scholarly and social activities similar to those of the other language groups.

Beyond question the best known professor of language at Shorter during this time was the colorful Dr. John N. Ware, who was married to the German-born, former Miss Dora Anna Elizabeth, baroness von

237

Turckheim-Baden. His doctoral dissertation on Bernardin de Saint-Pierre was published in 1927 by Johns Hopkins University. Possessed with a "boundless supply" of jokes and puns, he conducted numerous summer tours to France that were as popular with the students as were his classes. He published two books, *How to Find Old Paris* (London, 1927) and *The Familiar Guide to Paris* (London, 1928), that were urbane, breezy, witty, relaxed, entertaining, and informative. A devoted lover of the city and its residents, whom he sometimes termed "Parisites," he followed in the line of "Gregoire of Tours, who was one of the earliest Tourists of recorded history." Even in Paris, however, he could not always forget Shorter and its affairs, referring to the R.O.K. motto, *Haec olim meminisse juvavit*, Toonerville, "Mudville's Grand Uproar season, as the Chattanoogans rather cattishly call Atlanta's musical week," the Athletic Association, and his students' skirts that "barely *did* make it . . . down to the knees . . . ." One writer in the *Periscope* composed a letter on his behalf reminding Santa Claus that "I deserve a lot this year, for you yourself said that my book, *How To Find Old Paris*, had helped you considerably . . . ." Already he was composing thoughtful, little poems; four of them concerned experiences at Nice, Fontainebleau, Chartres, and Paris, each concluding with the refrain, "So runs my catalogue of lovely things." Because of his growing reputation, he was elected president of the South Atlantic Division of the Modern Language Association.

History and Social Science. With the coming of Miss Mildred Mell, dean of women and professor of social science, the department of history and political science was divided. Under Miss Clara Kellogg, the continuing department of history offered 55 s.h., while the new department of social science scheduled only 10 s.h. of sociology and 5 s.h. of economics. Miss Kellogg spent many summers traveling in France, Italy, Germany, Turkey, Egypt, England, and Romania, as well as studying at several American universities. A constant exponent of the A.A.U.W., Dean Mell was president of the Georgia branch and once addressed the national convention in Boston. The International Relations Club met monthly; one year a Shorter student was elected vice-president of the Southern States Conference on International Relations held at Duke University.

Mathematics and Science. Instruction in the sciences and mathematics grew slightly during this period to a total of 46 s.h. in biology, 36 s.h. in chemistry, 32 s.h. in physics, and 40 s.h. in mathematics. Four professors provided vigorous leadership: Dr. Bertha Martin in biology, Dr. Everett E. Porter in chemistry, Dr. Lawrence E. McAllister in physics, and Dr. Ruby Hightower in mathematics. In 1927 the latter received the Doctor of Philosophy degree from the University of Missouri, becoming the first Shorter graduate to earn that highest academic award. Six other alumnae were assistants more briefly in these fields: Misses Odelle Moore, Hilda Jackson, and Mabel Thompson in mathematics and physics; Miss Marion McGinty in mathematics; and Misses Margaret Mustin and Dorothy Morton in biology. It could be said that one of the junior music majors happily joined the chemistry department and thereby postponed her graduation; Miss Hazel Myers was married to Professor Porter in 1924, receiving her degree seven years later. Kappa Gamma Tau, a club for science and mathematics majors, was organized at Shorter in 1922, providing monthly professional programs and two or three socials each year. For a time the annual weekend biology camp was scheduled each spring on Mount Lavender.

Music. Clearly stating that Shorter was not a conservatory of music, the college nevertheless offered a consistent 31 s.h. of classes in musical history and theory and four years of individual instruction in piano, organ, voice, and violin. Four courses of 2 s.h. each were added in 1932 dealing with public school music. Throughout, attention was given to the training of young ladies as church organists and choir directors. Serving as director of music during most of this time, Arthur Sackett Talmadge was on the faculty for twelve years. Wilbur H. Rowand began a nineteen-year period as teacher of organ and theory and later as director of music. Miss Unnie Christine Ramsey gave lessons in piano for thirteen years. Miss Louise Bennet taught voice for five years and another alumna, Miss Marion Bush, was assistant in piano for two years. Apparently "The Wedding March" was a favorite with some members of the department: Miss Ethel Brown, shortly after her graduation in 1927, was married to Professor Talmadge, and Miss Anne Evelyn Simmons, soon after her graduation in 1931, was married to Professor Rowand. Two years later Mrs. Rowand received the first Bachelor of Music degree to be awarded on the present campus, with a major in organ.

As many as thirty recitals were scheduled annually—by students, faculty members, visiting artists, and the musical organizations of the college. The MacDowell Choral Club, which became the Shorter Choral Club in 1929, presented special programs at Christmas, Easter, and commencement. The Camerata Club, organized in 1922, normally had a most serious purpose for its frequent meetings, but starting in

1924 the Camerata Follies were annually given. Employing the talents of faculty and students alike, the group staged elegant numbers with such titles as "No Bodies," "Four Yards of Gingham," "a l'Armuchee," "Felix—The Grave Yard Kitty," "Tramp Tunes," "Hiram goes a' Courtin'," and "Hash." One enthusiastic girl wrote: "We would never need a trip to New York for anything in the 'follies' line . . . . What a shame those follies are only a yearly affair." Much more painfully formal were those recitals given by juniors and seniors in partial fulfillment of graduation requirements—but at least the senior sufferer might look forward to congratulatory gifts of flowers, jewelry, clothing, and perhaps even $20 from her favorite Uncle Floyd. In the Rome city auditorium and in Atlanta the young ladies were able to hear music of a quality sometimes superior even to that heard on the campus. Several Metropolitan stars, the Minneapolis Symphony Orchestra under the direction of Eugene Ormandy, Fritz Kreisler, José Iturbi, Ignace Jan Paderewski, and various operatic companies furnished such opportunities to them—as well as an outing.

PHYSICAL EDUCATION. The new swimming pool effected a predictable change in the department of physical education: courses in swimming were quickly added to the curriculum—and the ability to swim, as a requirement for graduation. The 6 s.h. of required courses included some swimming, while electives were introduced in diving and lifesaving. The only director of physical education remaining a signficant length of time was Miss Willie Dean Andrews, a Shorter graduate, who served her alma mater six years.

PSYCHOLOGY AND EDUCATION. Formed in 1929, the combined department of psychology and education provided courses that had earlier been offered by the separate departments of education and philosophy. Despite his reservations concerning vocational training at the collegiate level, Dr. Furry taught psychology and education until his election as president. Later Dr. Cameron D. Ebaugh served as professor of psychology and education for thirteen years. Observing the requirements set by the Georgia State Department of Education, the department gradually expanded its offerings to 44 s.h. Eight courses in high school teaching methods were developed to deal with English, history, Latin, mathematics, modern languages, physical education, music, and social science.

RELIGION. Briefly under President Blocker and for thirteen years under Richard Hall, the department of Bible slightly increased its offerings to a total of 29 s.h., adding courses in New Testament and one in Christian history. Affectionately called "Dr. Bible Hall" in order to distinguish him from a biology professor who was designated "Dr. Bug Hall," Richard Hall was honored when the athletes who discovered five baby rabbits born near the tennis courts named one for him. "Dicky Hall," "Milly Mell," "Willie D.," "Cousin Paul," and "Johnny Ware" contributed much to campus life during the spring of 1927. More seriously, Hall was recalled by one student who had heard him speak concerning the necessity of praying clearly and distinctly. Thinking of the deacon in her church who mumbled interminably, she exclaimed: "I thought you prayed to God!" A separate department of philosophy listed two or three courses, but these were only infrequently offered.

SPEECH. Under Mrs. Allie Hayes Richardson, course offerings in speech declined from 34 to 24 s.h., but public performances sponsored by this subdepartment expanded. Each year the stages in the auditorium or the Play Shop on the second floor of the Music Building were crowded with recitals given by juniors and seniors majoring in speech, one-act plays and sketches, student-directed plays, original plays written by seniors, and three-act plays regularly presented each fall, spring, and commencement. The Shakespearean commencement play was held out-of-doors when weather permitted until the mid-twenties, after which the Bard of Avon was bypassed in favor of contemporary dramatists and the program was moved into the auditorium. Making history on March 6, 1933, the Darlington-Shorter Players staged the first co-ed performance on the hill in the form of two one-act plays. The Georgia Association of Teachers of Speech, of which Mrs. Richardson was first president, invited the Shorter girls to present a play at the convention held in Macon. It was reported by one actress that their trip did not take the anticipated five to six hours because Mrs. Richardson drove the lead car fifty and sixty all the way! It was also reported that on the return trip the girls had a glorious day and a half in Atlanta, "the city of Shorter's delight."

Administration and Staff

Outside the classroom, numerous persons contributed to the well-being of the college. Miss Virginia Wendell was dean of women for nine years, being succeeded by Miss Mildred Mell, who soon became dean of the college. "Because she seeks to understand our problems and to help us solve them," two different issues of the *Argo* were dedicated to Dean Mell, "whose untiring efforts in our behalf have given her a place of love and respect in the heart of every Shorter girl . . . ." Miss Louise Thompson was employed as secretary to the president in 1924, being permitted to take two courses each semester toward her degree. Graduating in 1930 as a member of Phi Sigma Alpha, she was aptly characterized in the *Argo* that year with this quotation, "Sympathy is the golden key that unlocks the hearts of others"—and shortly thereafter she became registrar. In the business office, Miss Tennie Rhinehart was for eighteen years the cashier.

Growing in size from about 8,500 to 12,000 volumes, the library was constantly curtailed by a budget that never exceeded $3,000 in any given year. For fifteen years Miss Parthenia George was librarian; it was she who, on the present campus, first completely catalogued the collection by the Dewey Decimal System.

Mrs. N. B. King was housekeeper or supervisor of the dormitories for fifteen years. A second wedding on the hill occurred in 1922 when her only daughter, Georgia, a graduate of the college in 1918, was married to George C. Tinsley before an improvised altar at the end of the Academic Building. The second funeral on the present campus was conducted in the college parlor at the death of Mrs. King in 1927. Coincidentally, Dr. Furry officiated at both of these services. For the next five years, Mrs. Cora W. Huguley was in charge of the dormitories. "Sister Maggie" Jacobs continued as resident nurse—in what John F. Stevens, the night watchman, called the "informatory."

Dieticians usually remained only a year or two, suggesting that there was some truth to a joke included in the *Argo*: "Miss Wendell: 'Mr. Cousins, will you ask the blessing?' Mr. Cousins (looking at the food display) : 'Sorry, but I cannot conscientiously do so.'" In 1931, however, Mrs. Jennie B. Hurst began a career as dietician that lasted almost twenty years. Senor Ortiz, affectionately dubbed "Willy in the Kitchen," came from Mexico with little knowledge of the English language, married an American girl, and eventually was cook at Shorter in the late twenties. An honorary member of the Hispanic Society, he entertained the girls with his original Spanish poetry and his guitar.

Designated the superintendent of grounds, Howard Hull actually performed a multitude of tasks on campus for a decade. Because he was postman, among other things, one senior class willed him "a three weeks' vacation, much needed because of the popularity of our class as shown by our heavy correspondence." Later, Lon Smith spent thirty-four years in much the same capacity. From 1916 to 1927 the night watchman was "Mr. Mac" MacDurmont, being replaced by John F. Stevens.

In the dormitories, kitchen, and yard, several black workers displayed their loyalty to the college through long years of service. The maids included Mrs. Alice Wood, Mrs. Callie Hale, Mrs. Mary Jo Lewis, Mrs. Jessie Wood, and Mrs. Delores Thornton. A long-time favorite of the girls, Mrs. Victoria Anderson continued as receptionist in the entrance hall of the Academic Building. Her severe illness caused much concern, and many at the college inquired about her, went to see her, and sent flowers. Fortunately she recovered and was soon back on the job at the main door, displaying her amazing memory for names and faces as she recalled the returning alumnae. Among the men were Roy Brannon, Steve Graham, Spencer Hughes, and Solomon Thornton, waiters; Roy Barton, chef; and Aaron Shelton and Berry Jenkins, yardmen.

Student Government and the Students' Hand-Book

The Student Government Association of Shorter College was comprised of each member of the student body, with a Student Council made up of representatives from the three upper classes and the day students. Each spring an installation service marked the entrance into office of the new leaders, and on alternate Friday evenings the entire association met. Membership was held in the National Student Federation of the United States of America and in the Southern Intercollegiate Association of Student Government, and Shorter girls sometimes attended the annual conventions.

Appointed by the president of the college, an advisory committee from the faculty conferred with the Student Council when the necessity arose. Furry observed: "The Youth Movement, so conspicuous in our day, has made its appearance in our college, and students are demanding the right, not only of self-government, but of determining the course of study and the conditions under which their work is to be done. During the past few years numerous cases of conflict of authority have arisen . . . ." As a consequence, monthly conferences were scheduled some years involving student and faculty leaders, "for the consideration of all criticisms of the college by the students and for the removal of legitimate occasion for dissatisfaction."

The *Students' Hand-Book,* issued each summer, contained much that related to student life. The newly established Honor System provided that each student would be responsible for her own observance of the rules and for reporting to the Student Council those whom she discovered disobeying them, "unless," the provision added, "you feel capable of dealing with the problem yourself . . . ."

Rules did not cease being detailed—and ridiculed or disregarded.

Quiet was specified for 18½ hours daily, leading one class to write new rules that included this one: "Make all the noise possible during study hour. It sounds so cheerful." "Regulations regarding the telephone will be posted at the opening of school," and they were rigorous. "Students are allowed to hold telephone communications only with members of their immediate families." "Students leaving the college on a visit home or elsewhere must have written permission from parent or guardian. This permission must be mailed direct to the Dean of Women or President of the college." Because of this rule, a Christmas letter was included in the *Periscope* on behalf of Dean Mell which concluded: "Let me add that I shall be looking in every mail for your written permission from Mrs. Claus. By no means let her call or wire, and have her state in the letter whom you are to visit." "Restricted students may not leave the college except to see a dentist or physician, or in case of necessity, and in every case permission must be obtained . . . ." This led one writer to surmise: "Soon Shorter campus will have to be greatly enlarged in order to make room for all the Shorter girls who are campused."

In the early twenties a group slipped away on a free Monday without signing out. News heard along the way that a couple of murderers were hiding on Mount Alto did not immediately deter them from their outing. One of them later admitted: "Some of the zest had gone from our adventure, it was obvious, but no one commented. . . . Famished and silently apprehensive, we called a halt in order to cook the eggs" which had been purchased. In the midst of the meal, a frightened girl exclaimed: "Gee, they could clobber us over the head and no one would ever find the bodies." Wrote the one telling the story: "Without further discussion we tossed out the remainder of the eggs and began the descent. I am sure that we set an all-time record for getting down Mount Alto . . . ."

Of course the question was soon raised concerning automobiles on campus, and the catalogue was quite clear: "Students are not permitted to have automobiles. During the opening and closing days of the college year automobiles may be used under such regulations as the Dean of the college may announce. Automobiles are difficult and expensive to provide for at the college and generally prove a handicap to serious college work."

Countless other regulations were on the books, some of which were these: "No student may hold conversation with men without special permission." "Students are not allowed to wear men's apparel except on authorized occasions." "Plans for public entertainments or stunts must be submitted to the Dean of Women for her approval." "Students are held responsible for the neatness and order of their rooms, which must be ready for inspection every morning at 8:30, except Sunday and Monday. No trash may be swept into the corridors or thrown out the windows." "Students dressed in bloomers or knickers may not enter the Academic Building."

In 1931 and 1932, President Furry wrote the parents of his charges, expressing his personal opposition to smoking on campus but asking what their attitude would be if he changed the rule and allowed it. An avalanche of responses resulted! Most of the respondents would have agreed with the one who said: "I much prefer the odor of violets to cigarettes." A typical request read: "If it ever becomes necessary for you to permit this character of conduct from your young ladies, please put my daughter on the train and start her home." Several agreed to abide by his judgment, indicating that they would not withdraw their daughters. One mother replied by admitting that her daughter smoked in her presence and with her permission, adding that she would nevertheless insist that her daughter obey the school rule. The rule was not liberalized at this time!

A Christian Ideal

For many years the college catalogue carried a statement of ideals that said: "From its beginning Shorter College has been an avowedly Christian College and has sought to build its work on the profoundest and most substantial convictions of Christian people. Its ideal has always been to furnish the highest educational advantage under positive religious influence. In truth, Shorter seeks to be both educational and religious in character, and proceeds upon the assumption that a college can be both at once without in any way jeopardizing or minimizing the place and influence of either . . . . The college is non-sectarian in its management and has made itself the servant of a wider fellowship. . . . The development and conservation of the religious faith of the students is a matter of primary concern, and a reverential attitude toward the Bible as the Word of God is always and everywhere maintained."

Religious services and organizations were a part of the practical expression of this ideal. Chapel was held daily at 10:30, usually led by the president of the college, other members of the faculty, or students, and included music by the chapel choir. Visitors included Dr. Edmund D. Soper, numerous Georgia pastors, and one young preacher who selected the same topic as his mother's Shorter graduation essay back in 1882, "Big I and Little You." On Friday the time was often devoted to Bible study groups taught by faculty members. John L. Hill of the Southern Baptist Sunday School Board delivered a series of talks on campus, as did the popular Dr. W. A. Smart of Emory University, but neither was a part of a regular annual observance.

The Y.W.C.A. continued to be active and useful. Each spring officers and committees were elected, being installed at a candlelight vesper service on Sunday evening. Before classes began in the fall, these leaders held a planning retreat, and early each fall another candlelight vesper service recognized the new girls who had joined the group. Later in the year six persons were elected to the Freshman Commission, providing the new students with a voice in the affairs of the association. Furnishing a physical focus for the association, a "Y.W. Hall" was maintained, containing a library of new and standard religious books for student use. Fifteen minutes after breakfast morning watch occurred. Named for Mesdames Shorter, Cooper, and Poteat, the three circles functioned for a number of years, dropping out of sight in the late twenties. The general meeting on Tuesday evening might feature a visiting Y.W.C.A. representative, Dr. Smart, young men from the Emory Y.M.C.A., a local pastor, or one of the Shorter members. Some years the group sponsored "Hilltop Views," a small religious publication. Two or three times a year the association gave a party at Maplehurst or in the gymnasium, including always some kind of entertainment at the beginning of the school year. Maintaining its attraction, the college-owned cottage at Blue Ridge, North Carolina, was filled with Shorter girls for ten days each June in connection with the annual Y.W.C.A. conference. In the early thirties joint state meetings of the Y.W.C.A. and Y.M.C.A. were held near Athens, and a Shorter pupil was co-president one year. Other conventions were attended in Tennessee and Indiana and at Wesleyan College. Each Sunday evening the girls attended a religious service that usually included music from the vesper choir and a talk by some invited guest. Just before Christmas and at Easter, the college choir presented during the vesper hour a concert that was widely publicized to secure general attendance. One December the college closed early because of an influenza epidemic; the Christmas carol program, which had already been prepared, was given the following January 6!

During the spring semester of 1926 the Y.W.C.A. president, Mary Long Calloway, was influential in organizing a group for the study of missions and world religions. After her unexpected death that spring, the members adopted a new name as a memorial to the founder. For several years thereafter, ten or twelve meetings of the Mary Calloway Study Group were scheduled each semester.

Comprised of young ladies expecting to become foreign missionaries, a local unit of the Student Volunteer Movement existed. Members had periodic meetings, attended state conventions at Shorter and elsewhere, and traveled to national conferences at Buffalo and Milwaukee. Only Miss Helen Meredith of the class of 1932 eventually saw mission service, although she was not contemplating it during her college years.

The Baptist Young People's Union again briefly functioned on campus, followed by another short-lived Young Woman's Auxiliary. Although the Baptist Student Union became more widely known in the late twenties, none was formed that early at Shorter. However, in 1928 a picture of the Academic Building was carried on the cover of the monthly *Baptist Student*.

For many years the Martha Shorter Sunday school class at the First Baptist Church enlisted the girls. Contributing to its popularity were Halloween and Christmas parties and spring barbecues, especially when young men in shiny sedans and sports roadsters provided transportation.

Chiefly through the Y.W.C.A., the girls exercised an influence beyond the confines of the campus, helping at the Open Door Home and other social service agencies. At Thanksgiving about twenty baskets of food were distributed to needy families, and the Christmas tree for West Rome children was a highlight. Collected in a variety of ways, including a Golden Rule Dinner and a Y.W.C.A. Delicatessen, funds were distributed to the Community Chest, the Salvation Army, and Near East relief.

Numerous were the rules covering Sunday observance. Students were "expected" to attend the Sunday school and church of their choice in the morning, and commercial transportation was made available to get them there on time. Attendance at the evening vesper was "required," with no more than three absences a semester. Only after explicit permission was given by the dean could the girls enter a store or make a purchase. Guests from out of town might be entertained from 3:00 to 5:00 P.M. in the college parlor—otherwise, the pupils were expected to maintain quiet in their rooms from 2:00 to 4:00 for the purpose of meditation. None could go to the lake, to the theater or picture show, to ride, or to Sunday dinner at the hotel.

Until 1926 the Sarah A. Faust Medal was annually awarded for an essay on some phase of Sunday school work, after which it was discontinued and the interest was allowed to accumulate.

Detailed figures regarding denominational affiliation or preference are not readily available, but enough is known to indicate that sixty-five to seventy-five percent of the girls were at least nominally Baptist. As during earlier administrations, doubtless the Methodists, Presbyterians, and Episcopalians were the larger minority groups.

Student Publications

Advertising itself as a bimonthly newspaper, the *Periscope* actually appeared no more than nine times each year under the direction of an editor elected by the student body. Measuring 14 by 20 inches, the four-to-six-page issues sold for 10¢ each or $1.50 per year. In the absence of a separate *Alumnae Bulletin*, occasional numbers were edited by the alumnae. A senior-sophomore number, with Whoop-Em-Up blue and orange, and a junior-freshman number, with High-Minded yellow and green, were issued, and also one honoring the two literary societies. Every issue carried about one page of advertising, and most of them reproduced photographs and cartoons drawn by students.

Appearing quarterly, the *Chimes* was the literary magazine published by an editorial board elected by the students. Available at $1.00 per year, it contained twenty-four to sixty pages. During the twenties each issue featured news articles as well as literary items, but the inclusion of news was virtually discontinued in the thirties. A writers' contest was usually held each year with a prize for the best short story, essay, and poem. It was once observed: "Chimes staff swamped with contributions to contest. Both manuscripts were good." In some of the issues, the General Alumnae Association included news notes, and individual alumnae contributed many poems and essays. The magazine was partly financed by advertisements, in the midst of which one playful editor inserted this sentence:

"I rather thought you'd do something like that!"

The senior class gladly accepted responsibility for the yearbook, the *Argo*. One of ten in the country so honored, the 1924 annual was given honorable mention by the Arts and Crafts Society. The first colored pictures appeared in 1930 as eight campus scenes were reproduced by a rather unsophisticated five-color process. Ordinarily the superlatives and beauties were selected by their fellow students, but in 1927 the beauties were judged by none other than Florenz Ziegfeld himself! Apart from the $5 subscription fee, the annual was financed by the sale of advertisements, and by many projects that included a benefit oyster supper and performances by the glee clubs of Mercer and Georgia Tech.

College Songs

Praises to the college abounded in new songs that were written. "Shorter Spirit" grandly announced:

> Shorter Spirit never dead!
> Shorter's gonna win again!
> Shoot 'em in the eye, and knock 'em in the head!
> Shorter's gonna win again!
>
> We know it, indeed we know it, Sisters!
> We know it! Shorter's gonna win again!

It then continued:

> She's got the rep,
> She's got the pep,
> She's always on the spot!
> Uphold your standards,
>   Shorter girl,
> And tell the world what's what!

"Dear Old Shorter Hill" was honored by Inez Rumble, class of 1929, who penned words that were used for twenty-five years:

> Up in North Georgia 'mong those hills
> You'll find it nestled there,
> A little spot to us so dear.
> More than any elsewhere—
> Each glad hour that's past now
> Brings a memory still,
> And we love our college,
> Dear old Shorter Hill!

For fifteen years "Alma Mater" by Mary K. Bruner had been sung to a familiar tune shared by many schools. In 1932 Wilbur H. Rowand, instructor of organ, composed a melody that has been used exclusively since then.

Intramural Sports

All members of the student body were urged to become a part of the Athletic Association, the aim of which was to promote interest in sports among the students and to develop true sportsmanship. A Sports Council was composed of the usual four officers, plus class representatives. Income for the association was derived from the annual dues of $1 per student and from admission to parties and programs—a masquerade ball, a minstrel, a "Movie Ball," or a swimming carnival. In 1929 the organization was recognized by the Women's Division of the National Amateur Athletic Federation.

Activities sponsored by the asssociation at one time or another were golf, tennis, archery, hiking, volley ball, soccer, basketball, swimming, water polo, baseball, track and field events, and horseback riding. For a number of years a three-hole golf course was in use on campus; Mr. Cooper's gift had found a second life.

While participation was advocated for the pleasure and benefit of the individual, much emphasis was placed on competition between classes. After noisy elimination tournaments, trophies were given annually to the winning teams in volley ball, basketball, soccer, swimming, and baseball, and to individual winners in archery, golf, and tennis. Arm bands were awarded to those most active, while Shorter sweaters were presented to girls having eight arm bands. Some years a Shorter "Fish" and a pillow cover were also included among the awards.

The "noble and dignified instructors" vied with student teams in basketball and volley ball, adopting pink and scarlet or purple and green as their colors. On one such occasion, "when everybody had assembled in the gymnasium, the Faculty marched in with their team leading. They were holding high the cup they had won in '23. . . . They yelled and sang to their own team and to their opponents, the All-Stars. The five who represented the Faculty on the team had plenty of support from the rest of the Faculty on the side lines. . . . When the game ended the score was 35-26 in favor of the Faculty. After the game the Faculty team marched around the gymnasium, jubilant over the victory and holding high the cup which they had not lost."

In 1926 the *Periscope* mentioned the issue of intercollegiate sports for women's teams, without taking a position either way. The official policy of the college was not changed, however: "Intercollegiate contests are not permitted."

The Two Societies

Abandoning all thoughts of being literary organizations, the Eunomian and Polymnian societies functioned almost altogether for the entertainment of their members. Rushing rules detailed acceptable methods of obtaining pledges, concluding with the statement: "It is to be considered highly unethical to discuss the merits or demerits of either society." On the first and second Saturday nights of the school year, the societies presented elaborate entertainments in the gymnasium designed to impress the freshmen. Written by Hazel Tuggle,

"A Woman's Might" told the story of the goddess Eunomia, sad because she must leave her home at the age of eighteen and rule over a land in the distant domain of her father. His words encouraged her to help this country which needed a wise leader: "A good woman's might is the gift of the gods." Promising sustained love one for the other, she and her beloved Eros tearfully parted. Five years later her work in the distant land had been completed and the crown transferred to a more willing head. Eros took Eunomia back with him, but her loving spirit lingered always near her former subjects who cherished the colors that symbolized her, "olive green for peace in the heart, and darker green for victory over all obstacles." "In Quest of Polymnia" portrayed a grieving Peter Pan who discovered his affection for the absent Polymnia. Searching through many countries of the globe, he was temporarily diverted by dancers and singers from Spain, Egypt, Japan, Iceland, a New York night club, the sunny South, and elsewhere. At length he heard the strains of "I Love the Name of Polymnian," and found Polymnia and Mammy on Shorter hill. Prominent in the skit were Poly the parrot and the society colors, "the red standing for red-blooded young women, the white for earnestness of purpose, and the green for unswerving loyalty." Of course each playlet varied from year to year, as did the overall motif of the evening, which might center on a ship, nursery, Japanese garden, toyland, or carnival. A throne was used for the president clad in white, and starting in 1924 a coronation ceremony was a part of the evening. Invariably refreshments were served, and music for dancing among the girls was furnished by a visiting orchestra.

By 10:30 on Sunday evening after the second program, all of the legal rushing had been completed and the old members could only sit up late and wonder how things would turn out. A line formed at 5:30 on Monday morning in the freshman dormitory. When the pledge bell rang at 6:00, "it sounded as if a drove of wild horses had been turned loose in the halls." Galloping into the vestibule of the Academic Building and hoping to be the first to arrive, each girl indicated her choice at a desk where the two presidents sat. "There you write Polymnian or Eunomian—entirely forgetting how to spell either name, but quite sure which you are." To the appropriate hall she sped, where she was greeted with open arms, an incredible amount of singing and shouting, and joyful tears. The remainder of the day was unusually quiet, but only because the older members would take the pledges downtown for breakfast, shopping, a visit to the drug store, a show, and dinner. Always attracting the greater number of new students, the Polymnian Society reached a high of 159 and averaged 120,

251

while the Eunomian Society had to be content with a high of 94 and an average of 73. Virtually every girl purchased a society pin, some of which were decorated with semiprecious stones.

The president of each group served for a full year, and the custom was continued of presenting her at retirement with a gift such as a silver loving cup or a platinum pin with a small bow knot centered with a sapphire. Pictured with white caps, red and black neckerchiefs, and sneering expressions, the Thugs were Eunomian leaders formed as a service organization. Their Polymnian counterparts were the H.O.T.s, smilingly wearing black skull caps with long horns.

Society programs came each Saturday evening after dinner, attended by some with long dresses and by others with flapper dresses. Seldom serious in nature, they took many forms: a wedding in verse; an entertainment "with the wonderful invention of television"; spoofs of a Student Council meeting, faculty meeting, the faculty table in the dining room, a classroom, or a birthday party given by "Willie Furry"; "The Vamp's Tragedy"; a fashion show; "The Shooting of Dan Mc-Grew"; "Polymnia's Him Book"; a debate on the topic, "If two can't sleep alone, why can't one sleep together?"; or a literary meeting at the home of Mrs. Poodedoode. The Eunomians enjoyed a weiner roast each fall for many years, and both groups observed the coming of Christmas and Santa Claus. In the late twenties the Polymnians sent money to China to help Mrs. Edwin McNeill Poteat, Jr. (née Miss Wilda Hardman, class of 1916), whose husband a decade earlier had written one of the favorite society songs. They also accumulated $350 for a scholarship loan fund, by selling "slumber pillows" or charging admission to a performance by the Mercer Players. Each hall was periodically renovated, new pieces of furniture were added, and the graduating seniors often joined to give a useful present.

Both societies were full of melody! A much-used song was written by Hazel Tuggle and Caroline Gray in 1923:

> Once upon the mount of Olympia
> Stood a goddess in love with green.
> To her the symbols peace and victory
> Were the sweetest she'd ever seen.
> The name of the girl was Eunomia,
> And she took her colors for true,
> And now upon old Shorter Hill
> She is loved and honored anew.
> The green doth stand for victory
> We'll win whate'er we do.
> The girls of Eunomia loyal shall be,
> So, Eunomia, here's to you.

Two others were soon added, beginning, "Eunomians, you are the best society in the east or west," and "Going back, going back, going back to Eunomian Hall." The Polymnians were no less vocal, but their three most popular songs had been composed in the decade before.

While it is true that rivalry was chiefly expressed by attempting to win the greater number of new members each fall, it was not always restricted to that. Every two or three years the alumnae offered a loving cup to the society earning more money at the annual Christmas bazaar, and great enthusiasm was displayed in attempting to win it. During the Blocker administration the inter-society debate was discontinued—"for the best interest of Shorter," as he said—and an effort to revive it failed. Probably at the same time the basketball game was halted, but in 1927 the Polymnians issued a challenge that was promptly accepted. The report was published: "No lives lost"—but the challengers lost the game by a score of 24 to 22. Their later challenge was also accepted, but a lack of interest resulted in a cancellation.

Classes, Generations, and the Crook

"Like a thunderbolt out of the sky, came the unexpected crash of initiation" each fall shortly after the freshmen had been made to feel so important and secure. Taking revenge upon the juniors by abusing their only children, the sophomores delighted in their claims of superiority. Perhaps the first notice would come in a note: "Freshman! Don't ask any questions! When the Rec. bell rings Wednesday night! You be in the gym! Bring 25¢ *Sure*. Your impertinence and lack of respect for our seniors and sophomores has been stood long enough. *Beware!!!*" Or sophomores might descend upon a hapless freshman at 11:00 P.M., blindfold her, and lead her to "a dark underground cavern" where she was told in detail of her insignificance and made to crawl in the dust. Or a student body meeting might be called for Tuesday night, not Friday, from which the juniors were excused because the business at hand did not relate to them. Thereupon rat court was held, where one dined daintily on a cake of soap, another chewed two or three packages of gum to the tune of "Alma Mater," and others presented orations, songs, dances, and readings, amidst jeers and taunts. For two or three days the ratting continued, although one reported that "it seemed like years." Her required attire might be a dress twenty inches from the floor, unmatched cotton stockings stuffed with newspapers "to give the effect of shapely legs," one oxford, one high heeled shoe, hair parted in the center and pulled back, with a green F on her forehead and paper rat ears on her head. Setting-up exercises before breakfast were popular, as were hikes on fly paper, snacks in the form of castor oil, and books carried in pillowcases. She was sometimes carefully instructed until she was proficient at singing various inane ditties. When she met a sophomore early in the morning, she was often required to greet her with this salutation: "May you fare well today, most high and mighty sophomore. I am but a lowly worm." At such a meeting later in the day, she might kneel, kiss the outstretched hand, and humbly admit: "I'm a lowly rat, 'cause look where I'm at." She could march up and down the road guarding the campus with a broom on her shoulder, count all the leaves under an assigned tree, or pull out all the tacks in the rafters of the gymnasium. Indoor exercise at times included rolling an onion down the hall with her nose or crawling on her hands and knees up and down the dormitory steps with her shoes in her mouth. Nor did the freshmen's problems disappear after ratting was over. Teasing could continue right up to the end of the year, when the seniors might include in their last will and testament the provision that "to the freshman class we leave our heartfelt wishes that they may improve."

The juniors adopted the freshmen, showing sympathy during and after ratting by giving them parties that would take their minds off their troubles. The freshman class was formally organized when the junior president called a meeting in the gymnasium or auditorium and supervised the election of officers. Also in the fall, the juniors presented the freshman banner to their young friends at a special ceremony, perhaps held in connection with a picnic at the Country Club. Food and dancing might be centers of attraction at a mid-winter social for which the freshmen might dress as flowers. One of them recalled: "Though some of our costumes would not have been regarded as successes from the standpoint of either beauty or botany, every one of us had the time of our lives." In the spring, a spend-the-night party might be held at Maplehurst, through the courtesy of its regular occupants, the Blockers or the Porters. Responding to the juniors' generosity, the freshmen might entertain with a "jazz party." To be examined later in this chapter is the even stronger relationship that existed between the seniors and sophomores.

The two generations, the High-Mindeds and the Whoop-Em-Ups, had distinctive colors, green and gold for the former and orange (now red) and blue for the latter. Each held meetings at which their songs were lustily rendered. The one group produced an "Odd Generation Whistle" and continued to adapt these familiar lyrics: "Junior Class is High-Minded. B'lieve to my soul they're double-jinted. They can work and don't mind it, all day long!" The Owl Club was composed of outstanding seniors who pledged to live up to the High-Minded standards and carry on the traditions that they had inherited.

In alternate years beginning in 1922, the Whoop-Em-Up junior-freshman wedding was solemnized at a formal ceremony held in the gymnasium or auditorium. A distinguished "clergyman" splendid in his frock-tailed coat officiated. Complete with music, an altar, ferns, large white chrysanthemums, a seven-branched candelabra with burning tapers, and many attendants, the bride and groom (the two class presidents) were joined in "the sacred bonds of sisterhood." Following the service, a brilliant reception concluded the festivities. This generation continued to sing about raising noisy offsprings: "And when at last we come to sit with chillun round the door, we'll teach them that the thing to do is Whoop-Em-Up some more." They almost lost the practice of issuing the *Blazer*, but after a ten-year lapse, one appeared during the spring of 1932 while the crook was hidden. The senior honorary organization was called the S.O.S. Club.

The midnight feasts that had been so popular during the Van Hoose years ceased to be fashionable in the eyes of the juniors and seniors, and by 1922 the two younger classes were alone contending for primacy. After the rules had been posted, each class tried to hold its feast without being detected by the other. Some years both were successful, but the first to make its announcement gained the greater glory. After a delicious repast of Hershey bars and pickles, one freshman gloated: "The next day we knew how Columbus felt when he discovered America." Once the sophomores held their banquet the first night even before the lights went out, with unsuspecting freshmen walking up and down the hall! Several times each class tried to hold its feast on the same night, but the result was usually a noisy argument in the courtyard that led one participant to record: "Freshman and sophomore feasts break up into riots." However, by the late twenties this kind of disorder was a thing of the past as even the freshmen and sophomores tired of the feasts.

Although other traditions might fall by the wayside, the annual search for the crook persisted with renewed spirit. Usually occupying a place of honor in Senior Den, it was brought into the dining room by the seniors and then carried around for three days so that all could see it. The stringent rules were read in the hearing of every student, followed by the crook's disappearance. Seldom was it found, even though the diligent juniors might unload the coal bins behind the kitchen or penetrate the many dark cellars. Creeping along in the attic of the Music Building, one young lady accidently pushed her foot through the ceiling above the organ. She might have examined the pipes of the organ, for it was sometimes placed among them. The area under the swimming pool was subject to careful scrutiny, as were the water tower, the vines covering most of the buildings, and the maids' closets. President Blocker cooperated one year by allowing it to be placed in his office, where its safety was assured! The sarcastic seniors encouraged the juniors by offering clues: go to Myrtle Hill's house, examine Miss Tennie's safe, open mail box number 745. The juniors once responded with a cartoon in the *Periscope*. The crook was being addressed by a policewoman who demanded: "Stop! I have a search warrant for you, and you must come with me, Mr. Crook!"

One spring it was almost captured. The juniors waited in the hall for it to be brought out of the suite where it was located. Pretending not to notice them, seniors entered and departed in a steady stream. Outside, brooms were being sent up to the room from the second floor. Eventually most of the seniors gathered in the suite. Suddenly they all came out two at a time, each pair carrying a broom covered with bed clothes. As they scattered in every direction, the bewildered juniors did not know which couple had the crook and it was again preserved from the enemy.

Relishing the taste of victory, "we, the senior class of 1933, wishing to express our joy on finding the crook in the spring of 1932, have desired to dedicate this . . . *Argo* to the crook. We admire the sporting manner in which the class of '32 has taken the loss, and we hope that this same fine spirit may prevail throughout the years, so as to make the crook a true Shorter tradition." During that fateful spring the crook was disguised as a mop and carefully hung in the ventilation shaft of a bathroom on Senior Hall. While the seniors were being entertained by their sophomores at the spring banquet, it was found by Jane Shannon, Freddie McDowell, Emmilyn Hunter, and Laura Houser. They quietly moved it to a new location, hanging it in a tree, and then taunted the seniors later that evening. The chagrined seniors quickly issued a *Blazer* carrying a headline: "Fear Al Capone's Influence Has Spread to Shorter Hill." The lead article reported: "One of the most famous crooks in the world is the Mr. Crook who has been a resident of Shorter Hill for generations untold. This person, while very retiring in nature and never given to seeking the limelight, is known to every member of the community. On Tuesday night when Mr. Crook's friends were out of residence, marauders entered his home and bore him away. Foul play is suspected. In fact there are a great many members of the community under suspicion. . . . Members of the gang will not be questioned as they have shown an inclination to give confusing clues." The senior effort to recover the crook was a failure, however, even though there were "sleepless nights, soft footsteps, flashlights, night watches, dawn breaking on the aspect of huddled figures about the campus looking for Mr. Crook— keeping sleepy eyes open for a glimpse of him or his companions." The juniors retained possession until Class Day, and photographs in their annual reveal their president, Emma Hardin Moss, proudly holding the prize. They almost came to grief the next year, however, when the crook was spotted in the physics laboratory by three freshmen and a junior. Fortunately a guardian senior got to it first, preventing the juniors from claiming possession, and it was hastily moved to another location.

Other Forms of Recreation

The four traditional parties continued to be popular forms of recreation and also expressions of class spirit and ingenuity. At Halloween the seniors might station a welcoming apparition at the gymnasium door, herd students and faculty members into a "Crazy House," and offer the services of a skilled soothsayer. During one program, "the fate, the doom, the future agony of many of the faculty members was read from parchment that had recently been brought up from the under world." Occasionally the lake provided the scene for the festivities. "Of course, there were ghosts and witches on the way, and every person crawled through barrels, shook the greasy hands of witches, and went through much misery before she reached the lake . . . ."

After a chapel service led by Dr. Furry, the juniors or sophomores were hostesses for the Thanksgiving celebration. Carefully decorating the dining room with Pilgrims and turkeys, they presented a skit—perhaps concerning the trials and successes of John Smith or John Alden —followed by a huge meal and numerous toasts. Often in the evening a dance was held in the gymnasium, with a visiting orchestra providing the music.

Although the college provided a bountiful Christmas dinner just before school was out and various organizations observed the season with a multitude of parties, no class took this day under its exclusive jurisdiction. For several years a few voice majors and their professor sang carols in the corridors and courtyard early on the day that all were to leave. Probably one student spoke for the entire student body regarding their thoughts: "Special train leaves for Atlanta at midday. Home!"

The Valentine party was sponsored by the sophomores or freshmen, who added sparkle to the dining room with hearts and cupids and signs proclaiming the importance of love. The original playlet had one unvarying theme, whether it was entitled "Heart's Shoppe," "The Land of Heart's Desire," or "Card Tricks." Usually an orchestra played throughout the banquet, while toasts and singing completed the program.

February 22 was a half holiday that included a special chapel service, a skit in the parlor or dining room, and a feast in the dining room which suddenly had been transformed into a colonial mansion. Usually the freshmen furnished the flags, the red paper hatchets, the make-believe cherry trees, and the dramatic and artistic rendering of Washington's life.

The May Day festival was a regular function, held near Lombardy Walk or between the Academic and Music buildings. Amidst much pomp and ceremony, the beautiful May queen reigned over the land, dazzling in her long white dress and sparkling crown. The theme might be a toyland festival, Robin Hood and Maid Marian, or Hansel and Gretel, but music and dancing were always featured. Once it was claimed: "Cheese cloth costumes and ice cream are inappropriate for the weather." Observing the two thousandth anniversary of Virgil's birth in 1930, the girls presented the *Aeneid* in pantomime, complete with the wooden horse and the cities of Troy and Carthage.

Providing many diversions for the campus-bound girls, social clubs existed almost without number. Each had its pledges, whose major purpose was to furnish more parties. Some of the groups were the Epsilon Delta Club, with formals, horns, and pitchforks; the Kid Club, with pink and blue bows and short dresses; the Dahm Club, with white bib overalls, pink shirts, Buster Brown collars, and large bow ties; Delta Chi, with elegant formals suggestive of the antebellum South; the Do Nothing Club, with top hats, monacles, and black bow ties; the Why Not, with a large black question mark; the D.S.A., with its pansy; and the K.A.T., with its ominous feline. Others included the Cliquot Club, D.D.D., Knowit Club, Beta Gamma, Kappa Theta, Bachelors, Barefoot Boy, Scoop Club, the Deacons, the Mummy Club, C.C., Coffin Club, the Three Musketeers, J.J.J., and Black Marauders. The Granddaughters Club, or Gamma Delta as it was later called, was comprised only of those whose relatives were Shorter alumnae. Promoting "the spirit of whoopee" at their dances in the gymnasium, the Cotillion Club was formed in the early twenties. Attendance was by invitation only, and if boys were present at all, they were in the band.

Much appreciated and enjoyed by their peers were the Shorter

Syncopators, entertainers at many dances and parties and between the acts at college plays. Saxaphones, flutes, violins, pianos, banjo-ukes, clarinets, mandolins, guitars, and ukuleles combined to contribute hours of pleasure to the instrumentalists and their audiences.

Equipped with marshmallows, coconut taffy bars, salted peanuts, sugar wafers, and other delicacies from the campus store in Hall One or the Music Building, the girls chattered away the hours in bull sessions. Some of them kept their victrolas wound up for such classics as "My Baby Ain't Come Home" and "I'm Gonna Buck Back to Kentuck." The girls scrupulously obeyed one rule, "No games may be played with regular playing cards," by using Rook decks for Mah Jongg, poker, and bridge. So adept was one that she was jokingly accused of writing a book, *How to Play Bridge in One Lesson.* Most of them reveled in the infrequent presence of snow. One diary included this entry: "Jan. 10. Few flakes of snow fall in court. Girls get out sleds and galoshes and Shorter threatens to rival St. Moritz as a winter playground."

Programs by any visitor on campus could break the routine, of course, but one variety of visitor was preferred above all others. The Georgia Tech Marionettes or the Mercer University Players merited a full auditorium and a reception afterwards. Glee clubs frequently performed, coming from the University of Alabama, Mercer, Davidson, Emory, or Sewanee. This statement described one such evening accurately enough: "Georgia Tech Glee Club come, ramble on, and leave us wrecks."

Since classes were not held on Monday, that was a popular day for going to town. A picture show might be seen at the Rivoli, Elite, or Strand; a shopping spree would probably include the store whose personnel could qualify "for such degrees as B.S. (Bachelor of Styles) and M.D. (Master of Dress)" if they were given; and a snack would be absolutely required at "the coolest fount in the city." The city auditorium presented a variety of talents attracting the girls: Sousa's band; Ruth St. Denis and Ted Shawn, dancers; Alexis Kosloff and his Ballet; and musicals such as "Blossom Time" and "Abie's Irish Rose." Three of the girls, hatless and in knickers, once borrowed an old Ford and drove it to Broad Street, where it promptly stalled. Of course they could not be expected to walk all the way back to the college. Indeed, they did not even dare get out of the car, because of their attire. Two obliging young men noted their distress, rescued them with overcoats that covered their unlawful clothing, and returned them to the campus in a new car.

Each October during Fair Week the girls were allowed to enter a float in the parade. Often given an entire day off from classes to complete it, they twice received second prize. One evening each year Mr. Carlson and his Toonerville Trolley took them to "the land of hot dogs and delight," but they were pulled away from the whip and ferris wheel by his departure at 10:00 P.M.

A favorite form of recreation was suggested by this dialogue printed in 1933: "Mother—'Is Shorter co-educational?' Frosh—'Only on Saturday nights from 8 to 10.' " Privileges were extended to the freshmen in limited numbers. They could leave the campus twice a week in groups of two or more and were always to wear hats in town. Two or three dates were permitted each month, provided written approval had come from the parent or guardian. Except on Sunday, they could have dinner at the hotel, take an automobile ride, or go to the theater (not the picture show) with a young man if properly chaperoned. Sophomores had the same privileges, except that they could leave the campus three times a week. Juniors could leave four times a week and have four dates a month. Comparatively speaking, the seniors enjoyed enormous freedom. They could leave the campus alone any day in the week, could receive young men callers any evening in the week (but not every evening in any given week), and could go unchaperoned to the picture show with young men. The Darlington boys provided some dates for the younger girls, while college men were always welcomed. When returning to the campus, the young ladies were instructed by one notice posted on the bulletin board: "Girls coming up the Hill please either ride on the college street car or walk up. The running board of cars is reserved for the family dog."

The requirement that each student "when she leaves the campus shall . . . file the date and hour of leaving, and when she returns, the hour of returning," was circumvented by some of the more observant girls. The night watchman rocked in the vestibule of the Academic Building, coming out to investigate only if a car stopped. Hence, those on a date without permission would be driven around the circle slowly, hopping out near the dormitory and slipping in without detection. One cold night a young lady jumped into a drift of snow and skinned her knees. At Sister Maggie's insistence, she missed a few days' classes; because of her own silence regarding the cause of her disability, she missed being campused.

Another girl was not as successful. Without signing out, she left the campus expecting to sneak in after hours. Caught in the act of returning, she was the center of an uproar. The next morning President Furry was seen pacing tensely up and down the hall repeating: "Young ladies, it simply isn't done." This particular girl was sent home.

As the twenties passed, several Saturdays each fall were declared holidays, enabling the girls to attend football games at Georgia, Tech, or elsewhere. Invitations to dances held on many campuses were accepted with alacrity, even though such affairs were not as yet held at Shorter. One imaginative writer in the *Periscope* bragged that 399 hearts had been "ensnared" that year by the "lovely sirens" from Shorter—and she wondered who the next one would be.

Because some of the day students felt separated from the extracurricular life of the college, they organized the Town Girls' Club. Their president asked President Blocker's permission to share more actively in social functions. At chapel the next morning he announced: "Whether you live at the foot of Shorter hill or at the top of it, you are still a Shorter student and may participate in campus social affairs." Many of them spent frequent nights on campus and were in the thick of things. Furnished a town girls' room in the Academic or Music building, they did not always use it! After repeated warnings by Dean Mell that they should not store their belongings in the society halls, they returned from classes one afternoon to discover that everything of theirs was gone. Following their initial panic and some discreet inquiry, they discovered that Victoria and Dean Mell had carefully hidden their possessions behind the ruffles on the window seats.

Seniors and Commencement

When senior rings arrived, the proud owners were graphically aware that their goal was growing ever closer. At the Class Day exercises of their junior year they were symbolically presented with their caps and gowns, but that somber outfit—complete with chokers until 1927—was not officially worn until Shorter Sunday three months later. When they occupied Senior Table in the dining room at the beginning of their last semester, they again put on caps and gowns, as they often did when attending their classmates' graduation recitals later that semester. Although frequently bewailed as a declining tradition, deference was shown the seniors by allowing them to enter or leave the dining room or the trolley car first.

If possible the seniors selected as a mascot the child of a faculty member—little Dan Blocker, Jean Porter, or Everett Porter, Jr. All year long the seniors gave parties for themselves at Maplehurst, in the gymnasium, or in Senior Den. Of course that den was constantly in need of new furnishings, and many an entertainment was sponsored, bringing in funds for that purpose. In the spring a service club often honored the seniors by inviting them to a noon meeting downtown.

Not every senior completed the year and received her degree. One *Argo* contained these words: "In memoriam of our beloved Mary, departed this state . . . to enter the holy bonds of matrimony." To a friend Mary wrote back: "How were your exams? Mine were easy; I just had one and the answer was I will! I made 100 on it." Most of them remained, however, maintaining a bulging scrapbook that might include Woolworth weight cards revealing that in four years the owner had gradually gone from 100 to 116.

During the twenties each senior continued to select "her" sophomore, perhaps sending her a note during dinner or asking her at "rec" period and perhaps taking her downtown to breakfast the next morning. Often the senior allowed her class ring to be worn by her sophomore. At Halloween or Christmas the seniors might have a party for their little sisters—and once they provided a notable outing: "Boat trip! To every sophomore and senior it conjures up memories of two cold nights spent on a river bank and an epidemic of ptomaine poison. But the river couldn't dampen the pep and the ptomaine poison couldn't kill the fun of it, for in spite of everything those girls had a good time." In turn, the sophomores gave pieces of furniture for Senior Den and informal spreads for its occupants.

Their principal function, however, was the banquet which the sophomores arranged for the seniors each spring at a downtown dining room. The invitations were cleverly designed and hand-drawn, the menus were commercially printed, and the table decorations were elaborately executed for the occasion. The food was virtually obscured by the program! Clan songs were officially transmitted at this time, much to the delight of the sophomores. Senior rings were usually returned, and each sophomore gave her senior a fine piece of jewelry. Toasts were offered and dancing concluded the evening.

For years the senior-sophomore sisters were pictured together in the *Argo*, and one annual was dedicated to "Our Sophomores . . . who have always given their loving cooperation in all we have done; whose devotion to us has been proved by many thoughtful deeds; who have always . . . shown themselves to be true 'Chillen' . . . ."

Commencement was heightened all the more by a junior prom that was planned for three or four years starting in 1927. The dormitories were full of expectation: "Oh, I'm going to have the loveliest dress—it's all fluffy and long and pink, and would you get brocade slippers or just plain?" "Oh, y'all! Jim said he could come. I'm so thrilled I can't stand it!" "See! But I hope Jack doesn't forget to send me a corsage." One typical year the juniors transformed the courtyard into "a veritable garden of the orient—a garden lighted by swinging, colorful

Japanese lanterns, and festooned with clambering vines of wisteria, and trees adorned with pink cherry blossoms. In the center of the garden a picturesque rustic bridge spanned the shimmering pool on whose surface floated white, pink, and golden water lilies." Resplendent in their black and white evening clothes, young men streamed into the Academic Building, met by French maids (an hour earlier they had been mere Shorter freshmen) who checked their hats and pinned upon their coat lapels bright boutonnieres. When the orchestra struck up the first tune, the promenade began, with couples strolling through the courtyard. "A silver moon, even more gorgeous than ever dreamed, beamed with a friendly smile upon this scene of beauty." Intermittently the couples returned to the building for cups of refreshing punch served by Chinese and Japanese maids (two hours earlier they also had been Shorter freshmen) . All too soon the supper prom came, after which yellow and white pieces of ice cream and cake were served and a program of musical and dance numbers was given by underclassmen, "clad in artistic costumes." At the hour of midnight, "loathe to leave, the boys lingered over fond farewells. Presently all was quiet on Shorter hill, but it was not until the wee small hours of the morning had come that the Juniors were asleep."

Extending from Friday until Tuesday early in June, the commencement schedule varied little from one year to the next. Presented by the Shorter Players, the commencement play was staged Friday or Saturday night. The Sunday morning baccalaureate sermon was preached at the First Baptist Church, ordinarily by a visitor, until 1926. At that time it was moved to the college auditorium, scheduled late in the afternoon, and usually delivered by Dr. Furry. For two years President Blocker included a Sunday evening address on Christian education at the city auditorium, inviting as speakers prominent Baptist pastors, Henry A. Porter of Atlanta and L. G. Broughton of Jacksonville, Florida. The annual musical concert was on Saturday or Sunday evening, and many years an art exhibit would be displayed at about the same time.

On Monday the alumnae made their annual visit to the campus, but for the students the day was notable because the Class Day exercise was held at Maplehurst, at the balustrade, or in the auditorium. For a week "sophomores could be seen picking daisies at any hour you looked out your window and at some hours that most people wouldn't be looking out, for no hour was too early or late . . . ." One historian said of her class members: "How their backs ached from picking daisies and how their hearts ached to see their seniors leave them." Another confessed: "We hunted daisies—we found daisies—we picked daisies— we made daisies—we hated daisies. But we made the largest and prettiest daisy chain we've ever seen . . . ." Singing "Hail, Dear Old Shorter," the seniors slowly marched to the appointed place, where their representatives read the class history, poem, prophecy, and last will and testament. Displaying a good deal of self-satisfaction, the seniors brought the crook out of hiding and passed it down to the juniors—except in 1932 when the gloating juniors simply retained possession! Established to promote student honor, maintain high standards of scholarship, and encourage allegiance to the ideals of Shorter, the Argonaut Society was formed in 1931, and new members were named at Class Day. With the singing of the "Alma Mater" and the pronouncing of a benediction, the program came to an end.

Tuesday was the day so long awaited. Dr. and Mrs. Furry often invited the seniors downtown for a sumptuous breakfast. At mid-morning in the college auditorium the graduation exercise was conducted and the degrees awarded. Speakers at this and the baccalaureate service included President E. Y. Mullins of the Southern Baptist Theological Seminary; Walter Pope Binns, pastor of the First Baptist Church, Roanoke, Virginia; William L. Poteat, president emeritus of Wake Forest College; John L. Hill of the Sunday School Board of the Southern Baptist Convention; and Edwin McNeill Poteat, Jr., who had returned from China and was then pastor of the Pullen Memorial Baptist Church, Raleigh, North Carolina. The latter recalled that sixteen years earlier he had delivered the address "to an audience of one excited person," Wilda Hardman, who soon became his bride! The thoughtful Dean Mell spoke for many of her companions on the staff and faculty —and for many of the graduates also—when she admitted: "From year to year we do not become calloused to the experience, but each June brings fresh regret which is, in its way, as keen as that which makes the voices of the seniors so unsteady on Tuesday of commencement."

During the Van Hoose years graduates had included two Cedartown sisters, Emaline Young (class of 1920) and Eve Young (class of 1922). Completing their work in the Blocker-Furry period were three more from the same family—Annie (class of 1925), Ida (class of 1925), and Mary (class of 1928). For the second time in the history of the college, five sisters had received their degrees at Shorter.

The General Alumnae Association

When the General Alumnae Association was organized on June 2, 1924, Mrs. J. P. Cooper was elected president, a position which she occupied for two years, becoming honorary president in 1929. Mrs. Harold N. Cooledge (née Miss Rebekah Clark, class of 1915) was recording secretary; Miss Cordelia Veal (class of 1897), corresponding secretary; and Miss Rosa Hammond (class of 1917), treasurer. Presidents of the local chapters automatically became vice-presidents or members of the advisory board. Completing the organization was an executive committee comprised of a few Georgia ladies. Following Mrs. Cooper as president were these: Mrs. Luke McDonald (née Miss Rena Brett), Mrs. Horton Askew (née Miss Mabel Owens, class of 1922; later Mrs. Robert Todd), and Mrs. R. M. Wyatt (née Miss Elizabeth Betts, class of 1916). Among others furnishing leadership were Mrs. J. J. O'Neill (née Miss Margaret Cummings, class of 1920), Miss Yeteva Rogers (class of 1917), Mrs. W. F. Barron (née Miss Mary Sue Jones, class of 1924), Mrs. Aubrey Matthews (née Miss Sue Earnest, class of 1919), and Mrs. Emil K. Mann (née Miss Myrtle Arnall, class of 1922). For three years Miss Veal was the unsalaried alumnae secretary, being assisted two years by Miss Louise Bennet, the field secretary. Becoming the first salaried alumnae secretary in 1929, Miss Bennet significantly stimulated this aspect of college life.

The General Alumnae Association convened annually at the college on Monday before graduation for a business session, a luncheon downtown or on campus attracting as many as three hundred persons, and several class reunions. One member of the class of 1879 ruefully observed: "All the king's horses and all the king's men couldn't bring our class together again!" More successful was the class of 1883—all four of its members attended their golden anniversary reunion. After a toast by Miss Louise Bennet, one of them responded "with entertaining reminiscences" and all of them sang "the 1883 class song" which had been written for their graduation fifty years earlier. Several years an evening al fresco party was given in honor of the alumnae. Once they placed daisies on the graves of Martha and Alfred Shorter, and two or three times they had a "balustrade singing" when the old songs were revived. In 1927 they were delighted to present a program over WIBJ—and the announcement carefully specified, for the benefit of radio fans, that the wave length was 209.9 meters or 1470 kilocycles.

The first alumnae reunion away from Rome occurred at Atlanta in 1925, and two years later the first fall luncheon was held there. Three different years WSB carried thirty-minute programs featuring President Furry, Dean Mell, Governor Hardman, and various Shorter musicians, leading to the suggestion that local branches meet at the same time and tune in on the radio.

In 1924 local alumnae groups were already existing in Rome, Atlanta, Columbus, and Cartersville. Others were formed in Georgia, Alabama, Tennessee, Kentucky, and Florida, and a total of twenty-nine was finally reached. Meeting monthly, quarterly, or less often, these local chapters sponsored activities that contributed to the overall program of the association.

The alumnae brought to successful conclusion a number of projects that were of value to the college. They contributed $1,000 to the library just before the Southern Association accepted Shorter's petition for membership. From 1922 to 1929 the ladies assiduously raised funds for the swimming pool that had been erected by J. P. Cooper in their name. After paying him the $15,000 that he had requested, the association formally presented the pool to the college at the graduation ceremony, June 4, 1929.

Six years earlier it had been decided that the next major project would be the Van Hoose portrait. Accordingly, Mrs. Harold N. Cooledge, Mrs. Mark A. Cooper, and others led the drive for funds. Charles Naegele of Marietta, Georgia, painted the portrait, which cost $1,013.25. Formally presented at a special service on June 2, 1930, it was unveiled by Mary Van Hoose, daughter of the late president. "As the veil was lifted from the face of the portrait a moment of silence was observed, and the air was tense with very sincere emotion as Shorter students, alumnae, and friends of Dr. Van Hoose looked upon the almost speaking likeness of this great man. The portrait is remarkable, for it is not only a striking likeness, but it seems to have caught the real spirit of the man." Mrs. Van Hoose, who was also an honored guest, thanked the association: "Within a decade the world often forgets, but it fills my heart with gratitude to know that it is not so in this instance, with the girls who loved him and whom he loved so dearly; to have the assurance that they still cherish his memory, and to realize that he and his influence will live on and down the ages, through the channels of their splendid lives."

In 1930 two further projects were initiated that were not satisfactorily completed during this period, the funding of the J. P. Cooper Memorial Loan Fund and the resurfacing of a tennis court. An alumnae suite was furnished for the use of guests, however, and the ladies were urged "to visit Shorter and enjoy YOUR SUITE!" Although frequently mentioned, an alumnae building was not constructed, and the "large amount" of money that they claimed to have collected was expended on the swimming pool.

Apparently almost $19,000 was raised during this eleven-year period by the association. The Rome chapter maintained the Martha Shorter Tea Room on the second floor of the Music Building irregularly for four or five years. Spring fashion shows in the city auditorium were twice sponsored, as well as a miniature golf tournament and four ly-ceum speakers. Calendars with pictures of the campus were distributed for a small fee at least two years. Copies of two college songs were sold at a profit, "The White and Gold" and the "Alma Mater" with Rowand's melody. The Christmas bazaar, usually held in the gymna-sium, annually brought in as much as $500. Rummage sales, Easter egg hunts, auctions, and benefit teas also contributed to the treasury. Starting in 1929, the Loyalty Fund sought $2 annually from each alumnae. A campaign was launched in 1932 to collect one million Octagon soap coupons, said to be worth $5,000, but the alumnae were too few to be capable of such astounding cleanliness and the campaign went down the drain.

An interest in students and potential students was obvious. Each fall the Shorter freshmen were entertained by the Rome chapter. Programs were conducted at a dozen high schools by several local chapters, teas were sponsored for young ladies thought to be desirable, and high school seniors from Atlanta and Rome were brought to the campus for College Day activities. At least once the Atlanta alumnae sponsored a social hour for prospective students at the governor's mansion, then occupied by the president of the Shorter trustees, Dr. L. G. Hardman.

Alumnae loyalty was sought in a number of ways, because, as Dr. Furry recognized, "Whatever resources may be available for the future development of Shorter College there is no resource of greater signifi-cance than the spirit of a united group of loyal alumnae." He en-couraged them in these words: "While not a multitude as numbers go, when weighed as alumnae ought rather to be, you are fast becoming a mighty instrument in the making of a greater and better Shorter." Each class named a secretary, whose task it was to secure news about and support from its members. Sustained efforts by Miss Bennet to organize local chapters resulted in growing interest. The Loyalty Fund, as its name suggests, was as much a measure for securing loyalty as for raising funds. Perhaps the finest contribution was made by the *Alumnae Bulletin*. Alumnae news had been carried in earlier issues of the *Periscope* and the *Chimes*, under the direction of members ap-pointed as alumnae editors. A special edition of the *Shorter College Bulletin* appeared in July of 1924, just after the founding of the General Alumnae Association, but this was not yet a continuing publication. With Miss Louise Bennet as editor, the *Alumnae Bulletin* was issued twice yearly beginning in May of 1929. That first issue was a directory of every Shorter graduate, with current addresses when known. Later issues carried news articles, pictures, announcements of coming events, and information from local chapters and the various class secretaries.

In other important ways the voices of the alumnae were being heard. Beginning in 1924 alumnae trustees were elected: Mesdames A. W. Van Hoose, John Wright, and W. A. Steed. Mrs. J. P. Cooper became a trustee four years later. In 1930 Mrs. R. M. Wyatt suggested that the college dormitories be named and that a committee be appointed to confer with the trustees. Comprised of Mesdames Aubrey Matthews, W. F. Barron, and J. J. O'Neill, the committee was entirely successful as the two were henceforth designated as Cooper Hall and Van Hoose Hall.

A Forty-one-Day Administration

For eight years Dr. Furry was president of Shorter College. He spoke with frequency in the churches of Rome and was sometimes teacher of the Scrap Iron Bible Class of the First Baptist Church. For two summers he was a visiting professor at the University of Georgia. In 1929–1930 he was president of the Association of Georgia Colleges. The *Argo* dedicated to him described him as "our friend, our president, our sympathetic advisor," and the girls expressed pleasure when he returned to his classroom one semester each year starting in 1929 to teach a course in ethics. One shadow of darkness appeared as his once-active wife fell prey to a crippling form of arthritis that often confined her to their apartment.

Without previous warning to the girls, Furry announced his resignation on Wednesday morning, March 29, 1933, at the first chapel service after spring vacation. A front-page, five-column headline in the *Periscope* read: "Dr. Furry's Resignation Blow To College." The accompanying article explained that his decision "had been hastened by the continued illness of Mrs. Furry, who has been an invalid for the past two years, and that notice of his intention to retire was given the board at the opening of the present academic year. Dr. Furry will, as soon as convenient, remove Mrs. Furry to a more favorable climate. He wishes also to have some time for rest after more than twenty years service . . . . As the students left the chapel, tears fell down unashamed faces." A page-two editorial concluded: "We love you, Dr. Furry, and we'll miss you." Shortly thereafter a writer in the *Chimes* spoke of "his love and interest in the college" and "his excellent leadership," adding: "I want to say, in behalf of all who have known Dr. and Mrs. Furry on Shorter Hill, our appreciation of their service is boundless and our wishes for their happiness and welfare in the future are limited only by the skies." More perfunctory was the resolution adopted by a part of the trustees: "Whereas, Dr. W. D. Furry has served the college for about eight [actually almost fourteen] years, first as Dean and then as President, during which time the academic standing of the college has been raised . . . therefore, be it resolved that the Prudential Committee of the Board of Trustees of Shorter College hereby accept with regret the resignation of Dr. Furry and take this occasion to express their appreciation of his services . . . ." The seniors petitioned that he remain until commencement and sign their diplomas, but their request was denied.

The Rome *News-Tribune* editorially reported "widespread regret" at his retirement, noting his "diligence and outstanding success" at Shorter. "A cultured gentleman, of fine attainments, he will be missed greatly." Furry's pastor, Bunyan Stephens, published "An Appreciation" in the *Christian Index*, saying in part: "During his term as president he has increased the endowment of the college, secured for Shorter the highest collegiate recognition and kept out of debt during the depression. He is primarily an educator, but it would seem that he is an excellent executive, as well. He is an indefatigable worker. He has successfully administered a college during as hard a period as schools and colleges have known. He filled numerous speaking engagements throughout the state, attended educational gatherings everywhere, . . . conferred with various denominational groups in our state—wherever there was a call for service he responded readily, performed his tasks efficiently and always had a good word for Shorter College and Christian education."

Moving to Maryland, Dr. Furry attended his wife until her death in 1939, while also preaching occasionally in nearby churches. He returned to Ashland College, Ohio, where from 1943 to 1957 he was professor of philosophy. At his retirement he was named professor emeritus and awarded the honorary Doctor of Laws degree by Ashland. Two years later he died, full of years and honor, at the age of eighty-five.

The trustees received Dr. Furry's resignation on March 28, one day before it was made public. At that time they appointed Paul M. Cousins acting president, a selection that pleased the students. Said one: "He is a very dear friend of each Shorter girl and each has pledged her loyalty, support, and cooperation to him during his term as acting president."

Almost a month later, on April 25, the trustees elected Dr. Clarence Rothwell (Clyde) Wilcox as the new president of Shorter. He was born at Elberton, Georgia, in 1888, and later received the Bachelor of Science and Master of Arts degrees from Davidson College and the Doctor of Philosophy degree from Johns Hopkins University. He was honored by membership in Phi Beta Kappa. For six years he was associate headmaster of McCallie School, Chattanooga, Tennessee, and for three, an officer in the United States Army. He married Miss Janie Blanchard Simpson, and they had three children. In 1921 he came to Rome as president of Darlington School, gaining the confidence and support of the community in general. According to the agreement reached with him and the Darlington trustees, he was to be

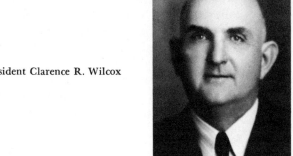

President Clarence R. Wilcox

president of Darlington and Shorter at the same time. Because of the college's critical financial condition, the Shorter trustees expected him to be responsible primarily for business matters.

The student body was told of his election at a brief installation service in the auditorium on April 27. Mrs. J. P. Cooper, Dean Mell, and Professor Cousins participated in the ceremony. President Wilcox addressed the students for a few moments, winning their "unbounded and vociferous approval . . . when he said 'and my first official act is to declare a holiday.'"

Editorially the *Chimes* supported the new leader, in these words: "We would like to express to Dr. Wilcox our sincere happiness over the fact that he has been chosen to occupy the place of chief executive for our Alma Mater. We want him to feel that the 'Shorter Spirit' is always his to rely on. . . . We are glad he is here and hope he will be happy in the service he will give to Shorter."

The Rome newspaper was even more vocal. The front-page editorial was titled "Shorter College Does Well." Its final paragraph proclaimed: "Dr. Wilcox is not only a great educator, enjoying a distinguished reputation throughout the country, but he is the type of man that appeals to every class—a soldier, a born leader, a genius for organization, and a man of great personal charm. He is eminently qualified to lead in an educational Renaissance in this beautiful and inviting field."

That Dr. Wilcox was an active member of the Presbyterian Church was widely known, and the support which he received took this fact into consideration. However, opposition to him was expressed within the board of trustees on the day of his election as votes were cast against him by Dr. L. G. Hardman, the president of the board, and by Luther R. Christie, a Baptist minister of Atlanta. The enfeebled and absent L. A. Dean later expressed his concurrence with their disapproval. Presumably to forestall further trouble, the prudential committee of the trustees named Paul M. Cousins as vice-president in charge of administrative affairs and announced that Dean Mell would continue in charge of internal discipline. It was made clear that Wilcox would virtually be the business manager of the college.

Altogether on the basis of his denominational affiliation, Dr. Wilcox received sustained and vigorous opposition. Absolutely no objections were voiced concerning his personal character or his abilities as an administrator. A great many simply believed that a Presbyterian ought not to head a Baptist institution. Hardman and Christie issued a joint statement that argued the case with clarity and charity. "Shorter has never been sectarian in any sense." Nevertheless, the spirit of Colonel Shorter's will demands "that the administration of the affairs of the institution should be in Baptist hands." Again, Baptist support will be reduced after it is widely known "that the institution is slipping away from Baptist leadership." Finally, "we do not believe any member of another denomination, however capable in other respects, can run a Baptist college successfully. . . . He is supposed to interpret the Baptist spirit and idea in the world of education, to mediate the institution to our churches and our Baptist people and to exercise numerous other functions which would be difficult to the point of impossibility, as we see it."

Responding to the Hardman-Christie statement, the other trustees called attention to the silence of Shorter's will or the charter of the institution as to the denominational membership of the president, faculty or staff members, or other employees. "In the recent selection of Dr. C. R. Wilcox as President of Shorter by an overwhelming vote of the Trustees, we have obtained the services of a Christian gentleman of proved capacity and ability as an educator and executive. Under his administration, ably supported by Mr. Paul M. Cousins as Vice-President, and Miss Mildred Mell as Dean, Shorter may confidently expect its most successful era of academic and Christian education."

Public imperturbability marked the demeanor of the college and its trustees during the ensuing weeks. The printed announcement of the sixtieth commencement, to be held June 3 to 6, 1933, listed Wilcox as president. As reported in the Rome newspaper, he led the academic procession Sunday afternoon, although Cousins presided over the baccalaureate service. Monday afternoon at the alumnae luncheon Wilcox was introduced as the recently elected president of the college; his response was "followed by rapturous applause." That evening he honored the graduates with a commencement reception.

Behind the scenes, though, negotiations were secretly conducted in an effort to gain an honorable relief from criticism. Appraising the emerging situation, Wilcox and the local trustees sought the counsel of Ellis Fuller, pastor of the First Baptist Church, Atlanta. It was proposed that Cousins be elected president and that Wilcox be made director of business administration and field work. Fuller discussed the matter with a number of fellow pastors who agreed that "an admirable arrangement had been worked out . . . ." When the trustees met on Monday morning, June 5, they formally accepted this recommendation, Wilcox stepped aside after only forty-one days in office, and Paul M. Cousins was named the new president.

At the Tuesday graduation service, Wilcox presided, announcing the change in leadership. He presented Fuller, who described to the stunned audience some of the private conferences that had led up to the recent action by the trustees. Wilcox then introduced President Cousins, "whose acceptance was received with applause."

Within a week the trustees mailed to thousands of Georgia Baptists a reprint of the newspaper article telling of the new president. Later in June their letter to the editor of the *Christian Index* was printed, stating in part: "The members of the Board of Trustees who voted for Dr. Wilcox . . . did not have in mind at all the alienation of the college from Baptist influences, nor did he have any such idea in accepting the Presidency. . . . The present arrangement at Shorter College, with Dr. Paul M. Cousins as President, Miss Mildred Mell as Dean, and Dr. C. R. Wilcox as Director of Business Administration and Field Work, is not only fully satisfactory to the officials mentioned, but has the unanimous approval of the Board of Trustees. . . . Believing that old friends will renew their interest in the institution and that new friends will be won to her, the trustees, faculty and student body of Shorter College look to the future with all confidence." Included on the same page was a communication from Fuller that concluded: "We can look confidently to the future, believing that the Shorter of tomorrow will be greater than any Shorter of any yesterday." General denominational approval had once more been secured, and a large measure of peace—if not of prosperity—prevailed.

Dr. Wilcox remained as a part-time member of the Shorter staff and faculty until 1939, while retaining the presidency of Darlington. After the death of his first wife, he married Miss Amzie Newton of Waycross, Georgia, a graduate of Shorter College in 1935. They had one son, Ralph Newton, who is also a Shorter graduate. Dr. Wilcox became president emeritus of Darlington in 1954 and died six years later. The recently renovated Old Main on Darlington campus has been named Wilcox Hall.

6

Preserving Life and Traditions

In the spring of 1933 the outlook for Shorter College was indeed bleak. Attendance had fallen to its lowest level since the turn of the century. Faculty salaries were reduced by forty percent from pre-depression figures. The institution had removed $25,000 from its endowment to meet operating expenses. Financial support from the Georgia Baptist Convention was being threatened for all of its affiliated schools, Shorter included. At such a time as this, a man of intense loyalty to the college was elected president.

Paul Mercer Cousins was born at Luthersville, Georgia, in 1889, the son of the Baptist pastor in that village. After earning the Bachelor of Arts degree from Mercer University in 1910, he was instructor of Greek and English at Locust Grove (Georgia) Institute from 1910 to 1915 and vice-president for the last three years. In 1915 he came to Shorter College as professor of English literature, leaving two years later for service with the army. Following a year of study at Columbia University he received the Master of Arts degree in 1919, after which he was professor of English literature at Georgetown (Kentucky) College for a year. In 1920 he resumed his work at Shorter College. He married Miss Marjorie Nowell of Monroe, Georgia, in 1923, a year after her graduation from Shorter, and they had one son, Paul, Jr. For a total of fifteen years the senior Cousins was professor of English literature—methodical, thorough, quiet, unassuming, occasionally showing a keen sense of humor, sympathetic toward his students, and widely liked by them. A scholar of some sophistication, he could nevertheless adapt gracefully to persons of limited culture and education, being as much at ease in a rural church as at a conference on a large university campus. A member of the First Baptist Church of Rome, he was ordained as a deacon in 1925.

His election as president was hailed by the *Christian Index*: "While we congratulate President Cousins on the merited honor that has come to him, we congratulate Shorter College the more in securing the services of this able educator and charming personality as President." It was predicted that he would meet "with unanimous approval among Georgia Baptists."

As president of Shorter, Cousins displayed in his office a framed photograph of Van Hoose, whom he considered to be the ideal administrator. For the first five years, he was required by the trustees to share his position of leadership. Dean Mildred R. Mell was in charge of internal academic and disciplinary matters, Dr. C. R. Wilcox was the business manager, and Cousins was specifically responsible for attempting to improve the relationship of the college with the churches of the Georgia Baptist Convention. All major decisions were theoretically in the hands of these three as a group, although in fact each often acted autonomously. In 1938 Cousins was given full administrative control of the institution, whereupon he shifted some authority to the new dean, Dr. Everett E. Porter, who gradually exercised increased power. Furthermore, Cousins throughout his administration permitted each segment of the school a large measure of independence.

During the summer of 1933 the college advertised consistently and Cousins traveled over the state seeking new students. A net increase of

President Paul M. Cousins

thirty-one college students filled the dormitories as the downward trend was reversed. In subsequent years he was on the road a part of virtually every week from January through August, interviewing prospective students, visiting with alumnae, and trying to raise sufficient funds to keep the school in operation. Each fall he attended many meetings of Baptist associations and the annual sessions of the Georgia Baptist Convention. When possible he traveled in an automobile owned by the college, making use of a chauffeur since he had not yet learned to drive. At the close of the week, however, he returned to the multifarious demands of his office—faculty recruitment, student complaints, accusatory letters, and a budget that usually remained balanced only with great difficulty. He continued to teach one or two courses each semester until 1936, after which he devoted his full attention to his administrative duties. His Columbia doctoral dissertation concerning Joel Chandler Harris was reluctantly ignored.

Enrollment

An increase in student enrollment was experienced during the Cousins era. The total student body varied from 198 to 335, with an average of 256. Of these, special students numbered from 11 to 97. The number of college students ranged from 184 to 242, averaging almost 219. In a period when enrollment in American colleges almost doubled, this average was a seven percent increase over that of the previous administration. The dormitories were filled to capacity five or six years, and the average use was about ninety percent. In the fall of 1945 some potential boarding students were actually refused admission. When the first faculty apartment building was opened two years later, additional space was made available for students, but by then it was not needed.

Residents of Georgia comprised about eighty-two percent of the student body, although a substantial minority came from Tennessee, Alabama, and Florida. Four American girls whose homes were in Japan, the Canal Zone, or Brazil were also enrolled.

For the first time, international students were on campus. For three months in 1946 Anna and Cecelia Prieto of Bogota, Colombia, audited classes in English. In the year 1947–1948, June and Patricia Tandy of Colchester, England, were freshmen. During the war their family had befriended an American soldier, Robert S. Franklin, whose sisters Helen and Ruth attended the college. When asked about schools in the United States, he proved to be a most persuasive spokesman for Shorter!

Each year from one to 22 of the special students were male, and from 1946 to 1948 Walter E. Bryant, pastor of the Gilmer Street Baptist Church, Cartersville, was a full-time student. A married man in his mid-thirties, he was the first male student to earn a place on the honor roll, and would have graduated from Shorter if the college had then been awarding degrees to men. Failing to become coeducational immediately after World War II, the college reaped little benefit from federal financing of an education for veterans that so markedly increased enrollment all over the country.

In an effort to secure students, at least eight persons from the staff and faculty toured the Southeast at different times, giving rise to a poem in the *Chimes* that began:

> Hello, my dear, and how are you,
> And is your mother home?

You see, I've come to talk with her
About a school in Rome.

So glad to meet you, Mrs. Jones;
Pray, is your evening free?
How marvelous! Now please consent
To sit and talk with me!

Its conclusion indicated success:

Just sign your name upon this line,
And be sure to remember
To sign in when you first arrive.
I'll see you in September!

Many a speech was delivered with an increased student body in mind
—to the Georgia Education Association, the Georgia Association of
School Superintendents, or a Beta Club convention—and students
presented dramatic and musical programs to various high school
groups. When the Sports Council sponsored Play Day during the
spring, selected high school seniors were invited, and several nearby
chapters of the General Alumnae Association brought groups of girls
at other times.

At least five different viewbooks were published by the school,
carrying much information of interest to prospective students and
including an abundance of pictures, sometimes in color. Late in the
period the music department ran advertisements in the *Georgia Music
News* and produced one descriptive brochure with the familiar bust of
a glum Beethoven on the cover. Beginning in 1938 the practice of
having photographs in the annual catalogues was resumed.

Tuition, Fees, and Student Aid

Costs for instruction and room and board continued to rise. The
basic charge for those pursuing the Bachelor of Arts degree increased
from $600 in 1933 to $975 in 1948. Additional fees for laboratory
sciences, speech, and music raised the total at first to a maximum of
about $750 and later to about $1,100. The Bachelor of Music degree
was always the more expensive to earn, ranging from about $800
yearly in the thirties to about $1,150 in the forties.

As the years passed, the amount of money available for loans and
scholarships also increased. For a time the Lewis H. Beck Foundation
of Atlanta offered loans and the National Youth Administration provided many scholarships, but these funds were not a part of the
Shorter endowment. While the Hardman-Sarepta Loan Fund con-

tinued to be under college auspices, other sources of student income were added: the J. P. Cooper Memorial Loan Fund, given by the Shorter General Alumnae Association; the Mary P. Cooper Memorial Fund, established by Mrs. Annie Scott Cooper of DeKalb County; the Sallie Pinson Steed Scholarship Fund, made available through the will of an 1881 graduate; the Pearl Ponder Ewart Loan Fund, provided by the will of an alumna of 1890; the Carter Harvey Scholarship, contributed by the Columbus chapter of the Alumnae Association in honor of this alumna who had been enrolled in the Shorter Academy from 1912 to 1914; the Galt Scholarship Fund, made possible by two Canton alumnae, Miss Martha C. Galt (class of 1915) and Miss Frances Galt (a student from 1912 to 1914), and later their brother, O. P. Galt; and the Bessie Acree Knight Scholarship Fund, furnished by the Woman's Missionary Society of the Second Ponce de Leon Baptist Church, Atlanta, honoring a 1909 graduate. Work scholarships were continued each year for those employed part-time in the library, book store, laboratories, and elsewhere. Discounts were maintained for two or more sisters from the same family and for daughters of clergymen. Eventually ten competitive scholarships covering part of the tuition were awarded to honor graduates of accredited high schools, and similar scholarships were also provided for the highest honor students in the freshman, sophomore, and junior classes at the college.

Income for the college rose from a low of $109,703.17 in Cousins' first year to a high of $227,775.81 in his last. During the same period the total national income significantly grew as the Gross National Product more than quadrupled. The college was able to operate on a balanced budget all but three years by practicing such economies as reducing faculty salaries, exercising care in the use of electricity and in the purchase of food for the dining room, and closing the swimming pool during some of the winter months. Especially, numerous renovations and improvements of the physical plant were postponed until the fifties—when they were completed by encroaching on the endowment and by using funds furnished by the Georgia Baptist Convention.

Trustees

Adopted by the trustees in 1938, an important resolution altering their status as a self-perpetuating body stated: "Be it resolved, that nominations of new trustees hereafter be submitted to the Georgia Baptist Convention for its approval or disapproval before final action by the board." That they continued to have the last word in their selection is evident enough, but it is also evident that the convention

279

was able thereby to exercise increased control over them and that the relationship between the college and the convention was further cemented. The term of office continued to be four years, and reelection was still possible without rotating off for a year or more.

Three men served as president of the board during this period. Former Governor L. G. Hardman of Commerce died in office in 1937 after twenty-six years as a trustee and nine as president. The resolution passed by the board at his death said, in part: "In his home-going this board loses a valuable member, Shorter College loses a loyal friend, and every worthy cause a staunch support. Be it resolved, therefore,

Dr. L. G. Hardman   T. B. Owens   Dr. W. P. Harbin

that we register our high appreciation of his long noble Christian life and service; our appreciation of his faithfulness as a friend of this institution; . . . and that copies [of this resolution] be sent to his family with the assurance that we share with them their loss and sorrow, and rejoice in the legacy of golden memories which a splendid life leaves to them and to us." T. B. Owens of Rome succeeded him for two years, resigning from office in 1939 and from the board three years later. A trustee since 1922, Aubrey Matthews of Rome next became president, retaining that responsibility thirteen years.

Five other notable members were lost to the board because of death or resignation. Upon the passing of Mrs. J. P. Cooper in 1938, the board observed: "The memory of John Paul and Alice Allgood Cooper is enshrined in the mind and hearts of an unusual number of people. It is not often that two people are enabled to touch with clear and lasting marks the lives of so many others. . . . Words are inadequate to express the devotion that we feel to the memory of Mr. and Mrs. Cooper. We cannot think of them separately because their work was one. May those who have been left in charge of the trust bequeathed to them by Mr. and Mrs. Cooper be given vision, faith and power to carry on their work." This distinguished graduate of 1884 was further honored in 1941 when the Alice Allgood Cooper Fine Arts Building was named for her. After serving on the board longer than any other person, almost forty-four years, L. A. Dean died in 1934. He was memorialized in these words: "For nearly half a century, Mr. Dean gave generously of his time to Shorter College. He was far-seeing in his ideas, constructive in his efforts, fair in his judgment, faithful to every duty assigned to him, and actuated in all his various services as a trustee by a thorough devotion to the success and progress of the college. We shall miss his counsel in our deliberations, but we shall be constantly grateful for his long record of unstinted service and unbroken loyalty." An oil portrait painted by Leiber Freidenthal of Atlanta was given to the college in 1964 by his daughters, Mrs. Pennington Nixon (née Miss Marion Dean, class of 1907), Mrs. George Miller (née Miss Jane A. Dean, class of 1909), Mrs. William Randle (née Miss Cobbie Mae Dean, class of 1914), and Mrs. Lee Dean Temple (class of 1921). Death also removed the Reverend L. R. Christie of Tallahassee, Florida, after twenty-three years, and A. S. Bradley of Swainsboro, Georgia, after twenty-two. In 1940 Dr. W. P. Harbin of Rome resigned after twenty-seven years.

Numerous alumnae were trustees: Mrs. Harry M. Arnold of Monroe (née Miss Sarah Glover, class of 1922); Mrs. Robert Arnold of Covington (née Miss Florence Turner, class of 1923); Miss Louise Bennet of Quitman (class of 1913); Mrs. J. J. Clyatt of Tifton (née Miss Josie Golden, class of 1919); Mrs. Harold Cooledge of Atlanta (née Miss Rebekah Clark, class of 1915); Miss Minnie Merle David of Columbus (class of 1906); Mrs. J. C. Dixon of Atlanta (née Miss Blanche Williams, class of 1919); Mrs. L. G. Hardman, Jr., of Commerce (née Miss Dorothy Shell, class of 1932); Mrs. Ryland Knight of Atlanta (née Miss Bessie Acree, class of 1909); Mrs. Alfred Thompson of Atlanta (née Miss Evelyn Sheffield, class of 1926); and Mrs. John C. Wright of Augusta (née Miss Alice Louise Hicks, class of 1907).

Dr. Lester Harbin and Claude H. Booker were two Romans elected to the board who were to be active more than twenty years each.

Because the college charter was soon to expire, the trustees again applied for a renewal and extension. This was granted by the Superior Court of Floyd County, Georgia, effective March 26, 1943. Since the charter was issued for a period of thirty-five years, the college is still operating under it, although it was amended in 1959.

The Campus

Dreams of expansion persisted through years of poverty and years of prosperity. The 1935 *Argo* was dedicated "to Greater Shorter . . . and to those friends whose lofty ideals insure for the institution growth and development. . . ." A decade later President Cousins had on the wall of his office an architect's sketch of the campus enlarged by four additional structures—a chapel, a gymnasium, a dormitory, and a library or administration building. Reality, however, was always less splendid.

Greatly appreciated by the students was the Rockery that was formally opened on May 2, 1934. Faced with girls who quickly tired of college food because it was served in the same dining room three times a day, Mrs. Jennie B. Hurst conceived of a plan for serving meals and snacks outside. The enterprising dietician secured some money as a gift from the class of 1932 and the remainder by preparing refreshments for various club parties, providing doughnut trees (a cup of coffee and two freshly made doughnuts for 10¢), and selling old egg crates and vegetable hampers. When sufficient funds were accumulated she had the area beyond the tennis courts—filled with underbrush, stones, and lost tennis balls—cleared, terraced into three levels, and planted with dogwood and crab apple trees, shrubs, and flowers that included petunias, nastursiums, iris, flag lilies, hydrangeas, and daffodils. Attractive green tables, chairs, and benches were added, as well as an outdoor oven. So much was given by friends of the college that Mrs. Hurst often referred to her "Friendship Garden." Places were provided for 172 persons—the faculty and guests on the lowest terrace, the seniors on the next, and the other students on the highest. A large cart with tall antique wheels donated by Mrs. J. P. Cooper brought the tea over from the kitchen, while stretcher-like trays borne by two men were used for other items not prepared in the Rockery. Desserts were available in red and yellow baskets hanging from iron hooks on the trees. In the evening improvised kerosene lanterns were brought out, until electric lights were added in 1939. There is little wonder that the girls welcomed the sound of the Rockery bell—and that hundreds of groups were entertained in the colorful garden for ten years.

Called the "Lumber Garden" by the night watchman, John F. Stevens, the Alumnae Garden was initiated in 1934, first completed in 1935, and later named in honor of Miss Louise Bennet. Located between Van Hoose and the Dining Hall, it was designed by a professional gardener, Nelson Crist of H. G. Hastings Company, and had beds of flowers, a variety of trees, a formal central plot containing a gazing globe, walkways bordered with shrubbery, and an adjoining stone terrace with new furniture. Miss Bennet long and lavishly cared for it.

Elsewhere on the grounds, improvements were evident. During the thirties Dean Porter changed into his overalls and worked many long, hot hours, planting and tending the sunken rose garden on front campus, laying stone walkways, and contributing much other manual labor when workmen were not available. In 1939 the faculty grounds committee utilized funds from the Atlanta chapter of the Alumnae Association to add rose bushes, crepe myrtles, magnolias, redbuds, and hundreds of other flowering plants and shrubs all over the area and along its two roads. Later a drinking fountain was placed in the courtyard, and the Gamma Delta Garden was planted near the Rockery. Paving around the college was completed in 1944. So attractive was the entire campus that the Garden Club of Georgia, convening in Rome, visited it and paid particular attention to the Rockery, which was pictured in the Atlanta *Journal*. Later a returning alumna seriously suggested that wide publicity should be given to the beauty of the campus and that signs should be erected on all highways near Rome. If other gardens could become tourist attractions, she reasoned, so also could those at Shorter.

An extension to the campus came when the Radio Springs cottage was bought for recreational outings in 1935. A swimming pool and two riding horses were provided on the premises. Students and their chaperones occupied the cottage virtually every weekend, signing up at the dean's office and purchasing $7.50 tickets that entitled the holder to ten rides. For more than thirty years this proved to be an enormously popular piece of Shorter property.

Soon after the death of Mrs. J. P. Cooper in 1938 the suggestion was made that additional buildings be renamed. This was done at the Founders' Day exercise held on October 30, 1941. "Honoring the many citizens of Rome who have joined in many ways to make the college what it is today," the Academic Building became Rome Hall, and First Commissioner John Yarbrough responded to the tribute. The Music Building was named the Alice Allgood Cooper Fine Arts Building, and one of her sons, F. S. Cooper, treasurer of the board of trustees, expressed the family's appreciation. The auditorium was designated the William Walker Brookes Memorial Chapel, and his widow was present to make a brief speech. Later she gave the red-bound hymnals that were in use for twenty years.

After extended discussion, a new gymnasium was again proposed when a $100,000 drive was announced on April 29, 1945. Several large advertisements in the Rome *News-Tribune* were sponsored by local business establishments, including one that affirmed: "Since Shorter was founded Rome has more than doubled in size. . . . Shorter has contributed in many, many ways to this growth. . . . Now Shorter needs to grow. . . . It is up to Rome now to help her." A slogan insisted: "A Greater Shorter Means a Greater Rome—Help the Building Fund." Led by Tom Lamar, president of the First National Bank, and Louis Shahan, president of the National City Bank, more than one hundred men attended a dinner at the college on May 21. Radio station WRGA cooperated by broadcasting a part of the proceedings directly from the dining room. Within three weeks about $56,000 in cash was raised and about $36,000 in pledges, and the trustees voted thanks for what they called a successful campaign. The project was then postponed, principally because building materials were unavailable, and partly in the hope that construction costs might decline. In 1947 Stevens and Wilkinson, architects of Atlanta, completed plans, and the J. P. Roberts Construction Company of Rome placed an acceptable bid in the amount of $101,176. That fall the Sports Council led in a ground-breaking ceremony, and newspapers carried pictures of a bulldozer being "operated" by two Shorter girls, each wearing an immaculate skirt and blouse. Formally presented to the college at the opening convocation of 1948, the building and its equipment initially cost $111,624.39. Of this sum, $1,000 came from the satisfied parents of two graduates who wrote concerning their children: "Of course we are proud of their success and feel that Shorter is directly responsible."

The feasibility of faculty apartments was investigated by the trustees early in 1947, and plans were secured from R. L. Townsend, a Rome contractor, for an eight-unit brick dwelling to be located down the slope from Cooper Hall on what was then called Hillside Drive. The sale of college land on Horseleg Creek Road yielded about $11,000, and some $20,000 was removed from the endowment. The first apartment house, costing about $30,000, was ready for occupancy in the fall of 1947. Soon thereafter the approach road was first paved. The building was financed mainly from the endowment, and the amount utilized has since been restored.

Although the physical plant did not expand as extensively as Cousins had hoped, it nevertheless did grow in beauty, serviceability, and value. In 1933 the land, buildings, and equipment were worth $484,011.47. Fifteen years and two structures later the campus was appraised at $610,058.59, an increase of twenty-six percent. Admittedly, not every year showed an upward trend, as revealed by the 1936 audit: "The decrease in these [plant] funds of $25.00 is the value of a mule that died during the year." Several pages later this was noted: "Carcass sold for $2.00 and proceeds turned over to Operating Fund."

The Endowment

In 1929 the Georgia Baptist Convention issued debenture bonds for several of its affiliated institutions, and Shorter was allotted $141,404.63 of them. From Cooperative Program receipts the college was to receive $7,070.23 annually for ten years, after which it would receive the entire face value of the bonds. As the depression deepened, payments lapsed. In 1934 the convention directed that the bonds be surrendered, agreeing to give Shorter about $14,000 within the next three years. In reality, over $17,000 was actually contributed to the college, for a total of about $39,000 from the Cooperative Program during the eight years that the bonds existed.

A state-wide campaign for endowment was planned by the president and trustees of Shorter in the early thirties, to be launched as soon as general financial conditions permitted. In 1934 the state convention gave its "hearty and enthusiastic endorsement" to this venture. When the debentures were removed and the endowment once again failed to meet minimum requirements of the Southern Association, a stimulus for action was provided. The field representative, Hubert T. Quillian, became vice-president in charge of endowment and expansion, traveling throughout the state. The immediate results of this canvass were termed "small," but the effort was continued. By 1935 the endowment regained its 1933 level, and the $25,000 encroachment was considered repaid.

Meantime, a drive for $150,000 in order to raise the endowment to $500,000 was initiated in Rome early in 1936. Throughout the month of May the project received much publicity, and one hundred men were invited to participate under the direction of W. F. Barron, John Berry, John Graham, Wilson Hardy, and Ralph Wilson. On Friday evening, May 22, they met for a supper in the Rockery, after which they adjourned to the auditorium for information, songs, acrobatic stunts, and humorous skits. The "Roaming Roman" expressed the wish in his column that he could write a check for a million dollars and have the banker cash it instead of saying: "I always knew that fellow had rhinolophus ferrumeguinum in the berefredus . . . which is a banker's way of saying one has bats in the belfry." Using as their motto "A Gift to Shorter is a Gift to Rome," the solicitors made their rounds until June 6. Unfortunately they found no million-dollar checks. Already on a reduced salary, the faculty nevertheless pledged $5,000. The local trustees added $7,500. Another $15,000 from the city at large raised the total to about $27,500 in cash and three-year pledges. During the years covered by these pledges, the endowment grew about $33,000, much of which apparently came from Rome, but the total was still less than $400,000.

Mrs. Columbus Roberts

Shorter was not included in the budget of the Georgia Baptist Convention from 1938 to 1940, a situation which the college took steps to remedy. While ultimately remaining self-perpetuating, the trustees agreed to present their new selections to the convention for approval or rejection. President Cousins' associates, Dean Mildred R. Mell and Dr. C. R. Wilcox, resigned from their administrative positions, leaving Cousins the sole leader. When Hubert T. Quillian assumed the presidency of LaGrange (Georgia) College, Edwin S. Preston became executive secretary at Shorter. Having led the Georgia Baptist Training Union Department for twelve years, he was widely known and admired over the state. With two popular Baptist men, Cousins and Preston, representing the college, it entered a new era of favor with the state convention.

Starting with an allocation of $2,500 for operating expenses, the convention resumed its support through the Cooperative Program in 1941. The figure steadily rose until it stood at $12,000 in 1948, and the eight-year total reached $48,000. On numerous occasions Cousins was careful to voice thanks for these funds which helped the school to satisfy the financial requirements of the Southern Association.

In addition to this, the convention developed a concern for enlarging the endowment of its affiliated schools that was expressed in two related ways. In the first place, the Georgia Baptist Foundation, chartered in 1941, provided a program of promotion for securing, managing, and investing endowment funds. An ambitious campaign to raise $5,000,000 in five years, of which $400,000 was earmarked for Shorter, failed to gain momentum in the absence of a full-time leader. After

Mr. and Mrs. Oakley M. Bishop

Arthur Jackson was elected executive secretary of the foundation in 1943, conditions gradually improved. Although he supervised a $200,000 drive for Shorter in 1944 and 1945 that fell far short of the goal, some funds were received and the necessity of endowment was again brought forcibly to the attention of Georgia Baptists. In the first eight years of its life, the foundation directly secured about $9,000 for the Shorter endowment. Of course its greatest success was to come later and was built on the work of these earlier years when Jackson was generating enthusiasm for its objectives.

Of greater immediate benefit to Shorter was a second action by the convention, the allocation of Cooperative Program funds directly to the endowment. Beginning in 1946 the convention annually placed in the Georgia Baptist Foundation to the credit of the institution an amount that in three years totaled $55,305.75. For this "forward looking type of financial support," Cousins quickly expressed sincere appreciation.

Although figures are sometimes only approximate, it appears that in twelve years, 1934 to 1937 and 1941 to 1948, the convention directly contributed over $120,000 for operating expenses and endowment.

Two large gifts were made to Shorter College by private individuals during the Cousins administration. Columbus Roberts, a Baptist businessman from Columbus, Georgia, first gave $25,000 to the endowment in 1943. Two years later he added another $25,000 as a memorial to his wife who had died in the interval. A classroom and adjoining office on the second floor of Rome Hall were redecorated and refurnished, a large picture of Mrs. Roberts was secured, and the Mrs. Columbus Roberts Department of Religion was designated as the first endowed department of the college.

In 1936, upon the death of Mrs. Oakley M. Bishop (née Miss Eva Phillips, class of 1914), the institution was notified that it would inherit her estate at the death of her parents. She desired that a memorial be set up in honor of her late husband who had taught science at Shorter from 1912 to 1917 and had later joined E. I. DuPont de Nemours and Company as head of the dye research department. For twenty years the college showed the Bishop Fund in its audit, but received no income from it. When the will was finally settled in 1957, $116,519.53 was added to the Shorter endowment.

In 1942 the federal government proposed the taxation of private colleges and charitable institutions. The Shorter trustees were apprised of this threat, a form letter was drawn up, and each member was encouraged to write his congressman and senators in opposition. The proposal failed to be carried out.

The General Education Board of New York was periodically approached for assistance, but the results were minimal. In 1948 a grant of $5,000 was made for laboratory equipment and library books, to be matched by the college.

The total assets of the college grew steadily over this fifteen-year period. Apart from the debentures, the endowment increased from $350,523.06 to $537,961.15. The total value of the college in 1933 was $847,247.25, plus debentures. By 1948 this had risen to $1,225,285.42, a growth of almost forty-five percent.

World War II

Because of Dr. and Mrs. John Ware, teachers of modern languages, a consciousness of the war came early to Shorter College. Visiting in Europe during the summer of 1939, they were separated when the conflict broke out. Their previously made plans to rejoin were thwarted by the general confusion. An uneasy Mrs. Ware sailed from Rotterdam, having failed to determine his whereabouts. Going to Paris, he tried unsuccessfully to communicate with her. When their daughter in America cabled him that Mrs. Ware was safely en route, he also headed home. His vessel remained a few hours in the English Channel to avoid traveling over a mine field at night, but otherwise the trip was without incident. Late for classes by 2½ weeks, they shared their harrowing experiences with several groups in Rome.

While in Paris that summer, Dr. Ware purchased many books for the college library. They had already arrived at Cherbourg when hostilities began and were soon stored under protective layers of dirt and cordwood there in a cellar. Two years later, without books or news, Ware wrote the American Embassy at Vichy and was advised that they were still safe. Silence during the next five years was made ominous by pictures of destruction in Cherbourg. Early in 1946 a letter came from the bookseller, asking if Ware still wanted the books. The relieved professor made arrangements for their shipment, and late that year they finally arrived—seven years late. He reported: "Even the bindings are in perfect condition with no trace of the blanket of dirt and no sign of a hungry roach." The volumes remain to this day as a part of the library collection.

American involvement in the war was supported by the Shorter community in many ways. The Shorter drill squad, forty girls dressed in white and gold, marched in Rome's defense parade on Friday afternoon, November 27, 1942, while other students took charge of the war stamp booths downtown. The Student Government Association appointed a War Council with committees in charge of gathering scrap metals, conserving critical materials, selling stamps and bonds, and fostering the first aid classes (their motto was "A first-aider to every suite"). The Sheffield Reading Room on the first floor of Rome Hall was converted into the War Information Center with maps, flags, and a bulletin board reporting the latest news. Chapel speakers frequently provided additional insights into the developing situation. Instead of spending Monday afternoons at the movies, many of the girls rolled bandages and knitted sweaters and blankets. Contributions were made to the Red Cross War Fund, and students donated blood at the Red Cross mobile unit. War stamps were given as favors at parties with a patriotic theme, the book store on the first floor of Cooper Hall had stamps on sale, and the Eunomians defeated the Polymnians in a stamp-buying contest. Defense bonds were bought for the endowment and for use later in financing the gymnasium. One year the Camerata

Club contributed the proceeds of its Follies to the bond drive. Later the Follies was repeated at Battey General Hospital, which then cared for soldiers, and Shorter girls spent each Monday afternoon entertaining in the wards with songs and dances. A few fortunate musicians were occasionally taken to the Columbus, Georgia, U.S.O. canteen, where they furnished programs and served as hostesses. The Whoop-Em-Up Wedding in 1943 presented the groom in uniform—and two years later all of the participants were in military attire. One year a male figure being kissed by one of the students was pictured in the *Argo* with the caption, "Man Shortage? Not at Shorter!"—but this "he" was made only of snow, not flesh and blood.

Two Shorter girls "decided to abide by the royal decrees," according to an Atlanta *Constitution* photograph and article in 1942. It was reported that King George had ordered bathtubs in Buckingham Palace and Windsor Palace painted with a line at the five-inch level to conserve water and fuel. The co-eds were pictured drawing such a line in their bathtub with lipstick! In a more serious vein, the student body later voted to eliminate bread from one meal a day, thus conserving food for famine relief.

The *Argo* was once dedicated "to our fathers, brothers, and friends who are giving their lives for us"—and in several heartbreaking instances this became literally true. Frequently it contained pictures of American GIs. Once the Thugs were shown flying an airplane with a bomb marked "For Germany," while across the page the H.O.T.s were supervising the punishment of Hitler and Tojo in the nether region. The wife of General George C. Marshall selected the beauties in 1944. Only one issue each of the *Periscope* and *Chimes* was printed from 1942 to 1944, and the money thereby saved went to the war effort.

The college catalogue announced: "Shorter College is cooperating in the general educational effort to prepare women for participation in government service." Accordingly, "Victory Courses" were publicized for seniors—concentrated offerings in physics, mathematics, and business English, together with a more rigid schedule in physical education. At least nineteen graduates enlisted in the Waves, Wacs, Spars, and Marine Corps. Dedicated to a faculty member who also volunteered, the 1944 *Argo* honored Miss Jessie Williams Gardner, First Lieutenant, Woman's Army Corps, who is now better known as Dr. Jessie G. Austin.

Community Relations

The winding road up to Shorter College continued to bear two-way traffic. Special students received instruction in a variety of subjects:

speech correction, drawing and painting, interior decorating, and art for children. For ten years Miss Clara Kellogg's course in current affairs attracted townspeople. As before, private music lessons were provided when possible.

Nearby churches benefited from their Shorter neighbors. Leading the music program of the First Baptist Church at various times were Miss Louise Bennet and Professor Wilbur Rowand. Miss Margaret Dennis and Mrs. Evelyn Rowand furnished music at St. Peter's Episcopal Church. Student choral groups performed at the local First Methodist Church, First Presbyterian Church, and Salvation Army, at the First Baptist and Druid Hills Baptist churches of Atlanta, and at various Chattanooga churches. Periodically President Cousins, John N. Ware, and the professors of religion spoke in local churches.

Professors A. S. Talmadge and Wilbur Rowand gave direction to the Rome Choral Club, and the latter was director of the Rome Men's Chorus and helped to reorganize the Rome Symphony Orchestra. The Rome Music Lovers' Club heard recitals and lectures and was furnished support and guidance by Shorter musicians. The club sponsored a women's choral group led by Mrs. Evelyn Harle. For a decade the club and the college cooperated in bringing visiting musicians to the campus for public performances. Concerts and speeches were provided by Shorter personnel for other music clubs in Atlanta, Cartersville, LaFayette, and Chattanooga.

The Junior Service League of Rome invited Professors Clara Kellogg, Bertha Martin, and Martha Griffin to speak at its meetings. Miss Louise Bennet was a member of and occasional speaker at the exclusive Nibelung Club. The local chapter of the American Association of University Women received the hearty participation of Dean Mildred R. Mell and others.

The Rome Rotary Club was regularly entertained by the Shorter Players and by school musicians, as was occasionally the club at Cartersville. The local Kiwanis Club heard speech students and Miss Kellogg, and the college sextet once sang for the Atlanta club. President Cousins addressed the Rome Lions Club and American Legion and Dr. Ware, the Exchange Club. At one time or another, these local service and civic clubs met in the Rockery or dining room, where students usually constituted the program.

Other groups also visited the campus, frequently being entertained by faculty members or students: the Floyd County Education Association, the district Junior Music clubs, the district Georgia Music Educators' Association, the Rome Music Lovers' Club, the A.A.U.W. of Rome, a bankers' convention, the Red Cross, the Georgia Press Association, and the Georgia Business and Professional Women's convention. A birthday party for President Franklin D. Roosevelt was scheduled for the dining room, with proceeds going for the Warm Springs Foundation. A Parent-Teacher Association convention in Rome had tea in the Rockery one spring afternoon. In colder weather, the Georgia Baptist Woman's Missionary Union convention was entertained in the parlors. Once providing the Chamber of Commerce with its president, Hubert T. Quillian, the school often provided in addition a site for the organization's annual meeting.

For ten years the Georgia Baptist Training Union Assembly convened at Shorter for a week or two in June, producing this comment in the *Christian Index*: "Certainly the beautiful setting on the top of Shorter hill lends itself admirably to the encampment type program." No less important to the youthful participants were the meals which the writer pronounced "unusually delicious and attractively served." The state-wide Baptist Young Woman's Auxiliary House Party was held for three years in the early forties, attracting as many as 200 girls for three days in April. A Presbyterian youth group utilized Shorter facilities in 1947, with more than 150 present.

Making good use of the radio, Shorter aired bimonthly or weekly programs over WSB of Atlanta until about 1943. Music, drama, speeches, interviews, and news items were included. A similar format was used for "The Shorter Hour" over WRGA of Rome each Wednesday or Friday evening while school was in session from 1936 to at least 1943. Occasionally a college group would perform at a station in Birmingham or Chattanooga, and once in 1942 the sextet sang on "The Baptist Hour" which was broadcast all over the South. Vitally interested in religious broadcasting, Edwin Preston gave impetus to this aspect of college life. Of long-term value was the recording studio installed in the Music Building in 1938; numerous records were produced during the following years that were used on radio stations over the state.

Making use also of the printed page, Shorter publicists produced articles and pictures that were included in the Atlanta *Constitution*, *Journal*, and *American*, the *Scenic South*, and the *Brighton Warp and Weft*.

Ever willing to enjoy a holiday that would keep the college in the public eye, Shorter pupils participated in the 1934 Floyd County centennial parade. A reported sixty thousand persons saw eighty floats, one of which was trimmed in gold and white, displaying sixteen of the prettiest girls on campus and depicting students dressed as Colonel and Mrs. Shorter giving the college charter to another student. The dedication of the Keel Levee five years later occasioned another city-wide celebration. A decorated automobile with four lovely girls represented the college in the parade, the Gadsden High School band played a special concert on campus in the early afternoon, and a special fireworks display that evening was clearly visible to the Shorter students from their lofty vantage point. National Education Week in the fall of 1948 was also marked by a parade that included a college float featuring a queen dressed in cap and gown, surrounded by her smiling court.

While the institution was raising money in 1945 for the gymnasium, advertisements in the Rome *News-Tribune* listed "a few of the many things Shorter contributes to Rome" and summarized rather well the impact of the college on the local community:

1. More than a thousand Rome girls have attended Shorter College.
2. Fifty-nine teachers in the Rome School System are Shorter graduates or former students.
3. Shorter furnishes an average of from two to three programs a week for civic clubs and other organizations.
4. Shorter students and faculty are active in the Sunday School and Church work of the Churches of Rome.
5. Shorter's Music and Speech Departments supply talent for almost numberless programs in the city.
6. Shorter's faculty members are constantly used as speakers for civic and Church meetings.
7. Shorter cooperates with the Rome Civic Concert group to make possible the Artist Series in Rome.
8. Shorter College Students and faculty cooperate in various civic campaigns, such as Red Cross, Clothing Drive, War Bonds, Blood Donors, etc.
9. Shorter College students and faculty are making a contribution in the way of entertainment, etc., at the Battey General Hospital.
10. Shorter's two hundred boarding students from all sections of the country pour many thousands of dollars into the trade channels of the community.
11. In addition to the amount spent by students, Shorter College brings annually to Rome more than $135,000, most of which is spent in Rome.

General Academic Matters

Although admissions requirements did not vary from those of the Furry years, some new elements were added to the opening days of orientation and registration. When the freshmen arrived on campus two or three days before most of the other students (one year the

S.G.A. leaders took turns meeting them at the station in a jeep), they received a mimeographed booklet detailing the schedule of events. Entertainment for them was plentiful—a party by the Rome alumnae at the Coosa Country Club, a weiner roast by the Student Council and the Y.W.C.A. at Rotary Lake or in the gymnasium (it was once recorded that "guests danced the big apple but were otherwise sane in their dancing and amusements"), and some years a breakfast sponsored by the Sports Council, a prom to which young men were invited, or a buffet supper given by President and Mrs. Cousins. Examinations were plentiful—general scholastic aptitude tests, psychological tests, and others dealing with mathematics, English, foreign languages, and (for proposed majors) music. Lectures were also plentiful—Shorter traditions, organizations, and rules were patiently explained, and a test was administered to qualify a new student for membership in the S.G.A. Faculty advisers were designated; one of them summoned an advisee with a note saying: "Please C me." In addition, some years each freshman was assigned a student counselor who frequently was sought out more often than the faculty member. Registration was held on Wednesday and Thursday, with instructors keeping office hours for consultation during the appointed time. Opening convocation regularly occurred on Friday morning, with brief talks by alumnae leaders, a local clergyman, and student officers. Almost always a guest delivered a major address: Editor Ralph McGill of the Atlanta *Constitution*, President M. L. Brittain of the Georgia Institute of Technology, John L. Hill of the Southern Baptist Sunday School Board, Ellis A. Fuller of the First Baptist Church of Atlanta, or Louie D. Newton of the Druid Hills Baptist Church of Atlanta. Introduced during this period were the ever-mystifying, opening day, twenty-minute meetings of all classes which enabled every teacher to make an assignment the very first day—to those students possessing enough genius to fathom the schedule. Completing the introductory events was Shorter Sunday at First Baptist Church, the "Mother of Shorter College," according to President Cousins.

Ordinarily classes met from Tuesday through Saturday, except before the war when football games in the fall usually caused the holiday to be shifted from Monday to Saturday. This change was made permanent by presidential action in 1947, and since then classes have normally met from Monday through Friday. The rising bell varied from 6:45 to 7:15; classes began at 8:00 or 8:30; chapel was held twice weekly at 10:00 or 10:30; study bell rang at 7:00 or 7:30; and lights were to be turned out at 11:00 or 11:30 (thirty additional minutes were allowed on Friday and Saturday nights).

At the close of each semester "Blue Books" were distributed by the faculty, and finals were inscribed therein. Moaned one victim: "Final Exams—They happen to the best of us. They will bring out the worst in us. We fear they'll be the last of us." Her judgment of the whole examination period was "Minnie-Meat," a familiar student phrase, usually designating meat of an uncertain origin, that in some years designated anything "ultra-inferior"! Since the Honor System was in effect, professors usually left the classroom once the examination had started. Many alumnae still recall the steady squeak coming from Dr. Hightower's office as she sat there and rocked. At the conclusion of the ordeal each January came a mid-morning Butterfly Brunch. With the dining room decorated by a multitude of paper butterflies, an abundance of delicious pancakes helped to give the event its name. One well-fed young lady explained: "The hot cakes were served and they make the butter fly!"

Regulations governing class absences and academic exclusion were altered from time to time. In general, one excused absence was allowed for each semester hour of course credit—although some years all seniors and those juniors on the honor roll were allowed unlimited cuts, while F students were allowed none at all. The penalty for each excessive absence ranged from a fine of $1 or $2 to the deduction of one quality point from the grade point total. At first, exclusion from school resulted when a student earned an F on more than half of her work in a given academic year. Later the rule stated that anyone who was "notably deficient in her work" would be asked to withdraw by a faculty committee appointed to deal with such cases.

Founders' Day was observed each fall and Honors Day each spring. For these events visiting speakers included Columbus Roberts, Dr. Goodrich C. White of Emory University, E. L. Wright of Darlington School, and some who had earlier been associated with Shorter: Dr. Mary Stuart MacDougall and Dr. Mildred R. Mell of Agnes Scott College, President Hubert T. Quillian of LaGrange College, and Miss Louise Bennet during her retirement.

After bringing to Rome Louis Untermeyer, poet and critic, and others, the lyceum series was altered in 1939, becoming the Student Lecture Association. Led by a student-faculty committee, the group sponsored a succession of authors, journalists, travelers, and radio commentators who dealt with significant affairs in Europe, South America, and the Pacific area. Interested students and faculty members were invited to after-dinner coffees in the faculty parlor on the first floor of Rome Hall to honor these and other guests.

By the spring of 1939 the first Sophomore Test was administered.

Initially covering English, general culture, and current events, this examination was continued with minor alterations through 1968.

Membership in the National Association of Schools of Music was gained in 1934 and in the Association of Georgia Colleges by 1940. All other forms of accreditation secured by Dr. Furry were retained, with one unavoidable exception. The college was on the approved list of the Association of American Universities for seventeen years before this list was discontinued in 1948.

The Curricula

Two degrees continued to be granted, the Bachelor of Arts and the Bachelor of Music. Allowing for greater flexibility, the freshman-sophomore requirements for the former were reduced from 61 to 50 s.h. and greater latitude was permitted in selecting these courses. Majors were offered throughout this period in ten areas: biology, chemistry, English, French, history, Latin, mathematics, music, physics, and speech. Sociology was added in 1934, religion and Spanish in 1937, art in 1946, and psychology and general science in 1947. Instead of a minor in one department, the concept of related work from several of them was introduced in 1936 and has been retained to the present. Of the 126 s.h. required for the degree, the candidate was required to offer a minimum of 66 s.h. with a grade of C or higher and a minimum of 126 quality points (an overall C average). All of the major and related work had to be passed with at least a C. Starting in 1937 the two-day comprehensive examination in the major field for seniors became an additional hurdle, leading one student to comment: "Comprehensives. . . . Although the faculty considers them Roast Turkey [a student phrase denoting "excellence"], the students opine 'Warmed Over Hash' [a phrase coined especially for this occasion and denoting something even worse than Minnie-Meat!]." Soon the senior survey course was introduced, and also a holiday from classes for the rest of the week after the test was concluded Friday noon.

The Bachelor of Arts degree was awarded to 446 persons during the Cousins administration. History, English, and sociology were the three most popular majors, each being selected by about one-fifth of the girls. Others attracting at least ten percent of the graduates were biology and speech.

The Bachelor of Music degree was retained without major alterations in its course requirements. Approximately one-fourth of the work was allowed in liberal arts; the remainder was in theoretical and applied music. This degree was conferred on a total of 42 young ladies during this period of fifteen years, with majors in piano, public school music, voice, organ, and violin.

Within the Departments

Meeting monthly on Tuesday evening, the faculty and staff numbered from 36 to 46, of whom 24 to 30 were full- or part-time classroom teachers. In the fall President and Mrs. Cousins usually honored new faculty members at a reception to which the returning members and the trustees were invited. In the faculty parlor various persons on the faculty and staff entertained at an after-dinner coffee on Sunday once each month throughout some of the sessions.

Faculty salaries rose from a high of $2,100 to $3,980, while the low ranged from $350 to $890. Often this was supplemented by free room and free or reduced board. For nine or ten years contingency clauses were included in faculty contracts. By their terms a basic salary was agreed upon, of which sixty percent was actually paid over a period of ten months. At the end of the fiscal year all bills were to be settled if possible and then any remainder divided among the faculty. During the period of these clauses, no more than seventy-five percent of the basic salary was ever paid. The figures cited at the beginning of this paragraph represent actual money paid, not the inflated basic salary. When the clauses were finally removed about 1942, the trustees began to discuss a retirement plan as a fringe benefit, and the Teachers Insurance and Annuity Association of New York was investigated. Although the college later reached an agreement with this organization, no retirement plan was actually initiated during the forties.

The faculty operated through the usual committees: executive, admissions and curriculum, registration, library, chapel programs and special events, radio, guidance, honors and awards, health and recreation, publications, and social. Mrs. Allie Hayes Richardson was secretary of the faculty.

President Cousins employed about 118 faculty members, of whom one-third remained only one year and about 26, no more than two. Of the 77 on the faculty for two or more years, the highest earned degrees were distributed as follows: bachelor's, 32 (sixteen of these claimed additional work on the next degree) ; master's, 30 (twenty of these claimed additional work on the next degree) ; doctor's, 15. Among the nonmusicians holding an advanced degree, the graduate schools most frequently attended were at Columbia and Johns Hopkins universities, the universities of Chicago, Michigan, and North Carolina, George Peabody College for Teachers, and the Southern Baptist Theological

Seminary. The musicians at Shorter two or more years had most often received their professional education at Oberlin and Cincinnati conservatories, Eastman School of Music, Shorter College, and several European schools, including the Conservatoire Fontainebleau.

Of course, from 25 to 35 other persons were on the payroll as maintenance workers, maids, and kitchen employees.

ART. Expanding the study of art history, the department of art continued to be led by Miss Martha Griffin, who earned the Master of Arts degree from Peabody during this period and published in the *Peabody Journal of Education* an article based on her thesis. A succession of persons assisted her in teaching, including Miss Susie Cunningham, a Shorter alumna. In 1936 the department was moved to the third floor of the Music Building, where the gymnasium was its neighbor for twelve years. Organized in 1947, the Art Club soon became the Art Students' League. Student art exhibits continued to be hung, including the annual May show that first presented the work of senior majors in 1948. Many other exhibits were borrowed from outside sources. A lending library was initiated in 1946, containing pictures usually purchased from Shorter students.

EDUCATION AND PSYCHOLOGY. For thirteen years Dr. Cameron D. Ebaugh headed the department of education and psychology, publishing essays in his field during this time. Sufficient courses in education were at first scheduled to permit professional certification in Georgia. After Ebaugh's departure, however, offerings in psychology grew rapidly, and, as the number of courses in education was reduced, only a provisional certificate was permitted to the graduate.

ENGLISH. Retaining the part-time services of President Cousins until 1936, the staff of the English department also included Dr. Mathilde M. Parlett, Miss Jessie W. Gardner (later Dr. Jessie G. Austin), Dr. Gertrude Ingalls, and Miss Barbara Monroe, a Shorter graduate. Dr. Parlett was twice selected as the best academic teacher in the college, and because of "the inspiration she gives her students to seek further knowledge" she twice had the *Argo* dedicated to her. Remaining active were the Phi Kappa Alpha Literary Club and Rho Delta, while Theta Mu, devoted to the study of poetry, existed for only one year.

Loosely associated with the English department, Alpha Delta Chi or the Debate Club was vocal from 1937 to about 1945. Debates were held with a dozen different institutions, including Winthrop College in South Carolina and the University of the South in Tennessee. Scholarly seriousness was not always present, as suggested by a debate sponsored by the club on the topic, "Resolved, that career girls are happier than married women." This impression was strengthened by the 1945 *Argo*: "Increased interest is being evidenced in this club. Perhaps it could be those exciting trips to Tech and Emory, etc., that are its drawing card."

FOREIGN LANGUAGES. Six different foreign languages were offered: French, German, Greek, Latin, Portuguese, and Spanish. Dr. Clara L. Thompson was professor of classical languages and Spanish. For a second time president of the Classical Association of Georgia, she experienced a marked decline of interest and offerings in the classics— except in the spring semester of 1947. At that time, much to the amazement of the public relations director, eighteen pupils signed up for elementary Greek, leading to the remark: "Maybe someone will dream up a Greek chorus for 'Open the Door, Richard.'"

The other modern languages were taught by Dr. and Mrs. John N. Ware, Miss Susie P. Brown, Miss Margaret Newhard, a Shorter graduate, and others. Dr. Ware remained the respected and popular professor of French, serving one year as president of the Georgia chapter of the American Association of Teachers of French. He was immortalized by one poetess in these words:

> I know he must be near somewhere,
> Of that there's surely no mistaking.
> Why, don't you see that smoke-screen there
> That his cigar is making?

Once termed a "Snake Doctor," he grabbed the tail of a large brown snake ("six feet as the tale goes, but only about three in reality") that had invaded the Academic Building and "gave it a jerk much as he would have done a whip and thereby cracked its neck or whatever part of the vertebra that would correspond to the place to break a neck." Concluded the writer: "Thanks Dr. Ware!" Not unexpectedly, the 1941 *Argo* was dedicated to him.

After many years of inactivity, the Classical Club was reorganized in 1938. El Club Espanol and Le Cercle Francais usually maintained monthly programs, and by 1945 the German Club was struggling for existence.

HISTORY AND POLITICAL SCIENCE. Two ladies gave extended service to the department of history and political science, Miss Clara L. Kellogg and Mrs. Eleanor Wilcox Willingham, a graduate of the college. "For her loyalty to the ideals of Shorter," the students dedicated the 1940 *Argo* to Miss Kellogg, after naming her the best liked academic teacher for three straight years. The International Relations Club met regularly and sent representatives periodically to regional conventions.

"Providing information, building public opinion, and supporting legislation," the League of Women Voters was formed about 1944.

MATHEMATICS AND SCIENCE. Instruction in mathematics, biology, and chemistry was provided regularly, while physics continued to be listed but was seldom offered in the absence of a regular professor. Dr. Ruby Hightower taught mathematics for twenty-eight years until her first retirement in 1947, after which Miss Margaret Baskervill was employed. Miss Louise Thompson was part-time instructor in this department. Dr. Bertha Martin continued to lead the department of biology, being helped by Miss Grace Wyatt and, starting in 1944, by Miss Emma Lewis Lipps. Dr. Everett E. Porter was professor of chemistry, also becoming dean of the college in 1938. That year the *Argo* was dedicated to him "for his loyalty and unselfish service to Shorter and her students." Of the many who were assistants in these areas for one to three years, seven were Shorter graduates: Misses Patricia Bradley, Florence C. Burford, Virginia D. Culbreath, Vaidee Guerry, Mary C. Martin, Mildred Morton, and Elisabeth Tarver.

Keeping white mice for experimental purposes, the biology department saw the birth of nine little ones late in 1940. A sign promptly appeared on the third floor of the Academic Building: "Maternity Ward—Tread Lightly."

Long remembered by her pupils were Dr. Martin's stories and poems that combined humor, hygiene, science, and religion. One nonscientific story concerned the artist who retouched several oil paintings in an ancient Belgian church. Required to present an itemized bill, he included the following: "For correcting the Ten Commandments, $5.12. For renewing Heaven and adjusting stars, $7.14. . . . For putting new stone in David's sling, enlarging head of Goliath, $6.13. For mending shirt of Prodigal Son and cleaning his ear, $3.39. . . . For putting new tail and comb on St. Peter's rooster, $2.20. For re-pluming and regilding left wing of the Guardian Angel, $5.18. . . ." One poem had a very practical point:

> I sneezed a sneeze into the air.
> It fell to earth, I knew not where.
> But when the germs were ten days old,
> Twenty classmates had my cold.

She preserved with approval these lines by Walter Rauschenbusch:

> In the castle of my soul
> Is a little postern gate,
> Whereat, when I enter,
> I am in the presence of God.

In a moment, in the turning of a thought,
I am where God is.
This is a fact.

She also preserved a sentence reflecting the understanding that she evidently had of her role at Shorter: "A teacher is a spiritual mid-wife who brings us to the birth of ourselves." One verse from the Bible she often quoted: "Ye shall know the truth, and the truth shall make you free."

The Science Club, sometimes called Kappa Gamma Tau, continued to further knowledge in the four scientific areas. Occasionally also the students increased their understanding by attending meetings of the American Chemical Society or the Mathematics Association in Atlanta.

MUSIC. Under two directors of music, Arthur S. Talmadge from 1924 to 1936 and Wilbur H. Rowand from 1936 to 1949, the department of music had the largest number of faculty members at the college. In addition to the directors, other notable members of the faculty were Miss Unnie C. Ramsey for thirteen years, Mrs. Evelyn T. Harle for seven, Miss Esther L. Howe for five, and Robert P. Sheldon for five. In 1947 Miss Carolyn Brown (later Mrs. Richard Willis) returned to her alma mater for an extended period. Other Shorter graduates who taught briefly were Misses Mary A. Chitty, Claire Davis, Clara M. Guerry, Margaret Swain, and Dorothy A. Ware. During this period Rowand earned the Master of Music degree from the Cincinnati Conservatory and later received the honorary Doctor of Music degree from that institution. He was dean of the Georgia chapter of the American Guild of Organists in 1934 and vice-president of the National Association of Schools of Music in 1947. Sheldon was voted best music teacher by the students one year, Miss Howe was most popular music teacher that year, and Miss Margaret Dennis was best teacher once and most popular teacher twice. Four years of private lessons leading to majors were provided in piano, organ, violin, and voice, while class courses more than doubled. Other majors were offered in theory and public school music.

The first Georgia school to be recognized by the National Association of Schools of Music, Shorter was voted provisional membership in 1934 and full institutional membership in 1937. This further step placed the college within a group of only twelve institutions in the Southeast which were so highly rated.

Opportunities to hear music in public performances were abundant. Visits to Atlanta and Chattanooga allowed the students to listen to the St. Louis, Philadelphia, and Minneapolis symphony orchestras, Lawrence Tibbett, Nelson Eddy, Lotte Lehman, Grace Moore, Kirsten Flagstad, Gladys Swarthout, Sergei Rachmaninoff, Vladimir Horowitz, Yehudi Menuhin, Jascha Heifetz, Fritz Kreisler, the Vienna Boys Choir, the Don Cossack Chorus, and performances by the Metropolitan Opera Association. Dragging into her room at four in the morning, one weary musician was greeted by a note on her bed: "Good morning, sweet thing. Welcome home! Have fun? I'll see you soon—too soon, as far as sleep is concerned, huh?"

For ten years the college and the Rome Music Lovers' Club jointly sponsored concerts at Shorter, and thereafter the college cooperated with the Rome Civic Music Association as it brought artists to the Girls' High School auditorium. Hence, without a long bus ride, Shorter persons heard Joseph Bentonelli, Julius Huehn, and Anna Kaskas of the Metropolitan, the University of Michigan Little Symphony, Artur Rubinstein, Isaac Stern, Virgil Fox, Blanche Thebom, Dorothy Kirsten, and the Cincinnati Symphony Orchestra.

From twenty to thirty-five concerts and recitals were given on the Shorter campus each year by visitors, faculty members, and students, and music majors were allowed one s.h. credit some years for attending them. Two public recitals—one of which came in the senior year—were required for the Bachelor of Music degree. A Franz Schubert Festival, consisting of five recitals, was presented in 1940 by visitors and faculty.

Almost every year the department brought to the campus for a two-day visit an artist outstanding in some phase of music, being sometimes assisted financially by the Rome Music Lovers' Club or the Carnegie Foundation. In this way the students profited from master classes and recitals by Egon Petri, Dutch pianist; Rudolph Ganz, pianist and conductor; the Britt String and Piano Trio; and Yella Pessl, harpsichordist. In 1946 Miss Helen Knox Spain, music and art critic for the Atlanta *Journal*, paid a two-day visit to her alma mater for lectures and conferences.

After her graduation in 1924 with majors in piano and violin, Miss Caroline Gray studied for eight years, chiefly at Fontainebleau and the Juilliard School of Music. Twice during this period she returned to Shorter for recitals. In 1932 she maried Harry Katzman, an eminent violinist for whom she became accompanist, and they appeared together in a recital at Shorter in 1935. Shortly after her unexpected death the next year, the Caroline Gray Memorial Library was proposed for the music department. Dedicatory services were held for it at the commencement of 1940, with members of the Alumnae Association taking a prominent part. The following year Harry Katzman came back to play a concert as a memorial to his late wife. Her picture and violin are on display at the college; on the door of the Gray Library is a metal plaque inscribed to a "gifted musician . . .[an] exemplar of the fine art of gracious living."

The larger robed Shorter Choral Club and the smaller robed Shorter Singers held tryouts in the fall for new members, performing many times on campus, at various churches, and over radio stations in Atlanta and Chattanooga. The annual program of Christmas music was usually scheduled in the chapel and once consisted of a cantata composed by Professor Sheldon. Choral emblems, a white S on a yellow lyre, were awarded in the thirties for satisfactory participation.

Starting in 1945 a spring festival of music extending over several days was presented. While art exhibits and dance recitals were included, the major contribution was made by local and visiting musicians. In 1948 the festival was replaced by a musical comedy, "Danny Dither," staged at the city auditorium and involving the work of artists, dancers, and musicians.

The Camerata Club continued to stimulate "a more genuine musical interest" among the departmental majors and to provide for increased social contact between them and the faculty. Added in 1939, the Camerata Room furnished a lounge and facilities for listening to records and conducting small classes. Highlighting the year was the Camerata Follies in the second semester. At least once it received a "Roast Turkey" rating: "Magnificent entertainment. Sufficient proof of the consummate talent tucked away in Shorter corners." Usually it displayed only the abilities of Shorter students and faculty members, although in 1938 "a batch of the darlingest of the Darlington boys" participated.

PHYSICAL EDUCATION. For fifteen years the department of physical education was staffed by Miss Harriett Garrett, who became Mrs. Wilbur Rowand in 1942, and by a succession of assistants who remained only briefly. Formed in 1939, the Dance Club gave at least one recital at the city auditorium, but evidently lost its vitality after two or three years.

RELIGION AND PHILOSOPHY. Richard Hall remained as professor of religion for thirteen years until his retirement in 1939. Two years earlier the girls had dedicated the *Argo* to him. The part-time professor of philosophy was Dr. C. R. Wilcox, who also left Shorter in 1939. Thereafter Dr. Ralph E. McLain occupied the combined chair for six years and Dr. Lawrence O. Grant for eight. The first endowed department in the college, it was named the Mrs. Columbus Roberts Department of Religion in 1945. The Religion Club was initiated that year, with membership open to all interested students, whether departmental majors or not.

SOCIOLOGY AND ECONOMICS. Given part-time leadership by Dean Mildred R. Mell and full-time leadership by several others, including Miss Bernice Allen after 1946, the department of sociology and economics enlarged its offerings in sociology and finally added one course in anthropology. A limited amount of practical training came from working with the children of the Open Door Home and by attending the county juvenile and superior courts. Interest was heightened by a murder case in which a woman was convicted of poisoning her husband to collect his insurance. "No one wanted to miss this case, so all who could arrange schedules attended. The class period the following day was devoted to a roundtable discussion." In 1942 the Sociology Club was formed among the majors "to promote actual experience in the field."

SPEECH. Receiving wide public exposure, the department of speech significantly expanded its offerings in radio and drama under the guidance of Mrs. Allie Hayes Richardson. Four Shorter alumnae were among the assistants who usually worked under her: Misses Lotis Freeman, June Pearson, Joyce Storey, and Paloma Wiggins. Mrs. Richardson retained an active interest in the Georgia Association of the Teachers of Speech and its regional counterpart, often being accompanied to meetings by some of her students. Off-campus trips were also made to Atlanta for performances by Katherine Cornell, Cornelia Otis Skinner, Kathryn Hepburn, Tallulah Bankhead, Lynn Fontanne, and Alfred Lunt. On one of them the car broke down and the girls returned at six in the morning. Their story was corroborated by the ethics professor who was a part of the group!

While continuing to employ the larger stage in the auditorium, the department was materially aided in 1935 when the Play Shop was renovated and much new equipment was installed. At that time the name was changed to the Little Theater. Under the auspices of the Shorter Players, three-act plays were scheduled each fall, winter, and spring. Numerous one-act plays and student recitals were presented, sometimes as many as twenty-five in one year. Majors were required to participate in group recitals as sophomores and juniors and to prepare a recital, produce a play, or direct an original radio broadcast as seniors. The Shorter-Darlington Revue was sponsored annually from 1933 to 1938. Starting in the spring of 1938, men from Rome occupied roles in

Shorter plays, and the practice was resumed in 1946 after being discontinued during the war.

Administration and Staff

During the Cousins era, Miss Mildred R. Mell was dean of the college until her resignation in 1938, after which Dr. Everett E. Porter, who had been professor of chemistry since 1920, was appointed. Two Shorter graduates occupied the combined positions of dean of women and alumnae secretary, Miss Louise Bennet until her retirement in

Miss Louise Bennet   Miss Margaret L. Jacobs

1946 after twenty-six years with the college and Mrs. Lydia Dixon Sheppard as her successor. Mrs. Sheppard, to whom the *Argo* was dedicated in 1948, was the author of the first extensive history of Shorter College, a 160-page master's thesis completed in 1941 and read rather widely in manuscript form. Miss Louise Thompson continued as registrar. Until 1938 Dr. C. R. Wilcox was part-time director of business administration and field work. The college cashier was Miss Tennie Rhinehart until her death in 1940 and Miss Lilly Mary Cain afterwards. Tribute paid to "Miss Tennie" in a *Periscope* editorial included these words: "In all her relations with students and faculty she revealed a charm and graciousness of manner, a joyousness and readiness to help anyone who came to her. These qualities combined to form within her a beautiful type of Christianity worthy of emulation. At a chapel meeting all the members of the college community stood in silence as they thought together of their beloved friend." Mr. and and Mrs. Hubert T. Quillian were with the college for five years; he was field representative and she was manager of the dormitories, book store, and student bank. Edwin S. Preston succeeded him as executive secretary for five years. A Shorter alumna, Miss Lucy Quillian, was personnel representative briefly. Another alumna, Mrs. Dickey Barron (née Miss Virginia D. Culbreath, who had earlier been assistant in chemistry), returned in 1946 as director of public relations. For about three years she prepared colorful and informative news releases that were read all over the state. Miss Virginia Wooten, a recent graduate, was secretary to the president for about a year. Since 1937 Mrs. Emmie Louise Lovell has occupied that position, becoming a graduate of the college twenty years later!

For fifteen years Miss Parthenia George was librarian. After her resignation in 1939, others served for brief periods of time. Holdings increased from about 13,000 volumes in 1934 to 24,500 in 1948, when the value was estimated at more than $36,000. Students returned in the fall of 1935 to discover that the library had been moved from cramped quarters on the first floor of the Academic Building to one-half of the second floor and that much new equipment had been installed. In addition to the general library, a reading room was maintained on the first floor of the main building where contemporary literature was available. This was designated the Evelyn Sheffield Reading Room in 1938 when Mr. and Mrs. I. M. Sheffield, Sr., of Atlanta provided funds in honor of their daughter, a graduate of 1926. This was moved to the second floor of the Library-Administration Building in 1961.

"Sister Maggie," Miss Margaret L. Jacobs, remained as resident nurse until her retirement in 1938 after twenty-eight years at Shorter. On her silver anniversary the alumnae had given her an engraved gold wrist watch. Three years later it was said: "Her fine personality, her unselfish years of service, her happy, friendly disposition endeared her to all Shorter students who knew her." Following a year in Texas, she returned to the campus where she resided as nurse emeritus without official duties until 1946. After her death in 1963, the trustees named the college infirmary in her honor and the General Alumni Association presented an oil portrait of her painted by Constantin Chatov of Atlanta. She was succeeded by Miss Meeta McDonald, an alumna of Shorter, for almost nine years. The school physician was Dr. Warren Gilbert.

The popular Mrs. Elizabeth V. Bryan served as house manager for eighteen years beginning in 1935. At times she offered a devil's food cake to the best kept suite. More often she left notes:

Beds and clothing all in jumbles,
The maid working as she mumbles,
Won't you please try to reform,
And really clean up this part of the dorm?

Sing a song of six pence,
A pocket full of guile;
Four and twenty garments all in a pile.
Who're the girls so guilty of such a messy house?
If they don't improve their ways,
They'll never get a spouse.

Georgy, Porgy, Jane and Clair,
How many dresses on that chair?

Mrs. Mabel Owens Askew (later Mrs. Robert Todd), an alumna, was social director for three years, and Mrs. Azalea Estes was student counselor for eight. Coming in 1938 as a student counselor, Mrs. Lila C. Elliott was honored by the 1942 *Argo*. The dedication was "to Mrs. Elliott, whose four years at Shorter have added richly to ours, who came with us and saw us through, who is a worthy addition to any school staff, and who is held with deep affection in every Shorter girl's heart."

Of the many maids working during these years, Mrs. Mary Jo Lewis and Mrs. Jessie Wood were particularly faithful. Mrs. Victoria Anderson continued as hostess in the Academic Building until her death late Saturday afternoon, April 3, 1937, while she was still on duty. The *Periscope* said: "Little of Victoria's life is known; all she has left is the memory of the greatness of her character . . . enshrined in the hearts of all who ever knew her." A full page in the *Chimes* was set aside for her, including her photograph and an essay titled "A Tribute to Victoria" that concluded: "With her passing, something that can never be replaced has been taken from us—something inextricably bound up with our love for Shorter. Life at Shorter continues as ever; we go on to our classes; we leave; new faces come to take our place; but behind it all something is missing. The little chair by the door is empty. Victoria is gone."

Famous for her Baked Alaska, Sally Lunn, cheese soufflé, and sizzling steaks, Mrs. Jennie B. Hurst reigned over the dining room and kitchen. For a time Charles H. Sigler was her baker. Long-time assistants included Mrs. Dolores Thornton, Roy Barton, Roy Brannon, Willmar Cammon, John Fielder, Steve Graham, Frank Harper, Spencer Hughes, Howard Miller, and Solomon Thornton. Three seated meals were served each day in surroundings made attractive by colorful table cloths and slip covers for the chairs. The Saturday dinner was by candlelight, with the girls properly attired in long dresses. Seating assignments were changed periodically, allowing each student to eat with almost everybody else in the course of the year.

Expending much effort to make her special meals effective and enjoyable, Mrs. Hurst displayed a clever knack for achieving the artistic and beautiful. In addition to the Butterfly Brunches, her Christmas parties were notable. The students sang—once to Cousins, Wilcox, and Quillian, employing the tune of "We Three Kings":

> They three men of Shorter are
> Seeking gifts they traverse afar
> O'er field and fountain, moor and mountain
> Seeking endowment par!

Gathered around the large Christmas tree under which gifts for them were placed, the servants sang spirituals. A college graduate, Frank Harper, once responded to the gifts in these words: "In behalf of the personnel of the dietary staff, allow me to offer you a few words of gratitude for this beautiful manifestation of the spirit of Christmas. Day after day as we go about our work in various capacities, we attempt to attain our maximum efficiency. The wonderful tribute you have paid us tonight will aid as a stimulus in helping us to attain that efficiency. The thought of tonight will remain with us throughout the years, as well as the realization of your unselfish spirit, and we will forever treasure it in the innermost recesses of our hearts. Again we thank you." President Cousins is said to have remarked quietly to those at his table: "I've got my commencement speaker."

Appreciatively called "Pop" by the girls, John F. Stevens was night watchman during this entire period. A bald-headed man, he frequently sat in the vestibule of Rome Hall. For good luck as she went up to the library, a girl would kiss her forefinger and then gently touch the top of his head. When informed of a malfunctioning coke machine, he promptly attended to the problem, later reporting: "I fotched back my foot and gave it a kick, and it belched out about six bottles." In response to a question concerning his wages, he is supposed to have admitted: "Well, I don't get paid too much. But, of course, I don't do too much, either." The girls would emphatically disagree with that last sentence, as indicated by the dedication to him and Lon Smith in the 1947 *Argo*:

Dear "Pop" and Mr. Smith,
  You were among the first to see us arrive on the hill back in '43, and among the last to see us leave this spring, but it is because of all you've been to us in the four years between these events that we have written this letter.
  Somehow you've always managed to provide for us the little things which

meant so much . . . Maypoles and platforms for our May Day . . . a way for luggage to be shipped to those of us who waited until the last minute to pack . . . help with our society and generation parties . . . those hard-to-get light bulbs during the war . . . the key to the swimming pool . . . your advice . . . and most of all . . . your friendship.

Supervisor of maintenance throughout the Cousins years, Lon Smith was assisted for ten of those years by J. W. Mellon. Negro workmen under their direction included Eugene Hutchins, John Perkins, Monroe Perkins, John Posey, and Jessie Posey.

By the mid-forties a mysterious lady took up residence in the attic of Van Hoose Hall. Known simply as "Mrs. Harper," she is listed in no college catalogue and no picture of her is ever included in an annual. Girls generously took her food that they had begged from the dietician, and freshmen were instructed to carry on intelligent conversations with her during ratting. She is said to have been responsible for removing objects from the dormitories and opening doors when nobody was in sight.

Student Government and the Students Handbook

In its constitution, the Student Government Association stated that its object was "to create, promote, and preserve student honor, to maintain high standards of scholarship, to regulate the conduct of the student body and enforce such regulations of the college as do not fall exclusively within the province of the faculty." The executive branch was the Student Council, the legislative branch was the student body, and the judicial branch was the Honor Board, subject to review by the faculty executive committee and the president of the college. Elections came in the spring, governed by the point system that divided the responsibility and opportunity of office-holding among many students. The new Student Council was installed in a March chapel program by the outgoing officers: oaths of office were administered, robes were passed on, and speeches were made by the old and new presidents. Starting in the fall of 1934 an evening ceremony marked the installation of the Honor Board and the accepting of the Honor Pledge by the student body. Guest speakers at this time included Dr. W. A. Smart of Emory University, President J. R. McCain of Agnes Scott College, Pierce Harris of the First Methodist Church of Atlanta, and President Josiah T. Crudup of Brenau College. Each student formally signed the following Honor Pledge: "We, the members of the student body of Shorter College, realizing that the Honor Board is powerless to perform its duties without the support of the student body, do hereby dedicate ourselves to the principles of the Honor System. We resolve, insofar as we are

309

able, to keep ourselves above reproach, to make known to the Honor Board, whom we have chosen as our representatives, any violation of the system that comes under our observation, and to do everything in our power to help the Board preserve and protect the Honor System of Shorter College." By 1946 Honor Week was observed prior to the installation service, when relevant chapel talks were made by spokesmen for the four classes, the president of the S.G.A., and a faculty member.

The student body met regularly on Thursday evening, with some business and much entertainment. Various classes and organizations were charged with producing the program, although occasionally the dean might put in an appearance. In 1936 an organization of all club presidents was begun, soon called the Key Club.

The student treasurer biannually received dues on behalf of all organizations until a general student activities fee, collected by the business office at registration, caused her job to be abolished about 1940.

The S.G.A. participated in the National Student Federation of America, the Southern Intercollegiate Association of Student Governments, and the Georgia Federation of Student Government Associations, and Shorter girls attended conventions in Atlanta, Florida, Louisiana, Virginia, Indiana, and New Jersey. In the spring of 1946 the Shorter S.G.A. president, Marjorie Joyner, was elected president of the regional association comprised of twenty-six institutions. Returning from one such meeting, a student leader concluded: "We have more privileges than most schools. Our student council has a wider scope and is more powerful. Our system of student government is quite up to date."

The practice was continued of issuing the *Students Handbook* annually. Greetings from the administration, pictures of and messages from the major student officers, a calendar of events, detailed rules, information about school organizations, songs, "Hilltop Hints," and advertisements extended to almost 120 pages. The foreword was comforting—and somewhat sanguine: "Don't worry if some of the rules seem a bit confusing because all misunderstandings will be corrected when your life on Shorter Hill begins." In the estimation of one student, this was a period of "some mighty good and intelligent changes." Legally leaving the campus still became increasingly difficult as the evening or the weekend approached or as an out-of-town trip was contemplated—and special permission was required for each and every airplane flight! Before the war students were not permitted to have automobiles, except under definite regulations during opening and closing days and (for seniors only) after spring vacation. Gasoline rationing temporarily removed the threat, of course, after which cars were allowed and riding limits were imposed. Card games could now be played with real playing cards, but not on Sunday and not for money. Dormitory rules covered lights, radios, and study signs—with examination week usually being characterized by a greater number of hours for lights to be left on and a greater disapproval of "*ANY* noise*," as one notice proclaimed. One guilty person, whose name probably should not be mentioned, smilingly remembers being called to her door by a Student Council member who gently told her: " 'Mrs. E.,' your radio is a little too loud." In theory at least, closed study was required for freshmen five nights a week from 7:30 to 10:30. Smoking was frankly discouraged, but in the late thirties rules were finally passed permitting it in suites, Senior Den, Student Council Room, and Town Girls' Hall. Telephones were provided in each dormitory and on the first floor of Rome Hall in the telephone room, and the severe restrictions of an earlier day were replaced by this: "A student should be considerate. . . . All local calls on any phone must be limited to FIVE minutes." One writer in the *Chimes* gladly approved: "Phone-talkers-for-more-than-five-minutes—remember there's a bare chance in ninety-nine that someone else might get a call. Minnie-Meat!"

Religion on Campus

The name of the central religious organization was changed in the spring of 1942 from the Young Women's Christian Association to the Shorter Christian Association. Its overall program, however, remained stable. Each spring the officers and other cabinet members were elected by the student body and installed at a Sunday vesper service. In the fall a planning retreat was often held at the Radio Springs cabin. Dressed in white and carrying lighted candles, the entire student body attended and new students were initiated into the association one Sunday evening each fall, signing and retaining a card that read: "As a member of the Christian Association of Shorter College, I pledge myself to uphold the purpose of that organization, namely, to realize a full and creative life through a growing knowledge of God, and to determine to have a part in making this life possible for all people. In this task I seek to understand Jesus and to follow Him." The association hymn, "Follow the Gleam," was always a part of the service. To identify new students with the organization, a Freshman Commission was named by the cabinet during the first semester. Usually its members kept the bulletin board in the Glass Corridor displaying "The

Thought for the Day." Worship services were sponsored by the association: optional daily morning watch, optional Tuesday vespers, and required Sunday vespers. Frequently a mimeographed order of service was provided for the two vespers, revealing that programs consisted of a large number of Protestant clergymen, an infrequent rabbi or Roman Catholic priest, furloughing missionaries such as Miss Helen Meredith (class of 1932) of Colombia, student speakers, campus musicians, one-act plays, and groups of young men from Berry, Emory, or the University of Georgia. A Y.W. or S.C.A. Room was maintained on the first floor of Van Hoose Hall, where a library of religious books was kept.

By 1939 the traditional Halloween party had turned into a fund-raising carnival which was first sponsored by the Y.W.C.A. that year. Admission was charged, and profits were realized from the House of Horror and other concessions. Each class nominated a candidate for Carnival queen, and the crown went to the young lady whose class box contained the most money. When class rivalry ran high in 1947, a near-tie resulted in the crowning of two queens, the junior and senior nominees. As much as $360 was netted by the association for use on its numerous projects. Each Thanksgiving fifteen to twenty baskets were personally delivered to needy families, and others were distributed some years at Christmas. A large party for underprivileged children from West Rome included a Christmas tree, Santa Claus, gifts, games, fruit, and ice cream. Frequently another entertainment for the same children was sponsored in the spring. Other forms of social service included work with the Open Door Home and with children's groups in the local churches. Money was also spent for Far East relief and for use by the World Student Service Fund.

Religious Focus Week was a regular element of the second semester when a visitor spent several days on campus. Pastors from Baptist, Methodist, or Presbyterian churches were usually invited— although Drs. Olin T. Binkley and Harold W. Tribble of the Southern Baptist Theological Seminary, Dr. B. Davie Napier of the University of Georgia, and Dr. Kenneth Foreman of Davidson College sometimes provided leadership.

"Hilltop Views," a weekly mimeographed news sheet that was continued into the early forties, usually contained a prayer meditation and announcements concerning religious events. Unwilling to remain solemn all the time, the association helped to prepare a weiner roast for the freshman each September and often put on a school-wide party in the gym or in the courtyard later in the year.

Throughout the thirties Shorter girls participated in Georgia con-

312

ventions of the Y.W.C.A.–Y.M.C.A. and traveled to Blue Ridge, North Carolina, for summer student conferences. In 1946 the S.C.A. joined the Georgia Student Christian Association, and Virginia Cline of Shorter was elected its president the following year.

Deputations necessitated additional travel for those who conducted vesper services at Wesleyan, Emory, and Georgia Tech. An engine failure occurred on one of these excursions when a young lady—later to become a learned member of the faculty—reached over to turn off the car radio, which she thought was controlled by a key.

Smaller denominational groups were created in the early forties: the Presbyterian Student Association, the Canterbury Club, the Methodist Student Union (Wesley Foundation), and the Catholic Club. Not surprisingly, Baptist groups were also active. Reorganized in 1938, the Young Woman's Auxiliary was named in honor of Martha Shorter and emphasized mission study and the Lottie Moon Christmas offering. Long before the Baptist Student Union was formed at Shorter in 1940, a few of the girls had been attending conferences in Memphis and at Ridgecrest Baptist Assembly of North Carolina. Once founded on the hill, the B.S.U. conducted a preschool planning retreat, publicized "Join the Church Day," stressed prayer and missions, gave campus-wide parties, and sent delegates annually to the state convention. By 1947 another effort was made to have a Baptist Training Union meeting each Sunday evening on campus. Throughout, the Shorter Sunday school class at First Baptist Church was provided for the girls.

Statistics are not readily available concerning denominational affiliation and the number of students preparing for church-related vocations. Without question the Baptists, Methodists, and Presbyterians constituted the largest groups. Including those interested in church music, perhaps as many as twenty young ladies in any given year were professionally training for work within the church. In 1946 the first ministerial student in the history of the college was enrolled, Walter E. Bryant of Cartersville, Georgia.

As the name implies, the twice-weekly chapel services were often religious in nature. Thus, addresses were heard from Dr. William Cannon of Emory University, Miss Juliette Mather of the Southern Baptist Convention, Sherwood Eddy, Mr. and Mrs. James L. Kraft of Chicago, Daniel A. Poling, Dr. Gunnar Westin, Swedish church historian, and Mrs. Grace Sloan Overton, marriage counselor. A solemn service followed the death of President Roosevelt at Warm Springs. Equally often, however, the programs concerned topics such as Indian life and songs, women in journalism, liquified air, Horace, Negro education, or modern painting. Congressman Henderson Lanham, Editor

Ralph McGill, Walter R. Thomas of Atlanta, and Morgan Blake, sports editor of the Atlanta *Journal*, were among those who spoke.

Widely appreciated during the Christmas season of 1941 was a nativity scene displayed by the college on the hillside near Maplehurst and facing Shorter Avenue. Each evening for a week various church choirs sang carols from the site, carried live over WRGA. The *News-Tribune* spread an eight-column picture of the scene across page one.

Student Publications

Elected by the student body or by the outgoing staff, the editor of the *Argo* and her chief associates produced the annual without a break even during the war years. The business manager and her assistants persistently sought advertisers, and at times sponsored programs such as a fashion show at the DeSoto Theater with an original skit about President and Mrs. Van Hoose. Fear was felt in 1942 that increased costs might force the omission of colored pictures—the staff even discussed the possibility of distributing the annual without a cover in order to save money!—but the finished product had both colored pictures and cover. Outside help was usually enlisted to select the campus beauties: annual staffs from men's colleges, Cecil B. deMille, or Glenn Miller and his band. One dedication was to the Shorter Girls' Creed, which "has guided us for four years and helped us to mold our personalities in a more pleasing and friendly manner." Recalling "When We Were Young" and modestly proclaiming, "Oh, What a Beautiful Baby," the seniors of 1934 and 1947 included shots that had not been taken by the visiting photographer!

The *Chimes* was issued three or four times each year until the war halted production in 1942. Beginning in the spring of 1944, only one number was subsequently published each year. Usually the editor was named in the student body election, but after the war the president of Rho Delta automatically became editor. Issues included poetry and fiction, some literary criticism, many book reviews, and block prints furnished by art students. Annually a contest was held to select the best poem, short story, and essay by a freshman and by an older student.

Published six to eight times each year, the *Periscope* was also affected by the war, being printed only once in the academic years 1942 to 1944. The leaders of the staff were determined at the annual spring election. Photographs were used in virtually every number, and often alumnae news was included in a special supplement. Maintaining membership in the Georgia Collegiate Press Association, Shorter sent representatives to the annual state convention.

314

The Sports Association correlated intramural sports, attempting to enroll every student in its membership and functioning through the Sports Council. After spring elections, the new council was installed at a chapel service, the first in 1938. Miss Louise Bennet's "The White and Gold," written back in 1918, became the official song of the association. A new club, also called "The White and Gold," sprang into existence when, in the mid-forties, the council selected a group of interested and capable freshmen to work on behalf of the association especially among their fellow freshmen. Some years a *Sports Association Handbook* was published.

Facilities were provided for competition between individuals, classes, societies, and generations in a wide variety of sports: volley ball, hockey, softball, basketball, soccer, swimming, tennis, hiking, golf, horseback riding, ping pong, track and field, fencing, archery, badminton, and water polo. A Sports Awards chapel was initiated, at which amazing numbers of persons were honored by amazing numbers of prizes. Announcement was made concerning those seniors whose names were engraved on the silver sports plaque. Distributed at this time were athletic letters, stars to be added to previously won letters, senior lifesaving certificates, the dance achievement award, and many cups that included the tall Parlett Cup for the class having the largest percentage of its members participating in intramurals.

Because student health was one concern of the association, a health contest was sponsored in the spring of 1934 and a health party four years later. Health Week was first observed in November of 1938, with points given for eating three meals a day in the dining room, getting at least eight hours of sleep at night, and exercising at least thirty minutes each day. An award was made to the girls on a dormitory floor or half floor accumulating the most points; once 3½ floors were tied for first place and each occupant got a free trip to the picture show. Probably it was one of the winners who wrote: "Health Week—More Roast Turkey loose for this, and it grabs a big one. It's a little incongruous to give a lot of gravy in addition, but we can break over from an iron-and-vitamin diet, because the idea deserves it. And Minnie-Meat to the non-cooperatives."

In the fall a picnic or Halloween masquerade party might be held for the freshmen. Stunt Night promoted rivalry between classes or generations, and a faculty performance usually contributed additional hilarity. The May Day celebration, sponsored in connection with other organizations of the college, was eagerly anticipated. Play Day was scheduled each spring, featuring track and field contests between classes, the traditional cap and gown race between the seniors and the faculty, and a picnic in the Rockery. Frequently high school girls were invited to watch the excitement.

The Sports Association held membership in the Women's Division of the National Amateur Athletic Federation and the Georgia Athletic Federation of College Women. Regarding the latter, Shorter girls regularly attended state conventions, two of which were in Rome, and at times were officers or council members.

Student-faculty sporting events were scheduled each year in basketball, volley ball, or softball. Some of these were termed "traditional" contests, resulting in what was called "tough" battles. Apparently the battle was tougher for the faculty, because they seldom seemed to win.

In 1940 the students again expressed themselves as favoring intercollegiate sports and were permitted to plan for competition in tennis, swimming, and golf with schools such as Agnes Scott and Georgia State College for Women. A tennis match played at Decatur with Agnes Scott in November of 1940 resulted in a 4 to 0 win for Shorter, and the following spring a Shorter group participated in a tennis tournament at Milledgeville. Evidently wartime restrictions curtailed further activities.

The Two Societies

The Eunolymnians and the Polynomians, to use Dr. Ware's designation, continued to occupy a prominent position in the life of most Shorter girls. Before arriving on the hill in September, each freshman received rush letters from members of both societies. On Thursday morning during orientation, all residential students were ordered into the gymnasium where the rushing rules were read. Giving one big scream, the older girls headed toward the wide-eyed freshmen, who had earlier been advised in the *Students Handbook*: "Don't be afraid! Those girls rushing at you with pencils and little books aren't going to hurt you; they want to date you up for the rest of the week." From Thursday morning until Sunday night they led the freshmen on a mad dash of events. Companions for breakfast, companions after breakfast, companions for lunch, companions from 2:00 to 4:00, companions from 4:00 to 6:00, companions for dinner, companions after dinner, companions for recreation—hardly a waking moment was spent without companions. Since the older students were not allowed to spend money on any prospect, the freshmen were cautioned: "Remember to take your billfold with you when you go downtown for a coke or a show." Just before tumbling into bed—without a companion—the freshman might find a "nighty-night note" on her pillow saying: "Hope you've had a perfectly swell time tonight—you looked so fresh and pretty—sleep good and I'll be seeing you bright and—maybe not *too* early tomorrow!"

Alternating the first Friday and Saturday nights of each fall semester, the societies provided coronation programs that were designed to dazzle the new girls. Utilizing the dining room and gymnasium, each gave its traditional play in which its president was crowned as queen, entertained with a variety show, served delicious food, and employed a small band for dancing. Some aspect of the plantation theme was always employed by the Polymnians, while the Eunomian decorations were varied: the "Lower Regions," an airport, a Dutch scene, or the Byrd expedition.

In 1936 the Polymnians first staged their play and coronation in the auditorium, followed by refreshments and dancing in the gym. Soon the play was also moved to the gym, and only the coronation was produced in the auditorium. The Eunomians followed suit in 1937 when the first Green Coronation was presented in the auditorium, after which "Queen Eunomia, Cabinet Member, Department of Happiness," reigned over "a swirl of entertainment in the Rainbow Room of the Eunomian Nite Club" that apparently included the traditional play. In 1940 the Eunomian ceremony was rewritten by Miss Lucy Quillian, a graduate the preceding spring, and for about twenty-five years her version was used. The Polymnians added in the mid-forties a coronation poem that is still recited:

> She is beautiful
> Because she lives in beauty.
> She has friends,
> For she is a friend who never fails
>   those in whom she believes.
>
> She is loved
> For she is loyal, steadfast,
> Because she, too, loves her school,
>   her friends, her life.
>
> She is happy
> For she can laugh, and love, and lift.
> She is our Polymnian girl.

As the freshmen walked through the first floor corridor of Van Hoose on their way to a coronation, the members of the opposite society lined the walls, often produced an arch with crepe paper, and sang their own society songs to them. Upon their return from the coronation, they might again be greeted by the older girls lining the corridor, this time holding candles as they sang. Each girl saw both coronations only in her freshman year; the other years she was busy distributing favors during the rival ceremony.

The Eunomians have proudly framed a telegram which has the appearance of authenticity:

QU150 70 NT-Washington DC Sep 18 1943
Queen Eunomia
   Shorter College Rome Ga
Sept 18, 1943. Have just created dept of happiness. stop
please accept post of cabinet member and be head of department. stop
have searched the entire country and think you and your group are the best
to lead in the spread of happiness thru out the U.S.A. stop
for your first project present floor show in Rainbow Room at Eunomian
Night Club at the Eunomian party, Shorter College tonight. stop
keep up the good work. dont stop
   FDR President of the U.S.

Rushing ended at 8:00 on Sunday night. One senior recalled: "Weeping buckets on pledge day—finally making our decision in the wee small hours." About 1940 an unofficial form of pledging was started. The girls shouted their choices from a Cooper window late Sunday evening. At six the next morning a bell rang and the freshmen sped to sign their names on the roll of the society of their choice. One of the biggest honors of the day was to be the first girl to pledge. As the new girls excitedly tumbled into Eunie or Poly Hall, they were greeted with shouts and songs and embraces and tears. Ribbons were displayed— green and green or red, white, and green. The day's fun continued as the Eunomians took their new members downtown for breakfast, followed in some years by a broadcast over WFDV when a bedraggled and sleepy group of girls tried to sing society songs with some show of spirit. The Polymnians treated their pledges to a luncheon downtown and to an afternoon theater party.

Society programs came regularly on Saturday evening immediately after dinner while most of the girls were still wearing long dresses. Gone were the days of literary addresses and serious debates; the programs were ordinarily meant to entertain. They furnished Shorter's version of *Pilgrim's Progress*, Kay Kyser's musical quiz, a preview of Judgment Day, a takeoff on Romeo and Juliet, a blues singer and jitterbugs, an insight into a faculty meeting, a skit entitled "Mars Views the Earth," or a contest with a Shirley Temple soap doll as the prize. They varied their schedule with fall and spring weiner roasts or picnics and parties at Halloween and Christmas. Santa Claus usually arrived through a window with fruit and candy for good little girls. One secretary recorded: "Then went home to bed to dream of Christmas holidays which were just around the corner." Each January the Polymnians celebrated their birthday with a cake, a recounting of their history, and a special rendition of their song, "I Love the Name of Polymnian." At times the two groups met together, with one in charge of the program.

Although most of their songs were ephemeral, the societies constantly sang just the same. "My Mammy" was an invariable part of each Polymnian meeting. Every year that society conducted a contest in which each class contributed an entry. The Eunomians produced a stately song still in use:

> Eunomian girls, where'er you be,
> We sing this song tonight to thee.
> The colors are waving here for you,
> Eunomian Hall calls you too.
> We love the traditions you left us here,
> And we will always hold them dear.
> Won't you come and sing with us
> In old Eunomian Hall.

The two societies selected new officers each spring, including two or three cheerleaders and three or four song leaders. Of course the Polymnians also picked a Mammy and several children. Each president was installed soon after election, being crowned and presented with the president's pin by the outgoing leader. As a gift from the society, the departing president might receive a tea-rose negligee, silver earrings, a gold watch, or something similar. Many of the queens remembered the members of their court with a small but treasured piece of jewelry. The graduating seniors were honored by a program—usually containing a wry prophecy concerning their activities ten years hence—and were sometimes given a small present such as a linen handkerchief. Loyal supporters of the aims and ideals of each society, the Thugs were "true Eunomians all" and the H.O.T.s were "one hundred percent Polymnians."

The two halls were continually being refurnished. The members bought a piano or a victrola for themselves at Christmas. The departing seniors gave needed pieces of furniture. When major renovations were required, alumnae members were written and invited to send in contributions.

Usually the competition existing between societies was serious but friendly, without antagonism, prejudice, or jealousy. Membership for the Polymnians ranged from 84 to 134, with an average of 107, and for the Eunomians from 63 to 123, with an average of 100. However, for the last half of this period the Eunomian Society was always larger, by an average of almost 20. Periodically one society would challenge the other to a game of basketball, volley ball, soccer, or hockey, and the victories were about evenly divided. The same cannot be said for the Student Council Scholarship Plaque instituted in 1937. Needless to say, both groups were proud of their members on the honor roll, but the truth is that the Eunomians maintained the higher average for fifteen of twenty-two semesters.

Classes, Generations, and the Crook

"Wow! in the middle of the night we realized how big and important the Sophomores were, for they suddenly became our Supreme rulers. We knew then that Freshman wasn't such a big title after all." "Three whole weeks of supreme importance filled with parties, registering, pledging, and getting settled, just to be unsettled . . . . Then two weeks of extreme insignificance." Thus did two seniors recall the beginning of their careers as rats. Without warning the sophomores would descend upon the youthful occupants of Cooper Hall. For a week or two the freshmen tried to satisfy all sorts of outlandish requirements. Upon meeting a sophomore or senior she might say, "I'm just a low vile rat, good for nothing but your door mat," take a swig of warm water from a bottle which she carried for such a purpose, and then depart "like a high-powered motor boat." She might join others in a chorus line, praising Allah, or playing choo-choo. She would instantly obey the command: "Button, rat!" or "Air raid, rat!" or "Blitzkrieg, rat!" Useful jobs might be assigned: dipping water from the courtyard pool with a teaspoon, preparing a five-thousand-word essay on "Why," or sweeping the dormitory floor with an eyebrow brush. Demands were made to sing a laundry list or "I Love You Truly" to the tune of "Yankee Doodle," bloom like a cross-eyed rose, smile and frown at the same time, throw a fit out the window, or be a symphony orchestra. All efforts were received with extreme contempt by the derisive sophomores. With her legs painted red and white like a barber pole and her white-chalked face decorated with pussy cat whiskers, wearing a stocking or a lamp shade as a hat, attired in articles of clothing worn upside down and inside out, and carrying her books in a waste basket or suitcase or pillowcase, the budding scholar pursued an education. One professor moaned: "Imagine teaching such wretched little creatures and not, like a mother cat, washing their faces as they shrink into class . . . ."

320

When the juniors serenaded the freshmen, some comfort was experienced, but the ultimate consolation came after the yellow and white rat caps were turned in and a huge bonfire was ignited. As punishment for being bad rats, caps were burned before the eyes of the tearful freshmen, who by that time had become sentimentally attached to them. Usually those caps on the fire were extras, however, and much rejoicing came when the freshmen finally got theirs back. This judgment was usually appropriate: "Freshmen—Roast Turkey; you took ratting in good fun. We noticed, and we think you deserve not apple, but cranberry sauce."

The pros and cons of ratting were discussed by the students—even by the older ones—and by the dean of women, who had to call in the sophomore president because of occasional excesses. In the thirties several decisions were made by the girls to reduce or abolish the initiation, but even the burying of a new hatchet one year did not halt the process when the next fall rolled around.

Freshmen were gently harassed even apart from ratting. Thus, they were thrown into great confusion when a notice appeared on the bulletin board: "All freshmen must turn in their mattresses to Mrs. Bryan before leaving for Christmas." Posted anonymously by the fun-loving president of the student body that year, it received such an overwhelming response that its authoress feared to gloat over her trick!

Maintaining a sense of identity, the four classes organized themselves by electing officers. Parties both planned and spontaneous were given for themselves and for their sister class. Teams represented the classes in the manifold sports events, and the cups that were awarded thrilled the victors, especially when they had already won in previous years and could claim a continuity. The crowning of the Halloween Carnival queen was made the more notable for the class whom she represented.

Each year the freshmen and juniors were automatically sister classes. Their elders helped the freshmen to organize by calling and leading a class meeting for them. Perhaps at a Hansel and Gretel party or at a Valentine program the juniors formally presented the freshmen with a banner showing the year of their graduation. The freshmen responded during the spring with a carefully planned party that might have as its theme a shipwreck, nursery rhymes, an Alpine lodge, a circus, or the Mardi Gras. Often they gave a piece of furniture to be used in Senior Hall the next year. The senior-sophomore relationship was closer; this will be described in a later section of this chapter.

The sister classes preserved the tradition of the generations, the odd-year High-Mindeds and the even-year Whoop-Em-Ups. The "double-jinted" High-Mindeds continued to sing about their remarkable condition, adding verses and other songs as the years passed. Members of their honorary club, the Owls, showed "their wisdom by being enthusiastic supporters of the High-Minded Generation" and "prominent in service to Shorter . . . ." In 1938 this generation adopted as a mascot Dr. Francis Peabody Dobitty, a white pigeon, which they later decided was really a white owl.

Dedicated to the Whoop-Em-Up spirit, the 1936 *Argo* appropriately included the sketch of a marriage license. In alternate falls the Whoop-Em-Up Wedding united a blushing bride, the junior president, to a handsome groom, the freshman president, in a formal chapel ceremony. It was preceded by a spinster dinner, a bachelor supper, and a rehearsal party—and one year the "men" got sick on cigars that were passed around. The generation wrote new songs, but continued to insist that, "with chillun round the door, we'll teach them that the thing to do is Whoop-Em-Up some more." The S.O.S. Club maintained a reputation of usefulness to college and clan. Rivalry was expressed chiefly when the generations clashed at a basketball or volley ball game or in a swimming meet—or when they tried to outsing each other.

The ancient crook became the object of attention during the spring of each year, for a period that was gradually reduced from one month to four days. Taken from Senior Den, it was brought to the dining room by the robed seniors at the dinner hour. Every student was required to be present, and all cars were halted at the foot of the hill. The senior president and her cohorts left the room and quickly scattered so that the underclassmen could not determine the direction of the hiding party. Since no one else could leave until the last senior had departed, those remaining seniors dawdled over their coffee until sufficient time had passed for their president to do a good job.

Rules were written by the students themselves. The crook could be concealed only on top of Shorter Hill—but not on the tall water tank and not in classrooms, grand pianos, faculty apartments, or the tunnel that housed electric lines. The rules finally decreed that no girl could cut classes or look between 11:00 P.M. and 6:00 A.M. Professors, administrators, and staff members could not be quizzed regarding the crook's location because they were not required to be in the dining room and might therefore unwittingly possess definite information.

Although two hundred girls could cover lots of ground in the time allotted, they seldom found the crook. The Atlanta *Constitution* carried a photograph of two seniors hiding it in a society hall; the caption read: "The hunt is now on, but the crook's not behind that curtain." Secreted under the back steps of Cooper Hall, on the far side of the swimming pool in a hole covered with straw, or as a part of an ironing board constantly in use by the seniors, it was usually safe from prying junior or freshmen eyes. One unconfirmed story tells of a junior who discovered the crook on top of a building, inaccessible except by a trap door which the seniors were guarding. The enterprising girl employed a pilot friend to fly low and secure the crook by lassoing it. He tried, but the seniors removed their treasure before he was successful.

The juniors took their failure with good grace. One *Argo* picture shows a girl crawling out of the basement with an object in her hand that was described as "only a rake." After days of searching, a junior might admit: "At least we know where it's not." The class once sang to the seniors: "Lost a crook as good as new. Now that crook belongs to you. . . . Seniors keepers, juniors weepers." On another occasion the juniors entered the dining room in black dresses and veils, singing a dirge as an admission of their inability to find it.

The search came to an official conclusion on or near the evening when the senior-sophomore banquet was held at a downtown dining room. In the early forties the freshmen took advantage of the situation by tearing up the sophomores' rooms while they were gone, receiving the assistance—or reprimand—of the juniors who sometimes made similar visits to the seniors' suites. Tied end to end, bed sheets were strung from Van Hoose to the swimming pool or the Fine Arts Building. Sometimes they were piled together in the form of a snowman. Metal head and foot boards from the beds were placed in the fish pond. Clothing was piled on the floor, lipstick smeared on the mirrors, and powder sprinkled all over the rooms. Saddle oxfords were strung up in the hall on a long cord. Tadpoles were placed in the bathtubs and frogs in the dresser drawers. Favorite pictures were exchanged, and pieces of furniture moved from one room to another. The house-mothers were all invited to attend the banquet, but at least one remained behind "to watch things." The crook was passed on to the unsuccessful juniors at Class Day.

Casting gloom over the senior-sophomore banquet of 1937 was the calamitous news that the crook had been found. On Monday night, April 19, at exactly 9:30 P.M., C.S.T., Helen Dent let out a scream as she spied it through a Van Hoose basement window facing the court-yard. The *Periscope* asserted that "in about $1\frac{3}{5}$ seconds the entire Whoop-Em-Up generation had gathered in a, to put it mildly, somewhat noisy group." Since Helen was a freshman and could not touch the crook, it was brought out by Mattie James and delivered to the junior president, Sara Davis. At nearby High Acres, Dr. George Smith heard the screams and got up expecting to see flames engulfing the college. Returning from their banquet, the seniors had already prepared a song with which they met the juniors. Precisely as printed in the *Periscope,* it confessed:

> Gee, but you're swell.
> We tried it last year,
> And we struggled like h---.
> We must admit you've worked and
> Worked at it well.
> An orchid to you!
> 'Cause you're about the cleverest
>   bunch that we ever knew.
> Oh, you detectives!
> Our hiding system must have been defective.
> You've shown us that we must be more reflective.
> From now on we'll be more objective.
> Honestly, gee, but you're swell.

At breakfast the next morning the jubilant juniors distributed what was obviously a hastily printed, orange and black *Blazer* acclaiming in large letters this "FIRST WHOOP-EM-UP CROOK VICTORY" because of Helen Dent, "HERIONE OF THE DAY."

Other Forms of Recreation

"Mareplay at Shorter" was the caption in the Atlanta *Journal* for a picture of four girls being initiated into campus clubs. Although a page in the 1935 *Argo* was devoted "In Memoriam" to the Delta Chi, Dahm Club, Kid Club, and Epsilon Delta, other clubs were retained. Why Knot, the X Club, D.S.A., and K.A.T. continued for a time, while the G.A.B. and 21 Club were born and died during this period. By 1948 only the long-lived Do-Nothing Club and the Florida Club, which started about 1944, were still present.

Special days provided highlights during the routine-filled semesters, but gradually the classes ceased to be responsible for the programs and banquets. The money-raising Halloween Carnival has already been described. On Thanksgiving a special program was presented in the chapel, followed by a huge dinner, the distribution of Y.W.C.A. or S.C.A. baskets, and sometimes a generation swimming meet, a society basketball game, a special program over WRGA, or an informal dance in the gym. Christmas was marked by the traditional visit of Mr. and Mrs. Claus to the dimly lighted dinner, by carols sung early in the morning as a dignified procession moved through the dormitory corridors, by society parties, and by a special bus heading for Atlanta. Valentine Day was the occasion of an Open House for one hundred young men in 1937, but usually it was observed simply by the banquet and girls-only parties. Both George Washington's birthday and St. Patrick's Day were largely ignored, except as they furnished the motifs for special banquets.

With a queen elected by the student body, May Day was annually sponsored by the Sports Council, with the cooperation of the art and music departments. The queen and her court were favorite subjects for the rotogravure sections of the Atlanta papers. In 1936 and 1946 pictures of the queen were given wide newspaper coverage, resulting in fan letters from Kentucky and Venezuela. Although the smiles were invariable, the theme of the program was altered from year to year: Scandinavian mythology, Old Mexico, medieval England, a modern city park, Alice in Wonderland, the circus, or the Old South. Once a pageant based on James Thurber's *The Last Flower* was produced. Held at the balustrade or between Rome Hall and the Fine Arts Building, after the war it was followed by a picnic in the Rockery and a dance to which young men were invited.

The idle hours were whiled away by reading the three favorite magazines at Shorter in 1938—*Life, Reader's Digest,* and *Good House-keeping*—and the ubiquitous movie magazines. Starting that year coke machines in the dormitories reduced the possibility of dehydration while also giving the girls something to do. "Who dealt this mess?" punctuated many a bridge game. Sun bathers were numerous, and were considered "Minnie-Meat" because they let the bugs in through the open windows. Beginning in 1940 the college owned a sound movie projector, and weekly or monthly shows were scheduled. Radios and victrolas blared when the rule was not being observed; "Hold Tight," "Three Little Fishes," and "Marzidotes and Doezidotes" split the air, while Wayne King was once voted the favorite orchestra leader and Joe Penner the favorite comedian. On the auditorium stage were presented a style show by the Student Council, a "Major Doze" amateur night by the speech department, and concerts by the Emory Glee Club. Senior Hall provided great excitement in 1934 when a midnight fire broke out in the waste closet and smoke came billowing forth in great clouds. Female fire fighters brandished extinguishers with such skill that the blaze was out before Companies One and Two arrived. Much later Cooper Hall furnished the excitement when a formal dress caught fire after being draped over an improvised closet light that had not been turned off. Having been asleep in another suite, the nonchalant owner arrived on the scene asking: "What's all the excitement about?" Equally as unpredictable—and fortunately more frequent—were snow storms. Eight inches of snow, a flood that prevented town students from reaching campus, and a low of three degrees above zero halted every class in Rome in 1936 except Shorter's, but at least several sculptors and military geniuses were permitted to display their talents outside in the afternoon. Four years later a foot of snow and weather that reached three degrees below zero paralyzed almost everything in Rome except its higher education. *Argo* pictures often reveal the girls shivering in the cold, enjoying their sleds, supplementing their diets with snowballs, and slipping on the ice with arms flying.

Students left campus, but their hats were left behind as soon as the requirement was deleted in the early thirties. Walkathon contests were promoted in Rome; while the Shorter girls did not enter, at least they attended. When the depression did not severely limit their spending money, they gladly went to town for bowling at a dime per game on Monday and Thursday, for shopping at the store where "they seem to have a youthful slant on clothes," for ice cream at the drug store "where you meet your friends," for barbecue and toasted sandwiches where "Shorter students are always welcome," or for a delicious meal at "Rome's leading restaurant." Movies were always popular: "Snow White and the Seven Dwarfs" was considered "Roast Turkey," and Norma Shearer and Frederic March were once voted screen favorites.

There is evidence here and there (and elsewhere too) suggesting that even when the girls were alone on the hill, young men were not far from their thoughts. Several years they selected "The Ideal Shorter Man," who often turned out to be a member of the military. They sang:

> Math and science are all right,
> And some of us take history.
> What we really want to know
> Is "Marriage and the Family."
>
> Girls who study art and French
> Will surely travel in "Paree."
> What we really want to do
> Is settle down and marry.

To the tune of "Ramblin' Wreck" they affirmed:

> And if I have a daughter,
> I'll dress her in yellow and white
> And send her up to Shorter
> To cheer with all her might.
> But if I have a son, then
> I'll tell you what he'll do—

He will yell, "Take me to Shorter"
Like his daddy used to do.

One girl dreamed: "Perhaps a wedding in Brookes Chapel will be as common as a sophomore meeting."

During this period dating rules were progressively relaxed, but of course there was plenty of room for relaxation without contributing to the delinquency of minors in the process. Freshmen were allowed four or five evening dates per month, plus any others that they were fortunate enough to arrange during the day or on Saturday and Sunday evenings. The allotment for sophomores was six to eight, for juniors, eight to twelve, and for seniors, six a week—plus the others. Chaperones approved by the dean of women were required for first semester freshmen dates. Second semester freshmen and first semester sophomores could double date without a chaperone. All others could date alone. The young men met the girls at the telephone room near the vestibule in Rome Hall, a room that was periodically redecorated whether the boys noticed it or not. A girl and her date were sitting in one of the society halls when Pop Stevens came in to turn out the light. Not noticing them, he did his duty and quickly departed. Unlikely as it may seem, the two were so startled that the young man jumped up—and turned the light back on! According to the rules, "Students may *walk* in the *lighted* area during dates at night. This does not include the path down the hill." Riding in an automobile was permitted to Darlington School, to Tubize (Riverside), to the airport, and to any destination within the city limits except the Country Club and Myrtle Hill at night. Special permission was needed to go elsewhere. No student was allowed to dance anywhere without written permission from her parent or guardian. Eventually it was specified that dancing on dates could occur in the recreation room and on special occasions in the dining room, society halls, or gymnasium. No student could leave campus during the hours of a dance, nor could she sit in a car during a dance or date.

The girls continued to leave campus for football games as far away as the Army-Navy spectacle in Philadelphia and for fraternity dances at Emory, Tech, and elsewhere.

A major attraction on campus was the Open House held several years, complete with promenades in the courtyard to the accompaniment of an orchestra, a punch bowl at the balustrade, lighthearted conversation in the Rockery, dinner at nine, and perhaps a program in the auditorium. With the addition of a hardwood floor to the gym in 1937, the girls began to ask for dances on campus that involved young men. Their requests went unheeded, however, and the format of the Open Houses remained unchanged. Signing the college guest book, one playful boy added his telephone number while another included his nickname, "Puddin'." A brilliant conversation sparkled as one visitor was being shown around the Academic Building. Said his hostess: "This is Poly Hall." Said the lad to the girl who happened to be standing in the doorway: "How do you do?"

By the early forties Open Houses included dancing in the society halls or the gymnasium. In 1947 the college officially sponsored a formal dance that was supposed to be held at the Coosa Country Club. When a downpour occurred, it was shifted to the campus dining room. The young lady wearing long lavender gloves had invited no less than seven men, and they all accepted. She took her choice and then easily got dates for the other six. The following year four Open Houses were scheduled, of which those at Christmas and in the spring were formal. The Cotillion Club, that for years had given dances attended only by girls, finally sponsored a spring formal in 1940 when male dates were invited, but these functions were separate from the Open Houses planned by the college.

Formed in the fall of 1947, the Social Committee first consisted of eleven girls whose purpose was to plan the Open Houses and other social functions at the school. Soon to evolve from this were the Social Association and its Social Council.

Sometimes called the Roman Legion, the Town Girls' Club sought to involve commuting students in the life of the college. Town Girls' Hall or the Roman Rendezvous in Rome Hall provided them with a headquarters, and the toaster and hot plate permitted them a limited amount of cooking at noon. Parties came at Christmas and in the spring when Rome seniors were honored.

Seniors and Commencement

"Gosh, we felt so 'SENIORERY' the first time we were recognized in the chapel," exclaimed one class historian as she wrote of that memorable September when the deans invested her group with caps and gowns. Two sizes were said to exist, too long and too short, and frequent cases of crossed eyes were alleged because of the swaying tassel on the mortarboard. Academic attire was worn for Shorter Sunday at First Baptist Church, for the senior music and speech recitals some years, and of course for the ceremonies related to commencement.

Each senior class elected officers, and many of them selected mascots who were pictured in the *Argo*. Some of these were children of former class members, although one turned out to be little Van Porter Enloe, III, with a sporty tam pulled down over his left ear. The class of 1939 changed the pace a bit by selecting their saddle oxfords and bobby socks as their mascots. A class song might promise: "When we leave Shorter, we will ne'er forget our class so strong and true." Senior deference was still practiced, although some years were filled with groans because the tradition was being ignored by the "ignorant" or "insolent" freshmen. Monthly coffees were held for some of the senior classes. Some years each girl brought her own cup which had frequently been presented to her as a special gift from her roommate, her little sister, a favorite rat, or her predecessor in an office to which she had been elected.

Seniors had parties for each other—especially popular were those given by the town girls at their homes out in town. The ambitious class of 1948 produced talent shows, sold hundreds of doughnuts, served breakfasts in the Rockery, and staged a womanless wedding in the chapel to earn money for a spring excursion to Daytona Beach. The entire wedding party except the bride and groom was publicized in advance. That the class was highly successful in its venture was established by the fact that most members were able to make the trip. In doing so, they happily broke a decade-long tradition of remaining in the dormitory throughout spring vacation to study for comprehensives. Members of the Duke student body furnished an eminently acceptable substitute by offering to instruct them in the finer points of softball. This form of study did not damage senior scholarship— they all passed the comprehensives. The chaperone for the week was Mrs. Rowand—not the bride and groom, Dr. Porter and President Cousins.

A special relationship existed between the seniors and their "little sister" class, the sophomores. Using Halloween, Thanksgiving, Valentine Day, or George Washington's birthday as an excuse to give a party, the sophomores honored their elders. During other years no such excuse was needed, and the party might be built on the theme of heaven, an artists' ball, the Near East, or the Wild West. Generous to their big sisters, the sophomores frequently contributed a gift for Senior Den—$50, a radio, or a rug. The spring senior-sophomore banquet was sometimes the event at which generation songs were transmitted and always the scene of fancy decorations, rich food, and carefree entertainment. As the seniors sang to them for the last time, one sophomore admitted to "the achey feeling inside when graduation draws nearer and we know the seniors are really leaving . . . ."

During May and early June the seniors were involved in a frantic

329

round of social events. The DeSoto Theater invited them to a free show, Miss Bennet was hostess at tea in the faculty parlor or the Alumnae Garden, and the societies might honor them with a bridge party. Mrs. Hurst gave them breakfast in the Rockery, and Dr. and Mrs. Porter held a buffet supper at Maplehurst. President and Mrs. Cousins always entertained the graduates, at a breakfast or luncheon downtown or at a buffet supper in their home on Sherwood Road.

Commencement was reduced in length from four to three days. The children's party, given by the Granddaughters Club, came on Friday or Saturday, and the commencement play on Saturday. The annual alumnae meeting convened on Saturday or Monday morning, with the luncheon following. Later in the afternoon the Class Day exercise was held at the balustrade or in the Rockery. Asked one sophomore: "How many daisies does it take to make a chain? . . . You tell us, we lost count after the first three or four million we picked." Carrying their daisy chain and singing "Hail, Dear Old Shorter," the sophomores escorted the robed seniors to the program. Featuring the class history, poem, prophecy, and last will and testament, it sometimes included presenting a gift to the college and always included presenting caps and gowns to the juniors. In 1935 the baccalaureate service was returned to the sanctuary of the First Baptist Church and was held at 11:00 A.M., having been scheduled on campus in the afternoon for the preceding ten years. A Sunday afternoon tea and evening concert were continued. The actual graduation ceremony was conducted in the college auditorium, beginning at 10:30 A.M. on Tuesday, later being changed to Monday. Visitors were invariably invited to address the graduates at the two major services, including Governor Ellis Arnall of Georgia, President J. H. Rushbrooke of the Baptist World Alliance, Dr. Edwin Mims of Vanderbilt University, President Rufus Harris of Tulane University, President Harmon Caldwell of the University of Georgia, Dr. Doak S. Campbell of Peabody College, Dr. W. W. Pierson of the University of North Carolina, Searcy S. Garrison of the Bull Street Baptist Church of Savannah, Monroe Swilley, Jr., of the Second Ponce de Leon Baptist Church of Atlanta, and James W. Middleton of the First Baptist Church of Atlanta.

In connection with commencement, many awards were made. The Sarah A. Faust Award in religion, the Susie Buttolph Medal in art, and Phi Sigma Alpha for general scholarship were continued. The three class scholarships, the French Award, the Imogen Coulter Award in English established by Claire J. Wyatt, Sr., and the Y.W.C.A. Award for the student possessing the best private library were all instituted by 1939. Beginning that year the Cincinnati Conservatory Scholarship

330

provided six weeks of study for the musician showing the most progress during the year. The Alumnae Award for music was begun in 1946. Initiated the next year were purchase awards in art, whereby paintings were added to the lending library. Several new awards were first given in 1948: the Presser Foundation Scholarship, the Sophomore Music Scholarship, the Freshman Music Award, and the Walter R. Thomas Award for the best actress of the year. Briefly, other awards were offered in biology, mathematics, economics, art, and music.

Three other honors were annually presented, although not at commencement. The Argonaut Society was perpetuated, gaining from one to five new members each year from the senior class. Late in 1937, for the first time, six Shorter students were named by the faculty to *Who's Who in American Universities and Colleges*. Dated May 12, 1938, the constitution of the Sophomore Sabots established a group composed of approximately ten percent of the outgoing freshman class whose purpose was "to stimulate interest in all college activities, to intensify the spirit of cooperation between the Student Council and the student body at large." Selected by the Student Council and the outgoing Sabots, its members remained anonymous until a special recognition service in the spring.

The General Alumnae Association

Eight ladies were elected president of the General Alumnae Association during the administration of President Cousins: Mrs. R. M. Wyatt (née Miss Betty Betts, class of 1916), Mrs. J. J. Clyatt, Mrs. J. C. Dixon, Miss Martha C. Galt, Mrs. Robert Arnold, Mrs. Lydia Dixon Sheppard, Mrs. Aubrey Matthews (née Miss Sue Earnest, class of 1919), and Mrs. Harry M. Arnold. For greater efficiency in enlisting supporters, President Galt in 1939 divided Georgia and Tennessee into nine districts, each with a regional vice-president. Except for the two years that she was president, Mrs. Matthews was general treasurer. Others in places of leadership for three or more years were Miss Mabel Thompson (class of 1924) and Miss Elizabeth Bradley (class of 1918). Unofficially, Miss Cordelia Veal (class of 1897) was publicity director until her death in 1943. Miss Louise Bennet was alumnae secretary and dean of women until 1946, being succeeded by Mrs. Lydia Dixon Sheppard. In 1948 Miss Barbara P. Monroe was named full-time alumnae secretary, but worked for only a few months chiefly in student recruitment.

Local chapters numbered as many as thirty, scattered throughout Georgia, Alabama, Tennessee, Kentucky, Florida, and New York.

Those most active were located in Rome, Atlanta, and Columbus. Monthly or quarterly meetings were usually scheduled, some luncheons were held, groups of prospective students were brought on tours of the campus or entertained in their own community, and parties, programs, and rummage sales were sponsored to raise funds. Forming afternoon and evening groups, for a time the Atlanta chapter published a monthly newsletter, *Shorter Sass and Seriousness.* Columbus was especially interested in adding to the Carter Harvey Scholarship Fund. The Rome chapter entertained the freshmen each fall, held a Christmas bazaar, and honored the high school seniors in the spring. Each of these three local chapters usually prepared yearbooks for the guidance of their members.

Every November the General Alumnae Association attracted over one hundred Shorterites to the breakfast or luncheon in Atlanta. WSB broadcast portions of the program for a few years, and those alumnae unable to attend the Atlanta meeting were urged to listen in over their radios. From 1934 to 1940 three to five regional luncheons were scheduled each spring to reach more ladies, being held at various times in Albany, Augusta, Savannah, Elberton, Macon, Columbus, Tifton, Waycross, Athens, Cedartown, Chattanooga, and Brunswick. When Edwin Preston produced his 1939 movie, "A Day at Shorter," it was projected at these regional luncheons and other alumnae gatherings, using the machine donated to the college by the Rome chapter.

The Alumnae Association held its general meeting on Monday or Saturday during the commencement period. Reunions came for those who had graduated fifty, twenty-five, ten, and two years earlier. A reunion of music graduates came first in 1937, but apparently this was not repeated in later years. The luncheon was held in the dining room or at a downtown hotel, although sometimes the meal was a picnic in the Rockery. Prominent at those campus affairs were the members of the Gamma Delta or Granddaughters Club, current students who were related to Shorter alumnae. For several years they directed a children's party during commencement, and at other times were hostesses at receptions for local high school seniors.

Starting in the spring of 1935 the Alumnae Institute was conducted for two days on campus, with conferences led by faculty members, recitals by the music department, productions by the Shorter Players, sporting events, periods of alumnae swimming, and several fellowship meals. Initiated and promoted by Miss Bennet, it was held for seven years, but was not resumed after the war.

Other projects benefiting the college claimed the attention of the association. One of the three tennis courts was surfaced at a cost of about $1,000 in the early thirties. The Louise Bennet Alumnae Garden was completed in 1935 and was subsequently restored once or twice. The Ten Dollar Club in 1938 assisted the drive for endowment. The J. P. Cooper Loan Fund finally reached a total of $2,500. In the early forties the study in each suite was repainted and refurnished with rugs, chairs, and couches. A complete set of flat silver and some pieces of china were placed in the dining room. Throughout the war, defense bonds were purchased for eventual use on the gymnasium building. Numerous other expenditures were made for the music library, the current expenses of the college, scholarships, other renovations, and the endowment. Altogether, the ledger shows that the alumnae raised $15,403.62 during the Cousins years.

The Loyalty Fund was supported by annual gifts of $1 or $2, being used to finance alumnae publications. Due to the depression, Miss Bennet was permitted to edit only one small twelve-page *Alumnae Bulletin* in 1934. Thereafter, one to four issues of the *Periscope* each year had a two-or-four-page insert that was mailed to the fifteen hundred known alumnae. Mrs. Sheppard early expressed the hope that she might prepare a separate publication, and finally in May of 1948 a large twenty-four-page alumnae edition of the *Shorter College Bulletin* appeared.

A popular "Alma Mater" was composed in 1936 by Miss Martha C. Galt, who dedicated it to President Van Hoose. The first of its five stanzas says:

> Deep within white petaled daisies,
> You will find a heart of gold;
> In the heart of ev'ry daughter,
> Loyalty and love untold.
> May we ever in devotion,
> Seek to hold thy standards high.
> Alma Mater, may our song
> Of thy praises never die.

This was later adopted as the official song of the Social Council.

The alumnae secretary estimated in 1937 that the college had about 4,350 living and dead alumnae, of whom the occupations of about 950 were known. As listed in a college brochure, the principal groups were these: married, 547; teachers, 200; business, 36; musicians, 13; religious, 8; doctors and nurses, 5; and newspaper workers, 5. Seven years later another report was made in the pages of the *Christian Index*, where it was asserted that forty-three professions were represented among Shorter alumnae. The three largest groups were said to be teaching, social service, and religious work. A total of 251 was claimed for the first group, but no other figures were given. Forty-seven were listed as taking professional part in the war that was then being conducted.

The Departure of Paul M. Cousins

Longer than any other man up to his time, Paul Mercer Cousins remained as president of Shorter College for fifteen years. In 1936 his alma mater, Mercer University, conferred on him the honorary Doctor of Letters degree. Two years later he became president of the Association of Georgia Colleges. A member of the Rome Kiwanis Club, he was its president for one year. At the First Baptist Church he was a deacon and teacher of the Scrap Iron Bible Class, which was carried over WRGA each Sunday morning. Among the girls of Shorter he was held in respect and devotion, as indicated by the dedication of the 1946 *Argo* to him, "because of what he is doing to fulfill the dream of a Greater Shorter"—thereby becoming the only person in the history of the college to have three annuals dedicated to him.

Looking toward Shorter's seventy-fifth anniversary, the trustees approved a resolution in 1946 calling for a state-wide drive that would raise $500,000. Half of this would go to the endowment, while the other half would provide for a new gymnasium, library, and dormitory. As it turned out, all of the money actually received was spent in erecting a gymnasium.

More modest plans were subsequently made for observing the anniversary. Transcribed in Brookes Chapel by the department of music, three broadcasts were heard during the spring of 1948 over stations in Rome, Bainbridge, Moultrie, and perhaps elsewhere. The *Shorter College Bulletin* and *Chimes* issued that spring were considered a part of the celebration.

The atmosphere was changed on April 6, when President Cousins announced in chapel that he was resigning effective June 30 to become professor of English at Mercer University. A veritable deluge of commendations followed. Aubrey Matthews, president of the board of trustees, immediately commented: "Shorter College . . . has enjoyed a wonderful growth and expansion and the board and the citizens of Rome are deeply indebted to him for his leadership." The Rome *News-Tribune* carried an editorial that said in part: "Thousands of Romans learned with regret the decision of Dr. Paul Cousins to relinquish his administrative duties as President of Shorter College. . . . It is hard to realize that his decision means that he can no longer be actively identified with the progress of Shorter and Rome. . . . He has done a magnificent job . . . . Shorter has enjoyed an unparalleled growth, with increased endowment, an expanded curriculum, construction of additional buildings and far greater support from the Georgia Baptist Convention as a result of his efforts as President. We can fully sympathize with Dr. Cousins in desiring to be relieved of this vast responsibility, however, and his wish to return to his first love, teaching."

The 1948 *Argo* had been sent to the publisher before the announcement was made public. When the finished copies arrived on campus the editors pasted in the back a printed letter addressed to President Cousins: "Thank you for everything that you have done for Shorter and for all that you have meant to Shorter Girls, both those of the present generation, and those who came before us. Thank you for devoting thirty-one years of your life to the bettering of Shorter and for your devotion to the ideals for which it stands." A simple statement of dedication was included in the *Chimes* issued that April.

When the trustees met at commencement, their official statement included these words:

For the past thirty-one years Dr. Paul Cousins has been associated actively with the affairs of Shorter College. Guided by his devotion to work, his excellence of character, his keen intellect, his fraternal spirit and worthy ideals, he has served that institution long and well. During the past fifteen years, in which he was President, he gave generously of his time and substance in the interests of the College and he has merited and enjoyed the gratitude of all for his useful living. He has lived at Shorter, to see many of his dreams come true. Dr. Cousins is bound to us in many fine ways. We love, respect, and admire him. We will miss his constant friendship as he leaves . . . . We extend our very best wishes for much happiness and continued success in the days to come.

Urging the alumnae to attend the immanent commencement, Cousins had written: "One of the last things Dr. Van Hoose said to me was that it takes more than one generation to build a great college. What has been achieved is a worthy incentive to even greater accomplishments." On Alumnae Day, June 5, a large group gave the Cousins a silver vegetable dish. Two days later at graduation, the trustees presented a silver tray, pitcher, and goblets in the name of the college. The day has been described as a very wet one—although no rainfall was recorded—because of the tears that fell.

In the autumn of 1948 Cousins assumed his new position. Before becoming president of Shorter, he had completed one-third of a doctoral dissertation that necessarily remained untouched for fifteen long and arduous years. He resumed his research at Mercer and brought it to a successful conclusion, with two notable results. In

1966 he earned the Doctor of Philosophy degree from Columbia University at the age of seventy-six. Two years later a revision of his dissertation, a scholarly volume titled *Joel Chandler Harris,* was published by the Louisiana State University Press. The Rome alumni sponsored an autograph tea in the society halls. After his retirement from the Mercer faculty in 1969, he and Mrs. Cousins remained in Macon, where they still live.

In an era when many American colleges died, Shorter was characterized by increases that were modest in light of the nation's overall economic and educational conditions, but were sizable in light of Shorter's earlier history. The annual income more than doubled; the value of the physical plant grew by twenty-six percent and the endowment by fifty-three. Baptist support was enlarged, as suggested by one measurable criterion—financial support totaled more than $120,-000, of which almost $30,000 was contributed in each of Cousins' last three years. Academically, the institution increased its offerings by adding six new major programs, and its department of music was accorded full membership by the National Association of Schools of Music. Locally, the regard of the community for the college was maintained, as shown by the construction of the gymnasium with funds coming mostly from Rome.

One less tangible aspect of the Cousins administration must also be recognized. Returning to the campus for Founders' Day in 1947, Miss Louise Bennet titled her address "The Gift of Giving." After discussing the contributions of Shorter, Gwaltney, Pennington, Simmons, Cooper, Brookes, Bass, Van Hoose, Furry, and others, she spoke of Paul M. Cousins: "May I say in tribute to him that I *know* his deep love and concern for Shorter, and that we are all grateful for the progress Shorter is making under his leadership. Many of us feel that his great gift is his knowledge of Shorter and Shorter traditions, which enable him to carry forward in the spirit of our founders, the ideals of Christian Education, for which Shorter stands." In the words of Miss Bennet, his had been a time of "understanding development."

7

Coeducation Comes to Shorter College

At his inauguration as the eleventh president of Shorter College, Charles W. Burts set the tone for his administration, asserting: "We shall go forward with the realization that education must be vital. Adaptation must be pioneering, and a college's program must be scrutinized continually to determine that it is doing everything possible to equip its students for effective lives in a changing world." Under his direction, the college was to tread pathways largely unexplored in earlier years. Young men were to be admitted in increasing numbers. Courses in business administration, economics, and education were to be multiplied. Evening classes and summer school were emphasized. As he later reminded the trustees, Burts was convinced that "education should be a . . . dynamic program which brings students in touch with the best of the past and the present with a view to equipping them to understand more adequately and live more effectively in the world of their day."

Born at Anderson, South Carolina, in 1907, Charles Watson Burts was the son of a distinguished Baptist clergyman and denominational leader. From Furman University Burts received the Bachelor of Arts degree and from Yale University, the Bachelor of Divinity and Doctor of Philosophy degrees. Except for forty months on leave in the United States Navy, where he eventually held the rank of lieutenant commander, he was an active member of the Furman University faculty from 1933 to 1946. There he advanced to the rank of professor of psychology, head of the department of psychology, and assistant dean of the college. For two years he was dean and professor of psychology at Meredith College, Raleigh, North Carolina. He and his wife, the former Miss Ruth Parker Littlejohn of Gaffney, South Carolina, had one son, Watson Lee. Formally elected president of Shorter College on May 27, 1948, Burts assumed his new position the following July 1.

The *Christian Index* marked his coming with a photograph and a long article. Described in the local newspaper as "a tall, fortyish man with blue eyes, reddish hair and a sincere glad-to-see-you smile," he was welcomed to Rome at a buffet supper given by the trustees at the home of their chairman and his wife, Mr. and Mrs. Aubrey Matthews. Burts and his family joined the First Baptist Church, where he was a deacon and frequent teacher of the Scrap Iron Bible Class. Entering his new position as college president with enthusiasm, in three months he covered six thousand miles visiting students and their families. His formal installation on Founders' Day, November 10, 1948, featured a colorful academic procession comprised of almost fifty visitors representing various schools and educational and religious organizations, plus members of the faculty and the senior class. Brief statements were made by Elizabeth Sparks, president of the student body, Mrs. W. F. Barron (née Miss Mary Sue Jones, class of 1924), president of the General Alumnae Association, James W. Merritt, executive secretary of the Georgia Baptist Convention, and others. Dr. James R. McCain, president of Agnes Scott College, delivered the main address. Representing the University of Georgia, one remarkable guest was Eugene P. Mallary, who had been born in 1878 on the Shorter campus when it was downtown. The *Christian Index* soon ran a picture of the installa-

President Charles W. Burts

tion ceremony on its cover and accorded Burts editorial support.

When Burts was secured and Maplehurst was found to be unsuitable for his use, a president's home became necessary. Plans were selected by the president-elect and his wife, and construction was begun that spring. At the same time, two further apartment houses were planned, one with eight units and the other with four. Hence, in the spring and summer of 1948, R. L. Townsend, the Rome contractor who had built the first apartment house a year earlier, erected these three additional brick buildings at an initial cost of $76,820.49. These were financed mainly from the endowment, and the amount utilized is gradually being replaced. In 1961 the president's home was named Bass House, becoming the dean's residence when High Acres was acquired the following year.

The annual income for the college during the Burts administration ranged from a high of $250,059.82 his second year to a low of $216,863.48 his last, at a time when the Gross National Product was

Bass House

increasing about forty percent. Each year the expenditures exceeded
the income, by as little as $5,902.49 the first year and as much as
$47,606.69 the last. Several factors help to explain this situation. Stu-
dent enrollment decreased because of the lower birthrate in the mid-
thirties, the Korean War, the recently introduced twelve-grade public
school program in Georgia, and certain disagreements within the
faculty and administration—soon to be examined—which reduced
internal stability. The Southern Association continued to press for
increases in faculty salaries. Prices persisted in their upward trend.
Especially costly were numerous capital improvements. The gym was
suitably equipped. The heating plant was overhauled and a new stoker
installed. General repairs were made in the dormitories, kitchen, and
Fine Arts Building. Fire escapes and fire doors were added in the
chapel and the dormitories, and the wiring in both dormitories was
partially replaced.

Although the cumulative operating debt grew to about $72,000,
three factors kept it from going any higher. It was held down when
about $15,000 was realized from the sale of timber cut from school
property. Again, one very quiet canvass was conducted in Rome by
the trustees from 1948 to 1950, producing a total of $13,490.75. They
seriously discussed a state-wide campaign for $380,000 and received
Georgia Baptist Convention approval in 1950, but the project was not
carried out because of disagreements within the college that reduced
public confidence. Finally, the convention provided $12,000 to $18,000
annually for the operating budget, an amount that totaled $72,000
during the five Burts years. In this connection, it should be observed

341

that President Burts advocated a Capital Improvements and Repairs Program, although he had left Shorter by the time such a plan was set in motion.

The declared value of the college grew by almost $95,000 to a total of $1,319,673.73. Actually, this figure might have been raised by an additional $45,000, the approximate cost of renovations that was not added in the audits to the value of the property. Doubtless the depreciations were thought to cancel out the additions. The entire increase that was shown came within the endowment which received a bequest of $5,000 from the will of J. Boling Sullivan, a former Rome trustee, and appropriations of $70,454.06 from the Georgia Baptist Convention.

As the Burts administration continued, the leadership of the college increasingly polarized. The trustees, Burts, and most of the faculty and administration desired a strong liberal arts program, supplemented by a limited amount of vocational training, to be made available to any person qualified for admission. A minority group within the faculty favored a course of study limited only to the liberal arts, and some of them desired that the student body be comprised only of women. This clash of principle was further complicated by clashes of personality. Composed of men and women of goodwill, each side honestly felt that it represented the best interests of the college. Late in 1952 the trustees were visited by several students and faculty members who expressed strong disagreement with the president. A few days later the board unanimously adopted a statement favoring the academic policies championed by Burts, a statement which Burts read to the faculty just before the Christmas holiday. Within a month he came to the conclusion that he should leave Shorter, addressing to the trustees a letter of resignation dated January 16, 1953. Two weeks later the full board met in Atlanta, deeply troubled by the unfortunate turn of events. While recognizing the long and faithful service rendered by some members of the minority group, the board nevertheless could not agree with the position that they and their colleagues had taken. After agonizing discussion, it was therefore decided, first, to inform the minority "that their resignations would be welcomed, and, second, that if these are not received within fifteen days, they will be requested." It was decided, also, "that Dr. Burts' resignation be accepted, with regret." Three of the minority group soon resigned, and the contract of the fourth was terminated in June. Both the Rome newspaper and the *Periscope* expressed regret that Burts was leaving, and the trustees later hosted a private dinner in honor of him and his wife, attended also by President-elect and Mrs. George A. Christenberry.

Returning to Furman University, Dr. Burts was for a decade chairman or dean of graduate studies and professor of psychology. In 1962 he became chairman of the department of psychology, a position that he still occupies.

The Christenberry Administration

The youngest man ever elected president of Shorter College, George Andrew Christenberry was born at Macon, Georgia, in 1915. He received the Bachelor of Science degree with highest honors from Furman University and the Master of Arts and Doctor of Philosophy degrees from the University of North Carolina. For three years he was head of the department of biology at Meredith College. In 1943 he joined the faculty of Furman University, eventually becoming professor of biology and dean of the men's college. During the war he served almost two years as an ensign and lieutenant in the United States Navy while on leave from Furman. An active Baptist layman, he was a leader also in civic and scholarly organizations and a consultant to the Atomic Energy Commission. He and his wife, the former Miss Elizabeth Reid of Greenville, South Carolina, had three children, Becky, George, Jr., and John Reid.

Formally named by the trustees on June 6, 1953, Christenberry was honored at a reception by the board in the college gymnasium on the evening of September 24. During the first year, the General Alumnae Association sponsored eight regional luncheons that involved the new president and his wife. Requesting that no elaborate installation ceremony be held, he was quietly inducted into his office at the graduation service of 1954 by the chairman of the trustees, Dr. Lester Harbin.

Christenberry inherited financial problems which the best efforts of the trustees and Burts had not been able to solve, but he was assured by the trustees that he was not expected to make up the deficit from operating funds. They felt that this would be removed either by a vigorous fund-raising campaign or by encroaching on the endowment, and they named a commitee to suggest an acceptable course of action.

Meantime, the strain within the operating budget was not immediately alleviated. Enrollment continued to be down, only a small increase in student charges was made, salaries and other operating costs

mounted, and endowment income dropped. Thus, while the annual
income rose from $235,483.88 during Christenberry's first year to
$295,085.88 the last—thereby keeping pace with the growth of the
Gross National Product—a deficit was experienced each of his five
years, ranging from a high of $64,089.38 his first year to a low of
$17,522.18 the second. Contributing a total of $204,560 to the operating
budget during these five years, the Georgia Baptist Convention thus
significantly increased its support—due in part to Christenberry's
prodding.

While realizing that their action was undesirable, the trustees finally

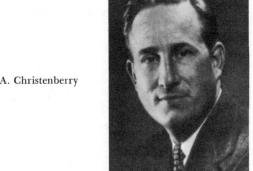

President George A. Christenberry

decided to petition the Superior Court of Floyd County for permission
to encroach upon the endowment. Asserting that the college had suffered a loss each of the past ten years and that additional capital
improvements were absolutely essential to its operation, they sought
$196,721.19. The court approved their request on July 2, 1954. Over
the next two years improvements were made. Installation of a new
heating system was begun. Cooper Dormitory and Rome Hall were
rewired. Both dormitories, Rome Hall, the infirmary, and the music
practice rooms were redecorated. Numerous fire doors were hung, and
another fire escape added. A hard surface was applied to the three
tennis courts. Approximately $54,000 was expended on these items;
the remainder liquidated the debt.

Unfortunately, however, the plunge was not halted, because the
undermining influences stubbornly resisted removal. By the spring of
1957 a three-year debt had accumulated in excess of $80,000. Once
more the trustees approached the Superior Court of Floyd County,

seeking to encroach upon the endowment. Permission was granted on July 22, 1957, allowing $88,000 to be removed, after which the college was again solvent.

Within a period of five years almost $285,000 had been taken, legally but reluctantly, from the endowment. Interestingly enough, though, the endowment actually experienced a net growth during that time of about $14,000, increasing to a total of $706,226.10. Six additions were largely responsible. First, a lot on Horseleg Creek Road was sold for $12,000. Second, the Georgia Baptist Convention added $20,000 in 1954 before turning its energies to the Capital Improvements and Repairs Program. Third, late in 1955 it was announced that Shorter would receive a grant from the Ford Foundation, the interest from which was to be used during the next ten years for increasing faculty salaries. The foundation had invited each accredited college in America to apply for a grant, and Shorter took advantage of the offer. A total of $98,500 was received, $50,000 in 1956 and the remainder the next year. Thirteen other colleges and universities in Georgia shared with Shorter in similar Ford gifts. Fourth, funds already held for the benefit of the college by the Georgia Baptist Foundation, probably contributed in earlier years by the convention, were first shown to be a part of the endowment in 1957, raising the total by $37,380.89. Fifth, the Oakley M. Bishop Fund became the property of Shorter in 1957, and the stocks valued at $116,519.53 were worth almost twice the amount of their initial appraisal that had been carried as a special fund in the college audit for twenty years. Finally, the Columbus Roberts Fund grew in value. In 1943 and 1945 Roberts had presented the college with stocks then worth $50,000. Subsequently they had apparently been sold and the proceeds reinvested. By 1958 the fund had almost doubled, and the addition was then for the first time shown on the audit. By a revocable contract completed in 1956, the trustees began transferring portions of the endowment to the Georgia Baptist Foundation. Hence, the Ford, Bishop, Roberts, and smaller funds were gradually placed with the foundation, which has subsequently handled most of the endowment.

Appointed by the executive committee of the Georgia Baptist Convention, a special committee to make a study regarding support and allocation of funds to Georgia Baptist schools recommended in 1952 that an in-depth investigation be made in order to reach a fair and adequate conclusion and that a Commission on Education be established as a supervisory body. Accordingly, under the direction of R. Orin Cornett, executive secretary of the Education Commission of the Southern Baptist Convention, an eight-man committee of edu-

345

cational administrators from outside Georgia made extensive preliminary studies and then visited each campus in October of 1953.
Among other things, they pointedly inquired about improving relations with Rome and with the Georgia Baptist Convention and about
increasing the number of male students. Two months later Cornett
met with the heads of the six schools, and they reached an agreement
for the distribution of funds. In 1954 the first illustrated pamphlet
publicizing Georgia Baptist Convention schools was issued. Also that
year each of the campuses was carefully appraised by an Atlanta
construction man who estimated the cost of minimal repairs needed on
existing buildings. The presidents were requested to prepare a list of
additional structures made absolutely necessary by enrollment as con-
servatively estimated for the next ten years. It was finally determined
that Shorter's needs amounted to $950,000: repairs, $130,000; Library-
Administration Building, $400,000; Men's Dormitory, $300,000; heating plant, $100,000; classroom adaptation of present library space,
$20,000. An ambitious Capital Improvements and Repairs Program
with a six-school total of $5½ million was adopted by the convention
in 1954, whereby special allocations above and beyond the fixed appropriations for operating expenses would be made available each
year to the schools. This money was to be distributed according to
the formula that allowed 16.58 percent of the total for Shorter, but no
more would be given than the college could match by its own capital
improvements expenditures. Since this took the place of earlier convention interest in increasing endowments, a crestfallen Arthur Jackson of the Georgia Baptist Foundation wrote: "There never will be
a convenient time to raise endowment funds." The 1955 report on
Christian education reflected the more widely held attitude of ela-
tion: "At that session of the Convention [in 1954] we voted to do
something concrete in the field of Christian education."

The reaction in Rome was immediate and positive. Although fund-
raising had been recommended by Christenberry from the first, the
trustees officially adopted a ten-year development program that sought
$2½ million for the objectives specified by the convention, plus new
equipment and increased endowment, faculty salaries, and scholarship
funds. Directed by Marts and Lundy, a thirty-month drive for $200,000
was planned as a part of this long-range effort. The only known
casualty was the faculty parlor in Rome Hall which was quickly
converted into the campaign headquarters and soon became the
office of the director of development and the location of a new telephone switchboard. One hundred fifty local residents and alumnae
filled the college dining room on April 29, 1955, as W. Forrest Lanier,

pastor of the First Baptist Church of Rome, spoke to the canvassers at the kickoff banquet. Barry Wright, Jr., the general chairman, presided, and Mrs. Victor Yeargan (née Miss Martha Collins, class of 1934), alumnae co-chairman, presented an original address in rhyme. Others in positions of leadership were Rome businessmen J. T. Roe, E. M. Reese, Tom Berry, Jr., and George Griffin; Shorter alumnae Miss Mabel Thompson (class of 1924) and Mrs T. A. Lamar (née Miss Sarah Bryan, class of 1923) ; and Shorter trustees W. F. Barron, C. H. Booker, Lester Harbin, Fred R. Johnson, Sr., and Stokes Walton. Throughout much of May an intensive campaign was waged, being continued during the remainder of the year with somewhat less vigor. A total of 612 pledges for $156,483.45 was received. Actual money contributed in the initial months was $204,022.77, of which $75,833.26 came from Rome and Floyd County, $42,889.51 from the Georgia Baptist Convention, and the remainder from the Ford Foundation. A four-page leaflet, "What Makes our City Great?" and a sixteen-page brochure, "To Meet a Challenge," pointed out the cultural, religious, and financial contributions made by Shorter to the area and encouraged wide support for the canvass. To lead the extended effort, Cecil Lea became director of development on October 1, 1955. Already on the staff, Mrs. Ima Jean Dempsey Kerce, an alumna, became his assistant. In this capacity he also supervised alumnae affairs, prepared publicity releases, and recruited students.

For several additional years the drive was maintained. Early in 1956 the Columbus area was canvassed with some success. The alumnae promoted a Living Endowment plan producing some revenue. By 1958 $177,968.73 had been received from the drive and $175,404.77 from the convention. (A convention appropriation later in 1958 raised its four-year total to $249,804.50.) The buildings were repaired, painted, and brought into compliance with most state fire laws. Much new furniture and equipment were secured. The kitchen was renovated and further storage area constructed. A new fifty-thousand-gallon water tank was erected. Work was started on the Glass Corridor which was doubled in size by the fall of 1958.

In response to a $27,500 gift from Mrs. W. W. Brookes, the chapel was completely remodeled for the first time in forty-five years and a new organ was installed. Costing $34,375, the thirty-five-rank Holtkamp organ was the only one of its kind in the state and the third one to be placed in a Southern school. As the presentation plate indicates, it was "dedicated to the glory of God in memory of W. Walker Brookes." Arthur Poister of Syracuse University gave the dedicatory recital on April 15, 1957.

Two familiar structures were removed in 1955 when W. M. Clemones of Rome was contracted to raze Maplehurst and the white frame cottage near the college entrance on Shorter Avenue.

Other structures were discussed but not erected. An application was filed with an agency of the federal government for $400,000 to build a dormitory for one hundred men and six dwelling units for faculty members. Although convention approval was secured and hope was expressed for occupancy in the fall of 1956, the request was allowed to lapse by an administration made uneasy because of the uncertain financial future. Early in 1956 plans were prepared for a two-story Library-Administration Building expected to cost $400,000. The architect's sketch—different from the four earlier ones and from the one finally constructed—was printed on the cover of the *Alumnae Bulletin* for July of 1957. It was Dr. Christenberry's goal to occupy the building within four years, but of course he was not around when that took place in 1961.

Participating in the organization of the Georgia Foundation for Independent Colleges in 1956, Shorter shared with eight other institutions in its program of fund-raising. "Free Enterprise" was their motto as the presidents of the cooperating schools solicited support from industry and business throughout the state. Included in the *Bulletin* was a photograph of the first check, in the amount of $1,004.55, for Shorter College. Additional payments raised the two-year total to $6,521.12. As might be expected, the greatest results of this foundation were not felt until the sixties and seventies.

On August 31, 1958, the value of the college was declared by the auditors to be $1,396,568.07. Since the appraised value of the land, buildings, and equipment remained unchanged at $609,362.82, this increase of about $80,000 in five years was shown only in the endowment and the unexpended development fund. Renovations and new equipment costing at least $234,000 added to the value of the plant, but the audit did not take these into consideration. Probably it was felt that depreciations offset the additions.

Dr. Christenberry announced his resignation from the Shorter presidency effective July 1, 1958. Popular among the students, he had been given recognition in 1955 when the *Argo* was dedicated to him: "A curl of smoke, a tennis racket, a chuckle, our friend. A figure of vigorous solidity, a firm handshake, a discerning eye, our president. His understanding, our respect. His judgment, our guide. His devotion, our affection. His leadership, our cooperation." Off campus, he had been a deacon of the First Baptist Church and teacher of its Scrap Iron Bible Class. Several local civic, cultural, and service groups had profited from his membership. For one term he had been president of the Department of Higher Education of the Georgia Education Association. At his departure the trustees adopted this statement: "The Shorter College Board wishes to record its respect and admiration for Dr. Christenberry as an educator and administrator, its regard for him as a citizen of strong spiritual and moral influence in his church and throughout the community, its affection for him as a man, and its appreciation to him for his services to the college in its advancement under his administration." Honored at a meal attended by faculty, staff, students, alumni, trustees, and other friends, Dr. and Mrs. Christenberry were presented with a silver service.

After leaving Shorter, Christenberry was for six years administrative director or vice-president for development at Furman University. From 1964 to 1970 he was at the Woman's College of Georgia (later called Georgia College at Milledgeville), first as chairman of the department of biology and later as dean. Since 1970 he has been president of Augusta College, Augusta, Georgia.

Trustees

The board of trustees continued to be comprised of eighteen regular members elected for a four-year term and two alumnae members elected for a two-year term. Each person was named by the board at its commencement meeting and formally approved by the Georgia Baptist Convention at its November session. It will be noted that official control was retained by the board. After investigating the method of electing trustees at each of its cooperating schools, the convention adopted a uniform practice taking effect with those trustees appointed in 1953. Under these terms the Shorter board nominated three persons for each vacancy, from whom the convention chose one. Soon thereafter the board formally elected the one so chosen. The term of office was raised to five years for the eighteen regular trustees, remaining two years for the two alumnae trustees. After his or her term, each trustee was to rotate off the board for at least one year.

Early in 1957 the trustees voted to "take steps satisfactory to the Georgia Baptist Convention to put Shorter College on the same basis with the convention as the other colleges." The convention that November agreed to accept Shorter if the charter were amended so that trustees would be elected directly by the convention. The resolution explained: "While the legal title to the property would remain in the present corporation [the board of trustees], the corporation itself would be controlled and operated in all respects as other convention in-

349

stitutions . . . ." In 1959 the trustees made a formal request to the Superior Court of Floyd County asking that its charter be altered. As approved by the court on July 30, 1959, the changes related to two major areas. First, the college was accorded "the right and power to offer and give the same educational advantages and training unto young men as . . . for . . . young women . . . ." Second, the trustees were to be elected by the Georgia Baptist Convention, which would fix their number at twenty to thirty, and were prohibited from borrowing money, creating debts, and seeking to amend the charter without convention approval. Henceforth they were required to hold

Aubrey Matthews   F. S. Cooper   Claire J. Wyatt, Sr.

membership in "a Baptist Church which is affiliated with the Baptist Convention of the State of Georgia . . . ."

Three men headed the board as its chairman—the term *president* was no longer frequently used. In 1952 Aubrey Matthews resigned as chairman after thirteen years. Dr. Lester Harbin, a Rome physician, served his first term during the next five years. In 1957 Walter R. Thomas, an Atlanta jeweler, was elected to the post.

The board observed the departure of valued members. Resolutions of appreciation were passed for Mrs. Azor W. Van Hoose, who was a trustee for twenty-five years until her death in 1949, and for Columbus Roberts, who died in 1950. Claire J. Wyatt, Sr., resigned in 1952 after twenty-six years. First to rotate off the board was its senior member, Aubrey Matthews, who had been active for thirty-one years. The following year Mrs. John C. Wright of Augusta (née Miss Alice Louise

350

Hicks, class of 1907), of whom no portrait is available, was retired after twenty-nine years and F. S. Cooper of Rome, after thirty.

Several ladies who had graduated from Shorter were on the board of trustees: Mrs. Robert O. Arnold of Covington (née Miss Florence Turner, class of 1923); Miss Louise Bennet of Quitman (class of 1913); Mrs. Harold Cooledge of Atlanta (née Miss Rebekah Clark, class of 1915); Mrs. Theodore Forbes of Atlanta (née Miss Mary Christie, class of 1920); Miss Martha C. Galt of Canton (class of 1915); Mrs. L. G. Hardman, Jr., of Commerce (née Miss Dorothy Shell, class of 1932); Miss Helen Harvey of Columbus (class of 1936); Mrs. Frank

Mrs. Azor W. Van Hoose

Leavell of Nashville, Tennessee (née Miss Martha Boone, class of 1915); Mrs. Aubrey Matthews of Rome (née Miss Sue Earnest, class of 1919); Mrs. E. H. Peniston of Newnan (née Miss Mildred Arnall, class of 1918); Mrs. John C. Wright of Augusta; Mrs. R. M. Wyatt of Rome (née Miss Elizabeth Betts, class of 1916); and Mrs. S. H. Yarbrough of Columbus (née Miss Martha Hays, class of 1933).

Over a period of three years the trustees, with faculty encouragement, considered assuming control of the Rome off-campus center of the University of Georgia. In 1954 it was finally decided to abandon the proposal as not being in the best interests of the college. Two years later President Christenberry announced several times to the faculty that a possible merger of the Southern School of Pharmacy in Atlanta and Shorter College was being studied by both boards of trustees. However, the Shorter trustees were informed in January of 1957 that negotiations had been halted by the other school, and no further action was taken.

As was true throughout America, the enrollment at Shorter College dropped in the early fifties and then began to climb by the middle of the decade. The total student body for twelve months varied from 258 to 476 during the Burts-Christenberry years, and the average was 347. Classes were offered during eight of the summers, attracting as many as 159 students and averaging about 109. Almost seventy-five percent of these were public school teachers enrolled only in the summer; the remainder were regular college students wishing to accelerate their course of study. The full-time students enrolled during the regular academic years varied in number from 170 to 243, averaging 196 under Burts and 209 under Christenberry. The women's dormitories were utilized at about seventy-five percent of their capacity. By 1957 the rising birthrate of the 1940s was being felt in the nation's colleges, Shorter included. That year the high for this period was experienced, a figure unequaled during the previous thirty years of Shorter's history. Of course the influx of male students accounted for some of this growth; in 1957 one-third of the students were male.

Ninety percent of all students were residents of Georgia, and in 1957 nearly half were from Floyd County. During these ten years, the greatest number of other students came from Alabama, Florida, and Tennessee. Nineteen foreign countries were represented. Several young ladies were sponsored by various Rotary clubs and by the Institute of International Education. One from Mexico and another from Japan selected Shorter after hearing about it from alumnae living in their respective countries. Much comment occurred in 1949 when, as a newspaper picture caption announced, "Nobility enrolls at Shorter College." Baroness Inge Von Gemmingen, an eighteen-year-old German girl, remained one year, evoking this appraisal from a classmate: "She is sweet, natural, and friendly—even if she is a baroness!" Frequently called on for speeches, many international students traveled widely over the state. For the first time in 1953, two of them, Marta Castellanos of Mexico and Evi Keskkula of Sweden, received Shorter degrees. Six others graduated during Christenberry's administration.

The college continued a vigorous program of student recruitment. Two house parties were held each year on campus. The alumnae sponsored luncheons encouraging prospective students to enroll. Full- and part-time admissions personnel visited high schools and private homes throughout the Southeast, and the Choral and Dance clubs performed before many high school audiences. Posters were displayed in schools all over the state, and news releases were sent to their newspapers. Describing Shorter's offerings in music, speech, science, art, teacher training, business administration, and religion, small leaflets appeared in profusion. Two large, illustrated booklets were aimed at prospects, being later replaced by a descriptive folder. In their news and feature stories and pictures, many newspapers publicized the institution. Frequent advertisements were placed in nearby papers—and occasionally in *Good Housekeeping, Vogue,* the Georgia *Beta Club Journal,* and the *Christian Index.*

Male Students

By the fall of 1957, the Shorter of old was decidedly a thing of the irrecoverable past. Sixty-four young men were attending classes full-time, of whom 24 were living on campus. Almost thirty percent of all full-time students were male. A men's club had already evolved into two fraternities, a few major offices on campus were occupied by male students, and a basketball team engaged in intercollegiate competition was forthcoming. Servings in the dining room were being increased in quantity to satisfy the masculine appetite, and course offerings in the classroooom and gymnasium reflected the masculine presence. Ten years earlier the one full-time male student had attended classes in his solitary splendor, while the 22 special students had dropped in for instruction once or twice a week. What a metamorphosis had come over the campus on which the persimmons were so rapidly growing up among the peaches!

Officially the transition was permitted by the trustees who took two important steps, and by a change in the college charter. Although some alumnae and faculty opposed the admission of males, a motion offered by Miss Louise Bennet was passed in 1951 "that the president and faculty be authorized to grant degrees to men, upon completion of the necessary work." Without a dissenting vote the trustees agreed in 1957 "that Shorter College solicit men boarding students as well as day students, and that male students be housed in existing dormitory facilities under proper and appropriate rules and regulations." Two years later the charter was formally altered to cover the actions that had already been taken.

In 1948–1949 only 20 part-time male students were enrolled, none of whom was working toward a degree. The number steadily grew, and in 1957–1958 there were 74 full- and part-time students on degree programs and 20 unclassified students. For the first six or seven years of this period, about half of the regular male students were local clergymen pursuing an education while continuing to serve their churches.

353

This is reflected in the first male graduate, James Sanders, a Methodist pastor from nearby Kingston, who received his degree in 1953. Of the 25 who graduated during this period, at least 7 were or have become ministers. As the decade of the fifties concluded, however, a much wider range of vocational objectives emerged.

At first all male students were commuters, except for William Porter, who lived with his parents at Maplehurst. President Christenberry began talking immediately about the Men's Dormitory and, as already described, took action to secure a federal loan for its construction. Temporarily, part of the Dining Hall Building was converted to living quarters occupied by about 10 in 1956–1957 and about 25 the next year.

Reaction on campus to the male population was varied. Some of the girls expressed resentment and hostility, according to a Rome *News-Tribune* feature that mixed its metaphors while describing the "brave souls who . . . broke the ice and faced the stares of two hundred girls" within the "Shorter stronghold." Titled "Shorter Goes Coed . . . and the Girls Love It," a 1957 article in the Atlanta *Journal and Constitution Magazine* claimed widespread approval. "A few girls did voice complaints when the invasion of men started—partly because the invasion was too weak." Now, the story insisted, the college "has opened its arms to men." Three pictures in full color, including the big one on the cover, were full of pretty young ladies—and noticeably marred by several of their less glamorous classmates. With tongue firmly in cheek, one male respondent to a poll taken that year proposed to improve the college by graduating or expelling all the girls!

Tuition, Fees, and Student Aid

Saluting the support, financial and otherwise, of their parents, the 1952 seniors included this sentence in the dedication of their *Argo*: "Only with your abundant love and sacrifice have we been able to travel this path to become 'Shorter girls' and the future of tomorrow." Tuition and fees moved upward—but, claimed college officials, not as sharply as other goods and services. The student paid $895 in 1949 for all charges levied by the school, with $140 added for the most expensive type of instruction in music. By 1957 the charge was $1,080, with an addition of $180 for music. The catalogue that year was the first to include a plan whereby the amount could be paid in small monthly installments.

Discounts were regularly allowed for daughters of ministers or teachers, for two or more from the same family, and for dependents of Shorter faculty and staff members. Superior high school graduates were eligible for scholarships in all areas of study, although music awards received the most publicity. The student earning the highest average in each of the Shorter freshman, sophomore, and junior classes automatically received a fifty percent reduction on her next year's tuition.

Three new single scholarships were added to those initiated in earlier years. In 1949 the General Alumnae Association set up an award, usually for a sophomore. In 1954 the Edith Lester Harbin Music Scholarship was given in honor of their mother, Mrs. W. P. Harbin, by her children, Mary (class of 1932; Mrs. Warren Gilbert), Lester, Tom, and William. It honored also the golden anniversary of the Rome Music Lovers' Club, founded by Mrs. Harbin, and was combined with a scholarship which that club had been presenting for fifteen years. In 1957 the John Cleveland Dukes Scholarship Fund was provided by the estate of that educator from Dawson, Georgia.

With A. W. Ledbetter, Sr., as first president, the Shorter College Scholarship Fund, Inc., was established by a group of Rome business and professional men wishing to aid local students, mostly boys. Forty awards of $350 each were made in 1954–1955, the first year of operation. This corporation continues to function, having assisted a total of almost six hundred. Willingham Smith is now its president.

Another new source of help was the Georgia Baptist Convention, which appropriated $520 each year starting in 1956 to help Baptist young people preparing for church-related vocations.

Students continued to occupy positions in the library, music department, laboratories, and offices, for which small stipends were paid. When the dining room became a cafeteria in 1949, many girls were furnished work opportunities there.

Scholarship assistance amounted to $5,552.50 in the first year of this period and climbed to $26,388 in the last. Student positions initially cost $5,171 per year to fill, rising finally to $13,508.

Community Relations

Shorter personnel and facilities were constantly at the disposal of churches and other religious groups of the state. Each summer hundreds of young people were attracted to the campus for week-long assemblies conducted by nearby Baptist associations, Presbyterian youth organizations, and the Georgia Baptist Department of Church Music. Ben Shanklin of the music faculty assisted over the state with Baptist church music festivals and schools. When the Woman's Missionary Union state convention met at Rome in 1953 for the first time in sixteen years, some of the four hundred guests were housed on campus and all were invited to a reception by the local chapter of the Alumnae Association. The following year the Shorter sextet sang for the ladies at their convention in Albany. The state-wide Intermediate Girls' Auxiliary House Party was scheduled at Shorter each spring for four years. Occasionally the Floyd County Baptist Association convened in Brookes Chapel, and some years the local Baptist pastors' conference held its monthly meetings there.

Churches in and near Rome utilized the Shorter dining room for dinners, invited the Baptist Student Union and sextet to present programs, and asked various staff and faculty members to preach. Interim pastorates were served by Bruce Whitaker, Edwin S. Gaustad, and Cecil Lea. Nearby church musicians included Ben Shanklin, David Beaty, M. R. Rice, and Mr. and Mrs. John Ramsaur. President Christenberry spoke to the the Rome Ministerial Alliance and at one Easter sunrise service. Some years this was conducted on the campus.

Shorter musicians contributed significantly to a wide community. As members, performers, and lecturers, they related themselves to the Rome Music Lovers' Club. A reception and concert honored the Georgia Federation of Music Clubs in 1950. The Rome Symphony Orchestra and women's and men's choruses made use of Shorter musicians. Although the Civic Music Association presented its guest artists downtown, Shorter persons year by year provided leadership and purchased an abundance of tickets. Bringing large groups of youthful participants with them, the Junior Music clubs of Northwest Georgia and the Georgia Music Teachers Association of the Seventh District accepted Shorter hospitality. When the Rome Music Teachers Association was formed in 1957, Shorter faculty persons were among the charter members. The Choral Club, smaller student groups, and instructors performed with frequency before diverse audiences all over Georgia and at times elsewhere in the Southeast.

Civic and educational organizations called on the college for programs and meeting places. The annual Chamber of Commerce banquet was twice scheduled for the campus—at one of them Governor Marvin Griffin spoke. The Rome Rotary Club sponsored international students at the college, heard them and other Shorter persons at their weekly meetings, and twice held Ladies Night on the hill. The Civitan, Pilot, Quota, Elks, and Kiwanis clubs occasionally invited students and faculty members to inform and entertain them, and one music major sang before the International Kiwanis Convention at Miami in 1950.

A leadership training course was conducted at Shorter by the Junior Red Cross later that year. Beginning in 1954 the Audubon Society met in Brookes Chapel, and the Northwest Georgia Archaeological Society was started in 1957 in Rome Hall with leadership provided by faculty members. Addresses by various Shorter personnel were heard by the Rome Junior Service League and Garden Study Club, the League of Women Voters in Rome and LaFayette, and the Calhoun Women's Club.

Providing educational leadership for the area, the college furnished speakers to the Rome branch of the American Association of University Women, the Delta Kappa Gamma teachers' sorority, the Rome Education Association, and the Seventh District of the Georgia Education Association. Over a wide area of Georgia and Alabama, members of the music faculty served as judges for high school music events. High school literary meets and one-act play competitions occasionally used Shorter facilities and judges. At other times, district art teachers' workshops were conducted and children's exhibits were displayed on campus. Shorter professors spoke at many nearby Parent-Teacher associations and the Darlington Mothers' Club.

Weekly radio programs were aired in the late forties and then resumed in 1953 with Esserman's as sponsor. Thirty-minute Sunday afternoon broadcasts included drama, music, and college news. Carried live by WRGA, they sometimes originated from the campus and were transcribed for use elsewhere. Throughout the remainder of this period they were presented with some regularity during the winter and spring. For about a year Mr. and Mrs. Ben Shanklin prepared a Saturday afternoon program for WROM, dealing with the education of preschool children. While WROM-TV was still in operation, Shorter girls appeared once to demonstrate Christmas decorations and once on a telethon to benefit the United Cerebral Palsy Fund.

Keeping Shorter pleasantly in the public eye, three of its young ladies were crowned Miss Rome—Jean Carr in 1955, Jean Harper in 1956, and Pam Altweis in 1958. When the Atlanta *Journal and Constitution Magazine* ran a two-year series of pictures labeled "Georgia Peach," half a dozen were products of the Shorter grove. Davison's College Fashion Board included Jean Harper three years, and she became its chairman her senior year.

In 1950, for the second time, it seemed appropriate to the seniors that they dedicate their annual to "the people of Rome, whose unselfish interest and spirit of cooperation have contributed to the growth of Shorter College and to the happiness of Shorter girls . . . ."

Regulations for admission were unchanged until the faculty voted to administer the College Board Entrance Examinations (Scholastic Aptitude Tests) as a prerequisite for all new students in 1957. As a member of the College Board, Shorter became the third testing center in the state. The minimum number of required high school units was then raised from fifteen to sixteen.

Opening days in September were full of orientation lectures, tests, and socials. The Student Council conducted classes on the *Student Handbook* and concluded them with an event that one freshman recalled: "How we crammed to pass our orientation test . . . ." The administration gave English, foreign language, general achievement, and psychological tests to the hapless freshmen occuping desks scattered all over the gym floor. The Rome alumnae continued their entertainment at the Coosa Country Club or Callier Springs Golf Club. Often the Shorter Christian Association invited the freshmen to a picnic, and the presidents of the dormitories were hostesses at a pajama party. Tours of the county, a free, picture show, refreshments at local drug stores, open house at clothing stores, and a luncheon at the General Electric or Pepperell plants were included. Tuesday was "the day the 'old girls' started pouring in (or should we say 'screeching' in) . Who would have thought dignified college women could act so uncouth?" This "bedlam of arrival" soon gave way to the bedlam of registration—first in the gym and later in the library. Friday morning saw the beginning of classes and the opening convocation. With seniors and platform party wearing caps and gowns, the service usually included greetings by the presidents of the General Alumnae Association and the Rome chapter and a main address by the president of the college. Two days later the seniors again utilized their academic regalia, this time for Shorter Sunday at the First Baptist Church. Some years a Monday evening presidential reception honored new faculty and staff members and the new students.

Held from Monday through Friday, classes started at 8:30. Early in the fifties eight o'clock classes were provided for alert and grateful students. Each professor scheduled his own smaller quizzes, but in January and May a "flash," allegedly from "Thompson's Headquarters," might be worded thusly: "The terrible demons . . . are about to strike our college—the demon of exams." "Dead Week" first came in 1957–1958, wherein student meetings were prohibited and student studying encouraged. Each spring Sophomore Tests were required.

In order to remain in school, a student was expected to pass at least

16 s.h. during the previous year. In the 1956 catalogue this was significantly altered. Henceforth, freshmen were to pass at least sixty percent of their work; sophomores, two-thirds of it; and juniors and seniors, eighty percent. Failing to meet these minimal standards, a student was suspended for a semester. A second suspension rendered the student ineligible to return.

Founders' Day, coming near the birthday of Alfred Shorter in November, and Honors Day, when the members of Phi Sigma Alpha and the dean's list were named in March, continued to be cap and gown events for the seniors. Distinguished speakers included Senator Walter F. George, President George B. Connell of Mercer University, President Guy H. Wells of Georgia State College for Women, President Josiah Crudup of Brenau College, and E. Smythe Gambrell of Atlanta.

Previous types of accreditation were retained, and the college became a charter member of the Association of Southern Baptist Colleges in 1948. The faculty studied the question, "What is a Christian College?" under the auspices of the Association of American Colleges in 1952. During the year 1953–1954, Dr. Christenberry and Dean Gaustad led the faculty in a complete self-study, resulting in curricular changes, the thoughtful rejection of the quarter system, and a new statement of objectives: "The aim of the college is that its curriculum be utilized to attain certain desirable goals for each student. The college believes that the following are fundamental standards by which the growth of the individual may be evaluated: the development of physical and mental health, an appreciation of our cultural heritage, the establishment of the habit of educating one's self, the acceptance of moral and social responsibilities, and the attainment of a sense of spiritual values." Looking toward the future, Dr. Christenberry discussed the membership rules of the Southern Association at six faculty meetings during 1955–1956, but no document emerged. Two years later the faculty produced a twenty-five-page mimeographed self-study report that took many more hours to prepare than minutes to read. Although the report followed an outline furnished by the Southern Association, no visiting committee examined the institution. In that same year, however, the National Association of Schools of Music requested a limited report, which was prepared, and a committee then investigated. Accreditation of the music department was subsequently renewed.

Two or three sessions of summer school had been held back in the 1880s. President Van Hoose considered reviving it in 1919 but finally decided against the idea. Dr. Cameron Ebaugh, professor of psychology and education, led a noncredit teachers' course during the summer of 1942. Thus, the 1949 summer school was something of an innovation at

Shorter College. For six weeks classes were held for 88 students, providing courses and a workshop that enabled teachers to renew their certificates and several 3 s.h. courses for regular college students. After a lapse of one year, summer school was resumed, enrolling from 70 to 159 during the next seven years. Continuing to furnish teacher training, in addition to regular college work, it was advertised in numerous Northwest Georgia papers and attracted up to a hundred teachers in a single summer. Professors conducting the sessions grew in number from six to about twenty. Sessions expanded to twelve weeks and then finally contracted to six. Housing and food were usually available on campus, and "Some Air-Conditioned Classrooms" were noted in the ads. Scheduled in 1956, a six-week School of Fine Arts offered noncredit instruction for those desiring intensive work in art, dance, drama, or music. Several persons completed requirements for the Bachelor of Arts degree each summer, but had to wait until the following spring for graduation.

Special classes late in the afternoon and on Saturday continued to be scheduled, with greater emphasis than before. The first evening classes in recent years were initiated in 1948, with offerings from virtually every department at one time or another. New equpiment contributed to a fresh interest in ceramics. Children's art classes resulted in art exhibits open to the public. As many as seventy preparatory students took music lessons, giving group recitals in the spring. A course in fine arts, popular with the youngsters, met on Saturday morning and once produced "Snow White and the Seven Dwarfs."

The Curricula

The Bachelor of Arts and Bachelor of Music degrees continued to be conferred. Beginning in 1954, basic requirements for the Bachelor of Arts degree were increased slightly and particular courses were usually specified. Majors were always provided in art, biology, chemistry, English, French, history and political science, mathematics, music, religion and philosophy, psychology and education, sociology, Spanish, and speech. By 1954 Latin and physics had been dropped. A major was offered in orchesis from 1950 to 1958. Elementary education and business administration and economics were established as separate majors in 1954. From 1954 to 1958 an interdepartmental major in church activities was available. Other interdepartmental majors in fine arts and natural sciences were approved in 1957–1958. The two-day comprehensive examination was required of all seniors. One bystander reported: "A few days previous to D. Day (Doom Day), when even the password of 'T.H.W.C.' had been forgotten, something happened!" She explained it as "hystrocatodelusiphobia," a condition marked by extreme stress among the seniors. Of course the examinees were usually successful, often holding a banquet the night before and taking off afterward "for the unknown to enjoy a few days of restful, riotous vacation." The Bachelor of Arts degree was awarded to 273 persons during the Burts-Christenberry period. The most popular majors were elementary education, biology, history, and speech, as each was selected by at least ten percent of the graduates.

The curriculum for the Bachelor of Music degree required less than one-third of the work in the liberal arts and the remainder in theoretical and applied music. With majors possible in piano, voice, violin, organ, flute, theory and composition, and music education, this degree was received by 44 persons. Among the requirements were a rigorous examination in basic techniques at the end of the sophomore year, a sophomore or junior recital, and a senior recital and written comprehensive.

Following trustee approval, a special training program for General Electric employees was established during the year 1956–1957. Financed by the company, it included regular Shorter courses in mathematics, English, and economics, and several courses in physics that were added primarily for the benefit of those enrolled. Studying at Shorter while working at General Electric, 20 to 25 men participated in the program during the first two years of its existence. A certificate was to be awarded to those completing 60 s.h. of courses in four years, but of course no person was eligible to receive one this early.

Within the Departments

In ten years Presidents Burts and Christenberry employed about 120 faculty members, 87 administrative and staff members, and many others working in maintenance, the dormitories, and the dining room. The full- and part-time instructional and administrative group varied from 33 to 47 and averaged 40. Additional staff members numbered about 20 each year. A faculty-student ratio of one to nine was claimed in 1953–1954 and one to eight in 1957–1958. Of the faculty members, about 42 remained only one year or were part-time and about 18, no more than two. Seventy-eight were on the faculty two or more years, with highest earned degrees distributed as follows: bachelor's, 9; master's, 45; doctor's, 24. The nonmusicians had advanced degrees most frequently from the University of North Carolina, Duke University, the University of Florida, George Peabody College for Teachers, and

Brown University. The musicians had most often received their professional training at the Eastman School of Music, Syracuse University, Cincinnati Conservatory of Music, and Indiana University. Salaries for full-time faculty members ranged from $1,750 to $4,130 in 1948–1949 and from $2,800 to $5,200 in 1957–1958. A few were also provided free or reduced room and board. In 1951 a further fringe benefit was realized when the college came under Social Security. The long-discussed retirement plan was once again considered by the trustees in 1957. After approval by the faculty, the trustees activated a plan effective September 1, 1958. For all full-time faculty and administrative members, it was in cooperation with the Teachers Insurance and Annuity Association of America and the College Retirement Equities Fund. Hospital and surgical insurance was made available in 1956 at a saving because of a group rate. By 1952 the college had begun providing some financial aid to faculty members who attended meetings of scholarly societies. Sixteen received such help in 1957–1958.

For those who had taught at least five years, three of which were at Shorter, and who held the rank of assistant professor or above, tenure was granted. In 1958 the trustees passed resolutions endorsing the Statement of Principles on Academic Freedom and Tenure from the Southern Association. Faculty retirement was set at sixty-five by action of the trustees in 1953. Continuance after that age came only at the annual option of the college.

Meeting once each month in the Little Theater, usually in the evening, the faculty considered a wide range of academic and disciplinary matters. Having been secretary of the faculty for thirty-four years, Mrs. Allie Hayes Richardson resigned in 1956. For two years Dr. Ethel B. Colbrunn, professor of English, filled that position. Humphrey Olsen, the librarian, was her successor in 1958. Numerous faculty committees were appointed by the president and dean: admissions, chapel and religious activities, class attendance, comprehensive examinations, curriculum and objectives, guidance, health and recreation, honors and awards, library, publications, radio, registration, social activities, and student government.

ART. Assisted by Miss Rebecca Wall for five years and Harlan Sifford for six, Miss Martha Griffin led the department of art in such a way that the 1949 seniors dedicated their *Argo* to her because of her "untiring service to Shorter and love for all its girls." A member of the National Association of Art Education, she gave a paper at the 1951 meeting. She was a founder and charter member of the Southeastern Art Association and active in the Association of Georgia Artists. In

362

1949 she wrote the constitution and became the first president of the Art Education Division of the Georgia Education Association. Helping to establish the Georgia Student Art Exhibit, she frequently judged shows over the state. On campus, her department expanded in number of majors and in quality of facilities, taking over the area formerly occupied by the gymnasium. The Rich Foundation of Atlanta granted $6,500 in 1952 for new ceramics equipment. Student art shows each spring included many works by the graduating seniors and some by children and adult townspeople receiving instruction. Several traveling exhibits were displayed each year, including one with working models of inventions by Leonardo da Vinci that was viewed by two thousand. The Art Students' League maintained a lending library of pictures for campus use and often in the spring made a weekend sketch trip to the Cloudland area. Students attended lectures and shows in Atlanta and Athens. Entering their work in art exhibits at Columbus and Rome, several won prizes when they were offered.

BUSINESS ADMINISTRATION AND ECONOMICS. When the department of business administration and economics was expanded in 1954, the local newspaper voiced its approval. Eighteen courses were gradually added by Dr. Lewis E. Hill, who was the first to offer a major in this field. For many years typing and shorthand had been taught without academic credit, but now 3 s.h. were offered in the former and 6 s.h. in the latter.

EDUCATION. A program in education was proposed in 1948–1949 that, according to its defenders, would not be a departure from the traditional liberal arts objectives of the college. Later in 1949 a plan to offer a Bachelor of Science degree in elementary education reached the faculty, which returned it to the curriculum committee for the purpose of drawing up a course of study. This did not materialize, and the work in education was allowed as a part of the Bachelor of Arts degree. Offerings grew to 35 s.h. of regular courses, 6 s.h. of student teaching, and 6⅔ s.h. of sumer workshop. Starting in 1954 the college was approved by the Georgia State Department of Education to train professionally certified elementary teachers, elementary and secondary teachers in art and music, and secondary teachers in English, foreign languages, mathematics, science, and social studies. For six years Miss Mary Ellen Perkins was a part-time associate within the department, as was Miss Mabel Thompson for five. In 1956 J. D. Ramsay began a fifteen-year period of service. The John N. Ware chapter of the Future Teachers of America was formed in 1954.

ENGLISH. Headed by Dr. Gertrude Ingalls until her contract was terminated in 1953 and briefly by others after that time, the department of English provided popular offerings in composition, grammar, journalism, and literature. Rho Delta contributed leadership and literary works to the *Chimes*. For five years an English Club was devoted to trends in modern literature—and, admitted one president, "building houses."

FOREIGN LANGUAGES. French, German, and Spanish were offered each year, and Italian, Portuguese, Greek, and Latin, on a less regular basis. Dr. Clara Thompson taught classical languages at Shorter for thirty-four years, until her resignation in 1953. Miss Margaret Newhard, an

Miss Clara Louise Kellogg   Dr. Clara Louise Thompson

alumna of the college, was on the faculty in modern languages from 1947 to 1959, being one of eight in Georgia to receive the Southern Fellowship Foundation Award for graduate study, 1956–1957. Dr. Joseph Cedeyco belonged to the department for five years, and Marvin Harrison joined it in 1953. Usually the French and Spanish clubs met monthly.

It would be almost impossible to exaggerate the place of Dr. and Mrs. John N. Ware in the minds and hearts of their students. The 1951 *Argo* was dedicated to him, "not only for his guidance in intellectual fields, but for his genuine interest in all Shorter girls." Mrs. Ware retired in 1952 after twenty-five years on the faculty and died three months later. Her funeral was conducted by Russell Daniel of St. Peter's Episcopal Church in Brookes Chapel and, with trustee approval, interment was on the campus just east of the Fine Arts

Building. The *Chimes* included this tribute: "Her radiant countenance shed light just as sunbeams on a summer day. Her understanding eyes were symbolic of blue summer skies. Her bubbling smile lifted heavy hearts even as would a summer rose. Snowy white clouds resting in the heavens give an insight into her soul—for she was at peace with God and man." Two years later Dr. Ware had the Rockery restored as a memorial to her, placing new metal furniture there.

After twenty-eight years, Dr. Ware also retired in 1952, thereupon becoming professor emeritus. This did not dissolve his active relationship with the college. He moved from his home on Shorter Circle to

Dr. and Mrs.
John N. Ware

an apartment in the Dining Hall Building. The two societies adopted him as an honorary member. He wrote poems, "Shorter" and "To the Alumnae," describing "my catalogue of lovely things"—the "loveliest" being a "dear quiet grave 'neath trees' protecting shade . . . ." A brief article about the Civil War was printed in *American Heritage*. For thirty years he had written letters of appreciation and criticism to authors of books that he had read, receiving more than two hundred responses. Likewise, he had long sent birthday greetings to his former students. Both of these practices were increased after his teaching load was removed. In 1956 he went to a Rome nursing home, frequently returning to the campus for Sunday dinner. At his death three years later, he and Mrs. Ware were buried in Sewanee, Tennessee.

HISTORY AND POLITICAL SCIENCE. Because of "her scholarship and friendliness," the 1954 *Argo* honored Miss Clara Louise Kellogg, who taught history at Shorter for thirty-eight years until her retirement in 1955. As professor emeritus, she was living in Rome at her death in 1958. Among others in the department were Miss Jean Grubbs, a Shorter graduate, and Dr. Allen S. Johnson. The International Relations Club existed throughout the entire period and the League of Women Voters for the first three or four years.

MATHEMATICS AND SCIENCE. In mathematics, Dr. Ruby Hightower had become professor emeritus in 1947 but lived on campus and instructed part-time three more years before her death at Quitman in

Dr. Ruby U. Hightower   Dr. Everett E. Porter   Dr. Bertha E. Martin

1959. From her estate came $5,000, making possible the purchase of a Steinway grand piano and some classroom furniture. Miss Margaret Baskervill taught from 1947 to 1959, receiving the Doctor of Philosophy degree from Auburn in 1958 and having her dissertation published in an Auburn bulletin at that time. For eleven years Mrs. May C. Blackstock was in the department. Miss Barbara Cogdell, an alumna, instructed for a short period of time. When she married Richard Lamb at the First Baptist Church on August 4, 1951, the reception was held in the Alumnae Garden. After thirty-three years in the department of chemistry, Dr. Everett E. Porter resigned in 1953 and was presented a silver tray by some of the alumnae as a mark of their esteem. Dr. Bertha Martin was named professor emeritus of biology in 1954, after twenty-seven years at Shorter, and continued to reside in the faculty apartments for the last six years of her life. More recently she has been honored by a conference room in the library and a museum in Rome Hall initiated by a gift from the Oscar Braden family. Dr. Julian T. Darlington headed the biology department from 1954 to 1959. Miss Emma Lewis Lipps wrote and lectured in the area of earth science and was one of eight in Georgia to win the Southern Fellowship Foundation Award for graduate study during 1956–1957. The Science Club persisted, once initiating new members by giving each a "peachy goldfish" to consume.

Music. Three men functioned as director of music—Wilbur H. Rowand, 1936 to 1949; Joseph A. Burns, 1949 to 1951; and David Beaty, beginning in 1951. Teachers included Mrs. Charlotte McManamon (later Mrs. Charlotte Vane) for eleven years, Mr. and Mrs. Richard Willis (she was the former Miss Carolyn Brown, class of 1947) for ten years each, Mrs. Lillian Acree Bosworth (class of 1944) for eleven years, Willard Shull for ten years, and Mrs. Rebecca Shull for thirteen. Four were added to the faculty and remain to the present: Mrs. Elizabeth Buday, David Beaty, and Mr. and Mrs. John Ramsaur. Two alumnae assisted briefly, Misses Dorothy Ware and Jane Jones. Various faculty members played regularly with the Chattanooga, Rome, or Atlanta symphony orchestras, most of them gave recitals at other colleges and before music clubs in the Southeast, and Mrs. McManamon and Mrs. Buday were guest soloists with the Rome Symphony. On the programs at conventions of the Music Teachers National Association in Macon, Tallahassee, and Tuscaloosa, Shorter faculty members also helped to organize the Rome chapter. With her continental background, Mrs. Buday quite naturally conducted summer tours in Europe. A favorite with the students, Mrs. McManamon had the 1956 *Argo* dedicated to her. Richard Willis gained national notice as his compositions were played over the Mutual Radio Network by the Oklahoma City Symphony Orchestra and by other orchestras in New York, Kentucky, Texas, Alabama, Tennessee, and Georgia. Winning significant awards in 1953 and 1955, he spent 1956–1957 studying in Rome, Italy, as a recipient of the Prix de Rome.

Welcomed to the campus for obvious reasons were some guests, the Emory or Vanderbilt glee clubs. Other guests were sometimes invited as extensions of the teaching faculty. These persons presented recitals and master classes. They included Lewis Crowder, pianist-teacher; the University of Alabama String Quartet; Ernst von Dohnanyi, composer-pianist; Glenn Schnittke, tenor; Lionel Nowak, pianist; Jeno von Takacs, composer-pianist; Walter Robert, pianist; and George Lucktenberg, harpsichordist. Shorter musicians profited also by attending the opera and various recitals in Atlanta and programs brought to Rome by the Civic Music Association.

Faculty and student recitals and larger musical performances raised the total each year to an astonishing number. Wednesday afternoon recitals involved virtually every music student; formal evening recitals each year involved the seniors and each member of the faculty. For three years a faculty string quartet was also active. Operas included "Dido and Aeneas" and "Marriage of Figaro." Choral Club concerts at Christmas and Easter, May Day performances, and commencement concerts or fine arts festivals added much to the life of the institution—and to the burden of the department.

Although smaller ensembles such as the trio and sextet made contributions, the Choral Club was constantly before the public. The group sang at churches, high schools, and meetings of music clubs from one end of the state to the other. Almost every fall the club appeared before the Georgia Baptist Convention. A spring tour grew from two days in 1949 to ten in 1956—and the latter covered 2,200 miles in five states, consisted of sixteen performances before combined audiences of ten thousand, and included several shows on military bases of the sponsoring Third Army.

Raising funds to secure visiting artists, the spring Camerata Follies might be built on the theme of "Dreams," "Mardis Gras," or "The Seasons." Proclaimed the printed programs: "The Camerata Follies is a glorious stunt night program whose inevitable stigma is a polished performance of faculty foolishness." Other lighthearted productions included "Green Grow the Lilacs," "Roberta," and "Best Foot Forward."

An electronic practice organ was provided in 1948 by two alumnae, Misses Martha C. and Frances Galt, and their brother, O. P. Galt, of Canton, Georgia. Four years later Miss Martha C. Galt gave a Steinway grand piano.

Psychology. Increasing its offerings from 28 to 46 s.h., the department of psychology made the newspapers several times due to one of its professors, John A. Hornaday. His demonstrations of hypnotism were described in the Atlanta *Journal and Constitution Magazine*. His exposé of some Rome stores whose stocks of comic books were full of horror, sex, and crime ran as a series in the *News-Tribune*. For use in experimental psychology, he purchased a four-pound Rhesus monkey which the Rome paper declared to be "one of the most important members of the class . . . ." Organized in 1953, the Psychology Club once sponsored a lecture by Dr. J. B. Rhine, one of Hornaday's professors from Duke University. Dr. Stanislav Velinsky began a fourteen-year term in 1956.

PHYSICAL EDUCATION.   After fifteen years at Shorter College, Mrs. Harriett G. Rowand left in 1949. Miss Franziska Boas came in 1950 and also remained fifteen years. Helping in the department were two alumnae, Misses Anne Betts and Sylvia Shirley.

Under Miss Boas the department significantly expanded its offerings to 50 s.h. and an orchesis major was available for almost a decade. Formed at Shorter College in 1955, the Georgia Dance Association had Miss Boas as its first chairman. Later she was chairman of the Southern Dance Section of the American Association of Physical Education, Health, and Recreation. Photographs of three students accompanied an article about her views on the therapeutic values of dance in the Atlanta *Journal and Constitution Magazine*. Student appreciation was obvious when the 1958 *Argo* was dedicated to her. The Dance Club was reconstituted in 1949, subsequently providing lectures, concerts, and master classes by visiting artists, Emily Frankel and Mark Ryder, Jean Erdman, and Eleanor King. Its members performed for the Georgia Dance Association, at the Woman's College of the University of North Carolina, and over a television station at nearby Winston-Salem. Receiving a tremendous stimulus from Miss Boas, the May Day pageants and fine arts festivals usually involved her students.

RELIGION AND PHILOSOPHY.   Until his resignation in 1953, Dr. Lawrence O. Grant continued as professor of the Mrs. Columbus Roberts Department of Religion. While serving also as dean of the college, Dr. Edwin S. Gaustad next occupied the position. Honored by having the *Argo* dedicated to him in 1957, he published that year a definitive study, *The Great Awakening in New England*. Dr. Howard O. Eaton received appointment as John Hay Whitney visiting professor of philosophy in 1956–1957. Arriving in 1957, Dr. Robert G. Gardner remains to the present.

SOCIOLOGY.   Under Miss Bernice Allen, Dr. Hoy Taylor, and others, the department of sociology grew slightly in its course offerings and finally provided a major separate from economics. In 1949 the Sociology Club was reestablished.

SPEECH.   Preparing students for public school teaching and speech correction, for writing and directing radio programs, and for work in the legitimate theater, speech courses were taught by Mrs. Allie Hayes Richardson and various associates who included Mrs. Anne Whipple Alderman and Miss Ann Austin, a Shorter alumna. The Shorter Players produced plays in the fall and spring and, usually, at commencement. Their involvement with May Day was notable. A recital, the production of a play, or the preparation of an original radio broadcast were required of senior majors through 1952. The first use at Shorter of the "theater in the round" technique came in 1949 with a play staged in the gymnasium. On six occasions the Barter Players of Virginia visited the campus under the auspices of this department, presenting such dramas as "Macbeth" and "Julius Caesar."

Administration and Staff

After eleven years as dean of the college, Dr. Everett E. Porter was followed by Dr. Zed H. Burns, Dr. Edwin S. Gaustad, and Dr. Allen Johnson. Two ladies served as dean of women, Mrs. Lydia Dixon Sheppard (class of 1920), who was also alumnae secretary, and Mrs. May Blackstock. It was most appropriate that Mrs. Sheppard's daughter, Wilann (class of 1947), should be married to N. D. Powers, Jr., in the Alumnae Garden on August 5, 1950, by Bunyan Stephens of the First Baptist Church. Miss Margaret Baskervill was academic counselor for three years. The registrar continued to be Miss Louise Thompson (class of 1930), "who has so willingly given her time and who so faithfully served Shorter and her girls," according to the 1953 *Argo* which was dedicated to her. Cecil Lea, director of development for five years, was assisted by Mrs. Ima Jean Kerce (class of 1931), who became alumnae secretary in 1956. Mrs. Emmie Louise Lovell (class of 1957) remained as secretary to the president. For eight years Clyde F. McAlister was business manager, assisted for five years by Miss Mavis Bailey. In the book store, Miss Lilly Mary Cain (class of 1938) was manager until 1951, being succeeded by Mrs. Alberdena W. Cedeyco. Among the many admissions counselors were Mrs. Rhoda LaPrade for six years and four Shorter alumnae—Misses Nell Irvin, Louisa Ann Sandifer, Mary Hendon, and Angie Hudspeth.

The library was headed by a succession of persons, of whom only Humphrey Olsen remained for at least five years. The collection grew from about 25,000 to 33,000 volumes and finally included partial files of 182 periodicals and 5 newspapers. Varying from about six to ten thousand dollars annually, the library budget included no more than $2,500 in any single year for acquiring books and magazines. In 1957 metal shelves began to be installed, replacing the old and sagging wooden ones.

Called the "Guardian Angel," Mrs. Elizabeth V. Bryan was house director for twenty years until her retirement in 1955. Her jobs were numerous: delaying the laundry man on Wednesday so that the stragglers could send their washing, hemming dresses, adding zippers, cracking "a cheery joke to lift your spirits," and leaving inspection notes that might say:

> I am old and bent and cheated
> But name me not with the defeated.
> Tomorrow, I come again!

For eight years until 1950 Mrs. Azalea V. Estes was associated with her. Mrs. Lila C. Elliot was the gracious housemother whose smile was not diminished by the weight of successive titles—student counselor, assistant dean of women, and house director. During several of the summers she led tours to Europe. Maids who were faithful over a long period were Mrs. Mary Jo Lewis, Mrs. Jessie Wood, and Mrs. Lucille Taylor. Several nurses worked briefly in the infirmary, with Mrs. Margit Tamassy as assistant nurse beginning in the early fifties. Usually located above the dining room, the infirmary was moved to the first floor of Van Hoose when the male dormitory population increased in 1957–1958. The college physician continued to be Dr. Warren Gilbert.

Dieticians were Mrs. Jennie B. Hurst and Mrs. Willie R. Scarborough. Assisting in the kitchen and dining room for extended periods were Mrs. Evelyn Kelly, Spencer Hughes, Roy Barton, Roy Brannon, John Fielder, Howard Miller, Toney Penn, and Willie Morgan. After the seated meals were replaced by cafeteria service, dozens of students were given work scholarships. Major appliances were purchased and the entire area redecorated and enlarged. For the sake of the full-time employees, Sunday evening meals became sack lunches or buffets in the Rockery supervised by the councils or societies.

Night watchman John F. Stevens was described in these words: "Pistol Packin' Pop. . . . He is not a big man in size, but his heart extends out into the distance so far that miles won't measure it." His death in 1951, after twenty-two years at Shorter, was mourned—but he was not forgotten. Four years later some of his comments were still being printed in the *Periscope*: "I heard the moon was in a parcel clip last night"; "I got away from there so fast that I was a mile away before the grass straightened up where I'd been standing"; "I'm a setting on top of the world with both feet swinging." For nineteen years Janos Tamassy was also custodian. After reaching the rank of brigadier-general in the Hungarian army, he retired when the Nazis invaded his homeland and fled when the Soviet armies threatened. Surrendering social position and wealth, he and his wife valued freedom more and eventually immigrated to America. In 1952 both came to Shorter, where their popularity increased as that strange creature called the English language became a bit less strange to them.

The buildings and grounds were supervised by Lon Smith until his retirement in 1953 after thirty-two years at the college. He was succeeded briefly by Mrs. Hurst and she by Gilbert J. Davis for six years. Working with them were several men who spent a significant number of years at Shorter: Jessie Posey, John Perkins, John Posey, Carlton Morgan, and Sam Kemp.

Without consulting anyone, "cantankerous old Mrs. Harper" inexplicably moved from the Van Hoose to the Cooper attic, taking her "squeak machine" with her. In 1953 a long poem recorded an abundance of indispensable information concerning this rather shadowy member of the staff. She had nine children who had first appeared on campus only a few years earlier. A daughter Erleen (an earlier authority had spelled her name Erline) lived with her, and eight older sailor sons occasionally visited their mother and sister. At these times they usually moved furniture around in the freshman suites—always without being seen. At any time Erleen might slip the girls' possessions from their accustomed places. Each night footsteps could plainly be heard coming from the attic as Mrs. Harper and her daughter paced back and forth. Suddenly the noise subsided. As nearly as can be determined, the Harpers ended their association with the college in the summer of 1953, and they have not been heard of since.

Student Government and the Student Handbook

Significant changes came in the Student Government Association because of the boys on campus. The usual feminine officers of the Student Council and Honor Board were elected until the spring of 1955. Permitted by a change in the constitution, Jack Evans and Jimmy Ware became the first male members of the Student Council and Dan Chambers, of the Honor Board. Two years later the presence of more men and a men's dormitory made further alterations necessary. The Student Council and Honor Board dropped the requirement that a certain numbers of boys be included, and four young men won places solely on their own merits. Matters related only to dormitory life were handled by the newly organized Women's Dormitory and Men's Dormitory councils. Louise Mathis and Dick Starnes were the first to occupy the presidencies of these respective councils. Once hanging in the Student Council room on the second floor of Van Hoose, the large, framed copy of the Shorter Girls' Creed was relegated to a closet.

The student body met each Thursday at 7:00 P.M. for the occasional purpose of conducting serious business and the frequent purpose of being entertained. The Student Council usually met Monday at 10:30

P.M., when it planned for house parties, freshman orientation, various student socials, and May Day. Added in 1957 was a Freshman Council that assisted the parent body with its projects and conducted some of its own, such as cleaning up the campus and raising money by selling hot dogs.

The practice of emphasizing the significance of the Honor Pledge and Honor Board was retained. Honor Week came in October, consisting of two morning chapels with student and faculty speakers, group discussions one or two evenings, and a formal installation ceremony in the chapel on Thursday evening. Speakers included Ralph McGill of the Atlanta *Constitution*, Ernest C. Colwell of Emory University, and Ernest L. Wright of Darlington School. Another citadel fell in 1957 when the Honor Pledge first included an inclusive "him" instead of the dainty "her."

Composed of the presidents of all student organizations, the Key Club supervised a vast operation. It conducted all elections, formulated a schedule that allowed some students to attend more club meetings than classes, sponsored the ever-popular fire drills, and arranged for Sunday night suppers. In conjunction with the Student Council it maintained the point system that first took notice of the men in 1955. The Key Club had its first male president, Jack Evans, in 1957.

The S.G.A. held membership in the Southern Intercollegiate Association of Student Governments until 1955. Two Shorter girls usually went to the annual spring convention; in 1953 Ann Austin gave the opening speech at Dallas, Texas. Starting in 1954, membership was held in the National Student Association, and annual congresses were attended in Iowa, Minnesota, and Michigan.

Appearing each spring, the *Shorter College Student Handbook* included over a hundred pages devoted to greetings from administrative and student leaders, a calendar of events, songs, helpful hints, advertisements, and rules. For the first time, in 1955, a three-page section entitled "Regulations Concerning Written Work" was added.

Incapable of being overlooked within the mass of materials were the rules for the women students. Expanding from twenty-five to forty-nine pages, these regulations continued to govern attendance at chapel, vespers, and classes, the use of cars, card playing, dating and dancing, dormitory behavior, leaving the campus ("filing"), smoking, and wearing apparel. A prohibition of intoxicants was added in 1951. Bowing to advanced automotive design, the rule against riding on running boards was last printed in 1956—probably being dropped after the freshmen started asking what they were, in order to determine if the rule were capable of being broken. Further relaxations came with regard to turning out lights; the upperclassmen were finally allowed to keep theirs on all night if they wished and even the freshmen were sometimes permitted a 1:30 deadline. A complex system of penalties persisted, but at least the ambiguous "day" became a definite "demerit" in 1956.

Almost lost within the mass of materials were the rules for the men students. Growing from one-half page in 1954 to three in 1957, they prohibited alcoholic beverages and also governed smoking, various forms of recreation, wearing apparel, and acceptable hours for male town students to be on the campus.

Religion on Campus

Functioning as the coordinator of student religious life, the Shorter Christian Association maintained a varied program. Each spring the student body elected officers and other cabinet members, all of whom were inducted either at a candlelight vesper or during a morning chapel service. In 1955 boys were first named to the cabinet. As in years before, new members of the association were installed at a fall vesper service that started in the chapel and concluded with a candle-illumined circle on the lawn between the Fine Arts Building and Rome Hall. The pledge was read and the associational hymn, "Follow the Gleam," was sung. Later in the fall the cabinet selected a Freshman Commission. Early in this period an official seal was designed with a cross and open Bible as its focal points.

A mimeographed S.C.A. handbook outlined the regular activities for the new students who were its main readers. Much used was the S.C.A. room, attractively redecorated in 1951, which was located on the first floor of Van Hoose.

Although most Sunday and Tuesday vesper services were conducted by the girls, special guests contributed new faces and outlooks. Leo Aikman of the Atlanta *Constitution*, Dr. Paul McCommon of the Georgia Baptist Department of Church Music, the Darlington and Berry glee clubs, members of the Georgia Tech student body, and the film "Martin Luther" were featured at one time or another. Some years an evening fellowship furnished an opportunity for group discussions on relevant topics.

Raising money for as many as twenty-eight Thanksgiving baskets, the Halloween Carnival in the gym varied from year to year. At different times it consisted of games, candy, a faculty talent or fashion show, a white elephant sale, a jitterbug and costume contest, the selection of Shorter's ideal man, and a faculty auction. In the latter, the highest bidder might secure Mrs. Elliott to make her bed, a member of the music department to render a midnight serenade, or General Tamassy to kiss her hand. The queen was selected from the class which contributed the most money—and finally a queen *and* prince were crowned.

The S.C.A. often conducted a Thanksgiving service in one of the society halls. At Christmas children from the Open Door Home enjoyed a party that included gifts from the Eunomians and Polymnians. Some years an Easter egg hunt was sponsored for the same group. Religious Focus Week early in the second semester brought guests such as Carlyle Marney of Austin, Texas; Chester Swor of Jackson, Mississippi; Claude U. Broach of Charlotte, North Carolina; C. DeWitt Matthews of Macon; and Warren Carr of Durham, North Carolina. In 1956 a large team led by William Hall Preston of the Student Department of the Southern Baptist Convention provided seminars, class visitations, and discussion groups. Three Shorter alumnae returned to assist in various years: Miss Reid Maddox (class of 1952), Miss Clara Maddox (class of 1955), and Mrs. Norman P. Manning, Jr. (née Miss Ruth Parham, class of 1951), who was accompanied by her pastor-husband. A financial drive was conducted each year on behalf of the World University Service (earlier called the World Student Service Fund). Aiding students in depressed foreign countries with their education, Shorter annually contributed about $125. Other money was used to buy Christmas baskets for the poor, to help support an orphan under the Foster Parents Plan, or to furnish lunches for twelve grammar school children. Publication of "Hilltop Views," a weekly mimeographed news sheet, was resumed in the fifties. Throughout the period, morning watch was conducted five or six times each week.

Denominational clubs were encouraged, and several functioned during various years: the Wesley Foundation, Westminster Fellowship, Canterbury Club (which often included Lutheran students), and the Newman Club. Having the largest number, the Baptist Student Union often scheduled a freshman party, a progressive supper at several churches, Join the Church Sunday, and a Lottie Moon Christmas offering for foreign missions. Members were urged to attend the state-wide convention and the international students' retreat, and after 1950 a new blue school bus was available to transport the group that once reached twenty-five. In the spring, events included a big party, election of officers, an installation banquet, and a vocational emphasis week. Work days were annually held to assist the state B.S.U. in sending out summer missionaries. Dozens of Shorter girls participated in raising money; four participated as summer missionaries. Once a six-year-old lad from the Baptist Children's Home at Hapeville was adopted by the group. Deputation teams spread out, presenting programs at nearby churches and Battey Hospital. Each year the Young Woman's Auxiliary sponsored mission-centered activities, and some years a Baptist Training Union (said to be interdenominational) provided Sunday evening recreation and religious training.

The number of Shorter students interested in church-related vocations never fell below 12 in any single year and reached 40 in 1957–1958. These were divided as follows: ministerial, 15; missionary, 5; educational, 7; music, 13—and several were already pastors and ministers of music. In 1957 the Wright-Meredith Club was begun for the purpose of fellowship, instruction, and service. Honoring two Baptist foreign missionaries from Shorter, it was named for Miss Lucy Wright of China and Korea (class of 1916) and Miss Helen Meredith of Colombia (class of 1932).

Precise figures revealing denominational affiliations for the full-time students are known for only one year, 1954–1955. A total of 219 were distributed in this fashion: Baptists, 128; Methodists, 40; Presbyterians, 22; Episcopalians, 12; Lutherans, 4; Christians, 3; Congregationalists, 3; Roman Catholics, 3; Christian Science, 1; Church of God, 1; unaffiliated, 2.

Twice each week attendance at a morning assembly was required. Under the direction of the college administration, the program was often of a nonreligious nature but the term *chapel* persisted. Typical of these were presentations by Congressman Henderson L. Lanham, the Central Primary Boys' Chorus, Lamar Dodd of the University of Georgia, and a Wac officer. Dr. Gerald Priestly discussed India and Southeast Asia, and Edward Shorter, a third cousin of Alfred Shorter, lectured on modern painting. The major councils, the Honor Board, and various faculty members also participated. At other times, however, a religious service featured an American Bible Society representative, a nearby rabbi, Aubrey Hawkins of the Georgia Baptist Student Union, or a local pastor. Dr. Grace Sloan Overton spoke concerning marriage and the family. A concert was given by the School of Church Music Choir of the Southern Baptist Theological Seminary. One Christmas an English literature class staged a medieval nativity play.

Student Publications

Issued monthly from October to May, the *Periscope* was prepared by a student staff led by an editor who, during the Christenberry years, was removed from the point system and paid a small stipend. When the

Georgia Intercollegiate Press Association was formed in 1956, the *Periscope* secured membership. Always the issues included photographs and sometimes sketches or block prints. A red Santa Claus smiled from page one of the only two-color paper produced. Invariably carrying a few ads, the publication printed an occasional filler, "Patronize our Advertisers," when all else failed.

The literary magazine, the *Chimes*, was published twelve times in ten years, comprising eight to sixteen pages. Full of essays, short stories, poems, and book reviews, it utilized contributions from both students and faculty members. One remarkable item was a previously unpublished, unfinished autobiographical article by the eminent anthropologist and ethnologist, Franz Boas, furnished by his daughter. Covers were always made unique by block prints created especially for the periodical by art students. Rho Delta provided much of the leadership for this publication.

Under the direction of the senior class, the *Argo* appeared each spring. Unifying themes were sometimes selected—a motion picture; morning, afternoon, and night; autumn, winter, and spring; or college songs. The editors of two annuals gained inspiration by going back to Jason and his search for the Golden Fleece. Color faded from sight, except for one lone number that made some use of red. The ideal Shorter girl, various superlatives, and the most representative member of each class and the town girls' group were voted on by the students. In 1955 the most representative town boy was first named, Charles Williams. College beauties were determined by Ezio Pinza, Richard Rogers, Eddie Fisher, or young men from Emory, Georgia Tech, or the United States Naval Academy. Presumably because of increased local masculine insight, the 1958 beauties were cited by the Shorter students.

Intercollegiate Athletics Again—Permanently

Intramural athletic events were under the auspices of the Sports Association and its council. The officers and members of the council were elected each spring, followed by a brief installation ceremony in chapel that included the singing of "The White and Gold." Two male representatives were added by a 1955 constitutional change. Two years later that rule was removed, but two boys were elected just the same. The freshman counterpart, named the White and Gold, was formed by council appointment each fall. In addition to enlisting freshman interest, the members sold cokes and popcorn at games and once even cleaned out the courtyard fish pond.

The Sports Council published a mimeographed handbook several years and always invited the freshmen to a picnic and games each October. Also in the fall was Health Week, renamed Sports Week in 1953. Rules stressing proper diet, sleep, and exercise were to be followed, with a prize for the winning floor, class, or individuals—a party to initiate "Regain Your Health After Health Week Week," as a girl claimed. One specimen of good health composed "A Pome":

Eight more glasses and there won't be
Anything solid left of me.

At 4:30 each afternoon routine activities began: a whistle was followed by a yell, "Sports practice!" For the next ninety minutes, the injunction was usually observed: "Play carefully. The bone you break may be your own." Depending on the time of the year, the girls engaged in ping pong, horseshoes, badminton, archery, basketball, volley ball, softball, hiking, croquet, soccer, tennis, and shuffleboard. Fencing received a stimulus with the coming in 1949 of René Buday. A former Hungarian colonel whose wife was on the music faculty, he gave expert instruction. One club, the Aquamaids, was afloat in the early fifties. Several water shows were given, even though one blue member insisted: "Those icebergs floating in the pool were just a tad cool."

In May one chapel was devoted to Awards Day. A yellow S was presented to girls accumulating 220 points, earned at the rate of one point for every fifteen minutes of practice. Stars were added for those already owning letters. Trophies in remarkable variety were passed out for excellence in personal, class, generation, and society tournaments. A cup for the best all-round athlete was provided, and the names of two or three seniors were engraved on a plaque in recognition ("recognization," read one of the plaques!) of their sportsmanship, service, and participation.

A type of sweet revenge was gained as student teams played the faculty. A Play Day or house party often included such a contest—and if a faculty victory ever occurred, neither the extant school papers nor the faculty minutes mention it.

The association was a member of the Women's Division of the National Amateur Athletic Federation, the National Athletic Federation of College Women, and the Georgia Athletic Federation of College Women. The last named organization, composed of about fifteen schools, met at Shorter in 1951 and 1956, and Nancy Ann Chidsey was elected its president in 1953.

Intercollegiate sports returned to the college as a Shorter girls' all-star soccer team traveled to Carrollton in the fall of 1956 and played a West Georgia team to a scoreless tie. The return match was scheduled in Rome a full year later. When a rainstorm forced the girls inside, Shorter won four times in volley ball and lost once in basketball.

The boys' basketball team made its debut on Saturday night, December 7, 1957, in the college gym, with neither name nor uniform uniforms. Coached by William T. Jenkins, a history professor, Shorter easily defeated the Rome General Electric team 57 to 29. Two nights later on the same floor they battled a West Georgia team on even terms for 39½ minutes and then lost a heartbreaker, 63 to 62. In the early part of 1958, yellow and white uniforms were secured and games were played with Valdosta State, Berry, West Georgia, Oglethorpe, Troy State, and North Georgia. The season concluded with a disastrous 0–8 record against other colleges. Three other practice games with the Rome Y.M.C.A. team netted Shorter one more victory, giving them an overall 2–10 for the first year. To be fair, it must be observed that the coach and his boys were all volunteers, with no scholarships being given. In other intercollegiate action that year, the girls' basketball team lost to West Georgia and a mixed tennis team played matches with Berry, Piedmont, North Georgia, and West Georgia. Of continuing importance was the formation of the Georgia Intercollegiate Athletic Conference, occurring by action of Shorter and seven other schools announced in February of 1958.

The Two Societies

The Eunomians and Polymnians pursued prospective members with undiminished zeal. During the summer, rush letters were mailed and favors made. On the first Thursday of school the new girls received date books that were soon signed by members of the competing societies trying to make a good impression. They attended the Eunomian Perfume Party and the Polymnian Coke Party. Printed invitations were sent out for the coronations on the Friday and Saturday evenings of the first week. Prominently displaying its banner, each group lined the first floor hallway in Van Hoose and sang to the girls as they made their way to the other coronation. While they were gone, their beds were covered with "nighty-night notes" and various handmade favors—laundry bags, bath cloth dolls, and the like. Upon their return and after the freshman curfew, they were sung to a second time by the same society.

Held in Brookes Chapel, the coronations remained similar to those of earlier years. The Eunomian court appeared in pastel shades of the rainbow; the Polymnian, in white. Each group presented its traditional skit in the gym, where the queen and her court received the guests.

379

Rushing ended by 9:00 Sunday evening. The new girls spent the night in Cooper, while the old ones retired to Van Hoose and waited. One girl recalled "the tingly feeling we had when we leaned out Cooper window to shout 'Eunomian' or 'Polymnian'" about 10:00 P.M. Hanging out Van Hoose windows, the upperclassmen could hear the shouts and would know the approximate results in advance. During the remainder of the night the freshmen gathered in two groups, gave yells, wrote songs praising their new society, and just barely heard Mrs. Elliott suggest to no avail: "Isn't it about time to quiet down a little?" Sometime during the night each girl dressed in her society colors, and some of them spent the last remaining hours in the corridor near Van Hoose. One said: "After a night's sleep on the ice cream machine, we were in fine shape for the long dash." Because it was considered an honor to be the first to sign, the race began just as the bell rang and ended in Rome Hall where the pledge lists were located. The two winners wore the presidents' pins for the remainder of the day. Recognizing their pledges, the Eunomians went downtown for breakfast and the Polymnians, for lunch. Both had a theater party—and neither went to classes, because the Monday classes had been shifted to the previous Saturday or simply canceled. At a meeting in the fall, each society officially installed their new members who signed the scroll by candlelight. Six of the years the Polymnian Society had the greater number of members, averaging 89 to the Eunomians' 74 over the ten-year period.

Coming on Friday night, the society programs were marked by much singing. The Eunomians made frequent use of "Going Back" and "Eunomian Girl" and produced a new one in 1955, "Somewhere Over the Rainbow," that lasted until the color of the coronation dresses was changed eight years later. Across the hallway, "To Polymnian Queen" was newly composed and quickly popular. Programs were seldom entirely serious: a radio show sponsored by Cassey's Coffins, a Cave Woman skit, Ted Smack's Original Hamateur Hour, a Southern version of Romeo and Juliet, or one that "gave us much information we can carry on our honeymoons." Christmas parties included traditional skits and gifts of toys that were later turned over to the S.C.A. for the Open Door Home children. Santa Claus, Polymnia, Mammy, Amos and Andy, and Peter Pan visited one society; the other viewed a playlet, "Why the Chimes Rang" or later "The Littlest Angel." To perpetuate an earlier custom, the Polymnians observed their birthday in January with a large and lovely cake. Appropriately wearing green and singing Irish songs on St. Patrick's Day, the Eunomians introduced their own birthday cake in 1955. With frequency the meetings were punctuated with appeals to purchase stationery, monogramed bath cloths, mugs, shirts with society emblems, and pins. Members were advised to wear the S *above* the pin because Shorter was supposed to come before the society in their loyalty.

The respective society halls were furnished as carefully as finances would permit—the Eunomians were particularly proud of a piano purchased in 1951. When a complete redecoration was effected six years later, both societies sent a gift to Miss Griffin in thanks for her help.

Leaving their halls behind, the groups scheduled hay rides, had parties at the Shorter cabin, ate hamburgers in the Rockery, picnicked at Cave Spring, and gave swimming parties. Separately and together they sponsored sock hops the night before formal dances, since some of the boys had already arrived. To raise money for the new recreation room on the second floor of the gymnasium, the Polymnians put on a Chinese auction and the Eunomians charged for a picnic lunch. Providing diversion—and a chance to plan the next year's work—the Polymnians enjoyed summer house parties three or four times.

Elected in the spring, the officers were installed shortly thereafter at a dignified meeting where the outgoing queen made a speech and crowned her successor. For her year of leadership she was presented a piece of luggage or, more often, a silver tray. Each senior was also remembered with an inexpensive gift. Formerly made up of society leaders, the Thugs and H.O.T.s were allowed to lapse.

Constituting a major form of competition, the societies played softball, volley ball, basketball, and soccer. Cheerleaders led many a pep rally and urged the girls to attend the contests wearing society colors. In the spring the victorious society gained possession of the trophy which stayed in its hall—and which was *not* to be used as an ash tray, one president sternly announced to her group.

Another type of rivalry was furnished by the Student Council Scholarship Plaque for the society with the higher average. Of course each one had members on the honor roll, but it is true that the Eunomians won the plaque seventeen semesters and tied for the eighteenth.

A much-loved "joint society member" was the lonely Dr. Ware, who visited their meetings many times after the death of his wife. Inviting their dates to spend the night with him at the "Warehouse," he also offered to help the girls with their French or German homework. His 1956 illness was noted with concern and his recovery announced with relief. The older girls were encouraged to visit him—and to take the freshmen along so that they could get to know him too.

381

The Men's Club came into existence during the academic year 1951–1952, and the next *Argo* listed eight members. The group slowly increased, planning sock hops and student body programs by 1955–1956.

Emerging in the fall of 1956, the two fraternities were called the Alpha Lambda Epsilon and the Adelphians. Each one gave a party for new men, and a high percentage of the male students became members. In 1957–1958, 26 were ALEs and 18 were Adelphians.

The ALEs held a steak supper, a chicken fry, and a barbecue, made a fall trip to the Great Smokies and a spring trip to Allatoona, and "robbed" students and faculty members to raise money for the cancer drive. The Adelphians furnished Christmas baskets for two needy families, adopted a child from the Baptist Children's Home, helped to furnish the Shorter cabin, hosted a school-wide frankfurter fry, and enjoyed a Christmas party and a spring steak supper. During the spring of 1958 they selected their new name, Phi Delta Tau.

Competing for a men's sports trophy, the two groups vied in volley ball and basketball. First awarded in 1958, it was won by the ALEs.

Classes and Generations

"We shall always remember . . . those first few days on Shorter Hill and the lost feeling we had," admitted one student. Surely she soon discovered, however, that she had been found—by the sophomores. Another writer described her experience: "And then those sweet sophomores did an about-face, and we were plunged into the long dreaded 'Rat Week.' " Looking at the situation from the opposite vantage point, a member of "the sophomore pest control" confessed: "To begin the year with a bang we donned our black outfits complete with rat caps, scowls, and teeth clenched to hold back gales of laughter." Upon orders from their elders "all those cute little 'prospective rodents' " wore lamp shades on their heads, carried waste baskets for brief cases, painted their legs red and white in a barber pole effect, and displayed state-shaped signs around their necks. One year they appeared as fictional or historical characters—on that notable day Clara Bow, Captain Kidd, Superman, Napoleon, Pocahontas, and others visited the campus. Desirable postures were assumed as they obeyed orders: "Button down, rat!" or "Bow, rat!" or "Bird dog, rat!" Putting the new gym to a use not originally anticipated, the "blacksouled sophomores" conducted rat court, with the freshmen kneeling before them in abject lowliness. Yellow and white rat caps were distributed as a part of the proceedings, temporarily taken back in a way calculated to cause the greatest displeasure to the freshmen, and then later returned amidst much joy. Exuberance bordering on cruelty forced the dean of women some years to require that the sophomores present her a list of what they proposed to do with the freshmen. The custom spread to two distinguished rats in 1953. President Christenberry and Dean Gaustad were photographed in suitable attire and fishing in the courtyard pool. A student recommendation to drop ratting in 1957 fell on rocky hearts and the practice continued.

The four classes had rather similar activities, planned by girls in pajamas and housecoats bringing combs and bobby pins to roll their hair at class meetings. Athletic competition resulted in trophies being awarded each year. Greatly coveted was the inter-class sports cup for class interest and participation. Parties were held at the Shorter cabin. One year a "Yokel Square Dance" brought forth original performances from each class and a prize for the best one. An ambitious junior class decided to dredge "the Shorter Okeefenokee." Three months later the class spent a holiday at Fontana Village, North Carolina.

The relationship between the freshmen and juniors was quickly asserted as the older girls sang to their sister class during ratting. Later in the fall the freshmen elected their class officers under the watchful eyes of the juniors, who eventually made and gave them their class banner. Dressed as Christmas presents, the juniors might serenade the freshmen; usually consolation was offered during the first semester examinations as the juniors again presented a "Big Sister sing." Responding, the freshmen might gather in the courtyard, candles in hand, to entertain the juniors—and the sophomores and seniors listening in from the roof. Usually in the spring, a party honored the juniors. The relationship between the sophomores and seniors will be treated in a later section.

Riding on that New River Train, the odd-year classes were the High-Minded generation. Although they continued to be double-jointed, they composed new songs. With a silver ship as their symbol, the even-year classes were Whoop-Em-Ups. Indicating a persisting interest in the instruction of "chillun round the door," they added "Dreams" and other songs to their repertoire. The traditional wedding came to be called the Whoop-Em-Up Uniting Ceremony and was apparently last performed early in 1953.

The generation parties, planned by the younger class, included a sumptuous meal in the dining room and a presentation in the gym that might have as its theme a circus, Shorter State Fair, Uncle Remus, or

"A Modern Cindy Rella." In the fall of 1957 these were supplanted by a Stunt Night made up of twenty-minute skits by each class, thus reviving a practice last observed in 1951–1952. Victory no doubt tasted sweeter to the sophomores than the banquet that they would ordinarily have given to their seniors. By this constructive substitution, it was held, "the best of the clan functions has not been destroyed." The familiar colors continued, and generation names and numerals appeared prominently on the water tank. Although pages in the *Argo* were devoted to each group until the mid-fifties, the Owls and S.O.S. Club eventually disappeared. Both generations wore distinctively decorated shirts in 1955. Athletic rivalry focused on a trophy, awarded first in 1949 and won six of the ten years by the Whoop-Em-Ups.

After interest in the crook had diminished during the late forties, it virtually vanished from sight throughout the fifties. Last hidden in 1948, apparently thereafter it found ignominious lodging in a closet. Apart from a 1953 *Argo* photograph of it taken during a skit in chapel, it was seldom seen. Each year the *Student Handbook* ignored this forty-year-old tradition. Together with the running board, the crook had fallen by the wayside.

Other Forms of Recreation

Out of the Social Committee came the fourth major council as the Social Association with its Social Council was formed in 1949–1950. Its officers were named and installed in the spring. By a constitutional change in 1955, two boys were required to hold membership on the council; two years later this rule was removed. By that time, however, Budd Bishop had become the first male president of the organization. In 1953 the Cotillion Club was reorganized as a freshman adjunct to the Social Council. For a few years the council conducted an Etiquette or Social Week in an effort to develop social graces and pleasing personalities. Mimeographed booklets, "Socially Yours," were distributed in this connection.

The council sponsored three formal dances each year in the gym with decorations that might be suggested by Salvador Dali, the Old South, space travel, Dan Cupid, or a circus. Twice the recently paved tennis courts were used, but May air was found to be too frigid for comfort. Usually the dances were preceded by dinner in the dining room, accompanied by refreshments in the gym, and concluded by breakfast in the society halls. Many of the dates spent the weekend on campus, being fed in the dining room and housed in the basement of the gym where surplus Army bunks were placed. Beginning in 1957 these dances were held off the hill. In addition to these carefully planned formals, every year the Social Council sponsored numerous square dances, sock hops, and informal functions such as weiner roasts and hay rides.

That young men were occasionally thought about, even when the school was still only "-ed," was suggested by the *Argo* that included "Engaged, 4" or "Married, 4" along with other honors under some of the senior pictures. "Diamonds sparkling after Christmas holidays" were noted altogether without criticism, and a certain semimusical Peggy listed "Bach, Brahms, Beethoven, Bill!" on her bedroom bulletin board.

College rules related to dating young men gradually became less strict, at least in comparison with those of earlier years. The *Student Handbook* covered the subjects of chaperonage, dancing, filing, and riding limits in such detail that course credit probably should have been awarded for mastering the material. Instead, though, penalties were awarded to those who did not—or tried to skirt it.

During the first semester two events were anticipated with pleasure. A Thanksgiving party was planned for students and faculty. The traditional formal Christmas dinner with Santa Claus and gifts for the servants and faculty children was only one part of a second festive season. Robed choir members marched through the dormitories caroling. A contest might be held for the suite with the best decorations. Suggested by Mrs. Burts, Christmas cards were strung along the first floor corridor of Rome Hall. Sparkling trees in the society halls, a choral program that once consisted of "Amahl and the Night Visitors," and an art studio decorated with cherubs, cards, and mobiles—these all contributed to the occasion.

Although the traditional May Day program was omitted in 1949, it was resumed in 1950 with a humorous historical play, "Shorter Through the Years." Both artistic and scholarly, "A May Day Legend" was given twice, emphasizing the rebirth of nature and the victory of good over evil. Written and choreographed by Miss Franziska Boas, it included original music by Mrs. Charlotte McManamon (later Mrs. Vane) and utilized a setting and properties prepared under the direction of Miss Martha Griffin. Later productions were "Again We Wander" by Miss Boas and Mrs. McManamon, "Concerto Grosso" by Ernest Bloch, "The Playground" by James Broughton, and "As You Like It." The final May Day presentation came in 1958 with "And Winter's End" by Miss Boas, Mrs. Vane, and Richard Willis.

Other events provided brief surcease from classwork. The Shorter-Darlington talent show was once broadcast over WRGA from Brookes

Chapel. Sponsored by Fahy's or Esserman's, style shows in the gym utilized models chosen by student vote. A recreation room on the second floor of the gym furnished a juke box and various kinds of games, while a television room on the first floor of Rome Hall later furnished a quieter form of amusement. A popular gathering place was the book store in Rome Hall—but only because of its cokes, candy, ice cream, and sandwiches—and the nearby post office boxes. "Cooking the carcass out on the roof" between Cooper and Van Hoose was a pastime for "the patrons of the Rooftop Riviera." Vignettes of dormitory life were preserved in the *Chimes* and *Periscope*: water battles, pillow fights, "hen sessions," popcorn feasts, chow mein at 3:00 A.M., untold servings of toast and jelly, bridge games, "solid boogie woogie" over the radio, the happy laughter of a girl whose family or fiance had just called, reading the paper while waiting for the supper bell, and tending to the ever-present coffee pot. An unexpected fire in 1951 caused a Polymnian program to fall through because "all of the fire fighters took a nap." Three years later the campus was thrown into consternation when Don, a son of Miss Margaret Baskervill's dog Zipper, disappeared. Shorter girls and faculty members reported the case to the police, put up handbills, advertised over the radio and in the newspaper, and personally conducted a wide search. When the eighty-pound German police dog was located in Calhoun two weeks later—apparently he had walked the distance—he was accorded a gala welcome back to the campus, complete with a song in his honor. A flood in a junior suite came two years later on the "Night When the Lavatory Fell." It was reported that "Admiral Tamassy and the Bucket Brigade" hastened to the rescue. On some glorious days the snow fell, contributing to snowmen and sleds—and girls heavily bundled against the cold.

The Town Girls' Club was furnished a lounge, usually in Van Hoose Hall, where its members played canasta and bridge, studied a little, ate their lunches, and at least one year enjoyed a large picture of Marlon Brando. Parties were given for high school seniors, for the commuting freshmen in the fall, and for the entire club at Christmas and in the spring. When a town girl, Ann McCutcheon, was elected student body president in 1958, the group had a big celebration.

Seniors and Commencement

Symbolically vested with their caps and gowns at Class Day, the seniors officially wore them at several formal convocations and sometimes when their colleagues played their graduation recitals. Senior deference still appeared in the *Student Handbook*, at the dining room when the seniors entered first, and at least part of the time when they went up or down the stairways in front of the others or swept through a door held by a respectful underclassman. Senior Hall, Senior Den, and Senior Kitchen were under their jurisdiction. Dressed up and smiling for the photographer, they held coffees in the den. To set themselves apart from all the others, the "Forty-Niners" ordered green shirts with the Shorter seal on the front. Later, some seniors sold Japanese prints to remodel their den. In 1956 they earned $194 for the development fund by sponsoring a "Suppressed Desires Day."

Seniors and sophomores paid particular attention to each other as sister classes. Not unwilling to tease the others, one year the sophomores imitated the senior coffee—in the laundry room! At other times the seniors were treated with greater respect, receiving Whoop-Em-Up cups as Christmas presents. Centered in Snow White, the Wizard of Oz, or Candyland, a party each year until 1957 honored the seniors. Just before comprehensives jumpy senior nerves were calmed by soothing sophomore songs or by a party in the gym built on the theme, "The Lost Chord." Giving rise to many wisecracks, the daisy chain was the final sophomore tribute. Cars took the girls to distant fields for load after load that cost them briar scratches, mosquito bites, and blistered backs. Wrote one:

> Daisies, daisies, give me your answer true—
> Where, oh where can I find some more like you?

Wrote another: "After long periods of concentrated effort, daisy pickers have been known to pick daisies which were not even there. In fact, for days afterward they can see daisies everywhere—in bathtubs, books, and even in classrooms. Have you ever seen a professor who looked like a daisy?"

A time of "excitement, fear, sadness, confusion, and joy," commencement consumed two or three days. Usually the annual meeting of the General Alumnae Association occurred on Saturday in the chapel. This was followed by a luncheon, often in the Rockery. During the morning or afternoon the trustees held their annual meeting. Class Day in the Rockery came at 4:30. With the traditional procession, "Hail Dear Old Shorter," and the daisy chain, it provided moments both sad and funny as the seniors told their class history, dedicated their annual, and read their poem, prophecy, and last will and testament. Splendid in his white uniform, James F. West was commissioned as a second lieutenant in the United States Marine Corps at the 1958 ceremony. After dinner, a commencement play or fine arts festival occupied the chapel. At the First Baptist Church, the baccalaureate service Sunday morning included a sermon by a visitor. The Rome alumnae or the president of the college honored the seniors and guests with an informal reception late in the afternoon. A commencement concert and, often, another reception concluded the day. Graduation exercises, with an invited speaker, came at 10:30 Monday morning at Brookes Chapel. Commencement speakers included Senator Richard B. Russell, Mrs. Frank H. Leavell, Professor Paul M. Cousins and Dr. Willis B. Glover, Jr., of Mercer University, President Duke K. McCall of Southern Baptist Theological Seminary, Morris B. Abram of Atlanta, Searcy S. Garrison of Bull Street Baptist Church, Savannah, and Louie D. Newton of Druid Hills Baptist Church, Atlanta. The entire occasion was reduced to two days in 1957 when graduation was set for 2:30 Sunday afternoon and two receptions and one musical program were removed.

Awards in a multitude of academic areas were made during the commencement weekend. The best all-round senior and the senior with the highest average were recognized. In art, the Purchase, Buttolph, and American Crayon Company awards were usually given. The Imogen Coulter Award in English was continued by the Wyatt family. Prizes in music were maintained by the Cincinnati Conservatory and the Presser Foundation, and awards from the department were made to an outstanding sophomore and freshman almost every year. When deserved, Honors in Music were declared for graduating seniors. In dramatics, the Walter R. Thomas Award was usually given. Honoring excellence in religious writing, the Faust Award was reinstated and the Hazel Tuggle Ivey Award was initiated by that graduate of 1925. Established in 1956, the Helen Franklin Award was presented annually by Mrs. W. M. Page (née Miss Lucy Quillian, class of 1939) to the sophomore most nearly typifying "the radiant life" of an outstanding 1940 graduate, who, as Mrs. Jasper Hunt, died prematurely in 1955. In addition, other prizes were offered for brief periods in art, biology, French, German, mathematics, music, and speech. Earlier in the year additional persons were recognized—the two to four Argonauts, the four to six seniors included in *Who's Who Among Students in American Universities and Colleges*, and the small group of Sophomore Sabots.

The General Alumni Association

Because of an important twenty-five persons, the General Association of Alumni of Shorter College came into existence in 1958 as the earlier organization formally changed its name and included one alumnus, James W. Ware, III (class of 1956), on its executive board. The presidents of the association were Mrs. W. F. Barron, Miss Louise Bennet, Mrs. Harold N. Cooledge, Mrs. G. Eugene Ivey (née Miss Hazel Tuggle, class of 1925), and Mrs. Kenneth Olson, Jr. (née Miss Elizabeth Long, class of 1945). In 1952 Miss Bennet was named honorary president, a recognition accorded to only one other lady, Mrs. J. P. Cooper (née Miss Alice Allgood, class of 1884). Long-time officers were Mrs. L. G. Hardman, Jr., second vice-president, Miss Mabel Thompson, recording secretary, and Mrs. Aubrey Matthews, treasurer. Leadership was also furnished by Mrs. Lydia Dixon Sheppard, who was alumnae secretary from 1946 to 1955. At her departure the seniors and alumnae presented her with gifts and the seniors staged a "This is your Life" program. Miss Mary Hendon (class of 1955) was her successor for a few months, working chiefly with student recruitment. In 1956 Mrs. Ima Jean Kerce was appointed alumnae secretary, remaining to the present. The association joined the American Alumni Council in 1954. Since 1955 the alumni program has been financed by the college, and all alumni contributions have been channeled through the business office.

To draw the association together, two meetings were scheduled each year. Planned by the Atlanta chapter, the November luncheon attracted only fifty when subzero weather descended in 1950 and closer to one hundred when the weatherman got the Shorter spirit. Alumnae Day was held during commencement until 1956 when it was moved to May Day. In either case, the general meeting was followed by a luncheon in the dining room and an afternoon student program. Reunions were publicized for the graduates of two and five years and for earlier classes at five-year intervals. Beginning in 1954 the spring meeting recognized outstanding alumnae whose names were engraved on a plaque. Each was presented with a silver tray to mark the occasion. In the order of their selection they were: Miss Lucy Wright, Miss Helen Meredith, Mrs. W. Y. Quisenberry (née Miss Rosa Dykes, class of 1891), Mrs. F. W. DeFriece (née Miss Polly Massengill, class of 1917), Miss Minnie Merle David (class of 1906), Mrs. Harold N. Cooledge, and Mrs. W. M. Page. Golden anniversary certificates were first given in 1957, when the 128 eligible ladies either received them on Alumnae Day or by mail. Since then, they have been awarded to members of each class as their fiftieth year was reached. For a few years starting in 1948, an Argonaut alumnae breakfast was held at one of the downtown dining rooms. Composed of students closely related to Shorter alumnae, the Gamma Deltas went out of existence just before Dick Starnes' matriculation would have made appropriate a new name, the Gamma Chis.

Also serving to unify the association, about twenty-three alumnae issues of the *Shorter College Bulletin* appeared, ranging from a ten-page folder to a fifty-six-page magazine. Class news consumed much space, as did current college news stories and pictures. Edited by the alumnae secretary, the periodical was mailed to approximately two thousand persons.

By the very nature of their organization, the alumnae expressed an interest in Shorter's past. In 1950 the class of 1900 wrote a skit about their college years that was presented for them by several of the students, displayed memorabilia of their era, and led a memorial service at the graves of Alfred and Martha Shorter. At a 1952 meeting of the executive committee, after many yarns had been exchanged, Mrs. Rebekah Cooledge exclaimed: "Why don't we write a little book and call it *Do You Remember?*" Of course the present volume has neither the diminutive size nor the title contained in her suggestion, but at least its purpose is not dissimilar. A call went out two years later for memorabilia and for essays dealing with the earlier days of the college. To celebrate the eighty-fifth anniversary, Alumni Weekend, May 2–3, 1958, contained a pageant, "The Story of Shorter," presented in Brookes Chapel. Written in poetic form by Miss Mabel Thompson, it was accompanied by music composed by Richard Willis and choreography planned by Miss Franziska Boas. Further assistance was rendered by Mrs. Allie H. Richardson, Miss Martha Griffin, Miss Helen Dean Rhodes, and the Rome Little Theatre. The next afternoon more than forty antique cars, with many Shorter girls in period dresses, were driven down Broad Street, up the steep Clock Tower Hill, and back to the campus, where a picnic supper was provided in the Alumnae Garden. The pageant was again given on Saturday evening, May 30, in connection with the graduation ceremony conducted the following afternoon. With a picture of Alfred Shorter on its cover, the *Bulletin* issued in January of 1958 highlighted the anniversary. The Rome *News-Tribune* for June 1 included a special section congratulating the college.

The alumnae also expressed an interest in Shorter's present and future. During this decade they contributed in excess of $77,000, plus a significant amount to the development program. Stressed throughout the early fifties, the Loyalty Fund was designed to produce at least $2 annually from each member for financing the *Bulletin*. The alumnae proposed a campaign that was given urgency by an anonymous friend who offered $5,000 if they could raise $25,000. President Bennet wrote a Key Alumna in each important Georgia community, asking her to support a twelve-point program that included much more than merely the current fund-raising drive. Sixty responded to her challenge and three were named as Outstanding Keys: Mrs. Speer Burdette (née Miss Lotis Freeman, class of 1942), Mrs. George Burrus, Jr. (née Miss Effie May Pierce, class of 1900), and Mrs. J. C. Dixon (née Miss Blanche Williams, class of 1919). By 1952 the association had given or pledged only $14,000, but the friend remitted the full amount anyway. That year a $100-a-Year Club was established, but its membership roll seems never to have been crowded. Twenty-one joined in 1953 and eleven in 1954. During Mrs. Cooledge's presidency it was suggested that the alumnae refurnish the dormitories. "Bitter Suite" complained in a *Bulletin* that she had not owned a new dress in forty-four years and hoped that her name might soon become "Sweet Suite." Although the association was assured of a $5 profit on each Spra-Matic dishwasher that its members started to sell, most of the $5,000 actually received came from clean lucre and not because of sparkling dishes. Senior Hall received new metal furniture in the bedrooms as a result. Attempting to enlist each alumna in the Living Endowment program, which replaced the Loyalty Fund in 1957, the leaders of the association pointed out that if one could not contribute $1,000 to the endowment, at least she could contribute the equivalent, $30 annually. In the first year almost three hundred participants pledged $13,316.40, of which $7,527.65 was paid in cash. Other money was contributed at various times during this decade when Christmas cards and informal note paper with Shorter scenes were sold and when some of the reunion classes gave anniversary presents to their alma mater. Two gifts have been much used for almost two decades—a silver service, tray, punch ladle, and candelabra from an alumna, Mrs. F. W. DeFriece, and a silver coffee urn and tray from a trustee, Walter R. Thomas.

In another way the alumnae expressed an interest in Shorter's present and future. Well over half of the 1954 freshmen were influenced to come by graduates. A vice-president for each district in Georgia was appointed to work with the local high schools in planning their College Day programs. Local chapters of the association in Atlanta, Columbus, Tifton, LaGrange, Athens, and Rome brought prospects to the campus and held teas and luncheons in their honor.

Having earlier proved beyond dispute that Shorter graduates liked to eat, the association sponsored regional luncheons almost every year during this period. In 1953–1954 these were held at Thomasville, Perry, Chattanooga, Monroe, Columbus, Canton, Augusta, and Atlanta, with the new president, Dr. Christenberry, on each program. Ten were scheduled the next year at cities that included Tifton, Athens, Newnan, and Chipley. In other years, luncheons were also held at Albany, Savannah, Valdosta, Miami, and Jacksonville, Florida.

At one time or another, thirteen local chapters met in Georgia, Tennessee, New York, and the District of Columbia, of which three were consistently in thriving condition. Afternoon and evening groups in Atlanta worked on the fall luncheon and raised money by holding fashion shows, cooking schools, classes in flower arrangement, and benefit bridge and canasta parties. Issuing a gold and white printed yearbook, the Columbus chapter added to the Carter Harvey Scholarship Fund. Often on the campus, members of the Rome chapter feted freshmen each fall and seniors at some commencements. Seeking to contribute financially to the college, they sponsored a musical at the city auditorium, conducted rummage sales, and held benefit bridges. Not unlike the Shorter birthday parties of the following decade, a 1956 banquet under their auspices featured Clarence Walker of Atlanta as principal speaker.

8

A Revitalized College

The Coming of Randall H. Minor

Upon his election as president of Shorter College, Randall Hunter Minor said: "I am delighted to have the opportunity to go to Shorter. The fine reputation and esteem enjoyed by the institution, as well as the splendid faculty, will make it indeed a pleasure." Fourteen years later the chairman of the board of trustees, Lester Harbin, publicly commented on the event in these words: "Randall Minor accepted the position with alacrity because he was aware of Shorter's potential and her great heritage; but above all he was cognizant of the need for the special type of education that only an independent church-related college can offer. I have never known whether or not he knew what he was getting into when he accepted the presidency of Shorter, but I do know that shortly thereafter a little squib appeared in his office which says: 'When the going gets tough, the tough get going.'"

A native Georgian, Minor was born near Stone Mountain in 1908. He earned the Bachelor of Science and Master of Arts degrees from the University of Georgia. After eight years in the public school systems of Gwinnett and Jefferson counties, he transferred to Shannon, Georgia, in 1936. For twenty-two years he was principal of Model High School, and concurrently for nineteen years was in the public relations department of the Brighton division of Burlington Mills Company. He is married to the former Miss Eula Lewis of Anderson, South Carolina, and they have one daughter, Barbara (Mrs. P. Allen Dodd, Jr.), and two grandsons.

While living in Shannon, he and his family affiliated with the First Baptist Church of Rome, where he became a deacon and also a teacher and general superintendent of the Sunday school. He joined the Rome Kiwanis Club, and eventually was the local president. At various times he was president of the Rome and Floyd County Young Men's Christian Association, the local chapter of the American Red Cross, and the Rome United Givers. Membership in other civic and fraternal groups included the Cherokee Masonic Lodge. A leader in professional organizations, he was president of the Floyd County Education Association and the Seventh District Georgia High School

Association. In the spring of 1958, he was named president of the Georgia Education Association.

In April of that year a committee of Shorter trustees was appointed to secure a leader, and Minor was among those proposed. Faculty and staff members were quietly polled and indicated approval. He was thereupon elected president, effective July 15, 1958, and he and his family moved from Shannon to the campus.

Subsequently, Minor has maintained a position of religious, civic, and educational responsibility, and recognition has been accorded to him. Continuing as a deacon of the First Baptist Church, he was chair-

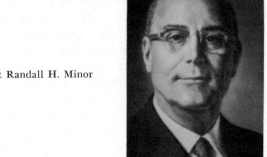

President Randall H. Minor

man of the board for a year. He has been lieutenant governor of the Eleventh District, Georgia, of the Kiwanis Club, president of the Bartow-Floyd-Polk Tuberculosis Association, and president of the Rome Civic Music Association. His leadership has been felt as president of the Georgia Foundation of Independent Colleges and of the Department of Higher Education of the G.E.A., as chairman of the endowment committee of the Georgia Baptist Convention, and as vice-chairman of the Education Commission of the Southern Baptist Convention. In 1959 Mercer University awarded him the honorary Doctor of Laws degree. He is listed in *Who's Who* and the *Dictionary of International Biography*. The students dedicated the 1962 *Argo* to him, describing him as one "whose faith in and devotion to Shorter College are surpassed only by his faith in and devotion to the students." "A decade of dedicated service" was noted in 1968 by the trustees who, as individuals, presented him and his wife with a three-week tour of Europe and the Holy Land. At that time the chairman of the board, T. M. Forbes, paid tribute: "We look forward to many more years of growth and progress at Shorter under the able administration of Randall Minor, educator, Baptist layman, and civic leader. It is with this trust that we thrust forward for a greater Shorter College." The trustees and some of the alumni gave an oil portrait of him, painted by A. Henry Nordhausen of New York City, to the college on Founders' Day of 1971.

The Campus

In 1958 conditions at Shorter College were showing mixed signs of prosperity and depression. Full-time enrollment had climbed to a thirty-year high of 243, part of the physical plant had been renovated, the endowment had grown in spite of two large encroachments, and Georgia Baptist Convention support had steadily been increased. On the other hand, as it had for more than a decade, the institution continued to operate at an annual deficit that in 1957–1958 amounted to about $25,000. Far from reversing this trend at once, President Minor fought a losing battle as he watched the deficit double during his first year. However, the institution has thereafter operated with a balanced budget each year except 1970–1971. The annual income has quadrupled. The student body, endowment, and annual support from the convention have each more than doubled. The value of the plant has risen eight-fold. An era of expansion has been experienced.

Enlargement of the Glass Corridor, started by Dr. Christenberry, was completed—in spite of the boys who swung monkeylike from the steel framework before the ceiling was installed—providing also a new sun deck for student recreation. Some new dormitory furniture was purchased. After the devastating ice storm in March of 1960, many small trees were set out to counteract the damage that had been done. About fifty thousand dollars was expended on these earliest projects. All of this was preliminary to a far-reaching financial drive that was to replace the 1955 development program which had virtually been concluded before Cecil Lea, director of development, left in 1960.

For a year discussions were carried on between the trustees and the president concerning the Library-Administration Building. Arthur Jackson, retired executive secretary of the Georgia Baptist Foundation, was secured as an assistant to the president in 1959. The trustees agreed to employ a professional fund-raising firm, and Phillip J. McLean and Ira C. Evans were brought in from Atlanta. Other positions of leadership were filled by W. H. Austin and Dr. Lee H. Battle.

A three-million-dollar development program was outlined in a number of brochures that included a handsome, yellow and white booklet entitled "Their Christian Future is in Your Hands." The immediate drive was for a more modest amount, $300,000, of which $230,000 would be matched by the Georgia Baptist Convention through a program devised in 1955. A local canvass was conducted, resulting in $139,264 in cash and pledges by June of 1960. Harvey and Elliott of Rome prepared plans for the building, and J. P. Roberts and Sons, Inc., of Rome presented the low bid of $306,294. The summer issue of the *Alumni Bulletin* proudly displayed a sketch and floor plan on its cover. During the same general period, Ledbetter-Johnson Construction Company of Rome paved a perimeter road, two new parking areas in front of the tennis courts, and another parking lot behind the new building, at a cost of $13,600. On Founders' Day, November 22, 1960, ground-breaking ceremonies were conducted. With small red shovels distributed for the occasion, everyone present assisted in excavating the basement. As construction progressed, pledges continued to be paid, and most of the $324,671 was made available when needed, either by the college or the convention.

The air-conditioned Library-Administration Building was occupied in the fall of 1961, although some classes and professors sat on the floor until all of the furniture and equipment arrived. Formally dedicating the structure on October 23, Dick H. Hall, president of the Georgia Baptist Convention, offered the prayer and Searcy S. Garrison, executive secretary of the convention, delivered the main address. Housing the library on the second floor and the administrative offices on the first, it was instantly popular with the students because of the snack bar and post office in the basement. Related to the former was the unsolved problem, often discussed by the Student Council, that *too much* student use was keeping it in constant disorder. Related to the latter was the *Periscope* report that when the Post Office Department finally required boxes to be kept locked, "campus communication temporarily collapsed." Along with the new building came an improved telephone system that extended service to virtually every office.

In addition, part of Rome Hall was renovated when the administrative offices and library were removed. At a cost of $20,900, Bradfield's, Inc., of Rome, altered all of the first floor and half of the second during the summer of 1961. Three hundred new desks were bought, together with some equipment for the science laboratories. An antique sale was advertised to dispose of the old classroom desks, but most of them apparently became kindling.

Although the new building was immediately the center of attraction, administrative attention was soon focused on the dormitories, present and proposed. In order to provide the radical repairs needed in Cooper and Van Hoose and a separate dormitory for the men, the college borrowed $650,000 from the Housing and Home Finance Agency in 1961. Approved by the Superior Court of Floyd County and the Georgia Baptist Convention, this sum is to be repaid with 3½ percent interest by the year 2001. A contract was awarded to Moses Construction Company of Rome, and half of Cooper Hall was renovated beginning in October of 1961. The girls doubled up, squeezing five or six into every available suite and making a shambles of closed study rules for freshmen. January 13, 1962, was moving day when fifty girls occupied new quarters with sparkling new furniture and bathrooms that elicited the exclamation, "Imagine, no rust spots in the tub!" More joyful young ladies were assigned to the remainder of Cooper during the spring. Half of Van Hoose was completed by the commencement of 1962 and the rest during the summer. The exterior appearance of the residence halls has been changed very little, but their interiors are, for all intents and purposes, those of completely new buildings. This portion of the building program cost about $300,000, plus about $60,000 for furniture and venetian blinds.

Meantime, the men were not being ignored. About 65 were housed in the Dining Hall Building on the top two floors. Utilizing plans drawn by Godwin and Beckett, architects of Atlanta, J. P. Roberts and Sons, Inc., erected a 126-man dormitory beyond the gymnasium, starting in the fall of 1961. Soon the *Alumni Bulletin* carried an architect's sketch of the new building on its cover. Ready for use and completely filled in the fall of 1962, it was dedicated on October 16. Hugh L. Smith of the First Baptist Church of Cedartown gave the prayer and Roy O. McClain of the First Baptist Church of Atlanta was the principal speaker. Some wondered how long this $390,000 building might stand, for the ceremony was held early in the week of the Cuban missile crisis—but the greater long-range threat, student occupation, has not yet weakened its foundations.

In the midst of this flurry of campus improvements, an unexpected opportunity was presented to purchase the George B. Smith home, High Acres, situated on seven acres adjoining the campus and facing Shorter Avenue. Designed by Pringle and Smith, architects of Atlanta, this Georgian mansion had been constructed in 1928. Asking $90,000 for it, the Smith family was willing to reduce the price by $15,000 if the college were interested. Early in 1962 various friends of the school were quietly approached by the trustees, and the convention quickly

High Acres

agreed to match their gifts. Later that spring the acquisition was announced, and a presidential residence exceeding even Maplehurst in
splendor was added. Hanging in the home are silhouettes of Alfred
and Martha Shorter cut when a French artist visited them at Thornwood.

Back on the main campus, the kitchen and dining room had been
repaired in the mid-fifties, but the other two floors had been left
virtually untouched. After consulting with Mrs. William J. Simpson
(née Miss Betty Altman, class of 1950), president of the General
Alumni Association, and other officers, President Minor proposed an
alumni-financed renovation to the trustees. Moses Construction Company was secured to do the job at a cost of $39,860. The Alumni As-
sociation in 1962 agreed to undertake a canvass with a goal of $20,000.
The Georgia Baptist Convention was to match these funds through
a new Capital Improvements and Endowment Program that had been
initiated in 1961. The remainder of the $650,000 loan was also ex-
pended. A carefully planned campaign among the alumni reached
its peak in November and December of 1962. The 350 pledges and
gifts exceeded eighteen thousand dollars, and $9,940 in cash was re-
ported in a public statement. Many of the other pledges have subsequently been paid. On December 1, 1962, the trustees voted to re-
name the building Alumni Hall "in appreciation of the loyal support
of Shorter Alumni." The invitation to attend Alumni Weekend in
1963 included this affirmation: "I know each of you will be interested

400

in seeing the two new buildings, and the renovations on the campus, especially ALUMNI HALL. We will be staying in Alumni Hall and what fun we'll have with our time of fellowship as we visit and re-live our college days." The third floor was made available for guests and an overflow of students, while the second floor once more accommodated the infirmary and faculty apartments.

For a full year changes in Rome Hall were discussed, and sketches involving half of the second floor and the entire third floor were prepared. During the summer of 1963 Bradfield's, Inc., completed these renovations and installed new laboratory equipment at a cost of $89,943. Although there were times during summer school when it seemed that classes on the first floor were being conducted in a machine shop or a boiler factory, reports of quality and convenience in the fall helped to heal the ruptured professorial eardrums.

The hyphen that was formerly in *coeducation* suddenly became two miles long in 1964 as the Greystone Hotel was purchased and converted into a men's dormitory. For two years the three dormitories on the main campus had been filled to capacity, making an expanded student body dependent upon additional living quarters. Built in 1934 on the site of the earlier Armstrong Hotel, with an eight-apartment annex constructed in 1936, the Greystone Hotel by the spring of 1964 had been closed to transient customers for eighteen months. With the approval of the Georgia Baptist Convention, the college bought the building for $225,000—said to be one-quarter the cost of erecting a new dormitory on campus. Private financing was secured at $5\frac{1}{2}$ percent interest, with payments to be completed by 1984. The seven-story, 123-room structure also includes apartments and a number of ground level business offices, the rentals from which are said to provide most of the funds for retiring the loan. After repairs and the addition of some new furniture, the dormitory opened that fall with 134 residents, housing a total of 153 during its first year of use. At that time, the former Men's Dormitory became Freshman Hall for women. Some boys have preferred to live on the main campus; in the fall of 1970 they finally returned when the third floor of Alumni Hall was again set aside for their use. This downtown acquisition has brought into daily prominence the yellow bus, sometimes called "the blond bomb," that had replaced "the blue goose" about 1962.

Under provisions of a will drawn by Ellis H. Peniston of Newnan, a memorial fund was established in honor of his late wife, the former Miss Mildred Arnall of the Shorter class of 1918. Accordingly, the new library was designated the Mildred Arnall Peniston Library and

401

an oil portrait of the honoree painted by Adolph Spohr of Cody, Wyoming, was given by Mrs. Peniston's sister, Mrs. E. K. Mann of Newnan (née Miss Myrtle Arnall, class of 1922). A service of dedication on May 11, 1965, included an address by Roger McDonald, pastor of the Central Baptist Church of Newnan, and the unveiling of the portrait by Miss Mildred Arnall Thomasson, a great-niece and namesake of Mrs. Peniston.

Unchanged but not forgotten was the Alice Allgood Cooper Fine Arts Building. Discussions concerning its renovation were instituted in 1962, Harvey and Elliott were employed as architects in 1963, and

Mrs. Mildred Arnall Peniston

a large loan was considered and rejected in 1964. During the spring of 1965, SOS came to the campus—the Spirit of Shorter campaign among students and parents, faculty and administration, alumni, and friends. Featuring Alfred Shorter (otherwise known as W. J. Neathery, the business manager) and his beloved wife (usually referred to as Randall H. Minor), chapel programs explained the drive. The classes competed in making pledges which amounted to about $10,000, with the sophomores emerging as the winners. Gifts from outside sources, matched by the convention, largely produced the requisite funds. At a cost of approximately $100,000, substantial alterations were completed during the summer of 1965 by Bradfield's, Inc. The basic plan of the building remains the same, but several changes are obvious— a permanently enlarged stage with new gold and white curtains in Brookes Chapel, new curtains and lighting in the Little Theater, an art gallery on the second floor, and an expanded art lecture room on the third.

With the last of the older buildings modernized and a second century of operation beginning in the immediate future, the Shorter College Fund of 1967 was conceived. Harvey and Elliott drew plans, while Ketchum, Inc., of Philadelphia, directed locally by Dallas Mackey, opened a campaign office at 310 Broad Street. Looking toward an immediate goal of $600,000 for a student center, every dollar of which would be matched by the convention, the plan also called for a fine arts auditorium, a library building, and recreational facilities. An attractive special issue of the *Bulletin* presented the project through a number of architect's sketches, and a large colored map of the

Walter Pope Binns

proposed campus was frequently displayed. Conducted early in 1967, the drive was led in Rome by Claude H. Booker, Albert C. Briley, Harry M. Oldham, W. H. Austin, Fred R. Johnson, Jr., N. N. Burnes, Jr., Victor B. Yeargan, Emory Ford, J. L. Todd, Howard R. Hart, W. R. Drew, and Glover Hogg. State chairmen were Alfred Lee Barron, W. F. Barron, W. E. Dillard, Sherman Drawdy, J. T. Roe, and W. D. Trippe. Initial gifts totaled $86,681, with pledges of double that amount. Other gifts and pledges have continued to be received; at the time of this writing about $516,000 has been contributed, with about $15,000 in outstanding pledges.

A contract was signed with Bradfield's, Inc., for $576,503, and the ensuing excavation soon received widespread attention. A 350-million-year-old Devonian fossil, the largest ever found in Georgia, was uncovered and placed in the Smithsonian Institute.

In August of 1967 a gift of $150,000 from the Callaway Foundation, Inc., of LaGrange, was announced—affording a total of twice that

The Walter Pope Binns Student Center was dedicated on October 23, 1968. Shown on the left is Mrs. Walter Pope Binns; in the center, Miss Alma Hunt; and on the right, Fuller E. Callaway, Jr.

amount because of the convention's matching program. At the request of the Callaway family, the structure was named the Walter Pope Binns Student Center, in honor of a former pastor of the First Baptist Church of LaGrange. This prominent clergyman-educator served churches in Georgia, Kentucky, and Virginia for twenty-five years and was president of William Jewell College, Liberty, Missouri, from 1943 to 1962. On October 23, 1968, a service of dedication was held in the large, cathedral-ceilinged dining room, with Fuller E. Callaway, Jr., and thirty-five Binns relatives in attendance. The main speaker was Miss Alma Hunt, executive secretary of the Woman's Missionary Union of the Southern Baptist Convention and a long-time friend of the Binns family. Unveiled by Mrs. Walter Pope Binns, the metal plaque reads in part: "Dedicated by Callaway Foundation, Incorporated, in memory of Dr. Walter Pope Binns, Pastor, Educator, Statesman of The Southern Baptist Convention. To know him was to know the meaning of the word integrity." A dedication issue of the *Bulletin* that fall contained an illustrated report of the event which included the text of Miss Hunt's address.

The air-conditioned $600,000 facility includes on the third floor additional space for the library and the Memorabilia Room of the Alumni Association. On the second floor are student and administrative offices, a recreation room furnished by Mr. and Mrs. J. R. Eubanks of Atlanta, a room with a color television set given by the Shorter Circle K Club, a locker room for the convenience of day students, a large lounging area, and a conference room. On the first floor are the book store, snack bar, post office, kitchen, and dining room. Until new equipment could be secured, regular patrons of the dining room consumed their meals from paper plates, using plastic utensils. Within six months the first floor of Alumni Hall had been redesigned to include faculty offices, classrooms, an educational materials center, a business machines room, and a $30,000 Raytheon electronic language

Mrs. Cully A. Cobb

laboratory that was installed under the direction of Dr. Frances Muldrow.

On June 24, 1969, a service of dedication was held for the Lois Dowdle Cobb Dining Room in memory of Mr. and Mrs. Lovett Pierce Dowdle. Mrs. Cully A. Cobb of Decatur (née Miss Lois Dowdle, a Shorter student in 1904–1905) made the presentation, accompanied by her husband who is now a trustee of the college. She honored her father, a Rome businessman, and her mother, who, she asserted, "raised me in a Christian home and knew the value of a Christian education." The dedicatory address was delivered by Louie D. Newton, pastor emeritus of the Druid Hills Baptist Church, Atlanta. An oil portrait of Mrs. Cobb, painted by Mrs. Grace T. Knapp of Decatur, hangs in the room which is located on the first floor of the Library-Administration Building.

More recent additions to the campus include much new carpeting in faculty housing. Because of this gift by I. V. Chandler of Dalton in honor of his wife, a 1929 graduate of Shorter, the middle faculty apartment building has been named the Ethel Meredith Chandler Building. A greenhouse and an archaeology laboratory have been built near the power plant. Between the gymnasium and the perimeter road a ninety-foot-tall water tank with a capacity of 165,000 gallons has been installed, and the old one will be removed. The tennis courts have been turned ninety degrees and resurfaced.

During the summer of 1972 several projects were completed. Air-conditioners were placed in some dormitory bedrooms. Some exterior and interior repainting was done on all five of the 1911 buildings. Some attention was paid to the grounds.

Significant additions to instructional equipment were made from 1969 to 1971 by the expenditure of $50,000, half of which came from the Educational Opportunity Grant program.

Twice in this period the land holdings of the college have been slightly diminished. In 1959 a lot on Horseleg Creek Road was sold for $9,250. Nine years later the Radio Springs cottage was disposed of for $1,400.

It is patent that important contributions have been made, enabling the college to expend almost $3 million on capital improvements since 1958. Four financial programs by the Georgia Baptist Convention have assisted this expansion. In each case, every dollar provided by the convention has been matched by the school. Completing the 1955 Capital Improvements and Repairs Program, the convention gave $227,137.83 from 1959 to 1961 for buildings. From 1961 to 1965 it sponsored a Capital Improvements and Endowment Program, adding to the Georgia Baptist Foundation $340,000 that continues to act as a part of the Shorter endowment, while the college raised a corresponding amount for campus improvements. A similar program extended from 1965 to 1970, when the convention placed $300,000 in the foundation as endowment and allocated $300,000 more for capital improvements. In 1970 the most recent program was adopted, being in operation less than two years at this time. $36,702.35 has gone to the college for the building program, $36,702.35 to the foundation for general endowment, and $73,404.70 to the foundation for a scholarship fund. In thirteen years the convention has contributed $563,840.18 for capital improvements, as a part of a total gift to the institution of over $2¼ million.

Many other sizable amounts have come from private individuals and organizations: Mrs. Robert O. Arnold of Covington (née Miss Florence Turner, class of 1923) ; Battey Machinery Company of Rome; W. C. and Sarah H. Bradley Foundation of Columbus; Mrs. Clarence

Cross of Colquitt (née Miss Mildred Pidcock, class of 1926) ; C. D. Ellis of Savannah; First Baptist Church of Rome; First National Bank of Rome; John and Mary Franklin Foundation, Inc., of Atlanta; Georgia Power Company of Atlanta; John H. Harland Company Foundation of Atlanta; Fox-Heyman Foundation of Rome (Mrs. Lyons J. Heyman is the former Miss Jo Marks, class of 1950) ; A. W. Ledbetter Foundation of Rome; Mrs. Emil K. Mann of Newnan; Massengill-DeFriece Foundation, Inc., of Bristol, Tennessee (Mrs. F. W. DeFriece is the former Miss Pauline Massengill, class of 1917) ; National City Bank of Rome; Patterson-Barclay Foundation, Inc., of Atlanta; Mrs. D. E. Pinkston of Hogansville (née Miss Martha Ware, class of 1919) ; Rome Coca-Cola Bottling Company; Edward S. Shorter of Columbus; Southeastern Mills, Inc., of Rome; Texaco, Inc., of New York City; Mrs. Alfred Thompson of Atlanta (née Miss Evelyn Sheffield, class of 1926) ; Trust Company of Georgia Foundation of Atlanta; Lawrence Willet of Atlanta; and two others wishing to remain anonymous.

At the beginning of the present administration, the physical plant was declared to be worth $609,362. In 1969 the first complete reappraisal in forty-six years was made by the Hardy Realty and Development Company of Rome. In the 1971 audit, the plant funds stood at $5,047,548.

Endowment

While the building program has been emphasized, the endowment has also been given considerable attention. Growing from $706,226 in 1958 to $1,880,444 in 1971, it has benefited from several notable gifts. The Georgia Baptist Convention has placed $750,107.05 in the Georgia Baptist Foundation to the credit of Shorter College since 1961 as a part of three Capital Improvement and Endowment programs. In 1968 the estate of Martin Clyde Roberts, a Shorter trustee from Ball Ground, provided stocks, valued currently at $83,266.50. The following year Judson Roberts, a brother of Martin Clyde Roberts, gave stocks now valued at about $100,000, the proceeds from which are used for scholarships. More recently his estate has provided additional assets for the general endowment, raising the total of his contributions to over $300,000. Honoring the Roberts brothers—these two, plus A. Webb Roberts of Dallas, Texas—Freshman Hall for women was named Roberts Hall in 1972. Announced in 1971, the Allie Hayes Richardson Trust Fund is comprised of $177,402 in stocks,

407

and functions as a revolving loan fund for educational purposes. Mrs. Richardson became professor emeritus of speech in 1961 after forty-three years at Shorter, willing her assets to a niece, Miss Cecil S. Ramsay of Toccoa, who later left them to the college. In recent months two further scholarship funds have been established within the endowment—one by Mr. and Mrs. Cully A. Cobb of Decatur in the amount of $20,000 and another by Mrs. F. W. DeFriece of Bristol, Tennessee, in the amount of $25,000. Since 1958 the total value of the college has risen more than five-fold to $7,910,957.

Martin Clyde Roberts   Judson Roberts   A. Webb Roberts

Enrollment

Classes opened in the fall of 1958 with 269 students. Each fall thereafter the number grew steadily until 754 full-time students were present in 1965. Thereafter the total diminished each year until the decline was countered in 1971 when 515 full-time students reported for classes.

The total number of full-time students in any single year has varied from 284 in 1958–1959 to 814 in 1965–1966, and has averaged 595 over a thirteen-year period. Part-time students have ranged from 47 to 137, with an average of 97. Summer schools have grown from a low of 162 in 1959 to a high of 365 in 1966, averaging about 295. The total student body for twelve months has averaged 820 thus far in this administration.

In the fall of 1958 almost forty percent of the full-time students were men. The male population grew to forty-seven percent in 1962–1963 and is presently about forty-three percent. For the first time, in 1971, men graduates outnumbered the women, 57 to 52.

Dormitory facilities for the men were filled to comfortable capacity from 1960 to 1966, although others could have been crowded into the Greystone. Overall, the men's dormitory space has averaged almost ninety percent occupancy. Only once or twice have the girls' dormitories been completely filled, and their rate of usage has been about

Mrs. Allie Hayes Richardson

eighty percent.

The number of full-time day students has risen and fallen, from 130 in 1958–1959 to 351 in 1966–1967 to 194 in 1971–1972. The percentage has likewise fallen, from a high of fifty-six to a current low of thirty-six. This may be attributed to the proliferation of low-cost junior colleges throughout the area.

The executive committee of the trustees on March 8, 1965, expressed "general concurrence" with a resolution that "the administrative officers of Shorter College be authorized to process applications from any qualified prospective students and to sign an Assurance of Compliance with Title VI of the Civil Rights Act of 1964." Although some Negro students had enrolled in summer classes during the early sixties, the first such graduate was Mrs. Agnes Rounsaville, in 1967. A few full-time students have been black, occasionally occupying rooms in the residence halls. Some have held the presidencies of the Honor Board and Shorter Christian Association, entered the Miss Shorter Pageant,

409

written for the *Periscope,* played varsity basketball, been listed in *Who's Who Among Students in American Universities and Colleges,* and been included on the dean's list.

Although Shorter has become increasingly cosmopolitan, about eighty-four percent of its students still come from Georgia. Florida has consistently furnished the second largest group. Outside of the Southeast, New Jersey and New York have sent numerous persons also. Ten foreign countries have accounted for as many graduates: Ecuador, Taiwan, Italy, Bermuda, Israel, Iceland, Argentina, Brazil, Norway, and France. At least twenty-three other countries have been represented.

Student recruitment has been carried on with vigor, with many persons traveling for the college. Brochures have been developed of restricted departmental interest, one was aimed at the junior college graduate, three were colored reprints of the opening pages of different annuals, and five were attractive mini-catalogues. The regular catalogues, usually containing campus pictures, have been widely useful. High schools over the state have heard programs by various music and speech groups. Talks for teachers' organizations, secondary school and junior college classes and assemblies, and parents' clubs have frequently been given. House parties on campus virtually every semester bring numerous prospects to Rome. Others have visited the school while participating in music festivals or literary, commercial, or home economics meets and when touring individual departments as a part of a field trip. Each summer since 1963 a rising senior in the top ten percent of his class from each nearby high school has been invited to take two Shorter courses free, with college credit given to those who later enroll as freshmen at Shorter. Approximately 120 have participated in this program. For several years a Science Career Day was held at Shorter in the fall. Alumni-sponsored coke parties in many cities have produced favorable publicity for the college. Advertisements have been placed with regularity in newspapers of the region—and occasionally in the *Christian Index,* the *Georgia County Government Magazine,* and the *Christian Science Monitor.*

Tuition, Fees, and Student Aid

In keeping with the direction and pace of the national economy, the cost of attending Shorter College has doubled. The average student in 1958–1959 paid $1,180 for a nine-month course of study, room, and board, with $150 added for music lessons and practice fees. The average cost in 1971–1972 was $2,120, with $300 added for music and

410

another $50 for a private room. Since 1962 medical and accident insurance has been required. For those driving automobiles on campus, a small fee has been levied for a parking sticker since 1961.

These charges are reduced for many who are awarded scholarships or occupy student positions. All of the earlier scholarship and loan funds have been continued, and others have been added. The Allie Hayes Richardson, Judson Roberts, Cobb, and DeFriece funds have already been described. The college offers academic, music, and athletic scholarships, not underwritten by endowment funds, that have totaled from $27,300 to $135,000 each year and have averaged about $42,500. Tuition has regularly been remitted for dependents of Shorter personnel—children, wives, and even one husband. Discounts are allowed to the children of ministers and to two or more full-time students from the same family. Beginning in 1967, Economic Opportunity Grants from the Department of Health, Education, and Welfare have been provided to about 100 students for a total of almost $62,000. In 1969 the Rome Council on Human Relations instituted a scholarship. The Georgia Baptist Convention continues to aid in the education of students training for church-related vocations, having given $48,440 in thirteen years. From the Georgia State Department of Education, money is available for those planning to teach in the state after graduation. Tuition grants from the State of Georgia were funded in 1972 for students attending nonpublic colleges—including Shorter, of course. Under its provisions, each Georgia student will receive up to $400 per year, starting with the 1972 freshman and sophomore classes.

National Defense Student Loans have been available since 1959, furnishing about $3/4 million to almost 900 students. Under this program, ten percent of the total has been allocated by the college and will eventually be repaid to it, while the remainder has come from the United States Treasury on the same basis.

In many parts of the college, students occupy positions for which they are paid. Receiving a total of $6,434 to $24,763 annually, these students have averaged almost $17,000 each year.

While the Gross National Product has doubled in the past thirteen years, the annual income of the college has quadrupled, growing from $301,739 in 1958–1959 to $1,319,394 in 1970–1971. Each year except two—the first and 1970–1971—the current income has exceeded the operating budget, and the annual average over the entire period has been about $78,000.

In addition to student charges and endowment income that have risen, several contributions have also helped to keep the budget bal-

411

anced. An anonymous grant of $100,000 has been made. Shorter's involvement with the Georgia Foundation for Independent Colleges, Inc., has produced total gifts of approximately $225,000. The Georgia Baptist Convention has increased its allocation to the operating budget each year, from a low of $44,992 to a high of $113,796, providing in this period $1,012,540 for this object. As has already been seen, to this must be added funds for capital improvements, endowment, and ministerial education, resulting in a thirteen-year grand total of $2,374,927.23.

One future contribution in this connection is already a matter of

John H. Jackson

public record. From the estate of the late John H. Jackson, a Rome real estate manager, more than $100,000 will be realized for current operations.

Trustees

Control of the college legally rests in the hands of its board of trustees elected by the Georgia Baptist Convention. Comprised at first of sixteen regular and two alumnae members, it was expanded in 1960 to thirty. The term of office is five years, and no person may be re-elected until at least one year has been spent off the board. Since 1962 the convention has required that at least one-fourth of the members be Baptist ministers. Meeting usually in May and November, the board appoints committees which assist in its operation: executive, finance, buildings and grounds, and development. Established by the trustees in 1967, an advisory board is made up of about thirty past trustees and

412

others, the purpose of which is "to aid the present and future program of the college."

Eight men have served as chairman of the board: Walter R. Thomas, an Atlanta jeweler (1957–1959) ; Norman N. Burnes, Jr., a Rome businessman (1959–1960) ; Claude H. Booker, a Rome banker (1960–1961, 1964–1967) ; Fred R. Johnson, Sr., a Rome businessman (1961–1964) ; T. M. Forbes, a retired Atlanta textile executive (1967–1970) ; Dr. Lester Harbin, a Rome physician (1952–1957, 1970–1971) ; and J. R. Eubanks, an Atlanta entrepreneur (1971 to the present).

| W. F. Barron | Walter R. Thomas | Norman N. Burnes, Jr. |

After twenty-nine years as a trustee, W. F. Barron resigned in 1959. The board has included eleven Shorter alumni: Mrs. Robert O. Arnold of Covington; Mrs. B. M. Blackburn of Newnan (née Miss Ruth Cole, a student in 1905–1906) ; Mrs. Clarence Cross of Colquitt; Miss Martha C. Galt of Canton (class of 1915) ; Mrs. L. G. Hardman, Jr., of Commerce (née Miss Dorothy Shell, class of 1932) ; Mrs. John Turner McCall of Rome (née Miss Annie Maude Wheat, class of 1938) ; Mrs. Emil K. Mann of Newnan; Mrs. L. T. Outler of Moultrie (née Miss Kathreen Coram, class of 1917) ; W. R. Simmone of Smyrna (class of 1958) ; Mrs. W. S. Taylor of Atlanta (née Miss Norwood Key, class of 1915) ; and Miss Mabel Thompson of Rome (class of 1924).

Aware of support given to the college by friends of the past and present, the trustees have seen fit to honor five such persons alive at the time of their citation. At the 1960 graduation ceremony, Bunyan

Stephens, pastor emeritus of the First Baptist Church of Rome, was given a certificate "In Apreciation for Faithfulness in Service, Leadership in the Denomination and Loyal Support of Christian Education." The board cited four men "for unusual service" at the 1971 Founders' Day ceremony: W. F. Barron, F. S. Cooper, and Aubrey Matthews, former trustees, and Paul M. Cousins, former president. Their photographs hang in the newly created Hall of Honor in the Library-Administration Building. It is anticipated that other persons will be selected for inclusion in later years.

Claude H. Booker   Fred R. Johnson, Sr.   T. M. Forbes

Community Relations

Because "Shorter College contributes to the religious life of the community, state, and nation," has had an "economic impact upon the city and county," and "continues to make a cultural contribution whose value to the area is immeasurable," local officials designated November 19, 1963, as Shorter College Day in Rome and Floyd County. Over a wide expanse, Shorter has attempted to occupy an integral—and sometimes scenic—part in the life of the community. The Miss Rome Pageant staged by the Jaycees had contestants from Shorter, two of whom—Janette Rossman and Dee Genet—won the crown. Musicians and speakers have provided programs at civic and fraternal clubs all over Northwest Georgia. The Rome Rooster Boosters Club breakfast and district Kiwanis rallies were held on campus. Students and faculty

414

members have appeared at nearby meetings of the Daughters of the American Revolution, the United Daughters of the Confederacy, garden clubs, and business and professional women's associations. The American Association of University Women, the Alpha Delta Kappa teachers' sorority, and many Parent-Teacher associations have heard a variety of Shorter personnel. Educators have used the Shorter dining room with some frequency: district art teachers, STAR students and teachers, district high school principals, and the Georgia State Board of Education. All sorts of high school competitions have been scheduled

Dr. Lester Harbin   J. R. Eubanks

on campus, and the faculty and student body have often furnished judges. At times the Rome Mineral Society has met at Shorter.

Numerous classes have been aimed at the local community. Saturday art classes were popular until they were discontinued in 1963. Music lessons for townspeople are available. Late afternoon and early evening classes have been scheduled by virtually every department, with concentrated offerings in education, psychology, humanities, and earth science. The 1970–1971 Shorter College Personal Enrichment Program provided twenty-six courses, ranging from noncredit classes in photography and Christmas crafts to full credit work in New Testament Greek.

In the early sixties the local civil defense agency was permitted the use of campus areas for fallout shelters. Later a sixteen-hour civil defense course was conducted on campus.

For many years the faculty has been canvassed for the American Cancer Society and the United Fund of Rome and Floyd County, with almost one hundred percent cooperation.

Extending Shorter's name beyond the state, a 1968 *Time* advertisement invited its readers in Southeast United States to "Stand with Shorter. . . . Home of Student Movements You'll Be Proud to Support!" The following year the art and geology departments entered displays at Atlanta's Lenox Square, suggesting that their viewers "Stay and See Shorter."

The Rome Little Theatre has frequently received Shorter support in the form of technical assistance and some cast members.

In the area of music, Shorter has consistently related herself to the region. The Camerata Concert Series has been open to the public, usually without charge. The Christmas and spring choral concerts have honored the Reverend and Mrs. Bunyan Stephens, Ernest L. Wright, Mrs. Edith Lester Harbin, the Rome Music Lovers' Club, Miss Louise Thompson, the religious workers of the county, and the city of Rome. Singing groups have been heard over local radio stations and seen on several Atlanta television programs. The Rome Music Lovers' Club has heard almost every member of the music faculty and many student groups, has met in Brookes Chapel, has been given leadership by several Shorter persons, and receives the cooperation of the college in observing National Music Week each spring. On occasion, the college has furnished programs for music clubs in Atlanta, Cedartown, and Chattanooga. Twice during this period the Georgia Federation of Music Clubs has convened in Rome and has each time visited the campus for a concert. The Rome Music Teachers Association often utilizes Brookes Chapel, and in 1961 the Georgia Music Teachers Association held its annual convention at Shorter. The college also hosted the Atlanta chapter of the American Guild of Organists in 1961. A co-founder of the Rome Community Chorus, John Ramsaur was its director for the few years of its life. More recently, Robert Jones has directed the Rome Boys' Club Choir. Students and faculty members have performed with the Rome Symphony Orchestra, which frequently rehearses on campus, and guest artists have been drawn from the faculty. Over the years the Rome Community Concert Association has benefited from Shorter leadership and has sold memberships to many college people. An anonymous donor has for two years made it possible for faculty and students to attend concerts without cost. In recent seasons, members of the music staff have previewed various operas to be presented in Atlanta.

In the area of religion, Shorter has also consistently related herself

416

to this region. Local churches have heard student music and speech groups. Professional church musicians have included Mr. and Mrs. John Ramsaur, David Beaty, Jerry Warren, C. Edward Spann, Robert Jones, and many students. The Georgia Baptist Department of Church Music has called upon Ramsaur, Jones, and Warren for leadership. Until 1964 the state-wide music camp brought approximately 150 participants to the campus each summer. Likewise, camps sponsored by local churches and Baptist associations have utilized college facilities. Almost every spring the regional Training Union Conference meets in the college chapel with as many as 200 visitors present. Usually the Easter sunrise service is conducted on the hill. Interim pastorates have been held by Cecil Lea, J. Samuel Johnson, Charles W. Whitworth, Joe R. Baskin, and Robert G. Gardner, and numerous pastorates have been filled by students. In the fall of 1958 the Northwest Georgia Baptist Ministers' Conference was formed at Shorter and has subsequently met there three times each year. The spring conference was often held in connection with the Church Vocations Institute that brought outstanding leaders to share their insights with students and ministers. Finally, hundred of students and faculty members have participated as laymen in the work of many local churches.

General Academic Matters

A statement of guiding principles for Shorter College was written in 1970 by Joe R. Baskin, was officially adopted by the faculty, and now appears in the catalogue under the title, "What we stand for." It asserts: "Shorter stands for excellence in the pursuit of knowledge. . . . Shorter stands for Christian values. . . . Shorter stands for the importance of the individual. . . . Shorter stands for respect for others, without which mankind can make no progress."

Admissions policies have changed in three important respects during this period. Early admissions was provided beginning in the mid-sixties for high school students completing their junior year whose academic records and standardized test scores merit special consideration. By 1969 a limited amount of college credit was being allowed for advanced placement tests based on superior high school courses paralleling Shorter's offerings. Some use has been made of the College Level Examination Program, and up to 30 s.h. are allowed for the successful completion of sufficient tests.

As the opening of school approaches, student leaders gather for a multitude of planning sessions. Arriving on Sunday, new students are greeted by sorority, Shorter Christian Association, or Baptist Student

Union welcome booths and refreshment stands. There follow assemblies in the chapel and orientation classes, accompanied most years by tests. Answers are often unpredictable—and not entirely accurate: the three branches of student government are the B.S.U., Student Council, and Honor Society; the name of the school paper is the *Periwinkle*; the yearbook is the *Yalbo*. Mixers partially fulfill their function, aided by innumerable other get-togethers.

The opening week includes matters of academic import also. Placement tests in swimming, mathematics, and languages precede conferences with the faculty adviser assigned to each freshman. Held in the gymnasium, the old student center (formerly called the Glass Corridor), or the new library, "the chaos of Registration" was alleged by one *Periscope* reporter to bring about "sore feet and frustration . . . ." Until the mid-sixties, the prior work of preregistration by the upperclassmen was undone at this time! As a part of the registration process, by 1963 the students received identification cards that in later years included photographs sometimes resembling the person whose name was shown.

Opening convocation provides a solemn sounding board for alumni leaders and President Minor on the first Friday or at the first regular chapel the following week. Dr. Robert W. Jackson, president of Tift College, was the featured speaker in 1971. Until 1969 the students— or at least those who were mentally agile enough to know what was happening—were given the privilege of meeting every class for twenty minutes all in one morning. Within a few days the president usually invites the college community and its friends to a reception at his home in honor of new faculty and staff members. Early in the semester, Shorter Sunday at First Baptist Church has included a sermon by Pastors W. Forrest Lanier or Floyd F. Roebuck.

Classes meet from Monday through Friday, ordinarily from late September through early June. In 1971–1972, the first semester extended from August 22 through December 17, a three-week vacation without term papers was enjoyed, and the second semester extended from January 10 through May 14. A similar schedule has been set for 1972–1973. Final examinations continue to be provided—even though Dead Week, during which student meetings were drastically curtailed, died in mid-decade. A Reading Day now separates the final day of classes from the initial day of examinations. Sophomore Tests were last administered in 1968, being replaced in 1972 by vocational aptitude tests at the close of the freshman year.

Academic progress regulations have been tightened only slightly, and that during the freshman year. First and second year students must pass two-thirds of the work for the academic year to avoid exclusion. All others must pass four-fifths of their work. Further, students must earn a minimum number of semester hours credit and quality points each semester on an increasingly difficult scale in order to remain off probation and at school. Theoretically, closed study remains for all first semester freshmen and all second semester freshmen on academic probation.

In 1969 a carefully considered academic guidance program for freshmen and transfer students was initiated, involving an assigned faculty adviser who is retained until a "Declaration of Major" card is completed and the student is turned over to his major professor. In 1970 the 4.0 system was adopted, by which an A is given four quality points and an F is simply given a zero. The following year a pass-fail alternative was added to the Bachelor of Arts program, allowing no more than one elective course each semester to be taken with a pass or fail grade that is disregarded when computing the student's grade point average. Class absence rules have varied from year to year without complete satisfaction at any time. The present system is much more liberal than in previous years: students in 100–200 level courses may have unexcused absences not in excess of the number of class meetings per week; students in 300–400 level courses may have unlimited absences, unless a below-C average causes them to be treated as members of freshman and sophomore classes.

Provisions have been made for gifted students. Honors sections in freshman history were provided for a few years, abandoned in favor of placement in the four-semester humanities sequence. A freshman English honors course has been retained. Superior language and mathematics students usually select sophomore courses. A small number of second semester freshmen are allowed to enroll in 300 level courses. In most departments, independent research is permitted for the more capable junior and senior majors.

Cap and gown convocations were held on Founders' Day, scheduled near Colonel Shorter's birthday on November 23, and at Honors Day in April, when members of the dean's list and Phi Sigma Alpha scholastic society are saluted. Usually these assemblies are addressed by guests, some of whom have been the following: Miss Marion Bush of Barnesville (class of 1927), Lieutenant Governor and Mrs. Garland Byrd of Reynolds (she was Miss Gloria Whatley, class of 1946), Jack V. Colwell of Adairsville (class of 1958), Dr. W. Nevin Jones of Shannon (class of 1957), Mrs. Everett E. Porter of Rome (née Miss Hazel Myers, class of 1931), Horace Stewart of Rome (class of 1964), Miss Mabel Thompson of Rome, Mrs. Robert Todd of Rome (née

Miss Mabel Owens, class of 1922), Joel Williams of Savannah (class of 1964), and Mrs. Victor Yeargan of Rome (née Miss Martha Collins, class of 1934). Nonalumni speakers have included President Noah Langdale of Georgia State College, Dr. Willis Glover of Mercer University, G. Othell Hand of the First Baptist Church of Columbus, and Hugh Smith of the First Baptist Church of Cedartown. Particular regard was given to the memory of Mr. and Mrs. J. P. Cooper in 1963 and of L. A. Dean in 1964.

Accreditation was renewed by the Southern Association of Colleges and Schools in 1962 and 1972, following the preparation of self-study reports and the recommendation of visiting committees. The National Association of the Schools of Music continued its accreditation after similar examinations in 1967–1968. A five-year approval from the Georgia State Department of Education was secured in 1967–1968. Membership is maintained in the Association of American Colleges and the American Council on Education, and all Shorter women graduates are eligible for membership in the American Association of University Women. Self-examination on the part of the college was also involved when its administrators cooperated with the Baptist Education Study Task of 1966–1968 and the related examination conducted for the Georgia Baptist Convention by Dr. Doak Campbell and the Associated Consultants in Education in 1968.

Evening and summer classes have been continued, with several special programs provided at one time or another. Into the early sixties an education workshop was scheduled each summer for in-service teachers. In 1960 a mental health and guidance workshop was also offered. An institute for secondary teachers of mathematics and science was funded by the National Science Foundation and held evening and summer classes from 1959 to 1964. Beginning in 1966, the Natural Resource Use Education Institute has been conducted each summer by the biology department for in-service teachers. Course credit was authorized in 1972 for work experiences under the auspices of the Georgia Intern Program, subject to departmental evaluation and approval.

The Curricula

Degrees have proliferated during the present era as seven new ones have been added to the familiar two. The Bachelor of Arts degree has consistently provided majors in art, biology, chemistry, economics, English, history and political science, mathematics, music, psychology, religion and philosophy, sociology and anthropology, and speech, and interdepartmental majors in fine arts and natural sciences. French and Spanish were suspended as majors in 1972. Business administration and elementary education were shifted to the Bachelor of Science program in 1970. Interdepartmental majors in the social sciences and liberal arts were added in 1961 and 1971, respectively. Starting in 1961 the two-day, senior comprehensive examination was replaced by the standardized Graduate Record Examination, which in turn was replaced by the Undergraduate Record Examination in 1970. The Junior English Examination was instituted as a prerequisite to graduation in 1961–1962, together with a writing laboratory for those who do not initially meet the standard. The Bachelor of Arts degree has been awarded to 1,204 persons from 1958 to 1972. The most popular majors, selected by at least ten percent of the graduates, have been elementary education, history and political science, English, business administration, and biology.

The Bachelor of Music degree continues to require about one-third of the course work in liberal arts and the rest in music. Majors have been available in piano, organ, voice, and music education. A church music major was added in 1961. Theory and composition was dropped from the catalogue as a major in 1966, violin and viola in 1967, and cello in 1969. Graduation requirements include applied music examinations at the end of the first five or six semesters, a junior recital for performance majors, and a senior recital. One hundred seventeen have been awarded this degree from 1958 to 1972.

In recent years more emphasis has been placed on programs leading directly to professional competency. The Bachelor of Science in Medical Technology degree was approved in 1961, involving three years on the campus and a fourth at Floyd Hospital. Fourteen have earned this degree. The Bachelor of Science in Business Administration degree was approved in 1970 and has been conferred on 14. The Bachelor of Science in Elementary Education degree was also inaugurated in 1970 and has been given to 15. A general Bachelor of Science degree was instituted in 1972 with majors possible in biology, chemistry, economics and business administration, mathematics, psychology, social sciences, and sociology and anthropology. At the same time, the Bachelor of Science in Business Administration degree was changed in name to the Bachelor of Business Administration degree. Four of these newest degrees were awarded during the first year of their existence. Encompassing courses already taught by the department, the Bachelor of Music Education and Bachelor of Church Music degrees were also introduced in 1972, but none will be conferred before 1973.

421

Established in 1956, the special training program for General Electric employees had run its course by 1960. Only one certificate was awarded for completing 60 s.h. of classwork.

Graduate work in biology has been offered on the Shorter campus since 1966. Under Dr. Philip Greear, the Natural Resource Use Education Institute permits graduate credit to be earned through Valdosta State College. In the spring of 1969 under the auspices of the Northwest Georgia Teacher Education Service, Dr. Rose Nell Horne and three visiting professors taught classes in education and psychology that earned graduate credit from the two sponsoring schools, the University of Georgia and West Georgia College. Shorter College maintains its relationship with this organization, and Dr. Floyd K. Moates has taught under its supervision at Calhoun.

Funded by the Ford Foundation, the Three-Year Master's Degree Program was guided locally by Thomas K. Lagow, head of the history department, from 1966 to 1970. Shorter students in English, history, modern foreign languages, and mathematics were provided undergraduate academic screening and direction enabling them to receive a stipend while earning a master's degree at the University of Georgia after one further year of study. Six persons pursued the program to a successful conclusion. Brought to the campus by the foundation were noted lecturers who included Hugh Holman and A. G. Engstrom of the University of North Carolina, Alex Dragnich of Vanderbilt University, and Frank Vandiver of Rice Institute.

Within the Departments

During the Minor administration, the college has employed about 154 faculty members, 89 administrative and staff members, and numerous other persons in maintenance, the dormitories, and (until 1963) the dining room. Full- and part-time teachers have varied from about 35 to 48 and administrators from about 23 to 29. Other staff members have numbered about 20 each year. The faculty-student ratio was one to sixteen in 1966–1967 and one to eleven in 1971–1972. Of the faculty members, about 48 remained only one year or were part-time and about 21, no more than two. About 106 were on the faculty two or more years, with the highest earned degrees distributed as follows: bachelor's, 11; master's, 55; doctor's, 40. The nonmusicians have had advanced degrees most frequently from the universities of Alabama, Georgia, North Carolina, and Tennessee, and Duke, Emory, and

Ohio State universities. The musicians have most often received their professional training at Converse College, Eastman School of Music, Indiana University, New Orleans Baptist Theological Seminary, George Peabody College for Teachers, Southern Baptist Theological Seminary, and Southwestern Baptist Theological Seminary. Median salaries for full professors ranged from $5,000 in 1958–1959 to $10,611 in 1972–1973 and for instructors, from $3,600 to $8,066 in the same period. Earlier fringe benefits were continued, with improvements made to the hospitalization plan in 1963 and 1970. In many years the college shared in paying the annual dues for faculty membership in the Shorter unit of the G.E.A. which was formed in 1959. Limited funds were made available by 1964 for faculty members wishing to study toward the doctorate. A sabbatical leave program was started in 1965 that has been utilized by several. A tax sheltered annuity plan is offered to those who want it.

Tenure is granted on the same basis as before, but, by specific action of the trustees in 1970, ends at sixty-five. Compulsory retirement has been set at seventy.

Monthly faculty meetings occur usually during a morning activity period, sometimes with invited student visitors and speakers. The secretary was Humphrey Olsen, librarian, from 1958 to 1961 and Dr. Paulina Buhl, professor of English, from 1961 to 1971. Dr. K. Lamar Hellams, assistant professor of chemistry and physics, was elected in 1971. Committees are named by the president and dean each fall. Varying from year to year, they now number sixteen: academic standards and awards, admissions, athletics, cultural events, curriculum and objectives, faculty legislative, financial aid, guidance, health, library, publications, public relations, recreation, religious activities, social activities, and teacher education.

A faculty guide was prepared for use in 1964. This nine-page, mimeographed pamphlet was doubled in size six years later, and continues to be distributed to new faculty members. Further subtle guidance is provided almost every year when a detailed grade study of each faculty member is compiled and made available to the entire group.

ART. Miss Martha Griffin led the art department for forty-one years in an era of expansion. Offerings grew to 67 s.h., supplemented significantly by studio instruction. To the third floor area in the Fine Arts Building were added a second floor gallery and a ceramics and sculpturing studio in the basement of Van Hoose. The collection of art history slides has expanded to more than three thousand. Miss Griffin's interest extended beyond the college community as she worked with the Rome Art League, the Junior Service League, and public school art teachers. Classes and exhibits were held on campus for local children, some of whom eventually graduated from Shorter, and adults not otherwise enrolled at the college. Her impact among the regular students was indicated by the ovations received at the 1968 Founders' Day and the 1971 Awards Day ceremonies. The grateful trustees spoke of her "capable and loyal service," observed that "the Shorter College Art Department is widely known and its graduates are recognized for their proficiency," and designated her professor emeritus at her retirement in 1971.

Others have taught in the department. Harlan Sifford was an assistant professor for six years until 1960. Miss Virginia Dudley was associate professor and artist in residence from 1963 to 1971, presenting one-man shows while at Shorter in Columbus and Rome and displaying works in Washington, D. C., and Chattanooga, Tennessee. She was listed in *Who's Who of American Women*, the *Dictionary of International Biography*, and other similar volumes. A part-time student at Shorter for a number of years, Mrs. Jane Miller McCord became an instructor in 1971. Since joining the faculty, she has had works accepted in juried shows in Georgia, Tennessee, and West Virginia, and has been awarded a $500 purchase prize in Chattanooga.

Art exhibits on the campus have included numerous visiting shows and works by faculty members, students, and alumni. Among these have been Mrs. Martha Ware Pinkston, Miss Claire Hollingsworth, and Larry Headrick. The spring student art exhibit features the output of departmental majors. Shorter persons have entered shows and won prizes at Rome, Atlanta, Columbus, Athens, and Chattanooga. Combining May Day and the Camerata Follies, a fine arts festival was held in 1959 and 1960, receiving the wholehearted cooperation of this department. The Art Students League maintained its lending library of pictures until the mid-sixties and sponsored art sales at Christmas in the early seventies.

BIOLOGY AND EARTH SCIENCE. Although the 1967 catalogue shows a skeleton in the biology department pointing out a relevant textbook passage to a questioning girl, there is a great deal of life elsewhere in that section of Rome Hall. Biology and earth science have experienced an upturn in student interest, resulting in courses that have significantly grown to 81 s.h. On the faculty since 1944, Miss Emma Lewis Lipps earned a second Southern Fellowship Foundation Award for graduate study and received the Doctor of Philosophy degree from the University of Tennessee in 1966. Her research was based on the

Marshall Forest, "Edgehill," adjoining Shorter College, and she was instrumental in having that area designated a Natural Landmark Site by the National Park Service. Listed in *Who's Who of American Women,* she has also been elected a fellow of the Georgia Academy of Science. She was first director of the National Science Foundation In-Service Institute that held evening and summer classes for teachers of science and mathematics in junior and senior high schools from 1959 to 1964. For a decade she has led in excavating fossil remains at Ladd Quarry, Bartow County, and has published two of the six resulting papers. She has read scholarly essays at several gatherings in the state

Miss Martha Griffin   Dr. Emma Lewis Lipps

Dr. Jessie Gardner (Mrs. James) Austin

and has spent two recent summers researching at the Smithsonian Institute. Because of her enthusiasm, the Shorter Geology or Caving Club began in 1967–1968. Its members have cut and polished native rocks, making jewelry, pen sets, and book ends that were started six hundred million years ago! The group is also involved in spelunking; as time passes, interest reaches ever greater depths. At Founders' Day in 1968 she was honored for her service to the college by a brief tribute that included these words: "Thank you for your knowledge and yourself."

Philip F-C. Greear entered the department in 1961, quickly earning the trust and regard of his students. The seniors of 1967 expressed their "special respect" for him because of "his interest in [his students] . . . individually." The 1969 *Argo* was dedicated to him, quoting

425

Matthew 25:40 in describing him as "a good man." He received the Doctor of Philosophy degree in botany from the University of Georgia in 1967. Author of several essays dealing with botanical observations in Northwest Georgia, he has addressed scholarly groups as far distant as Washington, D. C. In 1967 he was named a fellow of the Georgia Academy of Science. His interest in ecology has led him to enter the discussion on routing I–75. He was a founder of the Georgia Natural Resources Education Council and directed the first Natural Resource Use Education Institute in the state at Shorter College in 1966. This three-week summer conference for junior and senior high school science and mathematics teachers has been held annually since that time. Under his leadership a field trip was made during the spring vacation of 1969 and a study was made of coastal ecosystems on Ossabaw Island near Savannah. The Atlanta *Journal and Constitution Magazine* provided illustrated publicity, and the experience has subsequently been repeated with college credit for those who desire it. In cooperation with other Georgia institutions, Shorter helped to initiate the interdisciplinary Genesis project at Ossabaw in 1970, with Greear on its board of directors. Genesis is an effort to provide young people the opportunity to relate themselves to a wholesome natural environment while pursuing individual educational goals.

The third member of the biology faculty is Dr. Craig Allee, who returned to his alma mater in 1967. Specializing in entomology, he has presented a research paper at a national meeting of the Entomological Society of America and is listed in *Personalities of the South.*

Others associated with the department in the recent past include Dr. Julian Darlington, who was its head from 1954 to 1959, and Melvyn Ottinger, an alumnus. Mrs. June Mundy Blankenship, the recipient in 1964 of the first Bachelor of Science in Medical Technology degree to be given by Shorter, has been a lecturer in biology and a teacher supervisor in medical technology.

In 1963–1964 laboratory facilities were strengthened by a National Science Foundation grant that was matched by the college. The Georgia Academy of Science held its annual meeting at Shorter in the spring of 1968. The Science Club, combining students interested in biology, chemistry, mathematics, and physics, existed until 1961. Beta Beta Beta, biology honorary fraternity, was chartered at Shorter in 1965. Inspired by Earth Day in the spring of 1970, students instituted the Ecology Club the following fall.

CHEMISTRY AND PHYSICS. Although radically revised in recent months by Dr. K. Lamar Hellams, offerings in chemistry have remained at a stable total of about 50 s.h. Homer Blankenship has for a decade been a member of this department, and is listed in *Who's Who in the South and Southwest*. Always curtailed by the lack of a full-time professor in the field of physics, the college has reduced its courses to three. Some assistance was afforded by an Atomic Energy Commission equipment grant in 1962–1963.

ECONOMICS AND BUSINESS ADMINISTRATION. A powerful stimulus came to the college when the Callaway Foundation, Inc., made provision in 1968 to establish forty academic chairs in Georgia, one of which was to be at Shorter. From funds controlled by the foundation, an annual salary supplement is made. In 1970, the first Fuller E. Callaway Professor of Economics, Dr. W. Troy Anders, Jr., was appointed. Three degrees are now awarded, with offerings of 30 s.h. in economics and 35 s.h. in business administration. Earlier, instruction had been offered within the department of social science or the separate department of business administration and economics by Charles C. Thompson and others more briefly. Courses in secretarial science have not been taught since 1960. In 1959 the Shorter Business Club was organized.

EDUCATION. Supplying courses in education that doubled in extent to the present 59 s.h., the department of psychology and education for fifteen years included the genial, gentle, and jovial J. D. Ramsay. He was director of summer school for a decade. Since 1963 Miss Frances Ellen Porter has been an associate professor. For lesser periods of time others have offered instruction, including a Shorter alumna, Mrs. Merriam L. Smith. Accreditation was renewed by the Georgia State Board of Education in 1967–1968. Because of courses in this and other departments, Shorter assists students in gaining state certification as general elementary teachers, as elementary and secondary teachers in art and music, and as secondary teachers in art, English, French, mathematics, music, science, social studies, Spanish, and speech. A supplemental field, library science, is also provided, resulting from courses added in 1960. The Bachelor of Science in Elementary Education degree was introduced in 1970, removing all subsequent work in this area from the Bachelor of Arts program. The John N. Ware chapter of the Student Georgia Association of Educators, which is related to the G.A.E., continues.

ENGLISH. Since 1961 Dr. Paulina Buhl has provided leadership in the department of English that now offers 82 s.h. of work. The seniors of 1964 dedicated their *Argo* to her, "for outstanding abilities in the field of English. It can be said of her, that Shakespeare never appeared finer nor Browning more exciting than when touched by her wit." She has been president of the Georgia-South Carolina College English Association and the Georgia Council of Teachers of English and associate chairman of the 1970 National Council of Teachers of English convention in Atlanta. In 1958 Mrs. Jessie Gardner Austin returned to the department. The 1965 *Argo* was dedicated to her "for reminding us . . . that discipline and formality clarify communication between people, and that creative thinking quietly perceives reasons and establishes relationships . . . ." Two years later the University of Alabama awarded her the Doctor of Philosophy degree. Others teaching English include Mrs. Thelma Hall and Mrs. Lillian D. Jackson, the latter of whom is listed in *Who's Who of American Women*. Carl Griffin was active for five years and Wilson Hall, for seven. Griffin earned "the special respect" of the seniors in 1967 for "lending a hand when the going gets tough." Hall wrote brief essays about local history and the world of nature, and was honored when the 1968 *Argo* was dedicated to him. Briefly, Mrs. Gail Gray Jones, an alumna, was an instructor. In 1970 this department was made the nucleus of the department of language, literature, and speech, with Dr. Buhl as the head. The Rho Delta Club has met with some regularity, producing a *Chimes* once or twice each year through 1968.

FOREIGN LANGUAGES. Instruction in foreign languages has emphasized French and Spanish, both of which were suspended as majors in 1972. Two years of German and one of Italian are also offered. Latin and Greek were dropped from the 1962 catalogue, although 6 s.h. of Latin were restored to the 1970 catalogue only. Until 1968, Marvin Harrison was in this department, having the 1966 *Argo* dedicated to him. Miss Martha Lockwood has provided courses in Spanish since 1968. Two alumni, Miss Barbara Bradley and Marvin Taylor, taught briefly, as have numerous other persons. No language clubs have existed during this period.

HEALTH AND PHYSICAL EDUCATION. Until the retirement of Miss Franziska Boas in 1965, the department of physical education emphasized dance and sponsored the Dance Club. Traveling to Atlanta and Milledgeville to see famous individuals and troupes, members of the club also performed in Tennessee and often on the Shorter campus. The fine arts festivals of 1959 and 1960 had the support of this group. Dance recitals were given by visiting artists, Carolyn Gold and Daniel Nagrin, each of whom taught a master class.

Two other professors have remained for significant periods of time, William C. Foster for five years and Walter N. Attaway for seven years to the present. With the removal of most instruction in dance, the department now provides 29 s.h. of work. Four semesters of physical education are required for all degrees, including at least one semester of swimming for those unable to pass an appropriate test. Demonstrations of tumbling and modern dance are occasionally conducted by the various classes.

HISTORY AND POLITICAL SCIENCE.   Slowly expanding to offerings of 80 s.h., the department of history and political science was led by Dr. Allen S. Johnson until 1960. Since 1961 Thomas K. Lagow has been its head. Receiving his Doctor of Philosophy degree from the University of Georgia in 1968, Lagow has also gained recognition from the students who dedicated the 1971 *Argo* to him. Miss Dora Lee Wilkerson, a Shorter alumna, was a part-time lecturer for four years. Dr. Harold L. Grant taught seven years in the department. Continuing from 1965 to the present is Terry Morris, an alumnus of the college. The International Relations Club was reorganized in 1962, living for a couple of years. Pi Gamma Mu, a social science honorary fraternity, was begun in 1963. The History Club has been moderately active since 1970.

HUMANITIES.   Starting in 1962 under the supervision of Dean Charles W. Whitworth, an upper division humanities seminar has met biweekly, usually on Tuesday evening. Lecturers have been drawn from almost every department in the college, together with some visitors, and vary from semester to semester. Likewise, the topics for study are regularly changed. Themes have included the American black experience, Kenneth Clark's film series, "Civilisation," the relevance of academic studies, and utopias. A four-semester, freshman-sophomore humanities sequence was instituted in 1969 by the English and history departments. Conceived initially as an honors program, it has been team taught by members of the two sponsoring departments.

MATHEMATICS.   The mathematics department has been enlarged to include 66 s.h. of courses and has been staffed by a number of persons who include the following: Dr. Margaret Baskervill from 1947 to 1959, Mrs. May C. Blackstock from 1955 to 1966, Dr. Elizabeth Edwards from 1959 to 1970, Dr. Rosalie Seymour Jensen from 1966 to 1968, Mrs. Carol Holden Rudd from 1968 to 1971, and Dr. Richard Cowan from 1969 to the present. The last three are Shorter alumni. Dr. Jensen was listed in *Outstanding Young Women of America* and Dr. Cowan in *Outstanding Young Men of America*. The Mathematics Club was formed in 1960–1961 and Mu Mu Kappa, honorary mathematics fraternity, in 1966–1967.

MUSIC. Led by David Beaty and John Ramsaur, the department of music has had the largest group within the faculty. Remaining for an extended period of time to the present are eight. Mrs. Elizabeth Buday gives recitals throughout the Southeast. As president of the Georgia Music Teachers Association from 1959 to 1962, she was instrumental in bringing its annual convention to Shorter in 1961. A number of times she has led summer tours to Europe. She and her husband received an award in Americanism from the Xavier chapter of the Daughters of the American Revolution. David Beaty has presented recitals from Florida to Virginia. John Ramsaur was named Teacher of the Year in 1965 by the Southeastern division of the National Association of Teachers of Singing and was elected president of the Georgia chapter in 1967 and appointed lieutenant governor in 1969. Kenneth Josephson was included in *Who's Who in American Education*. An authority on Moravian music, Dr. Harry Hall has prepared new editions of some instrumental works. William D. Knight appeared at Carnegie Recital Hall in 1964. Robert W. Jones is now in his fifth year on the faculty. Mrs. Helen K. Ramsaur and Mrs. Mary Ann Knight have been part-time instructors in piano. Made up of Kenneth Josephson, William Knight, and Willard Shull, a string trio performed from 1963 to 1966.

Early in this administration, Mr. and Mrs. Richard Willis (she was the former Miss Carolyn Brown, an alumna of the college) taught until 1963. His compositions were played at Rome, Atlanta, Jacksonville State College, the University of Alabama, Washington, D. C., and New York City. In 1961 he won an American Music Award for a choral number, "The Drenched Land." Other former faculty members include Mrs. Charlotte Vane until 1959, Willard Shull until 1966, Mrs. Lillian Acree Bosworth (a Shorter graduate) until 1969, and Mrs. Rebecca L. Shull until 1971.

Music offerings have remained constant at about 110 s.h. throughout this period. Accreditation by the National Association of Schools of Music has been maintained, most recently being renewed in 1968. Each year members of the Shorter faculty give recitals on campus. Visitors also appear, often presenting private master classes in addition to their public performances. These have included Edward Kilenyi, pianist; Teresa Orantes, mezzo-soprano; James Barber, violinist, and Thomas Redcay, pianist; Jeanette Pecorello, soprano, and Eugene Talley-Schmidt, tenor (Mr. and Mrs. Gene Smith) ; Bedford Watkins, harpsichordist; Robert Goldsand, pianist; Béla Böszörmenyi-Nagy, pianist; Giorgio Ciompi, violinist, and Loren Withers, pianist; Helen

Vanni, mezzo-soprano; and Piet Kee, organist. Other concerts have been presented by alumni: Miss Jacquelyn Benson, Horace and Joyce Abbott English, William Krape, Mrs. Joan Hicks Hill, Tyler McGlamry, and Richard Shadinger.

Student vocal groups have been given many names: the Shorter College Chorus or Chorale, the Oratorio Chorus, the Mixed Chorus, the Freshman Women's Chorus, the Men's Chorus, the Shorter College Ensemble, the Double Quartet, the Goldtones (a girls' ensemble started in 1963), and the Shorter Gents (started in 1966). Performances come each Christmas and spring, together with brief appearances at various convocations, alumni programs, and the Georgia Baptist Convention. In 1959 and 1960 the fine arts festivals depended heavily on the music department for their success. Several short tours usually include about ten Georgia schools and churches, although in 1969 a ten-day tour extended also to Alabama, Mississippi, and Louisiana. In 1960 new blue and gold choir robes were secured. A preschool chorus camp, instituted in 1961, is still conducted. Long-playing choral records were cut in 1962 and 1967.

In the past several years, students have won honors in several competitions—the state and regional auditions of the Music Teachers Association and the National Association of the Teachers of Singing; the state, regional, and national auditions of the Women's Federation of Music Clubs; and the district, regional, and national semifinal and final Metropolitan Opera auditions. Original compositions by Shorter students have been performed before the Georgia and Southeastern Composers leagues. A few students have spent the summer studying at the Mozarteum Institute in Salzburg, Austria.

Presenting scenes from noted operas, a workshop has been held each spring since 1968. Later in the spring, members of the music faculty have sometimes previewed the operas to be presented in Atlanta by the Metropolitan Opera Company.

In recent years a new German tracker organ built by Rudolph von Beckerath and a new Baldwin electronic practice organ have been installed, as well as four grand and twenty-four practice pianos. Some of these pianos have been given by Mrs. Joseph K. McCutchen (née Miss Christine Bandy, class of 1936), T. Harley Harper, Richard H. Rich, and J. T. Roe.

Holding membership in the national and Georgia federations of music clubs, the Camerata Club is the general music organization. It sponsors recitals, receptions, music house parties, talent shows, picnics, and banquets. Virtually every year a printed brochure announces the

431

concert series. Founded at Shorter College in the fall of 1969, the Zeta Epsilon chapter of Phi Mu Alpha Sinfonia of America is a fraternity of men interested in the appreciation of music.

PSYCHOLOGY. Directed by Dr. Stanislav Velinsky until failing health caused his departure in 1970, the department of education and psychology has offered a course of study totaling about 45 s.h. in psychology. For many years Velinsky was consulting psychologist for the Child Guidance Clinic, Floyd County Health Department. In 1963 he published *Personality's Superstructure: The Cosmic Order and Our Mental Health.* From a philosophical, religious, and scientific standpoint, this volume discusses his "Protosubstantialistic Philosophy," in an effort to present "a guidepost toward interhuman friendship for the man of the space age." Under new leadership furnished by Dr. Floyd Moates, a program is available in cooperation with the Georgia Baptist Children's Home. In conjunction with the department of sociology, other comparable alliances are being explored with nearby social service agencies.

RELIGION AND PHILOSOPHY. The department of religion and philosophy has gradually developed a program of study emphasizing the Bible, the history of religions, and philosophy. Forty-two s.h. are offered in religion and 27 in philosophy, with a major provided in either area. Head of the Mrs. Columbus Roberts Department of Religion since 1957, Dr. Robert G. Gardner had the 1960 *Argo* dedicated to him. Author of published essays about Baptist history, he is currently president of the Georgia Baptist Historical Society. He is listed in *Outstanding Educators of America, Who's Who in the South and Southwest,* and other similar volumes. Serving also as dean of the college, Dr. Charles W. Whitworth has been professor of philosophy since 1962. Dr. Joe R. Baskin joined the faculty in 1966, wrote Sunday school lessons for the *Christian Index* one quarter in 1969, had the *Argo* dedicated to him in 1970, and is also director of religious activities on campus.

SOCIOLOGY AND ANTHROPOLOGY. With offerings growing from 37 to 54 s.h., the department of sociology and anthropology has left its former status as a part of the department of social science and has regained its autonomy. Earlier professors included Dr. Hoy Taylor, to whom the *Argo* was dedicated in 1963, "for his guidance . . . for his service . . . for his inspiration." His career was cut short by death in 1967 at the age of 87, and a memorial service in the chapel paid tribute to his perennial youth. Dr. J. Samuel Johnson taught for eleven years until his retirement in 1971. Miss Bernice Allen returned in 1963 and remains to the present. She has directed student work at the Youth Development Center and Open Door Home, has guided students in providing special tutorial service in the community, has led classes in compiling three social service directories, and has developed a curriculum in industrial sociology. Much of the expansion in this department has been under Patrick Garrow in anthropology. Aided by his students, he has excavated near the Chieftains, the early nineteenth century home of Major Ridge, and at a sixteenth century Indian burial site in Floyd County. The distinguished anthropologist, Margaret Mead, spoke at the college in 1964.

SPEECH. By dropping courses in radio and adding others in theater, the department of speech has retained a constant 58 s.h. of instruction. From 1918 to 1961, Mrs. Allie Hayes Richardson was in charge. At her retirement the trustees designated her professor emeritus and presented her with a television set. Before her death in 1966, she had the satisfaction of knowing that, in the renovated Fine Arts Building, the speech department had been named for her. Her generosity in founding a scholarship fund has already been described. Mrs. Mabel Rhinehart Milner and Mrs. Ruby Allen Murphy, Shorter alumnae, were instructors for a time. Charles J. Pecor, an accomplished magician who was called "The Wizard of Wit," taught for five years, having the *Argo* dedicated to him in 1967. From 1961 to the present, Mrs. Betty Zane Morris, a Shorter graduate, has been in the department. She was included in *Outstanding Young Women of America*.

The Shorter Players present two or three major plays each year, while several one-act performances result from various classes. Each fall and spring a festival features speeches and short dramas. Originating in 1968–1969, the Readers Theater performs for schools, civic groups, churches, and educational television—and has given a program in the governor's mansion. Junior and senior speech recitals, reinstated as a graduation requirement in 1972 after a lapse of twenty years, will serve to increase the programs furnished by this department. In the spring of 1972 the first drama focus week was staged.

Administration and Staff

Dr. Allen S. Johnson was dean of the college until 1960, followed briefly by Dr. Wesley N. Laing. Since 1962 Dr. Charles W. Whitworth has occupied that position, being honored in 1969 when the *Argo* was dedicated to him. Describing him, the editor quoted Aristotle: "A

433

good man is a man of practical wisdom. . . . His acts are good because they proceed from good will." Whitworth is listed in *Who's Who
in the South and Southwest*. Only Mrs. Maude M. Neill has been dean
of women for any extended period of time, from 1962 to 1968.
Clarence Roland returned to his alma mater as dean of students from
1963 to 1966. The registrar was Miss Louise Thompson, who was also
at times president of the Georgia Association of Collegiate Registrars
and Admissions Officers and of the Higher Education Department of
the G.E.A. On the campus her holiday decorations and her culinary
delights have been widely appreciated—and her virtual omniscience.

Miss Louise Thompson   Mrs. Frank R. Lovell   Mrs. Lila C. Elliott

"Ask Miss Thompson" became a frequent statement among the students and "Louise will know," among the faculty. After forty-seven
years with the college—longer than any other person—she was made
registrar emeritus in 1971 by the trustees who affirmed: "She has been
the epitome of graciousness, gentleness, and helpfulness. . . . All who
have come in contact with her, love and respect her." Her successor
in office has been Mrs. Lillian D. Jackson of the English department.
W. J. Neathery, the business manager since 1961, has been listed in
Who's Who in Commerce and Industry and *Who's Who in American
College and University Administrators*. Until 1961 Cecil Lea was
director of development; since 1963 C. T. B. Harris has been assistant
to the president and director of development. Clifford Cormany has
acted as administrative assistant and director of financial aid and placement since 1967. "You've always a friendly greeting and cheery smile"

was said of Mrs. Emmie Louise Lovell, executive secretary to the president, at Founders' Day of 1968. Mrs. Ima Jean Kerce has been alumni secretary throughout this period. These two sisters are alumnae of the college. For nine years the director of admissions was Kankakee (Buck) Anderson, assisted by Mrs. Bess Patterson and James C. Tribble. Four alumni worked in admissions briefly: David Bridges, Ronald W. Harris, William Moore, and George Weaver. The office staff has consisted of several remaining at least five years: Mrs. Mildred Sartin, Mrs. Carolyn White Coker, Mrs. Mildred Johnson, Mrs. Violet Vaughn, Mrs. Elizabeth Hicks, Mrs. Geraldine Turner, Mrs. Montine Bohannon, and Mrs. Myrtle Floyd. Miss Katherine Alford, an alumna, was a secretary for a brief time. Numerous persons have been in charge of publicity, including two graduates, Mrs. Avis Hardaker Ivey and James Penney. Since 1967 the postmaster and printer has been Sam Stewart, to whom the 1972 *Argo* was dedicated.

The library has been headed by Humphrey Olsen, Mrs. Lucelia Borders Henderson (an alumna), and Mrs. Mary Mac Mosley. At Mrs. Henderson's death in 1968, a memorial book fund was started. Others in the library include Mrs. Beulah Cormany and W. C. Owen. Three alumni have also been on this staff: Mrs. Madeline Smith Bridges, Mrs. Nita Read, and Tal Roberts. The annual budget has varied from almost nine thousand to over forty-six thousand dollars, being supplemented in 1970–1971 by an eight-thousand-dollar federal grant for books and periodicals. The collection has expanded to 57,320 books, 454 periodicals, 2,440 recordings and tapes, about 2,900 scores, and about 425 rolls of microfilm, microfiche cards, and filmstrips. As has already been noted, the library now occupies the top floor of the Library-Administration and Binns buildings and is named for an alumna, Mrs. Mildred Arnall Peniston.

Mrs. Lila C. Elliott, the house director or dormitory counselor, was honored in 1959 when the *Argo* was again dedicated to her: "Our helper in times of need; our confidant and guide in times of uncertainty; our mother away from home; our friend always—Mrs. 'E.' " The hostess for most college receptions and responsible for many lovely flower arrangements, she was thanked "for being you" on Founders' Day of 1968. Several summers she has left the campus long enough to lead tours to Europe. At her retirement in 1971 the trustees paid tribute to her: "Through her gentleness, understanding and concern she has been an influence for good on all with whom she has come in contact." Dormitory counselors have included Mrs. Cornelia Taylor, Miss Lilly Whitworth, Mrs. Rosa Cox, and John Caparisos, the last three of whom are alumni. Mrs. Mary B. Carper, Mrs. Ruth Payne, and

Mrs. Merle Buskill continue as counselors, and the last had the 1968 *Argo* dedicated to her. Among the maids working at the college have been Mrs. Mary Jo Lewis, Mrs. Lucille Taylor, Mrs. Mary Edmondson, and Mrs. Flonnie Morgan. The infirmary was on the first floor of Van Hoose until the renovation of Alumni Hall provided rooms on the second floor for the newly named Margaret Jacobs Infirmary. Mrs. Cynthia Primm was resident nurse for ten years, and Mrs. Margit Tamassy was assistant to her and others for nineteen years until her retirement in 1971. Dr. Warren Gilbert remains as school physician.

Mrs. Willie R. Scarborough was dietician until 1962, after which the food services were leased to Campus Chefs, Inc. The dining room was refurnished in 1961 by Lawrence Willet of Atlanta in memory of his mother, Mrs. Lucy Lester Willet. Erected in 1968, the Binns Building includes a commodious new dining area. When the Greystone was occupied in 1964, a cafeteria was opened for its residents. A snack bar has been operated in the Library-Administration or Binns Building. First employed in the snack bar and book store in 1962, Miss Bettie Satterwhite retained her nickname, Bettie Bookstore, even after joining the cafeteria staff in 1963 and becoming Mrs. Charles Reed in 1970. Several others have worked under Mrs. Scarborough or Campus Chefs for more than five years: Mrs. Onie Chapman, Mrs. Louise Daniel, Mrs. Louise Davie, Mrs. Evelyn Kelly, Walter Clark, Howard Miller, Willie Morgan, Toney Penn, and Charles H. Sigler.

Moving from Rome Hall to the Library-Administration Building to the Binns Building, the book store was eventually leased to Campus Chefs and in 1968 to Johnston and Malone. Several managers have remained briefly, including an alumna, Miss Bette King Britton, but Mrs. Mildred Johnson has supervised its operation under the present lease after leaving the business office.

Janos Tamassy served as custodian for nineteen years. An annual honored him and his wife, typically shown reading an overseas airmail letter. Said the inscription: "Mr. and Mrs. John Tamassy, whose smiling faces and helping hands are always near—to these two wonderful people, we dedicate the 1961 *Argo* in appreciation of their dedication to us through the years." The story of his remarkable career, together with a photograph of him as a Hungarian general proudly wearing his medals, appeared in a 1968 *Periscope*. A memorial service in the chapel shortly after his retirement and death in 1971 revealed once more the widespread respect and affection for him. Since 1968 off-duty policemen have regularly patroled the campus; of these, Philip C. Fowler has been employed almost the entire period.

For six years Gilbert J. Davis was superintendent of buildings and

436

grounds, a position occupied by Hugh Watkins from 1966 to 1971. Since that time he has been maintenance supervisor. After twenty-two years, mostly as janitor in Rome Hall and the Library-Administration Building, Carlton Morgan in 1971 was named supervisor of janitorial service. On the maintenance staff have been several men spending a significant number of years: Jessie Posey, James Glanton, John Posey, Boise Raiden, and Daniel Scales.

Student Government and the Student Handbook

Operating under a constitution revised in 1961 and 1968, the Student Government Association has placed its executive power in the Student Council or the student body president. Legislative power has rested in a student assembly or student senate and the faculty legislative committee. Judicial power has been retained by the Honor Board. The first male student body president was Mike Burdett in 1959–1960. From 1962 to 1968 a student parliamentarian supervised student activities and acted as an intermediary between the student body and the administration. Standing committees of the S.G.A. are as follows: executive, social, orientation, projects, sports, and parliamentary procedure. All elections occur in April, except those for freshman class officers, of course, and a point system is still utilized. S.G.A. officers are inaugurated at a chapel ceremony each spring. Until 1962 the Honor Board was installed formally at an 11:00 o'clock fall chapel, with speakers representing classes and faculty. Although this practice has ceased, the board is still much a part of campus life. In 1964 its rules of procedure were made public so that accused persons might know what to expect. The Women's and Men's Dormitory councils continue, although the former has been more active. In addition to enforcing rules, it has at times sponsored parties, a fashion show, the Halloween Carnival, and banquets for outgoing and incoming officers. The Men's Dormitory Council has often been practically inoperative, being revived most recently in 1971. In the early sixties the Key Club, the Freshman Council, and regular student body meetings passed from sight.

The S.G.A. has scheduled numerous events over the years—minstrel shows, house parties, movies, square dances, hay rides, and informal parties. It supervises the Homecoming and Miss Shorter events, to be described in later sections. The three main dances were planned by the Social Council and freshman Cotillion Club until 1961 when they were disbanded. For a few years the two fraternities were responsible for the fall and spring dances and the two societies, for the winter

437

formal. More recently the social committee of the S.G.A. has planned several school-wide dances a year and the fraternities one.

The S.G.A. retained membership in the National Student Association, sending delegates to its congresses almost every summer. Jerry Watson was the 1961–1962 regional vice-chairman of the N.S.A. In 1965 Shorter transferred to the Southern Universities Student Government Association, usually being represented at its conventions and co-hosting with Berry a convention in 1971.

Although Berry and Shorter had held joint Student Council meetings and dances in the mid-sixties, the Rome Inter-College Council was not formed until 1971, and Floyd Junior College was also represented. Joint dances and speakers have been sponsored, and most recreational activities on each campus have been opened to students of the other two institutions.

As is true of other schools, Shorter has liberalized its policies regulating student behavior. During the past decade some rules have quietly disappeared from the *Student Handbook*—relating to riding limits, hours for turning out lights, card playing and dancing, the number of dates per month, chaperonage, and getting to meals on time. One rule was retained—prohibiting alcoholic beverages—and three were added —prohibiting guns, fireworks, and unprescribed drugs. In that last connection a student-faculty committee has embarked upon a program of counseling and education. Most other rules have been relaxed—concerning room inspections, the use of cars, quiet hours, filing, and curfews. Men are permitted to visit the dormitories on Sunday afternoon from 1:30 to 4:30, but girls are allowed only in the lobby and mezzanine of the Greystone, during scheduled hours. Capable of broad interpretation, sports clothing has been approved for all events except Sunday dinner, special assemblies and convocations, and evening programs involving the general public. This being the case, classroom attire is now much more varied than in earlier years, although hair curlers are still forbidden. Worn by comparatively few, the bizarre costumes affected by some contemporary young people are nevertheless not unknown on campus.

The office of student personnel, with an assistant dean for student services and a director of student activities, cooperates with the S.G.A. and is responsible to the president and dean of the college. It supervises the college calendar, traffic control, special events, and discipline. An attempt is made to observe "due process," and an appeal to the president is always available.

Only once has student life been disrupted so completely as to gain state-wide publicity. In the spring of 1965, according to the Atlanta newspapers, thirty-eight Greystone residents were booked on charges of blocking traffic and disorderly conduct after refusing a police order to leave the scene of a traffic accident near the dormitory. Those considered to be innocent bystanders were bailed out by the college administration, which promptly issued an apology to the city of Rome for the whole event. Soon twenty-nine received suspended sentences; a few were allowed to withdraw from school, while the others remained.

Although charges of student apathy and administrative repression at times appear in student publications, the leadership of the S.G.A has generally been positive and responsible. There has been no radical disruption of the orderly process of instruction, no substitution of violence for the power of persuasion, no anarchy in the form of brute force. Dialogue between the association and the administration has been constant, and forward-looking compromises have been made on both sides.

Religion on Campus

The Shorter Christian Association and the Baptist Student Union have given important direction to the religious life of the campus. Working with them have been the chairman of the religious activities committee for eight years, Robert G. Gardner, and for seven years a director of religious activities, Thomas K. Lagow or Joe R. Baskin.

Its officers and cabinet elected and installed each spring, the S.C.A. in the fifties and early sixties scheduled a banquet honoring its leaders, distributed a mimeographed pamphlet containing an overview of the year's program, conducted a September chapel service in which new students were formally recognized as members of the association, led required vespers Sunday and Tuesday evenings, and sponsored a Christmas party for the children of the Open Door Home. Some functions have been retained. Evening vespers are often held, but attendance is optional. Each fall the Freshman Commission is appointed. Chapel programs are occasionally conducted by the association. In 1963, Horace Stewart became the first male president of the S.C.A.

Raising money for Thanksgiving baskets, the Halloween Carnival was sponsored by this group through 1959, after which Sherwood Forest Day was initiated. Each class elects its own Maid Marian and Robin Hood, and competition between classes and clans is scheduled— tricycle races, popcorn or pie eating contests, relays, talking marathons, egg tosses, powder puff football games, and others. Since 1963 a plaque has shown the winning class. More recently, some of the money has been used throughout the year for a few families periodically visited by small student groups expressing a sustained personal interest.

Each spring Religious Focus Week continues as a major event on the calendar. Services have become increasingly informal, often utilizing the skills of Christian laymen—airline hostesses, beauty queens, professional football players, the performance of a musical, "Natural High," led by one of its composers, Kurt Kaiser, and lectures by George Schweitzer of Knoxville, Tennessee. Other speakers have included J. Winston Pearce of DeLand, Florida; W. Forrest Lanier of Savannah; John Carlton of Southern Baptist Theological Seminary; Roger McDonald of Newnan; William C. Ruchti of Rome, Italy; R. J. Robinson of Augusta; Peter McLeod of Lexington, Kentucky; William Self of Atlanta; and Grady Nutt of Louisville, Kentucky.

The S.C.A. room has been replaced by prayer rooms in Cooper and Roberts dormitories. In 1971 a room in Rome Hall was set aside for this purpose by the B.S.U., with a small stained glass window made for the door by Dr. Thomas K. Lagow.

The B.S.U. has sponsored a program invariably including the election and installation of officers, a preschool retreat, mixers at the beginning of school and other socials throughout the year, a progressive supper provided by several local churches, a fall convention at Rock Eagle, and a spring retreat near Covington. For several years a Christian home week, a missions day, and a vocational emphasis day were scheduled. Deputations have been sent to Battey State Hospital and to churches requesting them. Since 1970 the B.S.U. has been increasingly presented as interdenominational in nature. It has alternated with the S.C.A. in planning evening programs called Encounter.

The Baptist Student Union and Home Mission Board summer mission programs have involved dozens of students who have contributed money or have participated in work days to raise money for the B.S.U. A few have actually become summer missionaries, serving in Arizona, California, New Mexico, Ohio, Pennsylvania, Texas, Brazil, Philippines, and Zambia.

About half of the time a Young Woman's Auxiliary has functioned, stressing missions and the Lottie Moon Christmas offering. Booklets have occasionally been issued detailing its annual program which has included white Bible ceremonies for prospective brides and some work with the children of the Open Door Home.

Published by the Y.W.A. or the Freshman Commission, "Hilltop Views" appeared as a news letter spasmodically from 1964 to 1969.

A monthly B.S.U. "Horror-Scope" provided information for a year, followed by "Hot Line To Glory" each month starting in 1970.

The Wright-Meredith Club has held from four to eight meetings each year during this period. Among its numerous speakers have been the Shorter alumnae for whom it is named, Miss Lucy Wright, retired medical missionary from China and Korea, and Miss Helen Meredith, evangelistic missionary in Colombia. The number of students preparing for church-related vocations has varied from about 50 to about 95. Of these, the largest groups have been comprised of those preparing for church music and the pastorate.

Other, smaller religious groups have met during some of the years: the Canterbury Club, the Ecumens, the Fellowship of Christian Athletes, the Jewish Fellowship, the Lutheran Club, the Newman Club, the Wesley Fellowship, and the Westminster Fellowship.

The religious affiliation of each student is indicated on his application and registration forms. This data was compiled at least once, indicating that sixty percent were Baptist, twenty percent Methodist, and eight percent Presbyterian. Smaller numbers of students were Episcopalian, Roman Catholic, or Church of Christ.

Chapels and assemblies have continued to be conducted periodically. Some have featured speakers whose interests have not been primarily religious, such as these: Kirtley Mather, Harvard geologist; E. Merton Coulter, University of Georgia historian; Richard Hocking and Charles Hartshorne, Emory philosophers; and several political figures: Herman E. Talmadge, John W. Davis, Carl E. Sanders, Jimmy Carter, Howard H. Callaway, and Hal Suit. Other guests have spoken on topics directly religious in nature: John Baillie of Scotland; Chester Swor of Jackson, Mississippi; Edwin S. Gaustad, former dean of the college, now of California; Charlie Shedd, authority on family life from Jekyll Island; Eric Rust, theologian-scientist from Southern Baptist Theological Seminary; William Holmes Borders of the Wheat Street Baptist Church, Atlanta; representatives from the Jewish Chautauqua Society; and choral groups from Southwestern and New Orleans Baptist Theological seminaries. Memorial services have been conducted in chapel for several persons: William F. (Sarge) Dahlstrom, manager of the book store from 1961 to 1965; Dr. Hoy Taylor; Dr. Frances Muldrow; General Janos Tamassy; and two students, Michael H. Knipper and Joseph A. Taylor.

Inaugurated with D. Swan Haworth of Southern Baptist Theological Seminary and H. Lewis Batts of Mercer University, Church Vocations Institute brought outstanding religious leaders to Shorter College from 1962 to 1971. They shared their insights with students and ministers of Northwest Georgia by appearing on chapel programs and conducting lectures and personal conferences. Among others leading the institute were William C. Bushnell, John W. Carlton, Kenneth L. Chafin, Findley B. Edge, and William E. Hull of Southern Baptist Theological Seminary; Olin T. Binkley of Southeastern Baptist Theological Seminary; Clyde Fant, Jr., of Southwestern Baptist Theological Seminary; J. Herbert Gilmore of Birmingham, Alabama; J. Estill Jones of Thomson; and Charles A. Trentham of Knoxville, Tennessee.

Student Publications

Composed of the three current editors and several members of the faculty, the publication board now chooses the new editors of the *Periscope*, *Argo*, and *Chimes*, although in earlier years the positions were usually filled during spring elections. Through 1960 the *Periscope* editor received a small stipend and remained outside the point system. Usually appearing monthly, the *Periscope* has assumed a diminutive size since 1971 due to its being printed on campus. In 1965 the paper joined the United States Student Press Association, while retaining membership in the Georgia Collegiate Press Association, but membership in both has since been discontinued.

The *Argo* has been published without fail each year, but no longer are the seniors responsible for it. An editorial and business staff is drawn from all classes, and the editor is sometimes a sophomore or junior. Colored pictures have been used extensively since 1963, when the first large annual since the mid-forties was issued. Campus beauties were again selected by guest judges—Bennett Cerf, the Kingston Trio, or Jimmy Dean—until the first Miss Shorter Pageant was staged by the annual in 1962 as a money-making project. One pharmaceutically inclined editor suggested that preparing the *Argo* is not without its problems: "To the next year's editor—the Excedrin are in the top drawer of the filing cabinet."

Once or twice a year through 1968 the *Chimes* was prepared by Rho Delta. Several creative writing contests provided items that were published—poetry, essays, fiction, and reviews of books and plays. Block prints and pen and ink sketches were often included. Utilizing contributions from students, faculty members, and outsiders, the magazine was printed at times commercially and at times on campus.

Irregularly between 1968 and 1970 the "Prism" and "Purple Prism" were produced on campus, editorially supporting racial equality, nonviolent civil disobedience in the face of wrong, and world peace. Some

442

poetry and dramatic criticism were printed, but most of the material related to current events.

Athletics

Although the intercollegiate sports program commands more public notice, intramural athletic competition at Shorter College is carefully organized and widely popular. The Sports Council continued as an autonomous body with its own constitution until the 1961 reorganization of the S.G.A. made it a part of the general organization and its name was officially changed to the Shorter College Intramural Athletic Association. It has retained a separate constitution, even though it now operates under the supervision of the S.G.A. sports committee. The freshman White and Gold is appointed each fall. In various years the Sports Council has planned picnics for the freshmen and for its own members, sponsored all-school folk dances, sold white and gold blazers, and mimeographed a handbook. The first male president of the council was Melvyn Ottinger, elected in 1961. Until the early sixties, membership was held in the Georgia Athletic and Recreation Federation for College Women.

The primary interest of the association is intramural sports. In the past, trophies were engraved with the names of winners in volley ball, swimming, badminton, tennis, softball, and ping pong. Others recognized the class with the greatest interest in sports, the generation and society winning the greater number of points, and the best all-round athlete. Through 1962 names of two or three seniors were placed on a plaque because of their sportsmanship, service, and participation. Until the early sixties, individuals were awarded letters for earning five hundred points. Currently, competition is listed in twelve team and thirteen individual sports. The sorority with the higher aggregate point total in the year is awarded a cup. Appropriate trophies for each sport are still furnished. In many of the sports, an all-star team is selected. During the spring a most valuable player award is presented to a girl from each sorority and to one outstanding male participant.

Occasional faculty-student athletic contests are held—usually raising money for various worthy causes at the expense of the faculty ego. At one volley ball game the Jennings ambulance crew removed by force the faculty member who forgot to collapse at the prearranged moment. Later two openly biased faculty referees still could not halt a basketball disaster that was obvious from the start. In recent years the *Periscope* has gladly given publicity to contests on the hardwood ending with twenty-point spreads favoring the students.

The early half of the sixties saw a limited amount of intercollegiate competition on the part of the girls. Volley ball, basketball, and tennis teams played against West Georgia College, Berry, and others, with results that the paper usually chose to ignore.

Since 1957–1958, male intercollegiate sports have attracted much local attention. Shorter has been identified with the Georgia Intercollegiate Athletic Conference and the National Association of Intercollegiate Athletics. During the first year of male competition, the Shorter teams had no name. In 1958 Coach Harvey Murphy provided a designation, the Gold Wave. When it was finally admitted in 1964 that this was impossible to visualize on an emblem, the athletic department sponsored a contest, and the current name, the Hawks, emerged. At that time, blue was added to the traditional white and gold as a part of the athletic colors. In addition to a consistent involvement with basketball, Shorter has some years sponsored teams in tennis, track and field, cross country, soccer, baseball, golf, and volley ball. Conference championships have been won in volley ball (1961–1962), track (1963), golf (1963, 1964, 1965, 1967), and baseball (1971), and several individuals have won all-conference and all-District 25 honors. Coach Douglas Rogers was named baseball coach of the year in 1971 within the G.I.A.C. and N.A.I.A. District 25.

Seven men have acted as head basketball coach during the fifteen years of competition thus far: William Jenkins (1957–1958), Harvey Murphy (1958–1962), William C. Foster (1962–1967), Joe F. Smith (1967–1969), William Moore (1969–1970), Douglas Rogers (1970–1971, three semesters), and Jerry Shelton (1972, one semester). Two alumni, Melvyn Ottinger and Ronald La-Pann, have been assistant coaches. The coaches' records are as follows:

coach	years	G.I.A.C.	overall
Jenkins	1957–1958	——	0–8
Murphy	1958–1962	29–23	42–52
Foster	1962–1967	43–11	110–33
Smith	1967–1969	9–18	18–36
Moore	1969–1970	10–4	13–15
Rogers	1970–1971	4–8	12–24
Shelton	1972	3–0	3–12
total	1957–1972	98–64	198–180

Individual players have won berths on the all-G.I.A.C. and all-N.A.I.A. District 25 teams, and the college has won the conference championship once, 1964–1965. In 1961–1962 it was conference co-champion, losing to Valdosta State College in the play-off. Two years,

1963–1965, Shorter was second on team defense in the entire N.A.I.A. Foster was voted basketball coach of the year in 1964–1965 within the G.I.A.C. and the N.A.I.A. District 25 and Area 7, extending from West Virginia to Florida. Moore was G.I.A.C. basketball coach of the year in 1969–1970.

Until 1959 all home games were played in the campus gymnasium. For a couple of years, some were held in the downtown Memorial Gymnasium. Since then, all home contests have been scheduled downtown, with Shorter's president and director of development usually occupying a corner and helping to officiate. The earliest printed basketball programs were distributed at games in 1962–1963, and the practice has been continued to the present. The annual Rome Tip-Off Tournament began in 1962, with Shorter emerging victorious the first four times. For six years beginning in 1965, the college participated in the Holiday Invitational Tournament in Rome, winning the first two. Made up of local boosters, the Hawkers was formed in the spring of 1965. From the sale of season tickets its members raised money for scholarships. The "Hawker Newsletter" gave coverage to the team in 1970–1971. A junior varsity basketball squad was initiated in 1965, and a team has been fielded each year since then. About 1969 video tape equipment was secured, enabling all basketball games to be taped for later analysis.

First elected in 1959, varsity cheerleaders were exclusively girls until one brave male appeared in 1962. Homecoming festivities were initiated in 1960—with many out-of-door displays, a pep rally, a dance, a queen and court, and a game with Valdosta State that Shorter lost by one point. More recently a crown has been added to make the reigning beauty a properly attired monarch. Since 1965 her name has been inscribed on a plaque. Beginning in 1971, smaller plaques have been presented to Miss, Mr., and Faculty Spirit. A Homecoming parade marched through town in 1972 when portable floats replaced stationary displays.

Until 1967 a varsity letterman's club was in existence, as a white and gold S was presented to each of the varsity stalwarts. Sponsored initially by the Circle K Club, the sports honor banquet first came in the spring of 1959 and continues under college sponsorship. At this time, awards are made in many areas. Later in the spring they are again announced to the entire student body at the Sports Awards program in chapel.

The Two Sororities

Greeted by rush letters during the summer and enthusiastic girls in the fall, the freshman and transfer students are immediately aware of the Epsilon Sigma and the Pi Sigma sororities. Known earlier as the Eunomian and Polymnian societies, they changed their names—but little else—in 1968. Coronations usually come the first or second Friday and Saturday evenings after registration. The Eunomian rainbow dresses were replaced by green ones in 1963, but the light and dark green society colors were retained. The Polymnian white dresses were changed to red in 1966, but the red, white, and green society colors were continued. As always, the queen has appeared in white—usually in what she hopes will be her wedding dress. The Eunomians have added a new song, "Hail Our Eunomian Queen," written in 1966 by Madeline Smith, and a new symbol, the white rose of friendship. The monologue says:

This rose represents an Epsilon Sigma friend.
A friend is someone who would throw cold water on you in the shower and
    make you laugh about it;
A friend is someone you take long walks with around Shorter Hill;
A friend is someone you just have to tell everything that "he" said;
A friend is someone who makes you better for having known her;
A friend is your heart whether heavy and chained or bubbling over and free;
To you, this is a rose; to us, it's our heart.

Both groups have added escorts to their ceremonies, and both have thoroughly redesigned the stage setting. In the gymnasium or cafeteria each holds a reception and produces a recently rewritten play suggesting its objectives and ideals. After several years of discussion, Mammy and her chillun were superseded in 1971 by Gran'ma, who lives in a house with red and green shutters, and has children named Loyalty, Purity, and Victorious Living. Before and after each coronation and reception, the other sorority sings to the new girls. During the program, members of the other group are busy placing all sorts of "nighty-night" favors on the beds of the new girls. Later in the evening the Ep Sigs burn their chain of friendship in front of the Freshman Dormitory, a practice that began about 1966. Because pledging has been postponed to November or December or February since 1968, the Eunomian Perfume Party, the Polymnian Bingo Party, and the joint talent show have been joined by other events that include a Thanksgiving Party and a Roaring Twenties Party. On the eve of pledging, each sorority treats half of the prospects to a banquet off campus. By 10:00 or 11:00 P.M. the new girls, dressed in sorority colors, are in Cooper Hall, where from designated windows they call out their choices. Noisemakers add to the din of shrieks and screams. Thereafter the freshmen retire to their dormitory, where each group spends the night writing songs honoring the sorority of its choice. These are sung

446

the next morning at breakfast in the college dining room—the special Eunomian breakfast and Polymnian luncheon were discontinued in the sixties, although the Pi Sigs still have an afternoon tea. Formerly, the first girl to sign each sorority's roll on pledge morning was allowed to wear the president's pin all day. The pledges continue to sign a scroll at an afternoon or evening meeting of the sorority—involving much solemnity, candles, and officers in Sunday dresses. More recently the Ep Sig pledge class president has worn the sorority president's pin the next day, and the Pi Sigs have secured a special pin to be kept for the remainder of the year by the pledge appearing to possess the most spirit. Under the watchful eyes of the pledge trainers, the pledges sponsor projects that make money for the sorority or improve the campus, give parties, and learn the lore of the sorority. Distinctive hats for the new girls are decorated by their big sisters. Since 1962 the Polymnians have worn white sailor caps; since 1966 the Eunomians have sported green leprechaun top hats. For a few days the pledges are subjected to initiation which includes mild harrassment that might involve sardines, raw eggs, liquid garlic, molasses, and mayonnaise— fortunately used only externally. At the end, refreshments and a small gift are often provided.

Weekly sorority meetings are held—occasionally having an entertaining program, but usually planning for some future event. Christmas parties are still scheduled—until the mid-sixties they included a skit for each society, "The Littlest Angel" for the Eunomians and Dickens' "Christmas Carol" for the Polymnians, and the giving of toys that soon went to the Open Door Home. Birthday celebrations come on January 27 for the Pi Sigs and on March 17 for the Ep Sigs. Starting about 1966, a rollicking scrub board band has been an honored part of Pi Sig life; since about 1969, the Ep Sig Singers have been melodious. Outings nearby are frequent, and trips to Gatlinburg, New Orleans, or Daytona Beach have been taken during longer vacations. After the Social Council was dissolved, the Eunomians and Polymnians jointly sponsored a dance each Christmas from 1961 through 1967. Rarely have others been held since then.

Money is furnished by the school and from dues that have grown from $4 to $25 annually, but the total never seems to be sufficient. "Sheckle-getter" ventures are frequent and varied: selling shirts, mugs, lavalieres, and stationery with sorority symbols on them; putting on an Ugly Couple or Ugliest Man on Campus contest; presenting the Halloween Carnival, a powder puff football game, or a spring fashion show; or holding a pickle or carnation sale.

The keen rivalry between sororities is usually shown in three ways.

First of all, the groups seek to pledge the greater number and to maintain the larger membership. Pi Sig success has been pronounced, as its membership has ranged from 74 to 174 and has been larger at least eight years. Ep Sig membership has varied from 72 to 125, being larger at least three years. Secondly, the sororities compete in intramural sports. A trophy is awarded to the group winning the greater number of points throughout the year. They tied for it two years, the Ep Sigs have won it twice, and the Pi Sigs have kept it the other years. Third, since 1969 several varsity basketball games each year have been designated spirit games, and a plaque is presented to the sorority having the higher percentage of members present.

Service projects are carried out by the girls. Some years Thanksgiving and Christmas baskets are provided, clothes are collected for Christmas, ditty bags are packed for troops in Vietnam, and Halloween or Christmas parties are given for underprivileged children. The groups sometimes help at the Rome Boys' Club or at the Open Door Home.

Late in the spring each sorority holds elections for new officers who are installed in tearful and staid ceremonies. The outgoing queen receives an engraved silver tray from her grateful subjects. Senior Day formerly came in May, when the coming graduates were served breakfast in bed and honored with a party or banquet. They are still teased with "gag gifts"—and sometimes pleased by serious gifts, such as a sorority charm. A Pi Sig awards night has been added in the spring, when the Pi Sig of the Year and the Most Spirited Pi Sig are recognized, along with other leaders. Replacing the earlier Eunomian Phantoms (some of whom turned out to be Polymnians anyway!), the Leprechaun was first elected in 1969 as a mascot with unusual spirit from the pledge class. Also honored in the spring are the Most Spirited Ep Sig and the Ep Sig with the highest scholastic average.

If the Thugs, Ep Sig secret group, have been revived, their existence is not widely publicized. The Pi Sig H.O.T.s have functioned irregularly since 1966, being joined by a sophomore group called the Spirits.

A modern counterpart of the earlier honorary members emerged in 1963 as the first society sweetheart was named by the Polymnians. Subsequently each group has annually named two to four.

Formed in 1966, the Inter-Society Council—now the Inter-Sorority Council, of course—is comprised of up to sixteen members before whom girls may pledge at times other than the regular period. Other business of mutual interest is also handled, including the inevitable pledging rules.

Almost every summer a house party or work weekend prepares for the rush of rushing. Whether at Van Hoose Dormitory, Jekyll Island,

Chattanooga, a mountain cabin near Clayton, or a Florida beach, the good times are said to be secondary to decorating cups and making pillowcases, laundry bags, octopuses, booklets, pencil holders, calendars—or whatever else will be given to the freshmen a few weeks later.

In recent years both sororities have redrawn their emblems and adopted new constitutions. The widespread use of pins was discontinued in the late sixties. Each group has an office in the new Binns Student Center.

The Two Fraternities

Seeking new members each fall, the Alpha Lambda Epsilon and Phi Delta Tau fraternities sponsor activities calculated to attract favorable attention. Free cokes often welcome the freshmen to the dormitory, and the brothers help to unload luggage for the long trek up to their rooms. Later events might include a smoker, mixer, deer barbecue, or banquet. Early in the fall each pledge signs the scroll of his newly selected fraternity, after which initiation lays its heavy hand on him. Molasses and feathers, mud baths, calisthenics, paddles, and feminine attire on Broad Street are at times replaced by cleaning up the student center and fish pond or selling candy downtown for a charitable cause. At least seven years the ALEs have been larger, comprised of 19 to 94. At least four years the Phi Delts have enjoyed the greater number, varying from 19 to 60.

The new brother quickly finds that seriousness is seldom a part of fraternity life. Recreation could be afforded by a picnic at Little River Canyon, hay ride and weiner roast at Cave Spring, water skiing party, chicken supper, or cookout at the Civic Center. Holiday trips have been taken to Daytona Beach, Nassau, the Mardis Gras, and elsewhere. Intramural sports furnish competition, with a trophy for the group accumulating the better record throughout the year. Since 1968 the varsity basketball spirit games provide recognition for the fraternity with the greater percentage of its members present. From 1961 to 1967 each organization sponsored one school-wide dance per year, alternating between the fall and spring formals. The Fraternity Night dance has been held annually since 1969. In addition, each schedules closed dances and parties and cooperates with the social committee of the S.G.A.

Each fraternity elects new officers in the spring. Since 1960 each group has vastly improved its appearance by choosing fraternity sweethearts.

An allotment from the college and dues paid by the brothers are usually supplemented by attempts to raise money each year. Car washes and waxes, doughnut sales, and the Phi Delt talent show (which was once taped for use over WLAQ) help to make the treasurers' jobs easier.

One segment of fraternity life answers the impulse for social service. The Phi Delts have had a Christmas party for children each year. The ALEs helped to purchase a Red Cross station wagon to be used overseas. Both contributed to redecorating the enlarged Glass Corridor and have raised funds for UNICEF and the March of Dimes.

Classes, Clans, and the Crook

Classes and clans have not been forgotten on the hill, even though they are not as prominent as in years gone by. Class officers are elected each spring, except for the freshman leaders who are named in the fall. Each class is represented within the S.G.A. and on the S.C.A. cabinet, and selects one of its number to enter the Miss Shorter Pageant and the contest for Homecoming queen. Sherwood Forest Day brings out much support each fall, and a class award is always presented amidst applause and shouting. At times a class sponsors a car wash or entertains its members and dates with a hay ride. Until 1960 Stunt Night called forth class artistry and ingenuity. The annuals through 1962 pictured the ideal and most representative members of each class. Trophies were awarded into the early sixties for class competition in badminton, softball, volley ball, and ping pong, and for class interest in sports.

Beyond question the most obvious group in the fall is made up of persons going through "the traumatic experience of RAT." A few elements have been added. The freshmen now display from the campus flagpole a homemade banner with many class members' names on it. Elected in secret by his fellows, the carefully disguised freshman Phantom or Flash Rat occasionally puts in an appearance, allowing his classmates to run away from the bothersome sophomores. Of course the sophomores attempt to capture him, thus putting an end to all legal escape. A rat talent show produces some good acts. Crowned by the assembly speaker, Carl Sanders, the rat queen and king were once enthusiastically applauded even by their tormentors. Rat auction often occurs when the black-dressed sophomores sell the rats, who thereupon clean up a suite, wash and iron clothes, or scrub the outside wall of the Greystone while singing Christmas carols. The value of this auction becomes instantly apparent to the sophomores when the bill for the rat caps is presented to them.

Some things seem altogether unchanging: dressing in odd combinations of wearing apparel, giving Indian war whoops in the circle, and scrambling like an egg. State-shaped signs still announce the identity of the wearer: Arbor Sacrifice, Dirty Butter, Religious Razor, Burton's Candy, Shakespearean Shoe, and the like. The results of scavenger hunts are never entirely satisfactory to the sophomores—even when the industrious rats bring in seventy-three toenail clippings, Miss Thompson's footprint, thirty-five faculty signatures, a picture of Rotary Lake, and all sixty-nine other things on the list. Eventually rat court is held, in the gym or in the auditorium, where prostrate rats—who by now have had their rat caps confiscated for some alleged misdemeanor—retrieve these prized possessions.

As in previous years, the pros and cons of ratting are still discussed. Although many town students and a few boarders simply ignore it, most would agree with the girl who wrote: "Rat was fun, but I can't wait until next year."

The clans—they are no longer called *generations*—are still Hi-Minded (the spelling has been streamlined) and Whoop-Em-Up. The juniors give the freshmen their class banner, and in the early sixties a dance often accompanied the occasion. Many songs and some clan history are passed down. In many years the classes of a clan fete each other, increasing clan spirit. Through 1963 they vied for a sports trophy, but this is a thing of the past. Clan wars were fought each spring in the middle and late sixties—with enough unscheduled "infantile vandalism," as one *Periscope* writer expressed it, to cause concern. Since 1970 a Clan Day has been the substitute, involving sporting events, a bubble gum blowing contest, a faculty talking contest (time limits are imposed), a pie eating contest, and a picnic in the Alumni Garden. Sherwood Forest Day likewise provides for some expression of clan partisanship. The speed bumps on the lower road are regularly repainted green and yellow or red and blue—and even the little statuettes recently erected near the fish pond have lost their pristine purity. The Hi-Minded symbol is the eight-pointed star, while the Whoop-Em-Ups have adopted as their symbol the owl—which many High-Mindeds thirty years ago will recall was *their* symbol! Great effort is still made to steal the opposing clan's banner, which then is returned with much ridicule at Class Day or the senior banquet.

As the fiftieth anniversary of the crook approached, an effort was made to revive this tradition. For almost fifteen years it had apparently been stored in various closets—sometimes virtually lost and sometimes quietly passed down from class to class. During 1963–1964 the sharp eye of Mrs. Elliott spotted it in a pile of debris soon to be thrown out.

451

Rescuing it from an ignoble fate, she displayed it in her apartment, where the girls came to see it. On Alumni Day the class of 1914 turned it over to the rising seniors, the class of 1965. They hid it in the spring of 1965, evidently without its being discovered. After a one-year lapse, the juniors in 1966–1967 challenged the seniors to hide it and the challenge was accepted. In the woods below the Rockery two juniors were avoiding Hi-Minded pursuers. As they sat on a log to rest, they noticed a "stick" that turned out to be the crook. After photographing the jubilant class officers with the crook in hand and holding a conference with Mrs. Elliott to determine the rules, they added to it a metal band engraved "Class of 1968" and proceeded to hide it. The frustrated Hi-Minded seniors did not look high enough to find it hanging in a tree near High Acres, and the juniors brought it out for Class Day. In the spring of 1968 it was again successfully hidden, and was decorated with red and blue for the second straight Class Day. Mrs. Elliott thereupon took charge of it, and that fall it was given a place of honor in the Memorabilia Room. Five times it has more or less properly been found: 1916, 1922, 1932, 1937, and 1967—although most of the traditional rules had been forgotten by the sixties and were not observed. A replica crook, made about 1940, has disappeared after circulating around the dormitories in the early sixties.

Other Student Activities

Stereos blaring, laughter and tears, snatches of conversation, popcorn exploding, the odor of hair spray or clothes being ironed—these too are a part of student activities. Four may sit on the floor and eat pizzas, or gather around a table for bridge, or talk on the sun deck, or join "a motley conglomeration of legs, backs, and sun glasses" in order to gain "the sought-after goal—a walnut-stained hue." The routine might be broken by a long walk around the hill, a bicycle ride, kite flying—or, in 1958 at least, gyrations inside a hula hoop. First in the gym, then in the basement of Cooper Hall, and now in the Binns Building, the recreation room has at times furnished television, a juke box, pool, ping pong, or just a place to chatter.

With coke bottles, clothes, and conversation, the town girls' lounge existed until the early sixties, when the new Library-Administration Building provided a general student lounge. After the food counter in it was replaced by the "Robot Snack Bar," the delicacies were not quite as warm, but the area retained its untidy usefulness. Occupying a part of the Binns Building, a similar facility attracts hungry, lonesome, and talkative students. A grill is open on a limited schedule, vending machines are supposedly capable of gobbling dimes, and a juke box is sometimes free and always loud.

Christmas time includes a chapel service appropriate to the season and a festive banquet or smorgasbord in the dining room with presents for the kitchen staff. Often an open house in the girls' dormitories reveals imaginative and colorful decorations. Starting in 1966, a tree lighting ceremony featuring the choir and the reading of Scripture has usually been held in the circle.

Originally sponsored by the *Argo* in order to raise money, the Miss Shorter Pageant was staged first in 1962 with Sara Beth Smith as queen. By 1967 it had come under the direction of the S.G.A. Miss Shorter of 1969, Jackie Alder, was the first to reach the finals of the Miss Georgia Pageant. Miss Shorter of 1971, Lisa Lawalin, who also reached the finals, was chosen Miss Peach Bowl in Atlanta later that year. Entering the 1972 state pageant as Miss Cedar Valley, she was crowned Miss Georgia.

A fashion show in Brookes Chapel, often under the auspices of the *Periscope*, selected Shorter's best dressed girls until 1969. The winner was always entered in the *Glamour Magazine* contest, but her charm and elegance failed to be appreciated nationally.

Never included on the school calendar is that ever-popular event, the coming of snow. *News-Tribune* pictures might show two girls brushing white flakes from their Florida license tag or others waving from cars covered with snow except where "Happy New Year" has been scraped off the windshields. Snow fights, snowmen, and sledding down the Shorter Avenue slope continue to be the consequences of a sufficient accumulation. Early in March of 1960 a paralyzing ice storm forced an evacuation of the dark and frigid campus. Lighthearted students stayed with friends in town or were bedded down on the Greystone and General Forrest dining room floors as classes were suspended for several days.

Some student activity has been of a more serious nature. The Circle K Club was formed in 1959 under the supervision of the Metro Rome Kiwanis Club, with J. D. Ramsay as its first adviser. It has since issued several student directories, sponsored campus cleanup weeks, worked with disadvantaged children in an East Rome mission and elsewhere, provided the color television set for the current recreation room, registered participants in Project Concern's Walk for Mankind, and raised money for the Hemophilia Association. In 1962 Democratic and Republican groups began to meet at Shorter, and these have functioned intermittently since. State political leaders have appeared at their meetings and on assembly programs. Faced with the Cuban missile crisis in October of 1962, some students held a prayer meeting in chapel. Peace Moratorium Day in 1969 resulted in a low-key demonstration. The assassinations of John F. Kennedy and Martin Luther King, Jr., were followed by memorial services conducted by students and faculty members in the society halls and later drew editorial expressions of grief and outrage in the *Periscope*. At a mock funeral on Earth Day of 1970, an automobile engine was buried behind Alumni Hall, but the grave marker has since been knocked down by cars parked in the area because of the overflowing lot nearby. The following year a display was built in the circle with caged-in students and professors identified with signs proclaiming "Homo Sapiens" and "Endangered Species!" The Ecology Club has been a continuing consequence of this interest.

Seniors and Commencement

The first expression of a new status, senior rings are ordered during the student's junior year and proudly worn—once they arrive, after what often seems to be an interminable wait. Symbolically presented that spring, caps and gowns are donned at opening convocation, Shorter Sunday, Founders' Day, Honors Day, and the appropriate commencement functions. By 1965 "senior deference" had been routed from its last bastion, the dining room, and seniors no longer break in at the front of the line. Until 1966 the *Argo* printed pictures of the senior superlatives and class ideals. A secret group first appeared in the 1967 *Argo*, the Shorter Senior Spirits, devoted to raising the spirit and enthusiasm of the college. An annual May event formerly occurred when the sophomores hosted the seniors at a social that often was a picnic. In various years the seniors have presented to their alma mater a gift, such as the new flagpole, the clock in the library, the statuettes in and near the fish pond, or the music system for the dining room.

The principal commencement weekend has been further compressed and has been joined since 1962 by a ceremony at the end of summer school. Graduation rehearsal at First Baptist Church on Saturday morning has some years been followed by an alumni meeting which seniors are requested to attend and a luncheon in the dining room honoring them and the alumni. Through 1969 Class Day at the Rockery called forth "Hail, Dear Old Shorter," a daisy chain one foot (more recently, six inches) in length for each graduate, and a program made different every year by new names and fresh quips. Since 1970 Class Day has been combined tastefully with a senior banquet sponsored by the sophomores. Some traditional parts have been mimeographed for distribution. The daisy chain and accompanying song persist. A Saturday evening reception at High Acres is given some years for graduates and their parents.

Sunday morning at the First Baptist Church the baccalaureate sermon is preached. In the afternoon at Brookes Chapel through 1959 and subsequently at the First Baptist Church, the commencement address has been delivered and degrees granted. A cap and gown reception has followed in the fellowship hall of the church since 1961.

Over the years distinguished guests speaking to the graduates have included these: Ellis Arnall, Newnan; Ashton J. Albert, Atlanta; J. Paul Austin, Atlanta; William R. Bowdoin, Atlanta; Harllee Branch, Atlanta; W. Lee Burge, Atlanta; Howard H. Callaway, Pine Mountain; Allen B. Comish, Columbus; E. Smythe Gambrell, Atlanta; Ben S. Gilmer, New York City; G. Othell Hand, Columbus; D. J. Haughton, Burbank, California; Brooks Hays, Little Rock, Arkansas; William E. Hull, Louisville, Kentucky; John J. Hurt, Jr., Atlanta; Robert W. Jackson, Dalton; Boisfeuillet Jones, Atlanta; J. Estill Jones, Thomson; John O. McCarty, Atlanta; Roger McDonald, Newnan; Richard H. Rich, Atlanta; Hugh L. Smith, Cedartown; Earl Stallings, Marietta; and J. Thornton Williams, LaGrange.

Numerous awards have been made annually, first at Class Day and by 1965 at Awards Day in Brookes Chapel earlier in the spring. Recognition is accorded the seniors in Phi Sigma Alpha, the Argonauts, and *Who's Who Among Students in American Universities and Colleges.* The Sophomore Sabots and the sophomore recipient of the Helen Franklin Award are noted. Long-standing awards are presented: the Freshman Chemistry Achievement Award given by the Chemical Rubber Company; the Claire J. Wyatt Award in English that has evolved out of the Imogen Coulter Award and continues to be given by the Wyatt family; the Freshman Mathematics Award given by the department; the Freshman, Sophomore, and Junior Music awards given by the department; the Presser Foundation Music Scholarship; the Edith Lester Harbin Music Scholarship; the Rome Music Lovers' Club Award; Senior Honor in Music, when merited; the Sarah A. Faust and Hazel Tuggle Ivey Religion awards; and the Walter R. Thomas Speech Award. Several new awards have honored Shorter persons from the recent past: the Bertha Martin Biology Award (named for the professor of biology at Shorter from 1927 to 1954) given by Mr. and Mrs. Oscar Braden (she is the former Miss Eugenia Rutland, class of 1934), Buddy Lam, Dr. Lewis Lipps, and Dr. Philip Greear; the Mathilde M. Parlett English Award (named for the professor of English at Shorter from 1935 to 1945) given by Dr. Jessie

Gardner Austin; the Sara Whitworth-Frances Muldrow Scholarship in Foreign Language (named for a 1969 alumna and the professor of languages at Shorter from 1966 to 1969) given by friends and members of the families; and the Ruth Barron Music Education Award (named for a 1933 graduate) given by the family of David Bridges. In memory of Allison W. Ledbetter, Sr., a senior who is outstanding in athletics receives his tuition and an engraved trophy. Other awards have been presented for brief periods of time in many departments: art, business administration and economics, education, English, French, geology, music, religion, and Spanish.

The Shorter College Alumni Association

Still largely under the leadership of the alumnae, the General Alumni Association changed its name in the spring of 1972 to the Shorter College Alumni Association. Its presidents during this period have been Mrs. J. Walker Chidsey (née Miss Margaret Haynes, class of 1927), Mrs. William J. Simpson, Mrs. Whitfield Gunnels (née Miss Louise Hudson, class of 1925), Mrs. Rosser Malone (née Miss Petrona Underwood, class of 1931), Mrs. Shouky Shaheen (née Miss Doris Bradshaw, class of 1955), Mrs. N. P. Manning, Jr. (née Miss Ruth Parham, class of 1951), and Mrs. Julius R. Lunsford, Jr. (née Miss Mary Vann, class of 1941). Miss Louise Bennet continued as honorary president until her death in 1968. The executive board usually holds a summer planning retreat, in addition to its meetings in the spring, on Alumni Day, and before the November luncheon in Atlanta. Men have been on this board throughout this period: Dr. James W. Ware, III (class of 1956), James F. Gray (class of 1957), William L. Morris (class of 1960), Dr. W. Nevin Jones, Sam Mitchell (class of 1961), Tal Roberts (class of 1962), Budd Bishop (class of 1958), Keith Taylor (class of 1969), and Horace Stewart. A men's division of the association was formed in 1964, but lasted only a few months.

Mrs. Ima Jean Kerce has been alumni secretary since 1956. With her cooperation, the *Shorter College Bulletin* is normally sent once or twice a year to the forty-three hundred members of the association. A comprehensive alumni directory was prepared in the spring of 1967, appearing as one issue of the *Bulletin*. Occasionally the organization sends Thanksgiving and Christmas cards, thereby expressing "gratitude and appreciation for those who are helping increase Shorter's stature in any way."

Under the auspices of the Atlanta Shorter Club, the November luncheon attracts from one to two hundred, usually includes examples of Shorter's musical or dramatic talent, and once was concluded with "A Minor Address."

Alumni Weekend has varied from early April in 1959 and 1960 to graduation weekend in 1961 to 1969 and to late April since 1970. Typical events include an executive board meeting, a reception at High Acres, a meeting of the general association, several class reunions, and a Saturday luncheon in the college dining room. In memory of Miss Imogen Coulter, an exhibit of paintings by Mrs. Jeddie Graham Mobley (class of 1916) was hung in 1968. Seminars led by various faculty members in 1970, 1971, and 1972 updated the participants' educational experience. (Similar sessions were held in connection with Homecoming the two previous years.) In addition to Golden Anniversary Certificates, a citation and gift are presented to the alumna of the year. These have been Miss Mabel Thompson (class of 1924), Mrs. Frank H. Leavell (née Miss Martha Boone, class of 1915), Miss Martha C. Galt (class of 1915), Mrs. J. Lucian Smith (née Miss Claire Davis, class of 1941), Miss Jane Arnold (class of 1948), Mrs. A. M. Arnett (née Miss Ethel Stephens, class of 1912), Mrs. Fritz Roberts (née Miss Mildred Pidcock, class of 1926; later Mrs. Clarence Cross), Mrs. Robert Arnold, Mrs. Whitfield Gunnels, Mrs. J. J. Clyatt (née Miss Josie Golden, class of 1919), Mrs. J. Curtis Dixon (née Miss Blanche Williams, class of 1919), Mrs. S. B. Kitchens (née Miss Montyne Shields, class of 1927), Mrs. Bryan Jolly (née Miss Rebecca Yeargan, class of 1925), and Mrs. Jeddie Graham Mobley. Since 1970 an alumnus of the year has also been named: Richard H. Wicker, Jr. (a student in 1955–1956), Richard L. Starnes, Jr. (class of 1958), and David H. McGowan (class of 1961).

Although President Van Hoose had spoken in 1920 of a Georgia Baptist historical museum at Shorter that would emphasize educational institutions, the project was carried no further during his administration. Shorter memorabilia was gathered as the years passed, but not until a committee was appointed in 1966 did the collection take definite form. Presidents Gunnels and Malone expressed keen interest in the project. Prepared by Mrs. Talbott Chandler (née Miss Frances Benson, class of 1929), Mrs. Warren Gilbert (née Miss Mary Harbin, class of 1932), Mrs. A. S. Hatcher (née Miss Helen Hardman, class of 1927), and Mrs. Douglas Milner (née Miss Mabel Rhinehart, class of 1946), an exhibit was placed in the foyer of Rome Hall in 1967. A Memorabilia Room was set apart in the new Binns Building, under the local supervision of Mrs. Gilbert and Mrs. Robert Powell (née Miss Virginia Cline, class of 1948), who have been assisted by Mrs. Robert G. Gardner. An attractive display has been arranged for the casual viewer, while all other materials have been painstakingly filed for the serious reader. At Alumni Day in 1969 Mrs. Gilbert was presented a certificate of appreciation by the association for her leadership in this project.

Local alumni groups have met and sometimes formed clubs. Many have sought prospective students by holding coke parties and by bringing some young people to the campus. These have included supporters in Albany, Atlanta and environs, Augusta, Brunswick, Calhoun, Cartersville, Columbus, Cordele, Covington, Dalton, Hogansville, the LaFayette-Trion-Summerville area, LaGrange, Macon, Marietta, Moultrie, Newnan, Perry, Rome, Savannah, Statesboro, Thomaston, Thomasville, and Tifton.

Through the mid-sixties and intermittently since, the Columbus club has held a spring luncheon. The afternoon and evening branches of the Atlanta Shorter Club meet regularly, issue a yearbook, and raise money in a variety of ways. Their contributions have included a book case for the alumni office, sixty coffee spoons and a silver tray, and twenty classroom chairs.

The Rome alumni have upheld the college in numerous ways. Money is raised by rummage sales, benefit bridges, and the sale of candy. Parties for high school seniors were sponsored through the early sixties. In 1961 a drive to provide classroom furniture was successful enough to call for placing two commemorative plaques. With Mrs. William L. Morris (née Miss Betty Zane Jones, class of 1955) as chairman, the club compiled and published a cookbook in 1965. Carrying a yellow and white decor throughout, it contained 151 pages of choice alumnae recipes. At $2 per copy, the project netted a profit of $1,108.04. Clad in white apron and chef's tall hat, a leading Shorter administrator accepted the check with a *News-Tribune* photographer recording the scene for posterity. Each spring since 1966 this club has marked the birthday of Shorter College with a banquet.

At various times, clubs have been organized also at Chattanooga, Tennessee, and Washington, D. C. The latter group is selling tea napkins and scarves designed especially for them by Frankie Welch. Teas and luncheons have also been held occasionally at Baton Rouge, Louisiana; Dallas, Texas; Greensboro, North Carolina; Jacksonville, Miami, and Ocala, Florida; Nashville, Tennessee; and New York City.

A plaque reading "Dedicated to the memory of those Shorter students who have died in the service of their country" bears the name of First Lieutenant Albert Judson Hayes, U.S.M.C., a graduate in 1964.

Two alumni weddings have made the campus even more beautiful than before. Miss Kathleen Smithey was married to Charles Hardaker on May 28, 1961, in Brookes Chapel with Dr. Robert G. Gardner officiating. Miss Ellen Payne and George Vinson Hellwig were married on August 7, 1966, in the Alumni Garden by the Reverend Tal Roberts.

Financial support from the alumni has been quite generous during this period. The Living Endowment fund was emphasized through 1966, totaling about $67,000. In addition, the alumni participated in drives for the Library-Administration Building, Alumni Hall, the Fine Arts Building, and the Binns Student Center. Through 1968 these contributions exceeded $122,000. In 1969 the association proposed a Tower Club for those giving $1,000, and 14 soon responded. Eight joined the Builders Club by sending $500, and 114 entered the Century Club with a $100 donation. As a part of the centennial, each graduate has been urged to be "one in a hundred" by participating in the 100 Fund of $100,000. Thus far, about $51,000 has been raised by these means. In fourteen years, alumni contributions have reached almost a quarter of a million dollars.

Looking Backward and Forward

"A Century of Service" is being completed at Shorter College. Ten years ago the trustees were already discussing 1973. Two years ago a special committee composed of community leaders, parents, alumni, trustees, faculty members, administrators, and students formulated recommendations covering a broad range of improvements. A centennial committee has initiated specific and appropriate action. The celebration during 1972–1973 will include addresses by R. J. Robinson of Augusta, president of the Georgia Baptist Convention; Admiral T. H. Moorer, chairman of the Joint Chiefs of Staff; Dr. William G. Pollard, executive director of the Oak Ridge Associated Universities, Inc.; Dr. O. B. Hardison, Jr., director of the Folger Shakespeare Library; Chancellor G. Alexander Heard of Vanderbilt University; Boisfeuillet Jones, president of the Emily and Ernest Woodruff Foundation of Atlanta; Colonel James B. Irwin, retired astronaut of Houston, Texas; Dr. Benjamin E. Mays, president emeritus of Morehouse College, Atlanta; and Dr. David Elton Trueblood, theologian-philosopher of Earlham College, Indiana. Commencement speakers will be Jimmy Carter, governor of Georgia, and Dr. William E. Hull, provost of the Southern Baptist Theological Seminary. A Christmas tour of the Holy Land and Rome, Italy, will be led by the department of religion. In the spring a historical pageant will be presented. Obviously this book is also a part of the centennial observation.

The total story of the college cannot yet be written—that part relating to the "Second Hundred Years." At the moment, these years can only be subject to guess and surmise. History is full of its discredited prophets. There is no need here to add another name to the list. Nevertheless, the future is not entirely unknown—at least in terms of hopes and dreams regarding it. Plans have been made to allow for a slow increase in student enrollment. The Second Century Fund will be pursued with energy, seeking ten million dollars for a men's dormitory, a fine arts auditorium, a library building, the installation of air-conditioning in all buildings not now so equipped, various other capital improvements, and a pronounced increase in the endowment. The curricula will be constantly evaluated and revised. The faculty will be further strengthened, as will the library holdings and laboratory equipment so essential to superior instruction. Practices relating to student recruitment, student personnel, and public relations will continually be subject to alteration and improvement.

President Minor has stated his purpose: "To direct our course between the traditions of the past and the inevitable of the future. . . . We are attempting to retain the customs and traditions which are worth retaining. By these I mean the eternal characteristics which mark a refined, gentle person. At the same time we are aware of the changes in cultural mores that are inevitable and with which we must cope. Essentially, we are trying to live in the twentieth century and prepare our students to live in the twenty-first." "We can only go forward or backward. If the time ever comes when we have no more dreams, no plans, no projections, then greatness and hope are gone. We must go forward." "It would be a mistake to bask in our past glories. We must use the first century as a foundation, as a taking-off point. Let our second century far surpass the first."

Shorter College looks to the past and to the future. Its stance is eloquently expressed by an inscription in the Walter Pope Binns Student Center: "Shorter College is grateful for all friends who have been a part of her glorious history—and for those whose vision and interest point to a greater future."

Index

469

472

473

476